Territorial Discontent

KRISTIN OBERIANO

Territorial Discontent

CHamorus, Filipinos, and the Making of the United States Empire in Guåhan

The University of North Carolina Press *Chapel Hill*

The University of North Carolina Press would like to thank the University of Guam Press for their collaboration on this publication. An edition of this book is available in Guam and Micronesia from the University of Guam Press. Visit www.uogpress.com for more information.

This book was published with the assistance of the Authors Fund of the University of North Carolina Press.

Set in Arno Pro by Westchester Publishing Services

Library of Congress Cataloging-in-Publication Data
Names: Oberiano, Kristin author
Title: Territorial discontent : CHamorus, Filipinos, and the making of the United States empire in Guåhan / Kristin Oberiano.
Description: Chapel Hill : University of North Carolina Press, [2026] | Includes bibliographical references and index.
Identifiers: LCCN 2026018202 | ISBN 9781463903 cloth | ISBN 9781469693910 paperback | ISBN 9781469688084 epub | ISBN 9781469693927 pdf
Subjects: LCSH: Chamorro (Micronesian people)—Guam—History—20th century | Filipinos—Guam—History—20th century | Settlerzcolonialism—Guam—History—20th century | Guam—Race relations—Political aspects—History | Guam—Ethnic relations—Political aspects—History | United States—Territories and possessions—Politics and government | BISAC: HISTORY / Indigenous Peoples in the Americas | HISTORY / United States / 20th Century
Classification: LCC DU647 .O24 2026
LC record available at https://lccn.loc.gov/2026018202

Cover design by Eurich Patacsil. *Background: Aerial View of Guam*, 1956, by Jeffrey Meyer. *Foreground: Hand-Stitched Tapestry*, 2025, by Joseph Certeza. Both used by permission.

Parts of chapter 6 were previously published as "The Quest for Indigenous Chamorro Self-Determination in the Age of Pacific Anticolonialism," in *The Anticolonial Transnational: Imaginaries, Mobilities, and Networks in the Struggle Against Empire*, edited by Erez Manela and Heather Streets-Salter (Cambridge: Cambridge University Press, 2023).

This book will be made open access within three years of publication thanks to Path to Open, a program developed in partnership between JSTOR, the American Council of Learned Societies (ACLS), the University of Michigan Press, and the University of North Carolina Press to bring about equitable access and impact for the entire scholarly community, including authors, researchers, libraries, and university presses around the world. Learn more at https://about.jstor.org/path-to-open/.

For product safety concerns under the European Union's General Product Safety Regulation (EU GPSR), please contact gpsr@mare-nostrum.co.uk or write to the University of North Carolina Press and Mare Nostrum Group B.V., Doelen 72, 4831 GR Breda, The Netherlands.

For Guåhan

Contents

Acknowledgments

This book started out as a simple question that launched a decade-long academic and life journey into understanding what it means to be Filipino from Guåhan. Along the way, I have met a countless number of people who have each in their own ways shaped the way I researched and wrote this book. I am grateful for each of them, even if they are not mentioned here. Dångkulu na saina ma'åse' and maraming salamat.

At Harvard, Phil Deloria, Genevieve Clutario, Erez Manela, David Armitage, and Walter Johnson gave me the intellectual grounding to write this history of Guåhan and the US empire. My colleagues in the Wesleyan University history department—Paul Erickson, Demetrius Eudell, Courtney Fullilove, Nat Greene, Erik Grimmer-Solem, Oliver W. Holmes, Bill Johnston, Ethan Kleinberg, Jeffers Lennox, Valeria López Fadul, Cecilia Miller, William Pinch, Gary Shaw, Joseph Slaughter, Victoria Smolkin, Ying Jia Tan, Jennifer Tucker, and Laura Ann Twagira—have collectively given me the time and space to develop this book to the best it could be. I must recognize my delightful and insightful colleagues A. George Bajalia, Roberto Saba, Antonina Woodsum, and Joseph Weiss for their unending support and guidance in my years at Wes. I also want to acknowledge the American Studies department and the members of the Indigenous Studies Research Network who have given thoughtful feedback for the introduction and several chapters in this book.

I have had the absolute privilege of learning from an insightful and generous network of scholars across the globe as well as from the people of Guåhan, who have shared their knowledge, their stories, and offered thoughtful feedback on this book. I want to convey my utmost gratitude to: Evyn Lê Espiritu Gandhi, Simeon Man, Moon-Ho Jung, Robert Underwood, Alvita Akiboh, Norman Analista, Jacob Anbinder, Chloe Babauta, Nita Baldovino, Samantha Barnett, Michael Bevacqua, Megan Black, Sony Coráñez Bolton, Michael Brenes, Auntie Carline Bello Bukikosa and Auntie Bella Bello Martinez, Keith Camacho, Christopher Capozzola, Seyoung Choung, Michael Clement, Auntie Hope Cristobal, Benjamin "B.J." Cruz, Frank Costigliola, Sasha Day, Brian DeLay, Adrian De Leon, Ariel Dimalanta, Tabitha Espina, Jana Lipman, Christine Taitano DeLisle, Vicente Diaz, Kevin Escudero, Andrew Gumataotao, Candace Fujikane, Alfred Peredo Flores, Juan Flores, Julian Go,

Vernadette Gonzalez, Anne Hattori, Rebecca Herman, Rebecca Hogue, Jane Hong, J. Kēhaulani Kauanui, Barbara Keys, Kenneth Gofigan Kuper, Patrick Luces, Carlos Madrid, James McDonald, Sarah Meiners, Tiara Na'puti, Lisa Natividad, Juliet Nebolon, Josephine Faith Ong, Paula Park, Ruben Payumo, JoAnna Poblete, Jewel Pereyra, Edna Rebanal, Aanchal Saraf, Dean Saranillio, Bernie Provido Schumann, Naoko Shibusawa, Brad Simpson, Erica Sterling, Heather Salter, Katerina Teaiwa, Nerissa Bretania Underwood, James Viernes, Kevin Vrevich, Brian Winston, Stephen Wesley, and Colleen Woods. The Filipinos for Guåhan—Tabitha Espina, Josephine Ong, Jamela Santos, Tressa Diaz, Ruzelle Almonds, and Vivian Dames—have been an incredible source of knowledge and strength. The nonprofit organization Guåhan Sustainable Culture, led by Michelle Crisostomo and my mother Marlyn Oberiano, has inspired me to keep the work of decolonization going.

In addition, this book has been shaped through the years by the questions and comments of dozens of scholars at many places, including Amherst College, New York University, Occidental College, Stanford University, University of California Berkeley, University of Chicago, University of Connecticut, and Yale University, as well as conferences of the Society of Historians for American Foreign Relations, the Organization of American History, the American Studies Association, the Association of Asian American Studies, the Marianas History Conference, and the Native American and Indigenous Studies Association.

Andreína Fernández at the University of North Carolina Press deserves my deepest gratitude for guiding this book into the world. I am indebted to Victoria-Lola Leon Guerrero and Vanessa Ochavillo at the University of Guam Press, who have so graciously and generously edited my writing and worked with The University of North Carolina Press to publish this book in Guåhan. Dorathina Herrero and Carmen Quintanilla Starnes, archivists and librarians at the Micronesian Area Research Center at the University of Guam, have been incredibly generous with their time and effort when I researched, wrote, and finished this book.

My family and friends have provided the foundation for me to write this book. I want to thank the Oberiano family of Guåhan, especially my "Nanay," Florita Oberiano. My aunties Rita, Lily, Luz, and Ning Ning's hilarious stories about getting into trouble with my dad, Ramon, in the village of Sånta Rita in the 1970s and 1980s were an inspiration for this history of Filipinos in Guåhan. This book would not be possible without Auntie Lisa and Auntie Mae's unwavering support for me. My brother Kevin has kept me grounded when I became too theoretical. Our family's more-than-human family members—Jazz, Charlie, Lex, Kiwi, and Jack—gave me much needed breaks during writing and revising sprints when home in Guåhan. I have no words that could convey how grateful I am for my dearest friends, Robin McDowell and Jilene Chua, for their influence on my academic and personal journey, and for my partner, Derek Chan, for bringing joy and love to my life. And to my mom, Marlyn, for everything, but most especially for being an example of how to use one's talents to serve and give back to the Guåhan community.

Note on Language

In recent decades, there has been a notable shift in the orthography of the CHamoru language in both academic work and everyday use. This shift reflects the ongoing movement to revitalize and standardize *fino' CHamoru* (CHamoru language) in Guåhan. In this book I have chosen to follow the orthography specified by the Guåhan-based Kumisión I Fino' CHamoru yan Fina'nå'guen I Historia Yan Lina'la' I Taotao Tåno (Commission on CHamoru Language and the Teaching of History & Culture of the Indigenous People of Guam). Therefore, I use "Guåhan," even though "Guam" is the most recognized and widely used on island and beyond. I have also chosen to use "CHamoru" instead of "Chamoru" or "Chamorro." However, at times the many primary and secondary sources I have incorporated into this history use "Guam," "Chamoru," or "Chamorro," consistent with the period from which they originated. Government departments and institutions may also use the spelling "Guam" or "Chamorro" in their titles. In these cases, I will quote directly with the term used. More information about the Kumisión I Fino' CHamoru can be found at https://kumisionchamoru.guam.gov/.

Additionally, I have chosen to use the general and ungendered term "Filipino" to describe those from the Philippine archipelago. The term "Filipino," as I contend in this book, is in active formation throughout the twentieth century, in which Philippine regional and provincial identities often took more prevalence in the lives of Filipino migrants moving to Guåhan. In the cases where it makes sense, I will use the more specific regional appellation that the primary source, secondary source, or oral history interviewee has used.

Timeline in Guåhan History

1521 The people of Guåhan encounter Ferdinand Magellan in his quest to circumnavigate the world. Magellan is killed by Lapu-Lapu in Cebu, Philippines.

1565 Spain claims Guåhan for the Spanish Empire.

1668 The first Spanish Catholic mission is established in Guåhan.

1670–1699 CHamorus resist Spanish colonialism in the CHamoru-Spanish Wars.

1872 The Cavite Mutiny signals a burgeoning anticolonial movement in the Philippines. Filipinos are exiled to Guåhan.

1896 The Philippine Revolution begins.

1898 The United States annexes Guåhan and the Philippines from Spain in the aftermath of the Spanish-American War.

1899 The United States establishes Naval Government in Guåhan and fights the Philippine Revolution.

1901 The first petition by CHamorus for civilian government is sent to the US Congress. (More petitions are sent in 1917, 1925, 1929, 1933, 1936, 1947, 1949, and 1950.)

1934 The Tydings-McDuffie Act sets date of 1944 for Philippine independence from the United States.

1936 CHamoru leaders Baltazar J. Bordallo and Francisco B. Leon Guerrero travel to Washington, DC, to meet with the US Congress and President Franklin D. Roosevelt and request US citizenship for those living in Guåhan.

1941 The Japanese Empire attacks and occupies Guåhan and the Philippines in World War II.

1944 The US military invades and reoccupies Guåhan and commences military buildup.

1946 The Philippines gains independence from the United States.

1947 The United States negotiates an Exchange of Notes with Philippines to transport Filipino migrant workers for military buildup in Guåhan.

1950 President Harry S. Truman signs the Organic Act of Guam, creating a civilian government and granting US citizenship to residents of Guåhan, including non-CHamoru people.

1959 The first tourism-focused hotel in post–World War II period opens.

1962 President John F. Kennedy lifts military security clearance that had been in effect since 1941.

1962 Typhoon Karen hits Guåhan, destroying island infrastructure and paving the way for the economic development of Guåhan toward tourism.

1965 The US Immigration Act of 1965 applies to Guåhan and opens the island to more immigration.

1969 The Guam Legislature establishes the Commission on Political Status to reconfigure Guåhan's territorial relationship to the United States.

1970 The Guam Visitors Bureau is formally established to organize tourism economic development.

1970–79 The Guam Constitution Movement seeks reform in island's territorial relationship.

1972 Philippine President Ferdinand Marcos declares martial law in the Philippines, leading to a rise in Filipino migration to Guåhan.

1979 The Guam Legislature establishes the Commission on Self-Determination to determine a new political status for Guåhan.

1980–93 The Guam Commonwealth Movement drafts, votes upon, and presents a new political status of Guam Commonwealth.

1997 The Guam Legislature establishes the Commission on Decolonization to advocate for United Nations decolonization process for Guåhan.

2006 The US Department of Defense announces the Alliance Transformation and Realignment Agreement expanding, once again, the US military presence on Guåhan.

Territorial Discontent

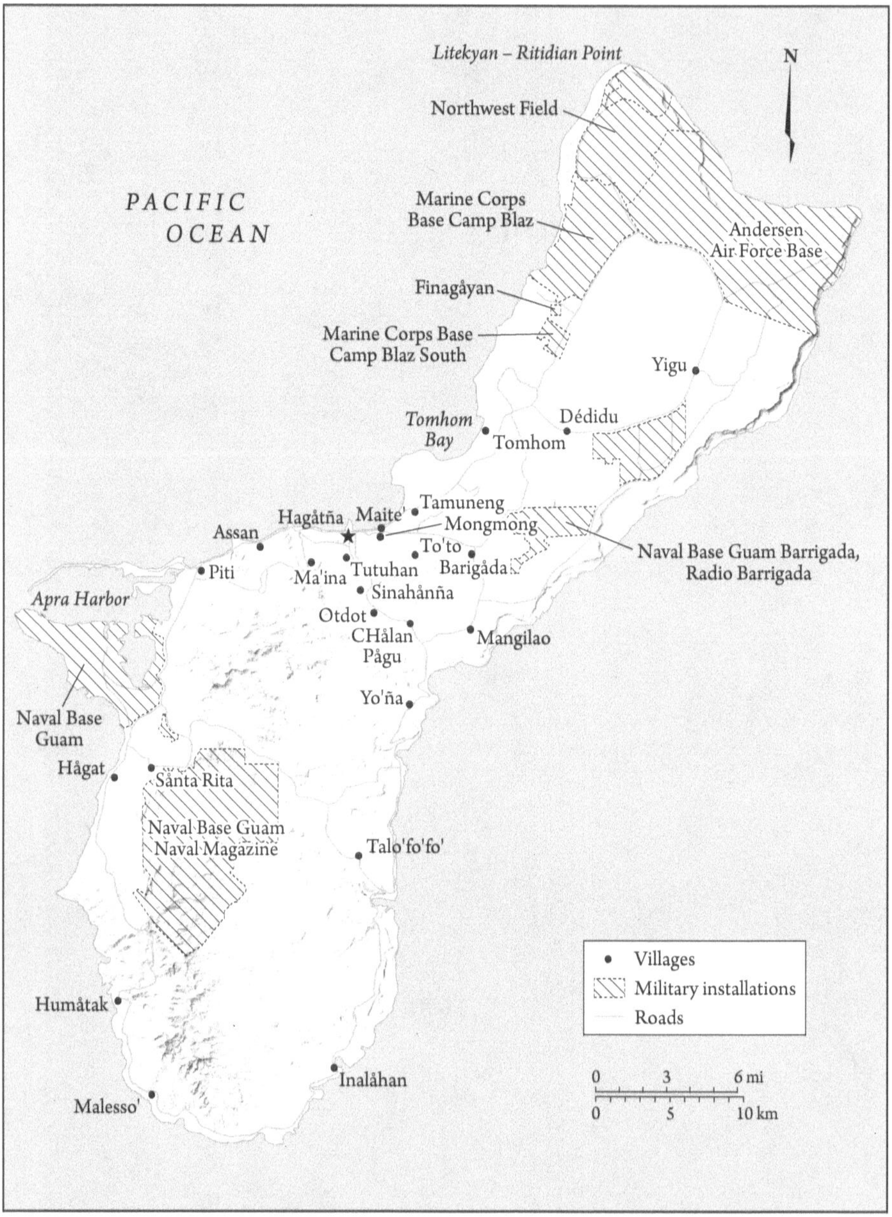

Map of the island of Guåhan with current villages and military installations (bases, stations, and camps) and military infrastructure (major road system on Guåhan).

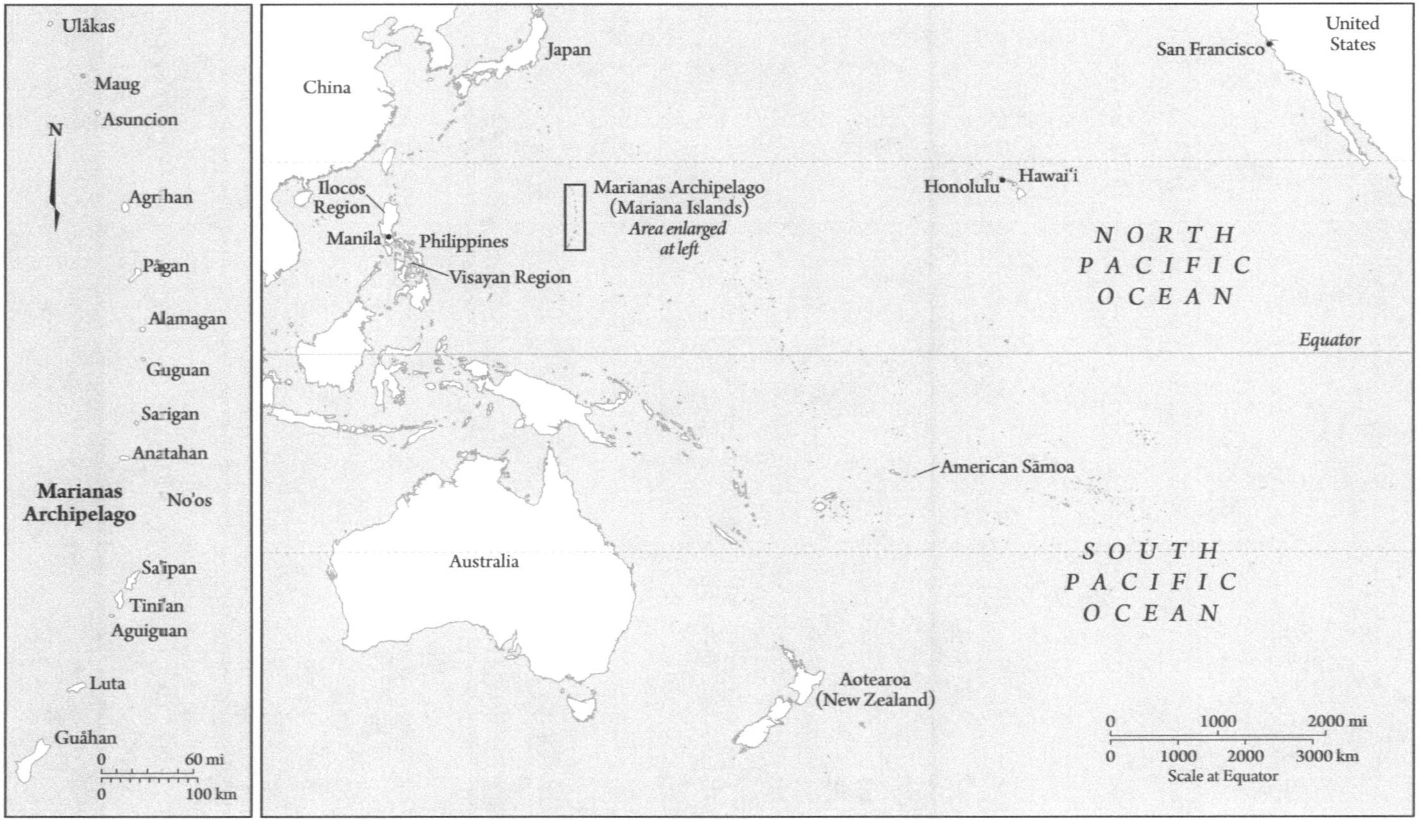

The Marianas Archipelago and the Philippine Archipelago in the context of the Pacific.

Prologue
Territorial Discontent

In 1947, a group of American academics visited the United States territory of Guam—Guåhan, a Micronesian island so far west in the Pacific Ocean that it was a whole day ahead of the North American continent. Led by Dr. Ernest M. Hopkins, the committee was created to research and offer recommendations to US Secretary of the Navy James Forrestal on what to do with the US Pacific territories of Guåhan and American Sāmoa, which had been US colonial possessions the Navy had governed before World War II.[1] The US federal government questioned whether it was necessary to reconfigure the islands' colonial statuses and confer US citizenship on their inhabitants amid the changing priorities of a postwar military. During their visit in Guåhan, the Hopkins Committee met with the Indigenous CHamoru leaders. US citizenship was frequently discussed during the proceedings, but it was not the only issue on the table. CHamorus sought access to land that the US military had annexed and transformed into the largest US-forward military base in the Western Pacific. The US military had condemned two-thirds of the island, and constructed military infrastructure, including roads, airstrips, harbors, and Quonset hut cities, to support the Allied front lines of the Pacific Theater.[2] Despite the end of the war, Guåhan was geographically positioned to become even more important to the United States projection of political and military power in the Pacific in latter decades. This militarized transformation irreversibly changed the political, social, and environmental landscape of the island.

One CHamoru man, Jose M. Flores, was livid about the US military's treatment of the CHamoru people. Two years after World War II ended, at which point Guåhan once again came under the control of the United States, Flores saw how the CHamoru people still could not move freely around their own island even after the so-called liberation of Guåhan by US forces. He testified before the Hopkins Committee, stating that "the people must know where to settle permanently as the government, more or less, owns or have [*sic*] the whole say of our lands and our whereabouts. Such a condition creates discontent." In the perspective of Flores and many other CHamorus, the US military had simply replaced the occupying forces of the Japanese military. Rather than bringing freedom to an island that was hit by war, Flores testified, US Army, Navy, and Marine "units at times occupying our properties won't let us come to such properties which causes ill-feeling also." "The products of the lands, as a rule are denied [to] us," he said, "such as mangoes, oranges, etc. Unsettled or restless people cannot work in harmony. Most [military] Units display signs—'Restricted Agana—Keep away.'" Flores reiterated to the Hopkins Committee, "The usual thing we were or are being told is that the properties are not ours. Imagine your feeling when told such a thing!"[3] Defying CHamorus' hopes and expectations, the US military had dispossessed and displaced the CHamoru people and continued to restrict their movements, brewing discontent within an increasingly important territory of the US empire. Before World War II, Guåhan had not been a place of violent anticolonial resistance. So Flores was unusually explicit about his dissatisfaction with US military operations on the island. He noted that because "the Island has been under Military Rule since its discovery," most CHamoru people would "naturally . . . abide with whatever the government wants, although we suffer silently."[4]

Other CHamoru leaders preferred to negotiate and engage in diplomacy to convey their discontent, often seeking gradual changes in the island's relationship to the United States. Yet Flores's testimony reveals a subtle, yet important, shift in the relationship between the US military and CHamorus on the island. CHamorus were no longer willing to quietly acquiesce to US colonial rule, and instead were ready to vocally express their discontent with the US empire. After listening to several testimonies, the Hopkins Committee recommended that CHamorus be given US citizenship, that their land and property claims be processed in a timely manner, that their heroic loyalty during World War II be recognized, and that at some future point the US Navy transfer jurisdiction of the island to another department of the federal government.[5] It was determined that the US colonies, where self-governance was not guaranteed, seemed to be antithetical to the American mission to spread democracy abroad. Moreover, CHamoru discontent could prove to be dangerous for US global power that paradoxically defended the rise of decolonization through the growth of US militarism.

Jose M. Flores might have garnered the courage to criticize the US military precisely because of his experience as a colonial subject moving across the US Pacific empire. Flores's early childhood reflects the imperial routes of migration and movement between the newly annexed Pacific colonies. Although born and raised in Guåhan, Flores attended school in American colonial Manila in the Philippines from 1911 to 1914, "at the expense of the

Filipino tax payers," as he put it.[6] His older brother Pedro Muña Flores also attended school in the Philippines, apparently sponsored by Silvestre Legaspi, a former Filipino revolutionary exiled to Guåhan who had been the general treasurer of the Philippine Revolutionary Government under Emilio Aguinaldo.[7] Legaspi was one of the approximately fifty "dangerous" Filipino revolutionaries who were exiled to Guåhan by the US Army in the Philippines from 1900 to 1903. Legaspi was exiled with the Filipino political philosopher Apolinario Mabini, also known as "the Brains of the Philippine Revolution," whose leadership heavily influenced the Philippine Revolution. These Filipino elites engaged with the CHamoru elites of Hagåtña, creating lasting friendships that spanned the Philippine Sea.

After living in the Philippines, Flores moved across the Pacific to California in the 1910s. He enlisted in the US Navy at the age of twenty-one and was a veteran of World War I.[8] After his release from the Navy, Flores passed the civil exams to become a worker in the postal service. Eventually he became a naturalized US citizen. While living in San Francisco, Flores met Marcello Sgambelluri, a man whose Italian name hides his connection to Guåhan, having married a CHamoru woman, Joaquina Camacho, after his tour of duty in Guåhan as a musician for the US Navy.[9] Taking Sgambelluri's offer to partner in business in Guåhan, Flores returned to the island, later becoming a well-known, well-traveled merchant whose advertisements adorned the *Guam Recorder*, the island's Navy-run and only newspaper. His business connections spread across the Pacific, including in Manila, Hong Kong, Shanghai, and Osaka. Flores became a leader in the Guam Congress as well as a judge in the Court of Appeals.[10] When he testified before the Hopkins Committee, Flores happened to be one of the few CHamoru people who already had US citizenship, a status that for decades CHamorus on Guåhan had fought for.

Flores understood his position within the US empire. He was so appreciative of the networks that had been created between his CHamoru family and the Filipino revolutionaries exiled to Guåhan, that he used his connections in the Philippine Chamber of Commerce to organize the installation of a monument in 1937 in memory of Colonel Lucas Camerino and Pio Barican, two Filipino revolutionaries who died during the exile.[11] He told the *Guam Recorder* that President Manuel Quezon of the Philippines had sponsored the monument. Leon Flores and Pancrasio Palting, two former Filipino revolutionary exiles who had settled in Guåhan, attended the memorial dedication. During the ceremony for the monument, Naval Governor of Guam Benjamin McCandish told onlookers that "this monument will serve as evidence of the bond that exists between Guam and the Philippine Islands," and that "the two peoples have kindred interests."[12]

Flores's life story connects the island of Guåhan, the Philippines, the continental United States, and the institutions of the US military and US Congress. His story is just one of the thousands of stories of CHamorus and Filipinos on Guåhan whose lives reflect the complexities and contradictions of colonial encounters, transpacific migration and movements, imperial negotiations, and social relations of colonized subjects within and throughout the US empire in the Pacific. In this book I have aimed to capture the political, intellectual, cultural, and social productions and oral histories of people like Jose M. Flores to tell a century-long history of US imperialism in the Pacific, and to elucidate how the United States made, governed, militarized, and controlled its Pacific empire—and how CHamorus and Filipinos resisted.

Introduction

CHamorus, Filipinos, and US Liberal Militarism in Empire

This history charts how CHamorus and Filipinos in Guåhan navigated, negotiated, and resisted the contradictions that arose out of different forms of colonialism and militarism that composed the basis of the US empire in the Pacific. Over the twentieth century, CHamorus in Guåhan experienced truncated political rights in an unincorporated territory, encountered ongoing land dispossession facilitated by the US military, and grieved over unfulfilled quests for self-determination. As an Indigenous people, they faced US settler militarism that threatened their presence in, and ties to, Guåhan. Meanwhile, Filipino migrants and immigrants, those more transient and those who settled long-term term in Guåhan, confronted the legacies of US colonialism in their home archipelago. US extractive colonialism, neocolonialism, and continued militarism propelled Filipino migrations across the Philippine Sea. As they arrived in Guåhan via political exile or economic opportunity, they faced an empire that continuously racialized them as outsiders and workers. These different forms of colonialism and militarism produced inequalities that shaped—and limited—what CHamorus and Filipinos understood freedom to be.

To resist the inequalities of empire, CHamorus and Filipinos on Guåhan sought greater inclusion *within* the United States throughout the twentieth century. They employed both a Western understanding of rights and the rhetoric of liberalism in their pursuit for political and economic freedom that they believed could be fulfilled with US citizenship and greater self-governance. To maintain control over Guåhan, CHamorus fought for political rights and power to counter unilateral US colonial governance, military land dispossession, and increased immigration. Meanwhile, to provide for themselves and their families, Filipinos sought US citizenship and permanent residency to protect their economic opportunities as immigrants and workers.

CHamoru and Filipino discontent—filtered through a rights-focused, liberal rhetoric framework—found expression in petitions, legal cases, protests, and demonstrations. Rather than partaking in outright anticolonial or decolonial movements against the US empire, they advocated for solutions predicated upon the continued colonization of themselves and each other. CHamorus often conveyed their sense of proximity to the United States through notions of race, loyalty, and civilization—even as they relied on and benefited from the racialized labor and exclusion of Filipinos from the United States. Conversely, Filipinos portrayed themselves as worthy immigrants and settlers by citing their ability to work and "rebuild the island"—even as they did so on annexed CHamoru land. Additionally, as evidence of the good in the US multicultural immigrant narrative, US settlers and colonial officials used the presence of Filipinos to oppose the CHamoru fight for self-determination. Both groups were critical of US colonial rule on Guåhan, but without a conscious realization of their common struggle under empire, their respective actions were rife with contradictions. While seeming to advance improvements for their communities, they only created further division and reproduced the foundations of US empire in Guåhan. What these contradictions reveal is not just the disparity between Indigenous rights and immigrant rights within empire, but the inherent limitations of liberal forms of "freedom."

The complicated history of CHamoru and Filipino relations demonstrates how two differently colonized groups were making the best decisions they could in an empire that offered them limited possibilities. By centering the history of CHamoru-Filipino relations in Guåhan, the following chapters relate—but do not conflate—the differing political, social, and economic motivations for CHamorus and Filipinos to elucidate how the past and present reliance on a limited liberal promise of freedom foreclosed alternative possibilities for anticolonial and decolonial resistance and solidarity against US empire. Yet this book also offers some inklings of how CHamoru-Filipino relations, rooted in a connection to Guåhan and the CHamoru virtue of *inafa'maolek*, "making good relations," can provide the foundation for the island's decolonization.

US Liberalism and Militarism in Guåhan

If CHamorus and Filipinos in the twentieth century advocated for liberal rights, it was because liberalism was the rhetorical terrain upon which the United States justified its imperial forays throughout the globe. In 1900, US Naval Captain Richard P. Leary issued a short proclamation that notified the "inhabitants of Guam" about the island's transition of sovereignty from Spain to the United States. As the first US Naval Governor of Guam, he lambasted the Spanish Empire for instituting a "labor-degrading system of human bondage and unjust, indefinite servitude or Peonage" that was "a system of Slavery" and thus was "subversive of good government, . . . an obstacle to progressive civilization, a menace to popular liberty, and violation of the privileges guaranteed by the Constitution of the United States."[1] Leary's proclamation is telling. Liberal "freedoms" have historically been constructed in opposition to slavery's "unfreedom"; liberal ideals and practices had the power to politically emancipate individuals from unequal forms of power and secure individual rights.[2] So when Leary called for the "absolute prohibition and total abolition of Human Slavery or Peonage," he suggested that the United States would facilitate the fulfillment of the promises of liberalism in the former Spanish colonies. It would do so through the development of "progressive civilization," "popular liberty," and the arrival of modernity through the "benevolent assimilation to the fundamental principles that constitute the basis of Free American Government."[3]

Leary's liberal rhetoric was compelling for CHamorus and Filipinos at this pivotal and uncertain time of revolution and imperial transition. Generally understood, liberalism refers to the Western political philosophy that proposes the "universal promises of rights," encapsulated by individual political rights, economic freedoms, equality among other peoples, and citizenship within a state.[4] Theoretically, liberalism is practiced within democracies where individuals can participate in political life, as opposed to monarchies, dictatorships, or autocracies where those without power are subject to the ruling classes. Liberalism also informs progressive historical narratives, where individuals, groups, or nations "progress" from an "uncivilized" past into civilized "modernity," or from an "unfree" past to the "free" present.[5] From this definition of liberalism—one that those on Guåhan would be familiar with—imperialism and colonialism seem to be anomalies or even in opposition to liberalism because the "universal promises of rights" were historically unevenly applied to colonial subjects in the geographic margins of empire, if they were applied at all.[6] Yet, historically, the exercise of liberalism depended on hierarchical modes of power and difference-making, including race, nation, gender, and class, that distinguished those who were "civilized," and thus worthy liberal rights, from those who were "uncivilized" and "not yet ready" for liberal freedom.[7]

By looking at different forms of US colonialism in Guåhan throughout the twentieth century, I show in the following chapters how liberalism's proclaimed universal rights of freedom and equality seemed to only further entrench the inequalities of colonialism for those living in Guåhan. As Leary's proclamation and the chapters of this book demonstrate, US colonial and military officials justified their colonial policies in the rhetoric of liberalism, assuring Guåhan's inhabitants that these policies were beneficial to them, the United States, and the world at large. In the Naval period, US education systems, health institutions, and infrastructural projects sought to prepare the island and the CHamoru people for liberal modernity. In their implementation, however, these colonial policies prioritized a US culture imbued with hierarchical notions of race, gender, and civilization that depended upon the erasure of CHamoru culture and language. After World War II, the United States further developed military infrastructure in the hopes of projecting and protecting liberalism and democracy against communist foes that sought to influence the Asia-Pacific region. This process relied on the simultaneous annexation of CHamoru land and the exploitation of Filipino labor in Guåhan.[8] Furthermore, in the late twentieth century, the United States bestowed citizenship on Guåhan's diverse nonwhite population, a strategic move that implied a US willingness to let go of its racist and segregationist past and move toward fulfilling universal freedom and equality for all peoples. In fact, however, the bestowal of US citizenship on CHamorus discounted their indigeneity, made them another minority group in their home island, and obscured the island's ongoing militarization for US Cold War interventions in the Asia-Pacific region. These contradictions play into the twenty-first century. In addition to the consistent repetition of Guåhan's inclusion within the United States—Guam is "Where America's Day Begins"—US military officials continually cite the continuous threats to the US "freedom and democracy" in the Pacific to justify its presence on island.[9]

Because the promises of liberalism—citizenship, infrastructure, modernity, democracy—seem beneficial, it has been easy to perpetuate the perception that the US military is the protector of freedom for the United States and the people in its colonies.[10] It is because of the language of liberalism that the violence of militarism—war, death, CHamoru land dispossession, Filipino racialized labor, environmental degradation—can sometimes go unnoticed or uncriticized. CHamoru scholars Michael Bevacqua and Manuel Cruz note that US militarism has become "banal." They write, "US colonialism, militarism, and imperialism all pass over and through Guam and do not emerge as smelling dubious or inequitable, but rather fresh and welcoming, or, much more commonly, like nothing at all."[11] Bevacqua and Cruz also observe, "Where there is actually an abundance of power at play, there appears to be nothing to be upset about, nothing to critique, nothing to inquire further into, nothing to see here."[12] In this book I seek to reveal that abundance of power by showing how liberalism, colonialism, and militarism coalesced into a cohesive form of imperial power that perpetuates violence even as it seeks to defend liberal rights.[13]

These various contradictions help illuminate why time and time again the liberal arguments that CHamorus and Filipinos had used to justify rights within empire failed to bring about the freedom desired. It is precisely because those liberal rights are dependent on continued US military and colonial presence in Guåhan. Thus, this history provides us with a vantage point to see how liberalism limits what freedom—being a full-fledged citizen of the nation—can look like, a solution to unfreedom that neither questions the premises of empire nor dismantles its inherent inequalities. This is why American patriotism and nationalism as part of CHamoru indigeneity and Filipino immigrant identity becomes particularly problematic. CHamoru and Filipino adherence to liberal freedoms wound up creating contradicting solutions that exacerbated CHamoru-Filipino tensions in a way that foreclosed possibilities for interracial solidarities against US empire.

Ultimately, by highlighting liberalism's limitations through a relational history of CHamorus and Filipinos in Guåhan, *Territorial Discontent* joins the robust conversation of scholars and theorists who ask what anticolonial resistance and decolonization can look like beyond liberalism.[14] I suggest that the historical kinships and solidarities formed between CHamorus and Filipinos—in spite of the pressures to vie for rights within empire—can inform present movements. If part of the liberal colonial project in Guåhan is defining "belonging" along the criteria of race, nation, and citizenship, then this book posits that looking for *inafa'maolek*, both harmonious and retributive, in historical CHamoru-Filipino relations can inspire alternative notions of relationality beyond those that empire prescribes.

Histories in/of Relation

CHamorus and Filipinos share a long history of colonialism. Both Guåhan and the Philippines were colonies of the Spanish Empire from the sixteenth through the nineteenth century.[15] They were both annexed by the United States in 1898 and were ruled, at first, by military governments. During the first decades of the twentieth century, the United States endeavored to teach CHamorus and Filipinos how to be modern liberal subjects via political and civilizational education. Both Guåhan and the Philippines were attacked by Japan on December 8, 1941, and the United States sacrificed both to the Japanese Empire in World War II.

The history of Guåhan and the history of the Philippines, while similar, have significant differences. In 1902 the Philippines transitioned into a civilian colonial government after Theodore Roosevelt declared the end of the

Philippine-American War, whereas Guåhan remained governed by the US Navy until World War II. In 1934 the passage of the Tydings-McDuffie Act slated the Philippines for independence. The United States, however, never seriously reconsidered the colonial status of Guåhan. After World War II, both the Philippines and Guåhan were thrust into a new imperial era; their colonial statuses changed as Cold War international politics demanded. The Philippines became an independent nation-state, while Guåhan was designated an organized unincorporated territory of the United States. Still, despite their different political statuses, both the Philippines and Guåhan remained immersed in the US military sphere in the Pacific. Under the dictatorship of Philippine President Ferdinand Marcos, the Philippines came under a neocolonial relationship with the United States.[16] At the same time, the United States transformed Guåhan into "the tip of the spear" for the US military in the Pacific.[17]

There have been too few scholarly discussions of Guåhan and the Philippines together—let alone CHamorus *and* Filipinos—because of the historiographical tendency to replicate colonial divisions within empire.[18] Conventional liberal histories tend to offer territorially bounded, progressive narratives of colonization to decolonization—or lack thereof—for either Guåhan or the Philippines. This separation ultimately obscures historically intertwined projects of militarism, connected forms of oppression, and grounded CHamoru and Filipino relationalities.[19] Then there is the other, though equally problematic, tendency of liberal narratives of empire to sometimes fail to differentiate the colonial experiences of various colonized peoples. These limitations of liberal histories are not just a problem for historical writing. Liberal narratives hinder alternative interpretations of the past, what Lisa Lowe describes as "past conditional temporality," that can inform present and future movements against the power of empire.[20]

To complicate these divisive or otherwise reductionistic liberal narratives of empire, scholars of Guåhan have called for histories of CHamorus and Filipinos to delve into the interconnected, yet complex, impacts of Spanish and American colonialism.[21] In the following chapters I address the lacunae and divisions in the historiography, by emphasizing how CHamoru and Filipino history are neither separate nor parallel, but instead, in the words of Vicente Diaz, a Filipino-Pohnpein scholar from Guåhan, are "kin of different colonial struggles."[22] Both CHamorus and Filipinos grappled with US empire, racialization, and decolonization, but from different directions. If CHamoru history in Guåhan is about land, indigeneity, and self-determination, then Filipino history in Guåhan is about labor, migration, and inclusion through US citizenship. These foundational differences meant that CHamorus and

Filipinos historically have had distinct and sometimes opposing reactions and responses to US empire.

To capture the complexity of this history in this book, I employ a "relational history" methodology. Relational history is a narrative approach that offers a way to view evolving imperial landscapes by paying attention to how communities were racialized differently both in relation to mechanisms of colonial control and in relation to other racialized communities.[23] Relational histories reveal the relations between different groups "in complex unity," as written by Dean Saranillio, "not flattening difference and assuming these groups are in solidarity, nor falling into the pitfalls of difference and framing them as always in opposition."[24] I believe that by juxtaposing and integrating the distinct experiences of colonized peoples into a *cohesive* historical narrative, relational histories evade binary categorizations, such as "the colonizer and the colonized," and instead reveal how power within empire is multidimensional and multidirectional rather than hierarchical or simply asymmetrical.

Taken to the scale of the family or individual, relational histories are akin to how those from Guåhan understand their place in island society. When people of and from Guåhan meet for the first time, it is common for us to offer information about ourselves, including our family lineages, the villages we come from, and the schools we attended, as a way of mapping a social network of relations that stretch from the present moment to generations past. Who you are is defined by a culmination of historical and ancestral relations. In this vein, I believe it is worthwhile here to foreground my own relationship to Guåhan. I am a third-generation Filipino born and raised in Guåhan. My paternal grandparents, Vic and Florita Oberiano, moved to Guåhan from Iloilo, Philippines during the post–World War II military reconstruction of the island. They lived for a short time at Camp Roxas, a labor camp for Filipinos created by military contractors. My father, Ramon Oberiano, was born in Guåhan and grew up in the village of Sånta Rita in a community of other Ilonggo families who worked for those same contractors. From Ilocos Sur province of Northern Luzon, my maternal grandfather, Manuel Buenconsejo Bello, worked for Andersen Air Force Base as a busboy at the Officers' Club in the 1950s and 1960s. And after he settled, he petitioned my aunt, Marieta Bello, to move to Guåhan; she in turn petitioned my grandmother, Leonor Quimino Bello, and her two younger sisters, Eliza and Marlyn. Marlyn is my mother and the younger of the two girls. Another sister, Pacita, was no longer a dependent and therefore stayed in the Philippines until much later. They bought a house and settled in the village of Barigåda in 1976. Although I grew up steeped in Filipino traditions in Guåhan, I did not learn either the Ilokano or Ilonggo languages and could only speak English fluently, a result of a US-centric education in Guåhan. I was educated at Saint Anthony Catholic School, Academy of Our Lady of Guam, and St. John's School, private institutions that had what could be considered racially diverse student populations, majority CHamoru and Filipinos. I then attended university and graduate school in the continental United States, where I now work in academia. My family's stories and my personal journeys back and forth across the Pacific have shaped my evolving relationship to Guåhan and ultimately influenced how I wrote this history as a Filipino settler from Guåhan. As an acknowledgment of my own genealogy and heritage, my family members' stories appear in this book.

Filipino narratives on Guåhan tend to follow the liberal migrant narrative, which traces an experience of exclusion to inclusion into US society through sacrifice and hard work without an acknowledgment of intersecting forms of colonial power, including Indigenous dispossession. The practice of recounting my own family's migration as part of the post–World War II militarization of Guåhan—one predicated on the annexation of CHamoru land and denial of CHamoru self-determination—is to complicate the liberal migrant narrative and instead place myself in relation to the CHamoru people, landscape, and history of Guåhan. As I have written elsewhere, to identify as a Filipino settler in Guåhan unsettles the image of Guåhan as a mixing pot of multiculturalism, a liberal narrative that equalizes all races at the expense of Indigenous peoples.[25] To identify as a Filipino settler in CHamoru land, furthermore, disempowers the structural antagonisms that are created by colonialism and instead emphasizes the centrality of CHamoru relations to Guåhan. Doing so does not discount the struggles of my Ilokano and Ilonggo grandparents have had. Rather, I partake in the call put out by Tabitha Espina, a Filipino scholar from Guåhan, for Filipinos to disentangle our identity from the US nation-state, "deconstruct" Filipino immigrant narratives, and align ourselves with the Indigenous CHamoru people.[26] Through a relational history, the following chapters lay bare the history of Filipinos in Guåhan to show how colonialism has separated Filipinos from CHamorus and how we can begin to create alternative relations beyond those prescribed by empire.

Employing a relational history method, however, does not mean we can approach CHamoru and Filipino history with the same analytical tools and interpretations. Doing so could flatten important differences in colonial experiences that shape CHamoru and Filipino political and social motivations.

As Diaz writes, "Chamorros have the right to decolonization, and Filipinos themselves have yet to be truly decolonized."[27] Transpacific histories of Asians in the US empire allow us to see Filipino migration and racial and identity formation in Guåhan as a legacy of the greater context of US imperialism and militarism throughout the Pacific.[28] However, relying on transpacific histories, which can sometimes gloss over the Pacific islands and Pacific Indigenous peoples in the service of Asian stories of migration, cannot be neatly applied to analyzing and interpreting CHamoru experiences on Guåhan. Without attention to Indigenous scholarship, ontologies, and methodologies, scholars risk sidelining Native and Indigenous peoples' unique experiences with settler colonialism, and unwittingly further the liberal and sometimes nationalist views expressed by some Asian American studies scholars who argue that inclusion is the solution for racial injustice and the inequalities experienced by nonwhite peoples.[29] Thus, in this book I place distinct CHamoru and Filipino colonial experiences in "critical juxtaposition" to bring into sharp relief what are often narrated as parallel and separate histories of US empire.[30]

Centering CHamoru ontologies and worldview allows for a better understanding of CHamoru history in the twentieth century. This book explores two key concepts in particular: the importance of land, and the CHamoru ethos of *inafa'maolek*. Land has always been a vital part of CHamoru culture and history. In the words of CHamoru politician Ricardo J. Bordallo, "Above all else, Guam is the homeland of the Chamorro people. That is a fundamental, undeniable truth. We are very profoundly 'taotao tano'—people of the land. This land, tiny as it is, belongs to us just as surely, just as inseparably, as we belong to it."[31] Bordallo was not speaking in metaphors. The CHamoru origin story describes how the universe was created from "the infiniteness of space" out of the bodies of a brother and sister, Puntan and Fu'una. Toward the end of his life, Puntan empowers his sister Fu'una to create the world. With his eyes, she created the sun and the moon. From his eyebrows, she created rainbows. Puntan's body was then transformed into the island of Guåhan. When it was her turn to pass, Fu'una transformed into a large natural rock formation called Fuha in the village of Humåtak. There, she birthed the CHamoru people of Guåhan.[32] This origin story demonstrates the significance of the land for CHamoru people. The land is inextricable from their existence. The land is the basis of livelihood, providing sustenance and the abundance that CHamoru people have had for millennia. Land, too, is how CHamoru people understand their relations to other families and clans across generations.[33] The twentieth-century history of US land annexation in Guåhan, then, is both a material and an ontological form of dispossession.

Secondly, *inafa'maolek* is the foundation of CHamoru social relations. Literally translated into English, *inafa'maolek* means "to make good."[34] CHamoru scholar Christine Taitano DeLisle writes that "*inafa'maolek* denotes balance and is based on mutual assistance, cooperation, reciprocity, interdependence, obligation, respect, peace, and reconciliation."[35] It also further shapes "how one behaves in relation to achafñak [family], community, and land."[36] *Inafa'maolek* is practiced in *chenchule'* where people give gifts and acts of service to keep harmony in the community. This *chenchule'* is expected to be returned at some future date, not necessarily by the individual, but by families and kin. The ethos is also observed when families help to raise children that are not theirs, in practices of *poksai*. These acts allow for community bonds across time and space, even through centuries of Spanish, Japanese, and US colonialism. *Inafa'maolek*, however, also has an inimical side as described by CHamoru scholar Keith Camacho, in which lapses to fulfill this responsibility are responded to with disdain, distrust, and sometimes vengeance.[37] To practice in *inafa'maolek*, then, is to understand how one's actions, obligations, and responsibilities impact the whole island and the island's community.

To recognize the significance of *inafa'maolek* as the basis of CHamoru relations and the importance of land as more than property for CHamoru people is to also recognize an Indigenous relationality that settler colonial logic attempts to destroy. *Territorial Discontent* demonstrates how the United States enacted settler military regimes through its Americanization programs to bring "modernity" to CHamoru people and expand its military presence with the aim of protecting liberal ideals in the Pacific. In doing so, the US military denied CHamoru people access to land and then eventually sovereignty and self-determination. Theorized by Patrick Wolfe, among other scholars of empire, settler colonialism is an analytic that elucidates how colonial regimes are premised on the "logic of elimination" of Native and Indigenous peoples for the purposes of acquiring land.[38] Regimes of settler colonialism seek to destroy Native life—including language, culture, institutions, and relationalities—through genocide, assimilation, and displacement in order to replace them with settlers and reproduce settler institutions and sovereignty.[39]

Expanding on Wolfe's theorizations, Juliet Nebolon offers a more precise way to see how the two imperial projects of settler colonialism and militarism can be co-constituted or even coalesce, such that the definitional boundary between the two becomes ambiguous.[40] Nebolon uses the term "settler militarism" to "refer to the dynamics through which settler colonialism and militarization simultaneously perpetuated, legitimated, and concealed one another."[41] Importantly, Nebolon notes how racial liberalism, an ideology that sought to rectify racial injustices through legal and social reform in the twentieth century, nevertheless "precluded a recognition of indigeneity, and elided the ongoing history of settler colonialism."[42] Drawing upon Nebolon's framework, the CHamoru historian Alfred Peredo Flores convincingly argues that the post–World War II era in Guåhan (1944–62) is a period of "settler militarism" based upon "a co-constitutive process that included CHamoru land dispossession, discursive justifications for remaking of the island, the racialization of civilian military labor, and the military's policing of interracial intimacies."[43] I expand on the work by Nebolon and Flores to show how settler militarism in Guåhan since World War II has relied on liberalism and liberal rhetoric to justify the dispossession of Indigenous CHamorus of their land, the unequal labor compensation for Filipino migrant workers, and the assimilation and settlement of non-Indigenous peoples. I also show how settler militarism made the rhetoric of liberal freedom the only available language for CHamorus and Filipinos to use in their fight against the injustices of empire.[44]

Even if CHamorus did not use the phrase or called for complete demilitarization, their discontent with military land policy echoes one of the critiques of settler militarism.[45] I follow the historical insight of CHamoru activists in the 1980s, such as Hope Cristobal, Robert Underwood, and Ron Teehan in the Organization of Peoples for Indigenous Rights (OPI-R), who observed and articulated the connection between US militarism, the rise in the Filipino immigrant population, and the multicultural narrative that subsumed CHamorus as "just" another minority within their home island. Their critiques suggest that "settlers" within settler militarism can be more diverse than just soldiers, military personnel, or colonial officials. Settlers can be racialized migrants, immigrants, and workers who have become imbricated in the process of US militarization.[46] Moreover, settlers do not need to permanently settle the island, either. As CHamoru ally and scholar Samuel Betances wrote in 1977, "the uniforms are always present, but different people wear them, as one group of soldiers leaves and another takes their place."[47] Filipino migrant workers, US soldiers, military personnel, and military contractors—although individually transient—still constitute a nebulous yet visible settler population necessary for the settled presence of the US military.[48] In addition, the colossal imposition of military installations, colonial institutions, and solidification of transient and settled non-CHamoru communities all participate directly and indirectly in the dispossession, displacement, and replacement of Indigenous CHamoru people and culture.[49] These non-CHamoru peoples helped to create a multicultural image of Guåhan that further reproduced and justified Guåhan's status as a militarized US unincorporated territory.

With this CHamoru critique of US settler militarism in Guåhan, conventional liberal narratives of immigrant Filipinos progressing from exclusion to inclusion fall apart too easily. I underscore in this book how Filipino immigrants and migrants—through the auspices of the US military—embodied a nonwhite settler population that came to physically and symbolically replace CHamoru people in Guåhan. From the Filipino revolutionary Apolinario Mabini, who was exiled to Guåhan in 1900, to the Filipino migrant workers recruited to build US post–World War II military installations, Filipino migration—whether for temporary work or permanent settlement—was a substantial part of how the US military secured, colonized, and governed Guåhan and the Pacific.

This happened in three ways. The first is with the labor that Filipino migrants performed to build and maintain the military installations that became the foundations of US settler militarism in Guåhan. The US military's continuous need for a heavily militarized Guåhan to project geopolitical power in the region made it so that military labor became a fixture of the island's landscape. The second is the sheer number of Filipino immigrants who settled on the island, including those who then used the island as a steppingstone for chain migration to the continental United States. Lastly, as explored in chapter 6, Filipinos and their constitutional rights as US citizens became a reason US Congress did not allow CHamorus self-determination and self-governance. Filipino inclusion into the United States was dependent upon their work for empire, and ultimately stymied CHamoru self-determination in Guåhan.

Yet, Filipinos who migrated to Guåhan were simultaneously grappling with their own set of colonial legacies under the Spanish and American empires. As scholar Candace Fujikane, who has roots in Hawai'i but is not Indigenous, writes, "Considering relationalities under the conditions of settler colonialism requires our expansiveness in articulating the simultaneity of overlapping positionalities."[50] If, on the one hand, Filipinos could hold the position as settlers in Indigenous lands, we must also understand that the phenomenon of Filipino migration is a legacy of US colonialism and racialization that positioned Filipinos as expendable and exportable workers for empire.[51] Filipinos were a reliable intra-imperial workforce that could replace other Asian peoples impacted by nineteenth- and early twentieth-century Asian exclusion laws. They were recruited to work the plantations in Hawai'i, agricultural fields in California, fisheries in the Pacific Northwest, and military bases throughout the empire.[52] This racialization influenced and reinforced the understanding among Filipinos that their ability to work (or, sometimes, invest capital) across empire was a tool to escape political and economic inequalities in the Philippines and secure liberal economic freedom outside the archipelago. Some Filipinos saw Guåhan as a physical location to fulfill that liberal promise of economic prosperity, a vision that had been inculcated by US education and cultural influence in colonial and neocolonial Philippines.[53]

In the chapters that follow, I examine how Filipinos navigated the uncomfortable and complicated circumstances created by the US empire in the Philippines and in Guåhan, including the shifting definitions of race, citizenship, and nationality. Their labor took them far from the barangays and barrios of their provinces. Those Filipinos who sought to settle in Guåhan as US citizens built a diasporic home and relationality that gave them opportunities that the home archipelago could not. They formed a Filipino identity within a place that is both Indigenous CHamoru land and a US territory. For those in the postwar migration, their experiences away from the archipelago shaped their Filipino identity. They came as Ilokanos, Ilonggos, Bicolanos, Tagalogs—but through their community building, search for affinity, and labor as overseas migrant workers for an independent Philippine national economy, they emerged as the Filipino community in Guåhan.

In these chapters I follow the astute observations of the Organization of Peoples for Indigenous Rights regarding the interconnections between militarism, Filipino migration, and multiculturalism to contribute a grounded, Guåhan-based history to the scholarship and theory of Asian settler colonialism. In recent years, scholars have created a robust literature inspired by Kanaka Maoli scholar and activist Haunani-Kay Trask's pivotal article "Settlers of Color and 'Immigrant Hegemony.'" Asian settler colonialism is an analytic that heeds the call of Native and Indigenous scholars and activists to show how Asian settlers and/or immigrants' desires for inclusion and assimilation in a racially liberal American settler state reify the dispossession and displacement of Pacific Islanders and other Indigenous peoples.[54] Drawn largely from the Hawai'i context, the Asian settler colonial phenomenon includes a higher population of Asians relative to Indigenous peoples, a greater number of Asian-settler-influenced political and economic institutions, and an emphasis on the liberal multicultural narrative that elides Native and

Indigenous sovereignty. In terms of population dynamics and voting power in local elections, Guåhan also exemplifies this phenomenon. According to the 2020 Guåhan census, the Filipino population (43 percent) has come to eclipse that of the CHamorus (41 percent). In addition, Filipinos, through their presence and their rhetoric, help to support the notion that Guåhan is a multicultural US territory, rather than a CHamoru island.

Yet given Guåhan's specific colonial history and the long-entangled history of CHamorus and Filipinos under empire, Asian settler colonialism manifests differently there than in Hawai'i. CHamorus continue to hold local positions of political and economic power, including governor, lieutenant governor, the Guam Legislature, and the courts.[55] Relatively few Filipinos have successfully run for local office; in recent decades there has not been an increase in elected offices held by Filipinos from Guåhan.[56] Understanding Filipino influence is further complicated by how, at times, some CHamoru leaders have pointed toward Guåhan's Filipino community as evidence of CHamoru hospitality; they have also recognized their own Filipino ancestors, and acknowledged the colonial history shared by Guåhan and the Philippines when they sought to shore up votes for an election or garner support for political or economic endeavors.[57]

But this dynamic—CHamorus pointing to Filipinos as kin when politically beneficial, but distancing themselves at other times—tells us something about how settler militarism works to transform articulations of relations. To combat settler military erasure, CHamorus have been articulating different forms of CHamoru identity and indigeneity over time to prove their relationship to the land and to provide the moral and legal basis of their political rights within the US empire and at the United Nations.[58] As they have done so, CHamorus often have had to redefine Indigenousness to distinguish themselves from outsiders coming into the island, using the legal and rhetorical tools rooted in the ever-evolving language and rhetoric of liberalism, all the while remaining grounded in CHamoru social relations.[59] Sometimes the use of liberal rhetoric has resulted in seemingly paradoxical actions, such as displaying CHamorus' "Americanness" and loyalty to prove their worthiness for US citizenship so that they could confront military land annexation. At other times CHamorus have had to rearticulate themselves as *fully* or *only* CHamoru and disavow or deemphasize their Filipino ancestors to assert Indigenous authenticity and thus legitimize their claims to self-determination in Guåhan. So while most theorizations on Asian settler colonialism (in the Hawai'i genealogy) focus on how Asians align with the settler state rather than Indigenous peoples, Guåhan presents an example of how Filipino presence pushes CHamorus to disavow their Asian kin who may undermine political claims rooted in Indigeneity. These observations only help to emphasize that Filipinos imbricated in settler militarism must be attuned to how inaction and apathy perpetuate a form of genealogical dispossession of CHamoru people.[60]

As a Filipino who calls Guåhan home, I believe that a critical historical engagement of how US imperialism affects different people differently can strengthen mutual understanding between the CHamoru and Filipino communities in Guåhan. Perhaps this understanding can then become the basis for CHamoru-Filipino solidarity for Guåhan's decolonization. My experience with researching and writing this book has been an exercise in historical empathy that I ultimately draw upon to understand my positionality in Guåhan and how I could contribute to an island and people who have given me much. In writing these chapters, I have hoped to be participating in what Espina calls for: "taking apart Western epistemologies and rebuilding a new foundation of decolonial options."[61] Perhaps through an acknowledgment of how US imperialism continues to influence the island's past and present, CHamorus can recognize the colonial legacies in the Philippines that impact the Filipino people in Guåhan and how Filipinos can build better relations to be in solidarity with CHamoru self-determination and decolonization movements. I hope *Territorial Discontent* offers a way to see the complex entanglement of colonial relationships between CHamorus and Filipinos and the limitations of liberal freedom, so that we can imagine alternatives modes of solidarity in pursuit of the island's decolonization.

Inflection Points

The following chapters cover approximately one hundred years of history in Guåhan, when US colonial rule was improvised, crafted, and changed in response to the island's evolving geopolitical military importance, and in response to CHamoru and Filipino discontent. After the island's annexation in 1898, the US military was the administrator and facilitator for the different iterations of colonial rule in Guåhan, where the needs of the US military dictated policies and regulations usually decided by civilian governments. The US military—its strategy and its needs—determined the applicability of federal immigration law, the creation of Guåhan's territorial civilian government, and the possibility of self-determination in accordance with the Charter of the United Nations. There are three phases of US colonialism that map onto the three parts of this book: military colonialism of the Naval era (1898–

1941), settler militarism of the post–World War II era (1944–1950s), and liberal multiculturalism in Guåhan (1960s–1990s). In describing these phases with historical hindsight, I do not suggest that there was a clean break between each colonial regime, nor do I imply that the development of one phase completely erased the previous. Rather, I suggest that each phase marks when US militarism had evolved to such an extent that different characteristics altered its colonial presence. By identifying these shifts, we see how the subtle logics of militarism and liberalism transformed in response to imperial pressures from abroad and within. This also highlights how CHamoru and Filipino struggles for more rights within empire were often working against a series of evolving manifestations of what freedom entailed. In addition, while instances of CHamoru-Filipino solidarity and intimacies are prominent in part 1, they seem to fade into the background in parts 2 and 3. This reflects how CHamoru-Filipino relations had become more rare or at least more difficult to forge and locate, and is thus an indication of how CHamoru kinship relations and *inafa'maolek* became overshadowed by other forms of belonging, such as race, nation, and citizenship.

The first part of this book explores Guåhan in imperial transition between the collapse of the Spanish Empire and the rise of an overseas US empire. Guåhan was essentially governed as a stationary naval ship in which a presidentially appointed Naval governor administered the island unilaterally and often at his own whims. At this same time in the Philippines, Filipino revolutionaries were fighting an anticolonial war against the United States to establish and defend an independent Philippine Republic. Chapter 1 recounts the little-told history of how the US military in the Philippines exiled Filipino revolutionaries to Guåhan to curtail the Philippine Revolution. In Guåhan, these Filipino revolutionaries met and hobnobbed with a cosmopolitan CHamoru elite who leveraged the transition of imperial rule to advocate for themselves. Although the archive does not divulge the conversations between the Filipino revolutionaries and the CHamoru elites, this episode highlights the intracolonial networks of elite colonial subjects within the US empire. Filipinos and CHamorus saw each other as colonial siblings and devised strategies to criticize US colonial rule through skilled articulations of liberal ideals.

Chapter 2 historicizes two inflection points, when CHamorus and Filipinos living in Guåhan had to navigate through shifting definitions and categorizations of race and nation in the early decades of US colonial rule. In 1926, in Manila, a Filipino representative in the Philippine Legislature of the American colonial government introduced a resolution that called for the annexation of Guåhan into the Philippines. Unwilling to join the Philippines and instead seeking greater integration to the United States, CHamoru leaders articulated a distinct CHamoru identity vis-à-vis their colonial sibling, the Filipinos, using rhetorics of race. In the 1930s, Filipino men married to "native" and CHamoru women appealed for Guam citizenship in order to protect their families' lands from alien land laws that the US Naval Government tried to enforce. By this point the United States and the Philippines had started negotiations for future Philippines independence, a process that created the possibility of Filipino-CHamoru families being considered foreign to Guåhan. In both cases, CHamorus and Filipinos expressed their discontent and advocated for their further inclusion into the United States by using a combination of racial logics that further entrenched US hierarchical and homogeneous categories of race. These inflection points reveal the contradictions that arose when CHamoru and Filipino notions of belonging, kinship, and family were overlaid with US liberal criteria for inclusion that were rooted in race, nation, and citizenship.

Part 2 charts how Guåhan became the forward-most military bastion for the US military in the Asia-Pacific region near the end of World War II and in the Cold War era. As chapter 3 shows, the United States projected power in the region by establishing military installations upon annexed Indigenous CHamoru land, which it did with Filipino migrant and immigrant labor. At this time, the Philippines became an independent nation-state in 1946 after the archipelago's decolonization from the United States. Both CHamorus and Filipinos became imbricated within the structure of settler militarism that was obscured by the military's humanitarian rhetoric to liberate colonized peoples and promote and protect global democracy. The case of Guåhan demonstrates that settler militarism manifested not solely in armed forces dispossessing Indigenous peoples through acts of violence, but also by shifting the terrain upon which CHamorus could articulate their relationship to land and how migrant workers from different regions of the Philippines became racialized and nationalized as "Filipinos" through their labor abroad. US settler militarism became justified and legitimized through racial liberal policies of the Cold War.

Chapter 4 investigates how colonial policies such as the Organic Act of Guam and US immigration law served to ensure US military presence in Guåhan. The Organic Act of Guam was a double-edged sword in which CHamorus finally attained US citizenship and a civilian government, but at the cost of the codifying of military land annexation. CHamorus voiced their discontent clearly, as demonstrated in "the Case of Radio Barrigada," where

129 families were ousted from the lands that nourished them. They, then, realized that US citizenship did not necessarily give them more rights to protect their claims to land. Likewise, the US immigration laws that were implemented in Guåhan in the 1950s and 1960s allowed some Filipino migrant workers a pathway to citizenship, all in a concerted effort by the US military and its contractors to ensure a stable labor force to build and maintain military installations. Filipino inclusion in the United States within the territory of Guåhan was predicated on their ability to work for the expansion of US militarism in the Pacific. The history of US citizenship in Guåhan serves as a potent example of the tenuous contradictions for colonized peoples when incorporated and included in a nation-state, especially when they are situated in an unincorporated territory (read "colony") of the US empire. Rather than a fulfillment of a liberal promise of equality, US citizenship helped to reproduce an *American* population for settler militarism in Guåhan.

Part 3 historicizes the emergence of a modern multicultural Guåhan. Even as the US military security clearance, which had been in place since 1950, came to an end in 1962 and Guåhan opened to the rest of the world, the island's civilian economy was inextricably tied to US military spending and a tourism economy based upon Guåhan's image as an American multicultural island paradise. The US military continued to maintain large bases in Guåhan to support its Cold War mission to contain communism in Southeast Asia. As discussed in chapter 5, the island experienced an influx of immigrants, many from the Philippines and the continental United States. This influx of outsiders consequently sparked fears in CHamoru leaders, who saw the rapid demographic changes as deleterious to CHamoru tradition, culture, and life. Yet Filipino migrants and immigrants were also adapting to the legacies of US imperialism—especially with the rise of President Ferdinand Marcos's martial law from 1972 through 1981—by seeking economic opportunities in Guåhan's military-tourism economy. By paying attention to how Filipinos, CHamorus, and white settlers held different perceptions of Guåhan as a place, this chapter elucidates how liberal multiculturalism worked to legitimize settler militarism.

US settler militarism and liberal multiculturalism coalesced by the latter decades of the twentieth century to deny CHamoru self-determination. Shortly after World War II, the United Nations had designated Guåhan as a non-self-governing territory. This required the United States to facilitate a decolonization process. Chapter 6 charts how CHamoru leaders and Indigenous rights activists led movements in the 1970s through the 1990s to change the island's colonial status of unincorporated territory to commonwealth. Drafted with input from residents throughout the island and allies across the globe, CHamorus believed that the Guam Commonwealth Act was the closest possibility for a political status that fit how they believed the island should be governed. The Guam Commonwealth Movement and the activist Organization of People for Indigenous Rights laid the rhetorical foundation for Indigenous CHamoru rights and self-determination and drastically shifted the tone of CHamoru activism from one of mere discontent to outright and vocal criticism of US colonialism and militarism. Because Indigenous CHamoru rights seemed to contradict the US multicultural narrative, opponents labeled CHamoru activists as racist and discriminatory. Yet there were a few Filipinos who stood in solidarity with the CHamoru movement, believing that CHamoru people had an inherent right to self-determination in Guåhan. Despite the support from Guåhan's electorate, the bill for the Guam Commonwealth ultimately died in the US Congress in 1997 because federal officials claimed that an exercise of CHamoru self-determination would be in violation of the US Constitution and civil rights and that it could threatened the US military presence in Guåhan.

This book's discussion ends with the demise of the Guam Commonwealth Movement, but these chapters reveal how CHamoru relationship to land and the ethos of *inafa'maolek* became the foundations for anticolonialism that sidestepped the ordinary rhetoric of individual rights and freedom. Even though there were many cases of Filipino antagonism toward the CHamorus, and vice versa, Filipino integration into CHamoru society in the first half of the twentieth century and political solidarity in the latter half was grounded in a relational and reciprocal practice, in which Filipinos understood their relationship to Guåhan, not through the US empire or nation-state, but through their relationships with the CHamoru people and the island of Guåhan. As another element in "relational histories," *Territorial Discontent* emphasizes these historical instances of *inafa'maolek* to give us insight into a possible decolonized future for Guåhan, what Josephine Faith Ong, another Filipino scholar from Guåhan, and I call "*inafa'maolek* solidarities."[62] To challenge the view that Guåhan is inevitably a US territory, and to recognize Guåhan as the land of the CHamoru people, is to substantially rethink the long-held notions of the historical permanence of the US empire—and begin to envision alternative futures.

Part I
US Naval Period (1898–1941)

CHAPTER ONE

Colonial Siblings

Filipino Revolutionaries and the CHamoru Elite in Imperial Transition

At about three o'clock in the afternoon on January 24, 1901, the USAT *Rosecrans* dropped anchor in Apra Harbor off the coast of Guåhan.[1] It had embarked fifteen days earlier from Manila Bay in the Philippines, carrying coal for steamships, canned food for Navy personnel, medical supplies for the hospital, building materials for infrastructure, and other things needed to establish a naval station on the island. Also on its manifest were thirty-seven Filipino men (along with their servants) whom US Army General Arthur MacArthur believed were the most influential and dangerous leaders of the Philippine Revolution. With the approval of US Secretary of War Elihu Root, these men, including "The Brains of the Revolution," Apolinario Mabini, were exiled to Guåhan in the attempt to "pacify" the uprising against the US empire.

A few months later and a few miles down the road in the capital village of Hagåtña, thirty-two men—a priest, a few cosmopolitan businessmen, former colonial officials of the Spanish government, and descendants of Spanish-era Filipino *deportados* (deportees)—gathered to sign a petition to be sent to the White House in Washington, DC. After three years under US rule, the islanders did not have an American-style representative democracy, so they petitioned for a permanent civilian government. They wrote that such a government would "enable us to mold our institutions to the American standard, and prepare ourselves and our children for the obligations and the enjoyment of the rights and privileges to which, as loyal subjects of the United States, we feel ourselves rightly entitled."[2] To them, the United States' arrival on Guåhan should have meant more political rights and freedom. Unfortunately, it did not.

CHamorus and Filipinos challenged US colonialism and sought greater self-government for their respective peoples, albeit in different directions. The Filipino revolutionaries exiled to Guåhan were the leaders in the decades-long anticolonial campaign for an independent Philippine nation.[3] Meanwhile the CHamoru elite of Hagåtña petitioned for more political rights within the US empire, believing in the US promise of liberalism and modernity that the Spanish empire had neglected to give to Guåhan. While Filipino revolutionaries like Mabini used liberal ideals as a way to theorize political independence and the formation of a Philippine Republic, the CHamoru elite had used those same ideals in the attempt to solidify their influence in Guåhan's colonial government. The differences between CHamorus' and exiled Filipinos' anticolonialism reveal the complex diversity with which colonial subjects negotiated the inequalities of colonialism in response to their different imperial experiences.

These differences, however, did not hinder CHamoru and Filipino elites from cultivating grounded relations and intracolonial networks ironically born out of the Spanish and US empires' carceral strategies of exile, deportation, and segregation.[4] When Filipino revolutionaries were first exiled to Guåhan in 1874 by Spanish colonial officials, elite CHamoru families housed Filipino intellectuals, military officers, and lawyers charged with insurrection. By the time US colonial officials arrived in Guåhan in 1899, CHamoru elites had honed their political acumen from their own experiences with Spanish colonialism, employed the lessons learned from exiled Filipino revolutionaries, and melded that with a keen sense of Indigenous CHamoru relations rooted in *inafa'maolek*. In 1900 the CHamoru elite welcomed the elite Filipino revolutionaries, including Mabini. How the CHamoru elite of Hagåtña navigated this transition of empire, especially how they influenced colonial policy vis-à-vis Filipino deportees and exiled revolutionaries in Guåhan, set the precedent for the subsequent decades of CHamoru negotiations with US Naval rule that couched itself in liberal rhetoric, positioned the island as a US territory, and demonstrated its people as worthy of US citizenship.

The archives do not divulge the political conversations CHamorus and Filipinos may have had, but we can speculate that they discussed their discontent regarding the Spanish Empire and the nascent overseas US empire. They may have learned from each other's successes and failures to garner more rights within empire, and they may have also quarreled about the best course of action for their respective political desires. Yet their letters, diaries, and petitions in the archives reveal the traces of their relationships and how they clearly and conscientiously vied for self-governance in a world of imperial transitions, shifting geopolitical power, and colonial revolutions.[5]

The CHamoru Elite of Hagåtña

The Spanish Empire claimed the Philippine Islands and the Mariana Islands—Guåhan is the southernmost island of the Marianas Archipelago—for nearly three hundred years, beginning with the voyage of Ferdinand Magellan in the sixteenth century. Between then and the early nineteenth century, Guåhan was a stopping point between Acapulco and Manila for Spain's Manila Galleons, which transported goods, people, and gold across the Pacific for nearly 250 years. The archipelagoes were governed via Mexico until 1817, when the Philippines and the Marianas became their own political entity ruled directly by Spain. The Mariana Islands were considered a province of the Philippines; Hagåtña on Guåhan was designated as their capital city. By 1871 the Marianas' provincial status was elevated to a "Politico-Military Government of the First Class."[6] Spanish officials for the Marianas were dispatched from ports in the Philippine Islands with orders from Intramuros, the walled capital city of the Spanish Philippines. Guåhan's Apra Harbor and the adjacent CHamoru village of Sumai became the hub of regional trade and commerce for Micronesia. The Spanish Crown's attention to the Marianas, however, was relatively insignificant. Without a strong export economy, the colonial government in the Marianas was susceptible to changes in funding from the Spanish Crown, sunken and missing ships that delayed or lost goods, and greedy Spanish governors or errant priests who took advantage of the island's people and isolated geography.

Nonetheless, the consistent circulation of military officers, soldiers, merchants, and intellectuals between the Philippines and the Marianas led to a cosmopolitan population on Guåhan. By the eighteenth century, the city of Hagåtña was racially diverse with *mestisu* families born out of the marriages between CHamoru women and soldiers from across the Spanish Empire, including Spain, Mexico, and the Philippines. These men's cultures and languages eventually mixed with those of their CHamoru wives.[7] Historian Michael Clement writes that in the neighborhood of Santa Cruz de Agadña (Hagåtña), "one can imagine that Kapampangan and other Philippine dialects were heard every day in the streets and in the homes" in addition to CHamoru and Spanish languages.[8] These *mestisu* families of Hagåtña experienced upward mobility linked to their proximity with the Spanish military and colonial government.[9] In the nineteenth century, Spanish leadership opened the island to more immigrants in response to a devasting smallpox epidemic and encouraged new settlers to develop an agricultural and trade export economy. These immigrants integrated into the mixed CHamoru community of Hagåtña.

Like many places at the edge of the Spanish imperial reach, the colonial governance of Guåhan relied on local Indigenous leadership and knowledge.[10] These positions included *gobernorcillos*, who led towns, and *cabezas de barangay*, who led village-level politics and tax collection. Indigenous leadership meant a melding of Spanish governance with CHamoru forms of relationality, most notably *inafa'maolek*, a system of relations grounded in mutual benefit formed and cultivated through *chenchule'*, gifts or acts of reciprocity. These bonds were generational, involved whole clans, and were dependent on access to land and resources. For the most part, the *mestisu* CHamoru elite were leaders in Hagåtña, while "ethnically homogenous indigenous" CHamorus led the smaller *reducción* villages outside of the capital city.[11] This distinction is important. When Spanish and US colonial officials arrived on Guåhan, they most likely interacted with CHamoru elites in Hagåtña, as their familiarity with Spanish imperial culture made it easier to converse and discuss matters of government. This also meant that the Hagåtña elite had a substantial influence on the politics of the island in a way that ordinary CHamorus outside the city did not have.[12]

Despite Guåhan's location, the CHamoru elite maintained networks across business, religion, and politics that spanned multiple regions.[13] For instance, CHamoru *mestisu* patriarch Luis de Torres used colonial networks to establish trade between the Caroline Islands in Micronesia, the Marianas, and the Philippines.[14] De Torres was the point of contact for European scientific expeditions in the Pacific. His wealth, ingenuity, and penchant for an intellectual life elevated his family to elite status on Guåhan. De Torres's grandson, Jose Bernardo Palomo y Torres, was the first CHamoru Catholic priest and an influential religious and political figure in the CHamoru community during the transition between Spanish and US rule. It is said that Spanish officials could not adequately enforce a law without Påle' Palomo's approval.[15] Educated at the Jesuit Colegio de San Juan de Letrán on Guåhan and ordained in Cebu, Philippines, Påle' Palomo represented the leadership, diplomacy, and cosmopolitan intellectualism of the CHamoru elite.[16] A polyglot, Påle' Palomo welcomed arriving European expeditions and other Pacific Islanders, and he offered outsiders critical insight into CHamoru and Marianas society.

Like the de Torres and Påle' Palomo, the CHamorus elite of Hagåtña took advantage of imperial routes, and in some cases these circuits brought information and knowledge that shaped how they interacted with world affairs. They were connected to Manila in particular.[17] Some traded goods from their large plantations on Guåhan in the Philippine market as well as sent their sons, who most likely attended the Colegio de San Juan de Letrán in Hagåtña, for further education at Philippine universities such as the Colegio de Santo Tomas (now the University of Santo Tomas) in Manila. With colonial subjects moving throughout the Pacific, CHamorus cultivated a political

Påle' Jose Palomo (1836–1919). From the Collections Division of the Guam Museum, a division of the Department of Chamorro Affairs.

philosophy influenced by events in the Philippines and the rest of the Spanish Pacific. When the Philippine Revolution began in the 1860s, Guåhan felt its reverberations.

The Philippine Revolution in Guåhan

The Filipino *ilustrados* were elite men who launched an intellectual, anticolonial campaign against Spanish imperialism. They were disgruntled with the Spanish colonial government that relied on the bureaucracy of the Catholic Church, exploited economic resources, and treated the people as colonial subjects rather than liberal citizens. The Propaganda Movement in the 1870s sought reform within the Spanish Empire, but those hopes went unfulfilled as the Spanish clamped down on any criticism of colonial rule, using violence, the execution of prominent leaders, and political exile.[18] By the 1890s an armed resistance struggle emerged with the Katipunan, a secret revolutionary group whose largely rural and peasant membership fought in the jungles and battlefields for the founding of a Philippine nation.

The Philippine Revolution echoed across the sea to Guåhan. In the nineteenth century, Spanish officials designated Guåhan as a penal colony for exiled convicts and anticolonial insurrectionists. Exile became a way to both control the peripheries of empire and support underdeveloped colonies through labor migration for public works and racial mixing.[19] For example, Filipino convicts from the more Christianized areas of the northern Philippines were exiled southward to the predominantly Muslim region of Mindanao.[20] In the 1860s, Guåhan and the Marianas became one of four penitentiaries in the Spanish Pacific, alongside one each in Zombanga and Cavite as well as the infamous Bilibid Prison in Manila. The famous leader of the Propaganda Movement, Jose Rizal, noted the carceral policies of the Spanish Empire in his novel *Noli Me Tangere*, where a Spanish friar warned the protagonist, Crisostomo Ibarra, "Let us give thanks to the Lord our God that you are not in *Marianis insulis comotes plantado* [the Marianas Islands planting sweet potatoes]."[21] Indeed, Guåhan received three waves of exiles from the Philippines: the first of convict laborers; the second of Filipino deportados associated with the 1872 Cavite Mutiny, widely considered the first violent rebellion against the Spanish Crown in the Philippines; and the last in the 1890s of Filipino revolutionaries who carried their revolutionary motivations to Guåhan. While some deportados were wealthy and educated, there were several hundred ordinary Filipino exiles, soldiers, laborers, and servants who put a strain on the finite resources of Guåhan.[22]

In 1861 the Spanish governor of Guåhan, Felipe de la Corte, attempted to use the labor of a hundred exiled *presidarios* (convicts) to develop the island's economy.[23] He asked for men who were physically fit and hardy enough to survive labor in tropical weather and well-behaved so that they could be housed among wealthy families on the island.[24] The plan quickly backfired. In November 1851 the convicts attacked a governor's patrol and attempted to take over the village of Hågat.[25] In response the governor deployed armed reinforcements who promptly subdued the rebellion. Fugitives were captured by the end of the week. In the aftermath, the governor noted to his superior general that the convicts' actions were an "atrocious plan" that "they had formed from their very first arrival . . . to pillage all the whites and the principal citizens of these islands."[26]

Nevertheless, policies of exile continued until the end of Spanish era. In the 1870s, Guåhan received Filipino political prisoners who were discontent with Spanish colonial rule.[27] On January 2, 1872, hundreds of Filipino rebel soldiers and workers attempted to overtake the Cavite arsenal in the Philippines to begin a separatist movement against the Spanish Crown. The rebels sought to kill all the Spanish there, including women and children, and declare independence.[28] But the Cavite Mutiny was quickly suppressed by the Spanish authorities, who punished the rebels with harsh sentences. Three priests—Mariano Gomes, Jose Burgos, and Jacinto Zamora—were executed in Manila. Other, more ordinary Filipinos were exiled to Guåhan.

Between 1872 and 1877, there were twelve hundred Filipino deportados living on Guåhan, which had a total population of a little over three thousand in 1856.[29] Free to roam the island, this new infusion of men and a few women caused trouble and incited paranoia among the Spanish officials and the CHamoru elite.[30] Catholic priest Father Aniceto Ibáñez wrote about these Filipino exiles, whom he characterized as desperate, hungry, and dangerous men vis-à-vis the virtually peaceful CHamoru people. In addition to the occasional runaways, convicts and deportados committed violent crimes. Ibáñez noted several violent murders that spread fear of Filipinos among the island's population.[31] "It seems that petty quarrels have been seething among the deportados," Ibáñez wrote. "They tend to settle things with knives and, regardless of the amount of blood spilled, the victims will not reveal or divulge anything."[32]

Spanish colonial officials speculated whether the Filipino deportados could instigate another insurrection on Guåhan, or worse, convince CHamorus to join the revolution. In 1874, for example, "a kind of powder bomb was tossed onto the roof of the house west of the houses of the

Tagalogs." The fire was extinguished, but this left Ibáñez to "hope it was not a native islander or a Filipino, which could mean something else."[33] Ibáñez's fears of a potential insurrection were confirmed when a twenty-two-year-old CHamoru man, José de Salas, assassinated Governor Angel de Pazos y Vela-Hidalgo in 1884. The Spanish guard armed themselves in preparation for an uprising, but none came. Upon further investigation, colonial officials discovered "a conspiracy among soldiers of the local guard company, nearly all Chamorros, to overthrow the government."[34] The presence of the Filipino exiles and the Filipino Revolution itself may have influenced the actions of the CHamoru guards in this act of rebellion. Forty-four suspects were apprehended and sent to Manila for their trial. Twelve were found innocent, thirty-one were found guilty and sent to prison, and four were sentenced to death.[35] The four were executed on Guåhan in April 1885, a warning to any person living on Guåhan willing to take arms against the Spanish Crown. This attempt to overthrow the Spanish government in Guåhan was CHamoru-Filipino solidarity in action.

CHamoru elites were influenced by the ideological underpinnings of the Philippine Revolution. Although most of the exiles were ordinary Filipinos, some exiles to the Marianas were some of the "leading liberal individuals" of the Philippine Revolution.[36] This wave included twenty-two upper-class and educated Filipino revolutionaries who arrived on the island in April 1872. These exiles, consisting of lawyers, clergy, and businessmen, were distributed among the elite houses in Hagåtña. Påle' Palomo housed four exiles, including Jose Maria Guevara Reyes, Mariano Sevilla, Toribio del Pilar, and Anacleto Desiderio.[37] These exiled elites took a calm approach to their exile in Guåhan, working with Spanish officials, the governor, and Hagåtña residents to make their stay as pleasant as possible. They brought along personal belongings that included large wardrobes and exotic jewelry, not to mention books and writing equipment that were rare in the Marianas.

These elite Filipino exiles also brought proof of a Spanish Empire on its last legs. Ironically, exile provided the foundations for an intellectual network of Filipinos and CHamorus from the latter half the nineteenth century and into the twentieth. Historian Carlos Madrid notes that the friendship between Filipino Dr. Antonio Maria Regidor and Påle' Palomo may have "facilitated the enhancement of their mutual positions of criticism regarding colonial authorities."[38] Because Filipino revolutionaries were involved in city life in Guåhan, it was very possible that they conversed with CHamorus about colonialism, exchanged political philosophies, and developed strategies for imperial reform and anticolonial rebellion. CHamoru elites took the opportunity to create diplomatic networks that aided their political goals. The fact that they formed such networks of intellectuals, however, does not mean CHamorus merely adopted Filipino anticolonial beliefs. As pointed out by historian Madrid, CHamorus had their own experiences in the Marianas that shaped their own political ideologies. Filipino perspectives instead "added to an already-existing political dynamic" of the CHamoru elite.[39]

More deportados were exiled to Guåhan when tensions escalated in the 1890s. As the Philippine Revolution grew more organized and Spanish authorities continued to deport revolutionaries to Guåhan, exiles came with the full intention to resist the Spanish government on the island. Most notably, on September 11, 1896, fifty-seven prisoners arrived on Guåhan after they were "captured in Manila during the revolt for independence."[40] In December, 207 more "rebel soldiers" arrived at Apra Harbor. Five of the deportados were women. Father Francisco Resano wrote in his diary that two CHamoru artillerymen overheard that the deportados "intended to kill the entire Spanish population, plus any Chamorros who interfered."[41] Two days after the deportados landed on Guåhan, "they began attempting to escape through the windows in the roof, but were stopped by bullets." One person was killed. Five others wounded. Not intimidated by the show of force, the prisoners attempted to escape again that night. They clambered onto the rafters or threw themselves against the prison doors to escape. Resano recorded in his diary, "The Chamorro artillerymen held to their posts, shooting them at close range, and they fell to the ground . . . the shooting continued for some time."[42] Word of the escaping prisoners spread throughout Hagåtña, and "armed with shotguns, machetes, and clubs, [the people] congregated at the vicinity of the prisón" to quell the rebellion. "When the prison doors were opened," Resano wrote, "there before our eyes, was a horrible sight: eighty persons lay dead and forty-five wounded, sprawled on the floor, bathed in their own blood."[43] These violent episodes of the Philippine Revolution in Guåhan shaped the perspectives of the CHamoru elites, many of whom detested the deportados' presence on the island.

Filipino deportados in the nineteenth century earned a mixed reputation in the eyes of the CHamoru elite. Elite Filipino exiles were lauded as symbols of civilization, intelligence, and cosmopolitanism and were useful for the CHamoru elite on Guåhan. With the right amount of diplomacy and hospitality, the CHamoru elite could establish networks that could benefit their families and community for generations. Påle' Palomo certainly understood the advantages of such connections. Meanwhile, lower-class exiles, especially those with revolutionary fervor, were seen as detrimental to the CHamoru society. Påle' Palomo told a former Spanish governor that those exiles were "nothing but a band of thieves, the very scum of Spain, ninety percent of whom could not read or write . . . wretches who only were good to corrupt the morals of natives."[44] Their unwanted presence threatened *inafa'maolek* and the balance of CHamoru relations that prevailed on the island. Nonetheless, the relationships between Filipinos and CHamorus of the Spanish period demonstrate how deeply intertwined the two archipelagoes were, politically, socially, and intellectually.

Imperial Transitions

Toward the end of the nineteenth century, Filipino *ilustrados* sought allies in different countries around the world to support their campaign for independence. Emilio Aguinaldo, Apolinario Mabini, and others in the Filipino Revolutionary Committee understood that a successful independence movement required recognition from multiple powerful nations.[45] Thus, they sent a diplomatic team to Japan, Hong Kong, France, the United Kingdom, and the United States to negotiate partnerships to support the revolution through military and economic aid.[46] Jose M. Basa and Antonio Regidor, two Filipinos exiled to Guåhan and the latter a good friend of Påle' Palomo, took part in this junta. The *ilustrado* junta successfully gained an ally in the United States due to their common enemy during the Spanish-American War. Emilio Aguinaldo worked with the US consul in Singapore to provide support for their revolutionary cause. As a result, on May 1, 1898, Commodore George Dewey sent to Manila Bay a squadron that decimated the Spanish Fleet.[47] For a short time, Aguinaldo was able to declare the Philippines an independent nation.

The United States, however, had different intentions. In August 1898, Spanish officers had secretly agreed to surrender their forces and the Philippines to the US officers in a staged battle to take place in Manila, without any Filipino representation. In this mock battle held on August 13, the United States had "won," leading it to declare that the United States—not the Philippine Republic—had sovereignty over the archipelago.[48] After several broken agreements, and with the ambitions of a rising global power, the United States turned its guns away from its Spanish enemies and pointed them toward the Filipino *ilustrados* and the Katipunan who had mobilized a mass movement for independence. On February 4, 1899, in the eyes of the United States, the Philippine Revolution became the Philippine Insurrection.

The Philippine Revolution was a brutal campaign for freedom and nation in the archipelago. The Filipino *ilustrados* needed to unite the diverse archipelago into a single nation despite the hundreds of different languages and dialects, the equally numerous regional and provincial identities and personalities, and the multiple cultural and ethnic groups. The coalescing of many different peoples into the notion of *bayan*—nation—was no easy feat, even within the group of Filipino elites themselves. Furthermore, the Filipino revolutionaries fought against an imperial power that believed that Filipinos were inferior in race, intellect, and civilization. US colonial and military officials villainized the intellectuals of the Philippine Revolution, despite the fact that they were educated not only at Philippine universities but in several countries in Europe. This racial ideology, in which the Philippine archipelago's linguistic, cultural, and religious diversity were seen as unfit for the creation of a nation-state, also justified US soldiers' brutal actions on the battlefield.[49]

While the US occupation of the Philippines was outright violent, Guåhan's experience of the Spanish-American War was, in comparison, quiet. US Naval Captain Henry Glass approached the island upon the USS *Charleston*, firing shells at the harbor along the Orote Peninsula, receiving no retaliation from Spanish officials. The next day the Spanish colonial governor, Juan Marina, surrendered to Captain Glass. On June 21, 1898 (less than a month before the mock battle in Manila), at exactly 2:45 in the afternoon, the US flag was raised and the "Star Spangled Banner" was sung. Shortly after this ceremonial event, the flag was lowered because Captain Glass was unsure if the United States could continue to hold Guåhan as a territory.[50] Nevertheless, Captain Glass corralled Spanish officials and military onto his ships and left Guåhan in a state of political uncertainty, which would only be resolved once the first US Naval governor arrived in 1899.

The first couple of years of US sovereignty over Guåhan were shaped by the improvisations of low-level US Naval officers and the strategic maneuverings of the CHamoru elite. Colonial authority was never quite clear. In the year between Captain Henry Glass's annexation of Guåhan and the arrival of the first official US Naval Governor of the island, there existed several exchanges of leadership between Spanish, CHamoru, and even American men.[51] On January 23, 1899, Captain Edward D. Taussig brought news of the Treaty of Paris notifying that Guåhan now belonged to the United States and that the Mariana Islands to the north belonged to Germany.[52] After ordering an inventory of the island's treasury and announcing that Apra Harbor was US Naval property, Taussig appointed CHamoru elites to leadership positions:

Joaquin Perez y Cruz as acting governor, Vicente Perez as secretary, and Vicente Herrero in charge of finances. This leadership remained intact until a US Naval captain, Louis A. Kaiser, arrived on the island. Despite his lack of official orders, Kaiser placed himself in charge of Guåhan, removed Perez as acting governor in July 1899, and appointed a friend, William Pritchard Coe, as governor. In response to Kaiser's actions, the CHamoru leaders created their own bicameral legislature to counteract policies created by Kaiser and Coe, but Kaiser disbanded what one historian describes as "what would have been the first legislature in Guam's history."[53] With the US empire consistently leaving gaps in local power, CHamoru leaders were reluctant to let total chaos reign over the island and took the initiative to take charge of their island's affairs.

In August 1899, Captain Richard P. Leary sailed up to Apra Harbor and declared Guåhan to be a US Naval Station. Together with his lieutenant governor, William Edwin Safford, and official orders, they administered the first of nearly fifty years of Naval rule on Guåhan. They were the first in a line of dozens of presidentially appointed Naval governors whose tenures lasted anywhere from one to three years. However, their presence did not mean a clean break from the Spanish Empire; it was a transition. From the beginning, it became apparent that Governor Leary wanted nothing to do with the island, seeking instead to hide himself on the USS *Yosemite*. Leary appointed Safford to be the judge of first instance, recorder of deeds and titles, and auditor of the treasury, all in addition to his position as the lieutenant governor.[54] On the night of the change of command, Safford lay down "to think over my new situation, not without the feeling of the unusual responsibility thrust upon me. But I also experience a sort of exultation in being in a position to help people who would need help, and I hoped that our coming would be a blessing to the island."[55] Originally from Ohio, the forty-three-year-old Safford arrived in Guåhan with about twenty-two years of service in the US Navy in the Pacific and Latin America. A reluctant military man, Safford was an intellectual, speaking several languages including English, Spanish, and German. While in Apia, Sāmoa, he obtained approximately two hundred books from Robert Louis Stevenson's collection. After his retirement from the Navy, he wrote and published several botanical studies on tropical plants he had encountered while on duty. His travels throughout the Pacific made him an exceptionally knowledgeable colonial officer in the eyes of the CHamoru elite. Safford's progressive tendencies and willingness to "help" the CHamoru people, rather than neglect or mistreat, came to represent, perhaps mistakenly, the possibilities of a liberal empire in Guåhan.

Unlike Leary, Safford made the effort to learn CHamoru culture and immerse himself in the CHamoru community. He bought a house in Hagåtña among the CHamoru elite, took tours of the island's smaller villages, studied the island's flora and fauna and how the natives used them, attempted to learn the CHamoru language, and treated the natives with respect. Safford visited CHamoru homes, met their families, visited their ranches and plantations, and often described them in his journal. Safford, in fact, celebrated Thanksgiving dinner with Påle' Palomo, Justo Dungca, Juan de Torres, Gregorio Perez, Lorenzo Franquez, and Jose Herrero. According to Safford, "it was the first real American fiesta that the natives had been called upon to celebrate, and they were not sure how to go about it."[56] Safford made sure there was an abundance of local food at the gathering, cooked and served by Susana, "a most important personage."[57] Safford wrote in his journal, "Nothing more beautiful than this island could be imagined; and no one could wish for more pleasant occupation nor kinder friends."[58] The way Safford described his Thanksgiving dinner with the natives of Guåhan, with the emphasis on friendship and cooperation, reflects how he saw parallels between his and the US Navy's presence on Guåhan with the first European settlers on the North American continent. Believing that US benevolent imperialism sought to "uplift" colonial peoples, Safford wrote, "Above all, I feel it a privilege to be engaged in work which really counts—work in which I can be of some use to people who need me."[59]

In some ways Safford's respect for the island's people could be interpreted and seen as a practice of CHamoru *inafa'maolek*—the CHamoru cultural practice of "making good," sharing in reciprocal practices for the good of the whole community. *Inafa'maolek* is the foundation upon which family and kinship relations are created and practiced through generations. It "gave the Chamorros an understanding of who they are in relation to others in their family clans and communities."[60] To be *taimamahlao* was "to have no shame." To be disrespectful was to break *inafa'maolek*, which brought shame upon a family. Safford, according to community historian Jillette Leon Guerrero, "was the most prolific and influential public advocate for the people of Guam in these years—introducing the American public to the island, its culture and people."[61] Safford's willingness to listen to the CHamoru elites, integrate himself into Guåhan society, and work to improve the conditions of the island made him the liberal, progressive face of the US Naval period at the turn of the twentieth century.[62]

While Safford was an exception to the often misguided and uninterested Naval governors who would pass through Guam during the first half of the twentieth century, he was by no means anticolonial. Safford and Leary were the first in a long line of military officers who based their governance on liberal imperialism, imposing Western values about land, labor, and government onto a racialized and colonized people.[63] For example, the administration's land policy, which transferred all uninhabited, underutilized land to the Naval Government, was the first US policy in the long history of CHamoru land dispossession on Guåhan. Their tax policy furthermore put a strain on landowning elites. They also implemented and enforced laws to prevent CHamorus from "over-indulgence" in village fiestas, which Leary and Safford believed distracted CHamorus from productive work.

Nonetheless, the CHamoru elite negotiated a delicate balance between the US Navy and the island's residents, engaging in diplomatic friendships with colonial officials that could benefit them in the long run. The CHamoru elite needed US officials to ensure their influence in island affairs, and Naval officials needed help from the CHamoru elite to implement colonial policies. For example, the CHamoru elite sought to deport misbehaving Filipino deportados from the Spanish era who could jeopardize their influence upon US officials in this pivotal time of colonial transition.[64] Exiled Filipino convicts and insurrectionists were still distrustful of colonial power, and even more, their lower-class status could not offer any political or economic aid to the CHamoru elite. So, on August 28, 1899, the CHamoru elite sent a petition to Leary regarding the deportation of these Filipino exiles—they perhaps broke *inafa'maolek*—to which Leary entrusted Safford the dirty work of exiling the Filipinos. Using information offered by CHamorus, Safford reported that Filipino deportados started a riot in December 1898 and engaged in general misbehavior that annoyed the CHamoru elite. Safford was also told that "there had been a disturbance between some Chamorros and Filipinos on Easter Sunday, and it was feared there would be an outbreak on the part of the Filipinos."[65] Safford learned that the previous officer in charge of the USS *Nanshan* issued curfews and "took list of those having firearms in their possession."[66] In addition, several lawsuits existed between CHamorus and Filipinos. CHamoru fears of misbehaving Filipinos were not unfounded, considering the CHamoru elites' experience with the violence of Filipino deportados during the Spanish era. Even more, the CHamoru elites' desire to ban colonial insurrectionists from Guåhan might have been a strategic move to demonstrate loyalty to the new colonial power.

To be a good citizen was to be a good colonial within the US Naval Government while participating in *inafa'maolek* among the CHamoru families. Thus, Filipino deportados' criminality was absolved if they contributed positively by becoming productive members of the island through work or family. Upon hearing the request to deport Filipinos, Safford found that "although many of those names were upon the list furnished me were bad or worthless men, yet some were thrifty, hard-working citizens."[67] Those who were deemed "the better class" of Filipinos were allowed to stay, while "orders were issued for the arrest of others, who were [then] confined in the tribunal for safekeeping to await transportation to Manila on the [USS] *Nanshan*."[68] The "better class" of Filipinos, according to Safford, were those who had valuable skills and could work to develop the island, including skilled cabinetmakers and rice planters. Furthermore, men who married CHamoru women and adequately cared for them were allowed to remain. Two poor women and their children visited Safford and claimed that their men "were good men and had never been law-breakers." As it turned out, a "respectable rice planter" was mistaken for a man of "bad character." He was allowed to stay. Safford used his discretion to discern between good and bad citizens—something that Naval Governor Richard P. Leary allowed him to do—but also listened to the CHamoru people who spent time among the Filipino men.

The next day the arrested Filipinos were marched to the *Nanshan*. In a letter to the secretary of the Navy, Leary wrote, "After investigation of the records of those persons, all who have completed their terms of imprisonment, I have decided to send back to their homes (per U.S.S. *Nanshan*) those who are a menace to the peace of this island and undesirable as residents."[69] The exile of these Filipino ex-convicts broke down familial and kinship connections that bonded them to the island. Safford observed a group of women who visited the jail, "some holding little children in their arms and weeping, running after the men as they marched out of town and handing them little baskets and bags of food."[70] The women also brought clean clothes so that the men would not have to "go on board in the working garments in which they had been arrested." Despite having families in Guåhan, these men were deemed irredeemable criminals, whose only future lied in deportation. The handling of unwanted Filipinos on Guåhan demonstrates how the CHamoru elite influenced colonial policy as well as how colonial officials wielded carceral strategies to maintain their hold on the island.

Not all of Guåhan's elite were satisfied with the deportations of the deportados. On October 22, 1899, Safford visited the copra plantation of Don Justo Dungca in Apotguan. Safford described Dungca as "one of the most thrifty citizens of the islands" because he exported copra to the Philippines and owned large grazing lands on the island. Dungca complained that one of his workers who "cleverly constructed" several houses on Dungca's plantation was "one of the Filipino ex-convicts sent to Manila."[71] Filipino labor was crucial to Dungca's commercial success. Dungca himself was a descendant of a Spanish-era Filipino deportado, Nicomedes Ascunsion, who was exiled to Guåhan in 1855. His family and descendants were "productive and turned out to be good citizens."[72] In the 1870s and the 1890s, he housed and employed Filipino revolutionaries exiled to Guåhan, including a Filipino woman who was a servant in his household.[73] Dungca himself became a prominent member of the Spanish colonial administration and easily transitioned into the US Naval administration as justice of the peace. Dungca's integration into the Guåhan elite was due to his entrepreneurial success and the bolstering of Guåhan's economy, which relied on Filipino labor.

Nonetheless, with this successful expulsion of Filipinos, the CHamoru elite saw the opportunity to influence more of the island's colonial affairs. Early on, CHamoru leaders understood that US sovereignty over Guåhan was legally undisputed; but they wanted certainty that they would be consulted in colonial policymaking. They had reason to believe that the new government would allow them to do this. In January 1900, Governor Leary posted a "Proclamation!" in English, Spanish, and CHamoru (perhaps translated with the help of the CHamoru elite) that emphasized that Spain had transferred sovereignty of the island to the United States. The Proclamation said the United States would bring "the surest and speediest route to success, prosperity and happiness for the inhabitants for this island" through "benevolent assimilation to the fundamental principles that constituted the basis of Free American Government."[74] In addition, the United States was to accomplish this task with "honest labor with just compensation" because the Spanish "labor-degrading system of human bondage and unjust, indefinite servitude or Peonage . . . is in fact a system of Slavery."[75] The United States sought to extinguish a regime that was "an obstacle to progressive civilization [and] menace to popular liberty."[76] This proclamation persuaded the CHamoru elite to see more opportunities and possibilities in a new liberal empire when compared to the Spanish empire, and they took advantage of it.

Four months after the proclamation, on April 3, 1900, twenty-eight residents of Hagåtña signed a petition to the president of the United States. The CHamoru elite acknowledged the transfer of the island's sovereignty from Spain to the United States, and they used a rhetoric of US liberalism. They explained, "The Chamorro people . . . hold the hope of entering, if has not done so already, the path of both moral and material progress by being governed by a nation that is eminently free in its form of government, and eminently commercial and industrious, and this legitimate hope gives them grounds to expect that the high authorities, even while distracted by vast matters that occupy them, might dedicate some attention to the advancement of the island, which is currently poor and nearly unproductive."[77] The CHamoru elite believed that the United States, with its "eminently free" form of government, could bring about political and economic prosperity through liberalism where the Spanish empire did not. They also believed that this progress depended on clear communication between the island's people and the colonial government as well as a knowledgeable governor capable of reconciling CHamoru desires with US colonialism.[78] They cited the political and economic developments in the eight months under Safford's leadership as evidence of the island's path toward "moral and material progress."

Of course, the CHamoru elite had a specific person in mind when they wrote this petition to the president of the United States. After demonstrating what they understood to be the characteristics of good governance, the CHamoru signers requested that Safford become the governor of Guam because he had "been working inexhaustibly for all the things regarding the common benefit and, without exaggerating or paying flattery, but on the contrary simply doing him justice."[79] They further elaborated upon Safford's progressive policies; he had put every effort into getting to know the island, including its environment, teaching English language in schools, learning Spanish legal codes, attending to the sick, as well as surveying land. In addition, Safford responded positively to the CHamoru request to remove Spanish-era Filipino deportados from the island.[80] Safford also did not see CHamorus—or at least the CHamoru elite—as any less than liberal individuals, capable of leading and thinking for themselves. The petition's signers were the closest of Safford's acquaintances. These men included Påle' Jose Palomo, Jose de Torres, Gregorio Perez, Luis de Torres, Vicente de Leon Guerrero, Atanasio T. Perez, among so many others.

The signers' request to have Safford as the governor, however, was not heard by the president of the United States. Safford departed the island in July 1900. He wrote in his memoirs, "As the ship weighed anchor and sailed away I felt real grief, as though leaving people of my own blood. I shall always look back upon the year I spent on this lovely island as one of the happiest of my life."[81] It also seems that the CHamoru elite considered him family, sending correspondence to Safford to keep him abreast of the latest news on Guåhan, activities from everyday life, to legal disputes, to marriages and deaths, to the Filipino prisoners, and about the petition to have him as governor of Guåhan.[82] Atanasio Perez sent a letter to Safford on July 5, 1902, detailing the marriages, births, and deaths in the families that had hosted him in

Guåhan.[83] Using these letters, Safford continued to publish about Guåhan's natural flora and fauna and collaborated on a CHamoru-English dictionary with Påle' Palomo, Pedro Duarte, and others.[84]

The first Naval administration of Guåhan demonstrates how the transition of empire, though relatively calm compared to the Philippines, was hardly organized or smooth. The United States embarked on an improvised colonial governance of the Philippines and Guåhan, using preexisting Spanish colonial infrastructure and policies, including Guåhan's status as a penal colony for Filipino criminals sentenced to exile.[85] As colonial elites who had economically and politically prospered under Spanish colonial rule, CHamoru elites of Hagåtña had much to gain from remaining close to US Naval officials. They were prepared to influence the new colonial government, emphasizing the liberal rhetoric that the United States espoused and Safford embodied. Despite lobbying the Naval Government to deport Spanish-era Filipino deportados, the CHamoru elite forged friendships with a new wave of elite Filipino revolutionaries who arrived on the island's shores a few months later.

The Last Wave of Filipino Revolutionaries

On December 10, 1899, in Cayupo, Nueva Ecija, Philippines, US military officials surrounded the house of Zacarias Flores.[86] The US Army had just spent a week surveilling the town after word spread that Apolinario Mabini was living in one of the homes.[87] An eyewitness who was a child at the time recounted that "many strangers were seen loitering about the *población* [population]" and that "these people had no business in Cuyapo." After about a week of spying, a US soldier asked the eyewitness if he had seen Mabini in town. The child, petrified, said nothing, his father having warned him "never to betray Mabini to the Americans." The US soldier, taking the child's silence as a clue to the whereabouts of Mabini, walked to the house of Zacarias Flores, found the front door "securely bolted," but found a way in, using the kitchen stairs. In one of the rooms, "a man with sallow complexion, sunken eyes and broad intelligent brow sat in a large easy chair in one corner." The US soldiers were unsure of Mabini's appearance, but knew that Mabini was paralyzed. They asked the man to stand: "'Up, up!' ordered the sergeant lifting both hands upward. . . . With one supreme effort he mustered all his strength and tried to stand, but he soon gave up the attempt. The Americans then knew they had their man."[88] As they carried Mabini out of the house, the townspeople shouted "Mabini! Mabini! Mabuhay si Mabini! [Long live Mabini!]." Mabini was transported in a hammock back to Manila as a prisoner of war, and for a year lived in a home in Intramuros, Manila, then the seat of the US government in the Philippines.

The US military in the Philippines had taken great pains to find Apolinario Mabini because he was considered the intellectual foundation of a liberal and independent Philippine Republic. A lawyer by training, Mabini was a leader of several revolutionary organizations, including the La Liga Filipina, the reformist organization founded by Jose Rizal in the 1892, and was the prime minister in Emilio Aguinaldo's government after ratification of the Malolos Constitution in the first half of 1899. Throughout his political life, Mabini was adamant that Filipinos should fight for the individual rights to nationhood, which he believed derived from natural law.[89] He wrote several influential manifestos and essays based upon liberal tenets of self-governance that incited fervor for the revolutionary cause and warned Filipinos of the potential ulterior motives that the United States might have had in helping Aguinaldo defeat the Spanish.[90] Mabini held meetings with General Arthur MacArthur and sent letters to the US Congress, including an anti-imperialist senator from Massachusetts, George Hoar. He published letters to convince the general US public that the Filipino Revolution was akin to the US anticolonial war against Great Britain. Mabini remained staunchly pro-independence even when other Filipino leaders believed it would be beneficial for the Philippines to be annexed by the United States and adopted the US-sympathetic "Paterno Plan" at the Malolos Congress in the summer of 1898. Mabini supported the Katipunan and the armed revolution in the provinces that wreaked havoc on the US military's plan to pacify the archipelago.[91] Mabini's subversive and revolutionary work was crucial to the continuation of the Philippine Revolution—or, from the perspective of US military officials, the Philippine Insurrection.[92]

While imprisoned in Manila, Mabini was caught sending correspondence to the last holdouts of the Philippine Revolution. Subsequently, General MacArthur labeled Mabini and his follow revolutionaries as dangerous to the US state-building efforts in the archipelago. As such, MacArthur believed that Mabini's deportation was "absolutely essential."[93] Secretary of War Elihu Root agreed with MacArthur's plan "to deport certain of the prominent leaders to the Island of Guam," in order to "emphasize the sincerity of the Government's purpose, and as a practical example to the natives [Filipinos]." Once again, Guåhan would serve as a penal colony as the US military officials in the Philippines adapted Spanish tactics of crime and punishment to curtail revolution.[94]

On December 26, 1900, Secretary of War Elihu Root commenced the process for exile, ordering the governor of Guam, Commander Seaton Schroeder, to prepare to receive the prisoners from the Philippines.[95] By January 14, 1901, Governor Schroeder received a note from Rear Admiral George C. Remey stating that Guåhan would receive Filipino prisoners that were "some of the most influential leaders of the Insurrectionist Party in these Islands." Remey emphasized to Schroeder that his "utmost endeavors are therefore imperative to prevent the escape of any of them from Guam."[96] With these revolutionaries set for Guåhan, the island was "in the same category as the Naval Prisons at Mare Island and Boston."[97] Ten days later, Apolinario Mabini arrived on the shores on Guåhan aboard the USS *Rosencrans*. The Filipino exiles were still aboard the *Rosecrans* six days after it arrived in Apra Harbor. In his diary, Mabini observed that "nothing has been unloaded from the boat, nor was there anyone disembarking, except the American commandant and officials."[98] Breaking the monotony of confinement, a Marine ship, the USS *Solace*, brought eleven more deportees from Ilocos Norte and transferred them to the *Rosecrans*.[99] Mabini inscribed their names in full in his diary: "With this last batch of deportees, there are now 57 of us, including the servants." For twenty-eight days, they were confined in cramped, suffocating quarters meant for soldiers. Occasionally they were allowed on deck to smoke a cigarette or have their meals.

Eventually, on February 12, 1901, the exiles were allowed to step onto terra firma and forced to walk—Mabini was probably carried in a hammock—to the village of Piti.[100] There they discovered that the Navy planned to house the prisoners in tents on the site of a former colonial Spanish leper hospital in Assan. Away from the capital village of Hagåtña, they were segregated to be forgotten. Poetically, Mabini wrote to his brother Alejandro on February 17, 1901, "they tell us the place could not be better suited, since our minds are suffering of a contagious illness, they are forced to separate us, like the leper, from the society of our fellow beings."[101] The Filipino desire for revolution and self-determination was pathologized as a disease that needed to be contained to prevent CHamorus from catching revolutionary fervor. "Nevertheless," Mabini wrote to his brother in July 1901, "we occupy a beautiful place." He found familiarity with the island, seeing the similarities between the Philippines and Guåhan. "If I face the North," Mabini wrote, "I have the ever raging sea, a steep hill covers my back and my left side, . . . the Barrio huts hidden in the coconut groves and half-destroyed by the last typhoon and farther on another naked hill."[102] He also mentioned the village of Hagåtña, and the native people

Apolinario Mabini, "The Brains of the Filipino Revolution," incarcerated as a political prisoner in Camp Asan, Guåhan. From the collection of the Richard F. Taitano Micronesian Area Research Center.

who "are of our race."[103] Although he was imprisoned, Guåhan's beauty and familiarity brought Mabini some comfort.

Prison life was regulated and disciplined. Major H. B. Orwig, the US Naval officer in charge of the Presidio of Guam, provided prison rules on February 12, 1901; these included the schedules for meals and baths, letter-writing, dress codes, roll calls, and curfews. Ironically, the US Navy created simulations of democratic processes within the Filipino exiles' prison. The Filipinos were allowed to air grievances to the Naval governor as well as elect a president and vice president "to be in charge of watching over the orderly and punctual execution of the orders and dispositions of the authorities relative to the welfare of the prisoners and internal regime of the same prisoners."[104] In March 1901, forty-eight prisoners took part in an election that Mabini presided over. Pio del Pilar won by eleven votes over the famously unwavering anticolonial revolutionary Artemio Ricarte.[105] Del Pilar, a former military general serving Emilio Aguinaldo, was hesitant to be the president because he did not know how to speak Spanish or English. Electing del Pilar rather than someone who could converse with the US Naval personnel suggests that the other exiles thought this position was neither diplomatic nor substantial to advancing the Revolution's goals on Guåhan.

The Navy separated the exiles from the local population, emphasizing the tensions between Filipinos and CHamorus. Mabini recorded that the prisoners "have also been told that our rigorous lack of communication is due to the request of the natives of the Island, who have been robbed by Filipinos confined for common crimes in during the Spanish government, who committed all kinds of abuses."[106] Governor Schroeder also hesitated to expand the prison because "recourse would probably be had . . . to condemnation proceedings against private property, as it is not believed that any Chamorro will voluntarily sell or rent land for the purpose of harboring Filipinos who are held in general detestation."[107] While it is true that the CHamoru elite were successful in deporting Spanish-era Filipino deportados a year earlier, the US Naval officials did not understand that the CHamoru elite welcomed the Filipino elite, as they did later with Mabini's cohort of exiles.

Despite the Navy's attempt to separate the two colonized peoples, the Filipino revolutionaries and CHamoru elite were able to nurture substantial friendships. CHamorus made it a priority to visit the Filipino exiles, whose lives were "so boring," according to Mabini.[108] The visitors included "Spanish mestizas from the prominent families of the district," the same people who attended to Safford in 1899 and 1900, including Pedro M. Duarte and Påle' Palomo.[109] On February 24, 1901, Mabini wrote that "Mr. Pedro Duarte, who was the captain of the civil guards and an old friend of mine from Manila," visited the prisoners. Påle' Palomo also visited the prisoners often, celebrating Mass on at least two occasions in 1901 and presiding over the Catholic burials of two Filipino prisoners, Lucas Camerino and Pio Barican, who died in exile.[110] Påle' Palomo catered to the latest wave of Filipino revolutionaries exiled to Guåhan, some of them inspired by and possibly related to those Påle' Palomo would have been acquainted with in the 1870s.[111]

The Naval Government of Guam was perpetually concerned about the lack of supplies for the island, and this scarcity was felt within the prison compounds. Mabini often complained about how the canned food negatively affected prisoners' health. Using the prisoners' right to appeal to the governor, he sent a complaint about the prisoners' hunger to Captain W. N. McKelvey in November: "We beg you to acquaint the competent authorities with this fact and induced them to preserve us from diseases by starvation. Do it for humanity's sake, if not for other motives."[112] The next month Mabini wrote in his diary, "The prisoners could no longer eat canned meat, no matter how they forced themselves, because they felt nauseated and wanted to vomit."[113] A few of the prisoners had already passed away due to sickness, and Mabini's preexisting poor health did not help either.

The CHamoru community was willing to step in when the Naval Government did not. Fellow sympathetic Navy officers and CHamorus brought various fresh foods and milk to supplement the prisoners' diets. The scarcity of food in the presidio was ameliorated when Mabini's companions in Hagåtña received from the community "gifts in kind, such as meat, fish and other things."[114] "Also during time we could order vegetables, chickens and other things, either by the Chamorro who brought milk every morning, or by our cook who [is] also Chamorro," Mabini wrote.[115] CHamoru gardens and ranches had enough to supplement the diets of the revolutionaries; CHamoru practices of *inafa'maolek* and *chenchule'* were extended to these elite Filipino revolutionaries.

Mabini's diaries and letters became more detailed about people from the local community. Mabini wrote about a night when the families of Mr. Herrero and Mr. Martinez visited the prison in July 1901. He recorded, "They are Spanish mestizos and their children are the prettiest in Agana."[116] Herrero and Martinez, patriarchs of elite CHamoru families, welcomed the most famous personalities of the Filipino Revolution. During a night filled with dance and the music of "a trio of two violins and a guitar," Mabini enjoyed "a show of the most powerful voice of all of Agaña." According to historian Tony Palomo, "during their 19-month stay here, the more prominent of the Filipinos hobnobbed with island society and were accepted by some of the most prominent families."[117] In fact, the feasts were remembered decades after they occurred. These events included the wedding of Thomas Andersen Calvo and Regina Martinez Torres. Calvo was an alumni of the University of Santo Tomas in Manila—a university that many of the revolutionaries, including Mabini and Artemio Ricarte, had also attended.[118] Pablo Ocampo, a wealthy revolutionary exile whose family owned land and plantations in the Philippines, "footed the bill for some of the most elaborate parties" held at the beginning of the century.[119] Monsignor Oscar Lujan Calvo described the exiles as "suave and debonair," bringing Philippine symbols and displays of class and wealth to Guåhan.[120]

The Filipino exiles and the CHamoru elites had more opportunity to spend time with each other. Slowly exposed to the CHamoru community outside the presidio grounds, Mabini's interaction with the island became more complex. By December 1901 some of the prisoners lived "on their own account and with more freedom in Agaña [Hagåtña] town."[121] They lived in close proximity to CHamoru families. Mabini experienced a Fourth of July celebration at the invitation of US officials, which would be the only time Mabini would see Hagåtña. Mabini even discovered the existence of some of the older generations of Filipino deportados from the 1896 cohort. In December 1901 Mabini wrote to his brother that he met a "woman of Santa Mesa, Segunda, deported here during the Spanish regime" who "is still alive and is staying at the house of a well-to-do family that have taken her in."[122] She had been unable to leave the island because of the travel fare, and Mabini hoped that she would be able "to embark with us because a woman without relatives or resources in a foreign land moves one to compassion."[123]

By March 1902 the Filipino prisoners petitioned for more freedom—"the expansion of soul and for a change in their food"—from the governor, including the ability to walk to Hagåtña during the day.[124] The prisoners finally received permission to head to Hagåtña in May 1902.[125] Unable to walk to Hagåtña due to his paralysis, Mabini stayed at the prison, but his companions brought him necessary supplies. Mr. Pressey, lieutenant governor of the island, offered to house Mabini in his Hagåtña home, but Mabini refused "because it is heavier for me to live at the expense of another strange person."[126] He wrote to his brother, "I cannot say anything about the island because I have not seen any of it except the expanse that my sight reaches from the prison windows."[127]

The CHamoru elite and Filipino revolutionaries shared common imperial histories—colonial siblings, from the perspective of the imperial powers that had colonized them. The sharing of food, the Catholic masses, the parties, weddings, and *lechonadas,* all point to meaningful connections between them. CHamorus cultivated friendships to create political and economic opportunities for the future.[128] Upon returning to the Philippines after his exile to Guam, Pablo Ocampo became a Philippine commissioner to the United States. On his way to Washington, DC, Ocampo stopped over in Guåhan, delivering supplies as well as horses to the friends he had made during his exile. Perhaps the petition the CHamorus wrote in 1901 was inspired by the presence of these revolutionaries.

Liberal Anticolonialism in Imperial Transition

During his incarceration on Guåhan, Mabini wrote a manifesto of freedom, *La Revolucíon Filipina,* where he deftly articulated the paradoxes of a liberal US empire. Mabini foregrounded his political beliefs in individual rights and the ability of Filipinos to govern themselves in an independent nation. Revolutionaries, he wrote, "fought in the conviction that our dignity and sense of duty required the sacrifice of defending our freedoms as long as we could, since without them social equality between the dominant class and the native population would be impossible to practice and perfect justice among us could not have been achieved."[129] He faulted leaders who succumbed to personal politics and greed for power for the Revolution's failure and further criticized Filipino leaders who acquiesced to US colonial rule.[130] When it became apparent that the United States was no longer open to the Philippines' quest for independence, many Filipino leaders acquiesced to annexation, citing the millions of lives lost in battles across the archipelago. Despite US actions in the Philippines, Mabini believed Filipinos should negotiate a binding agreement with the United States that included the nation's future independence. Additionally, Mabini paradoxically criticized and believed in the potential of US liberalism. He wrote that US colonialism was "an absolutist regime . . . contrary to the character and customs of the American people."[131] Yet he found it "interesting to observe [that] the Republican Party, led by Lincoln in its beginnings, freed many millions of slaves in the United States, while, led by McKinley in its greatest period of vigour and prosperity, it made the United States the absolute owner of many millions of Filipinos."[132] Mabini clearly understood the contradictions embedded in the liberal US empire.

While the Filipino revolutionaries were on the island, thirty-two prominent members of Guåhan society sent a petition to the US Congress in December 1901, the first of many petitions sent during the Naval era.[133] The signers, which included Påle' Palomo, Pedro M. Duarte, Atanasio T. Perez, Justo Dungca, as well as Naval sailor Charles Stimpson, petitioned the US Congress to pay attention to the island and determine a political status for Guåhan. The Hagåtña elite used their knowledge of the US government to request a survey to study "the situation and needs of our peoples, with instructions to formulate and present to Congress for its action such measures it may deem advisable for the establishment of a permanent government."[134] The petition was sent in six months after the first Insular Case, *Downes v. Bidwell,* created the category "unincorporated territory" to differentiate the islands annexed as a result of the Spanish-American War from those territories eligible for incorporation as states.[135] While it is not clear whether the Hagåtña elite knew of this important legal decision, from the perspective of US colonial law, Guåhan was designated "foreign in a domestic sense."

The signers of the petition penned their discontent with the military government, which they believed was antithetical to the liberal, republican ideals expressed by the United States and Naval officials. "A military government at best," they wrote, "is distasteful and highly repugnant to the fundamental principles of civilized government, and peculiarly so to those on which is based the American government."[136] Furthermore, they criticized the Naval governor, who "exercises supreme power in the executive, legislative, and judicial branches of government, with absolutely no limitations to his actions, the people of this island having no voice whatever in the formulating of any law or the name of a single official."[137] The Naval governor of Guam was the complete opposite of the type of government that the United States was supposed to represent.

On the local level, the CHamoru elite were very aware of the improvisational nature of the colonial government on Guåhan. They believed that the slow-moving bureaucracy of the US empire created uncertainty that harmed the residents of the island. Harkening to the past when Indigenous leaders maintained power in colonial and village affairs, the petitioners wrote, "It is not an exaggeration to say that fewer permanent guarantees of liberty and property exist now than when under Spanish dominion."[138] Despite the rhetoric espoused by the United States, CHamoru leaders pointed out, "the time that has elapsed with no apparent effort having been taken toward the establishment of a stable government." Furthermore, the CHamorus believed that US-appointed Naval governors, apart from Safford, were incompetent and unknowledgeable about how to govern the complex legal systems that merged in the imperial transition. They believed they were "fully justified in asking relief from a system of government that subjects a thoroughly loyal people to the absolute rule of a single person, who is to administer the very cumbersome and complex system of laws which has continued from the time of Spanish control, and which was not framed to suit local conditions, being the legislation for the whole Philippine archipelago, a system of laws which in principle is foreign to that to which he has heretofore been accustomed; and framed and administered in a, to him, foreign tongue."[139] Not only did the United States take away representation from the local peoples, the signers argued, but the new imperial power continued to use Spanish imperial law rather than implementing new policies that aligned with the US liberal mission and rhetoric to aid the people of Guåhan. In short they wanted better governance.

This petition demonstrates how CHamorus resisted what they believed was an illiberal form of government and attempted to influence colonial policy. Although the petition did not seek independence for Guåhan, its authors must have learned much from the experiences of the Filipino revolutionaries' successes and failures. They were able to hobnob with Filipino revolutionaries. They were able to persuade Safford to support their initiatives. They were able to convince Charles A. Stimpson, who was the US postmaster and a member of the Navy, to sign the 1901 petition with them. And they seemed to get the Naval governor of Guam to agree. Governor Schroeder fully supported the CHamoru petition. He told the president of the United States, "Their opinions are entitled to respect."[140]

The Revolutionaries on Guåhan

On July 2, 1902, Theodore Roosevelt proclaimed the end of the Philippine Insurrection and pardoned "all persons in the Philippine Archipelago who have participated in the insurrections," provided that they took an oath of allegiance to the United States.[141] This offer applied to the Filipino prisoners on Guåhan. Federal government officials believed that "the presence of these Filipinos in Guam is not considered desirable by the Governor, as there is racial antipathy for them among the natives of Guam. Their return to the Philippines after release from confinement would therefore seem to be desirable in the interests of Guam."[142] So Elihu Root permitted the Filipino prisoners to be released and transported back to the Philippines if they took an oath of allegiance to the United States.[143] Most of the prisoners, wanting to return to the Philippines, agreed.

Some Filipinos continued to resist in the Philippine provinces and in exile. Apolinario Mabini and Artemio Ricarte both refused to take the oath of allegiance. Mabini wrote to his brother Alejandro, "They [US Navy officials] are plainly convinced that I am an astute agitator and very dangerous, and it is very difficult to take away from them this conviction, as experience has proven."[144] Mabini was correct. In a letter to the secretary of the Navy, Philippine Governor William H. Taft warned that Mabini was "the most prominent irreconcilable" and that his return to the Philippines might reignite the Philippine Revolution. Taft asserted, "If he were allowed to come to Manila he would form a nucleus for all the discontented elements which he would be certain to encourage in every form and conspiracy against the existing government."[145] He further added that Mabini's dream to form an independent Philippines would reverse the developments made by the United States and bring "misfortune and hardship to the people he thinks he loves and would aid."[146] From Taft's perspective, Mabini's incarceration on Guåhan was necessary for United States colonialism in the Philippines. Ricarte refused to take the oath, opting to relocate to Hong Kong. Mabini finally acquiesced when he noticed his health failing considerably. He arrived in Manila a hero, but passed away a few short months after.

Before he departed for the Philippines, Mabini handed fellow exile Maximo Tolentino a letter "in a sealed envelope."[147] Tolentino, a servant to the Filipino exiles, decided to settle on the island. The letter contained a short poem Mabini wrote to remember his time on Guåhan.

> Adios, Asan; Adios, Agana!
> We bid thee adieu, We, the unfortunate victims of the love for a sacred ideal;
> We vow thee our loyalty for thy humanitarian hospitality.
> Adios, Asan!
> Our favorite village, on whose sands our pains have been sprinkled, and our tears spread;
> Your name I shall Never forget.
> Adios, Agana! Soon I shall leave thee;
> May heaven shower Happiness on thee;
> Adios, my brothers, sisters, of my soul
> Adios! Farewell! Adios!

Assan, the village that was once the leper colony that contained the "infectious" diseases of the Filipino revolutionaries' desire for independence, eventually became Mabini's "favorite village," where he experienced the island's "humanitarian hospitality." Mabini and his cohort of exiles felt a visceral connection to the villages of Assan and Hagåtña "on whose sands our pains have been sprinkled, and our tears spread." Wishing farewell to the connections he made to the CHamoru families that hosted him and his colleagues, he called them "brothers, sisters, of [his] soul" recognizing the close ties he fostered with the people of Guåhan.[148] Despite the ocean that lay between the archipelagoes and the imperial transition, this poem reflects the intimate networks of colonials exchanging ideas, establishing friendships, and becoming kin.

Maximo Tolentino kept the letter he had received from "Don Mabini" long after Mabini left the shores of Åssan. He was one of three revolutionaries who decided to stay; the others were Leon Flores and Pancrasio Palting, who were trained lawyers and who eventually became influential and prominent members of the Hagåtña elite. Tolentino, however, was a poor mess sergeant in the Filipino revolutionary army when he was arrested by US military patrols. While being questioned in the Philippines, the US military officials offered him the opportunity to "be in charge of [the exiles] meals" on Guåhan. In describing the revolutionary desire and high intellect of the other revolutionaries who served, Tolentino described himself as "least of them all."[149] Tolentino, Flores, and Palting decided to stay on Guåhan because of the strong connections they forged during their exile and the relationships formed with those on the island. Furthermore, the nascent American empire needed colonial elites to oversee its colonial bureaucracy. The three exiles-turned-settlers became part of the US Naval Government on Guåhan—Tolentino as a messenger, and Palting and Flores as island attorneys.[150] Flores's and Palting's command of the Spanish language and knowledge of the Spanish colonial system—crucial skills needed in the transition of empires—placed them at the top of the Naval Government's civil servant bureaucracy.[151] If Flores and Palting were previously part of the Philippine Revolution, they were now colonial workers of the US Naval Government on Guåhan.

Artemio Ricarte was disappointed by the three men. Ricarte refused to take the loyalty oath and moved on to Hong Kong after his stay in Guåhan. According to Tolentino, Ricarte tried to "induce [Tolentino] to get the Filipinos in Guam to start an uprising against the Americans."[152] Tolentino responded that he did not appreciate the content of Ricarte's letters, and noted in a 1961 interview that "General Ricarte did not realize at the time what he was asking of us Filipinos who had adopted Guam as our new home, in which we were contented and happy with our families."[153] Tolentino married Tomasa Crisostomo Lizama in 1906 and had a family. To continue the revolution in Guåhan was to risk the life he had made for himself in exile. Tolentino and the others now understood themselves as members of Guåhan's society and kinship network, no longer directly tied to the Philippine Revolution that Ricarte attempted to reignite.

By 1904, Leon Flores married Felicita Dungca, and Pancracio Palting married Soledad Dungca. Felicita and Soledad were both daughters of Justo Dungca, a signer of the 1901 petition, a friend of William Safford and the Filipino revolutionaries, and a man who offered his home to the Filipino revolutionaries throughout the nineteenth century.[154] Rather than seeing Flores and Palting as irreconcilable outlaws, Dungca perceived them as potential productive members of Guåhan's society, so much so that he was happy to welcome them to his family. Dungca wrote to Safford, "My two sons-in-law, who are from the same town and province in the Philippines, have been deported here in the year 1900 for political reasons and are now employed in the Government of the Island."[155] Filipino exiles' contributions to Guåhan's society allowed them to integrate into island society and, in particular, into the Hagåtña elite.

The intertwined nature of CHamoru-Filipino political acts at the turn of the twentieth century, though deeply complicated, shows us the significance of intellectual networks in the formation of political solidarity. The relations between the CHamoru and Filipino elite of this transitional period in Guåhan's history established the foundations for CHamoru-Filipino relations. The difference in political aims between the CHamorus on Guåhan and the Filipinos in Philippines demarcated the origins of the racial and national separation of Filipinos and CHamorus, so much so that shared histories as colonial siblings would be obscured by time. However, this chapter in Guåhan's history reveals the potential for alternative relationships that could inform the present. Though geopolitics were out of their control, the CHamoru elite attempted to influence colonial policy not only by advocating on the local community's behalf, but also by engaging in diplomacy with Filipino exiles and the military officials of the Naval Government. Exiled from their archipelago, Filipino exiles were grateful for the CHamorus who saw their humanity and offered them friendship in a time of incarceration.

In previous centuries Manila had been a locus of civilization for Guåhan and the rest of the Marianas, but the age of the US empire on Guåhan pivoted their gazes eastward. The CHamoru elite began to look toward Hawai'i and Washington, DC, for access to colonial networks. These connections, however, proved trying, because US racial hierarchies, the sheer distance, and the linguistic and cultural gaps made it difficult for them to advocate for their rights in the US empire. While Puerto Rico, the US Virgin Islands, and Hawai'i received Organic Acts early in the twentieth century, Guåhan remained just on the periphery of US Naval officers' consciousness. Nonetheless, the CHamoru elite submitted several more petitions, all of them asking for a civilian government, more representation in local affairs, and US citizenship. The CHamoru elites were often ignored, but what remained constant throughout the twentieth and twenty-first centuries was the continuing diplomatic effort to increase local self-governance on Guåhan.

CHAPTER TWO

Of a Separate Race

Race, Citizenship, and Belonging in Naval-Era Guåhan

In September 1926, a startling message from Manila arrived in Guåhan through the Associated Press (AP) and the Cable News Service. The message was so unexpected that the Guam Congress notified its representatives and called a special session to discuss its contents. Eduardo Mercaido, a representative in the House of the Philippine Senate, proposed a resolution declaring that, because "Guam is intimately linked with the history of the Philippines, and is largely inhabited by people belonging to the Filipino race," the island "should have its Representative in the Philippine Legislature." A subsequent line made matters worse. Mercaido also sought "to ask, and hereby ask, the President and the Congress of the United States to cede to the Government of the Philippine Islands, the Island of Guam."[1] As the message was read aloud in English and CHamoru, Jose C. Torres observed that "a solemn silence pervaded the assembly hall and from some dazed look which appeared from every face it seemed as if some dire catastrophe impended." A Filipino leader was attempting to annex Guåhan.

"The once quiet assembly," Torres wrote, "emerged into a tumultuous gathering by a simultaneously plea from all corners to voice the unanimous sentiment" that CHamorus "love and will always live to love the United States of America."[2] CHamorus saw the Philippines on a trajectory toward independence, but were adamant that Guåhan remain a US territory. Reluctant to make hasty decisions with heated emotions, the Guam Congress formed a special committee to review and draft a response to the proposed resolution. A week later the committee presented their findings. They believed that CHamorus and Guåhan should be treated as a separate political entity and territory within the US empire. In doing so, they declared that they were of a different race than Filipinos, called Filipinos un-American and uncivilized, used tropes of scientific racism, and described Filipinos as criminals and, in one moment, "infernal wretches."[3]

Although no further steps were taken on the resolution, the uproar it caused among CHamorus was a significant break in historical relations between CHamorus and Filipinos.[4] The 1926 Philippine resolution was a critical moment of identity formation for CHamorus, in which they embarked on a complex process of articulating the parameters of the CHamoru race by positioning themselves as distinct from their colonial siblings. They navigated contradicting intersections of three schemas of race and belonging—CHamoru, Spanish, and American—that operated in Guåhan. Although the US hierarchical and homogeneous categories of race conflicted with the realities of mixed-race and *mestisu* peoples of Guåhan and the Philippines, CHamorus had to redefine their identity using US racial logics that resonated with colonial officials. As a result of this redefinition, CHamorus reluctantly eschewed their *mestisu* identity and adopted a racial identity that was imbued with notions of whiteness, civilization, and modernity.

In a colonial society and a global zeitgeist that often saw race as a critical component of eligibility for liberal rights, both CHamorus and Filipinos in Guåhan had to engage with the logics of racial science to bolster their political claims. In this chapter I examine two precarious situations—the 1926 Philippine resolution and the Naval Government's enforcement of alien land laws in the early 1930s—in which CHamorus and Filipinos navigated and negotiated conflicting schemas of race. Firstly, when CHamoru members of the Guam Congress saw that claiming their *mestisu* race could be used against them to deny their distinctiveness as a people within the US empire, they used US racial rhetoric to differentiate themselves from Filipinos, to advocate for closer political relations to the United States, and to retain their claims to land, property, and the political future of Guåhan. Secondly, in the early 1930s, when the Navy threatened to dispossess "native" women and children of their land and property on the island because their Filipino husbands and fathers were considered "aliens" to the United States, the Filipino men—including two former Philippine revolutionary exiles-turned-colonial lawyers, Leon Flores and Pancrasio Palting—launched a legal battle to protect their families' land and property.

Read together, the two situations reveal how the complicated US definitions race, nation, and citizenship shaped the relationships between CHamorus and Filipinos. I argue that the way CHamorus and Filipinos used US rhetoric of liberalism to justify their claims further entrenched racial hierarchies and notions of civilization into Guåhan's political discourse. Although CHamorus fought against the injustices and inequalities of empire, the racial logics they had used to justify their inclusion in the US body politic, in their response to the 1926 Philippine resolution, became the same logics that excluded Filipinos as "aliens" to the United States. Yet the slippages in definitions of race and belonging also reveal the enduringness of CHamoru-Filipino relationalities that remained under the surface of these colonial negotiations.

Contested Boundaries of Race, Nation, and Kinship

In both Guåhan and the Philippines, the US imperial bureaucracy implemented colonial policies to placate, tutor, and discipline CHamorus and Filipinos. When in 1927 Representative Mercaido introduced the resolution to annex Guåhan for the Philippines, the Philippines was governed by the Insular Government.[5] Although the governor was presidentially appointed, the Philippines Assembly consisted of elected leaders who could draft and pass legislation. The Philippines also had a standing nonvoting representation to US Congress through the Philippine Commission, which sent delegations to Washington and engaged in diplomatic efforts across a range of colonial issues, including economic trade, culture, and Philippine Independence. Filipinos, thus, had a specific institution where they could voice concerns about colonial policy. CHamorus in Guåhan did not.

In the early 1900s a number of rulings by the US Supreme Court declared that the US Constitution did not fully apply to "unincorporated territories," including Guam and the Philippines. After these rulings, which are known as the Insular Cases, CHamorus and Filipinos were operating within the larger imperial context where one's inclusion in the United States through citizenship depended on one's race and one's location in "unincorporated" territory. A manifestation of liberalism's inherent inequalities, race arose as a "set of classificatory regimes" used to distinguish those peoples deemed "uncivilized" or unworthy for self-government from those worthy of the liberal promises of freedom. Ideologies of white supremacy supposed that nonwhite peoples were part of the former rather than the latter.[6] Furthermore, the Insular Cases at the turn of the twentieth century codified the creation of the category "unincorporated territory," by which the island territories of the US empire acquired after the Spanish-American War were denied pathways for incorporation as states. Despite the US desire to "uplift" colonial peoples through tutelary projects, Guåhan's political status as a "spoil of war" and the CHamoru people's racial classification as nonwhite made the CHamoru people ineligible for US citizenship.[7]

While the political structure of the two territories was dictated by the United States, CHamorus and Filipinos, in and of themselves, embodied the *mestisu* racial schema tied to Spanish imperial policies. As we saw in more detail in chapter 1, the legacies of the Spanish Empire led to an emergence of a mixed-race, *mestisu* CHamoru people in Guåhan. By the 1930s the village of Hagåtña had a population of about seven thousand (the island's total population was about ten thousand) and was home to *mestisu* families whose genealogies may have included Indigenous CHamoru, Filipino, European, Latin American, and even East Asian ancestors.[8] The Hagåtña elite earned their reputation and elevated social class due to their proximity to the Spanish, and subsequently US, colonial officials.[9]

When US Naval personnel first arrived to investigate the inhabitants of the island, they noted the racial mixing of the Hagåtña elite. In an 1899 *Harper's Weekly* article, Naval ensign C. L. Poor reported on a brief trip he had made to Guåhan, where, he said, the "blood" of the people of Hagåtña had "a considerable proportion of Spanish, South American, and American stock." He described them as "cleanly, intelligent, and peaceful" as well as educated, "modest and very courteous." In doing so, Poor described a people worthy of the US benevolent imperialism in contrast to their colonial siblings in the Philippines, a sentiment shared by Naval governor of Guam, Roy Smith.[10] Poor explained that "the natives of Guam are in pleasing contrast to the Filipinos." He wrote, "In personal appearance the natives resemble the Filipinos, though of greater stature and more robust, while the hair is not so bristling and porcupine-like, and brown or even blond hair is occasional evidence of the mixture of races." Poor also argued that CHamorus were superior not only phenotypically but also intellectually. "The intelligence, as indicated by their faces, is much more marked than in the native of the Philippines," he observed. For Poor, although CHamorus in Guåhan were mixed-race, their European-like qualities made them superior to Filipinos, and as his argument followed, their intelligence proved their worthiness of US tutelage. Poor's article demonstrates how race was integral to the imperial project, and how anthropological description was used to rationalize colonial rule.

The uncategorizable brownness of both CHamorus and Filipinos was an anomaly to the binary Black/white—sometimes Native/white—schema that was the premise of US racial hierarchies. In order to govern the territories, colonial officials strategically made porous otherwise rigid racial categories to justify their presence and control of Pacific and mixed-race peoples within the empire.[11] For instance, Kanaka Maoli scholar Maile Arvin argues that, by characterizing Native Hawaiians as white and delegitimating their nativeness, imperialists justified white settler colonial goals to claim Polynesia and further acculturate Pacific Islanders into "civilization."[12] In the same way, as noted by the CHamoru scholar Christine Taitano DeLisle, Naval governors and their wives in Guåhan repeated racial descriptions to legitimize their presence, to justify the US tutelage of CHamorus, and to argue that CHamoru proximity whiteness justified the United States' obligation to engage in benevolent imperialism in Guåhan, while simultaneously legitimizing their exclusion from US citizenship.[13]

The Guam Congress's response to the 1926 Philippine resolution reveals how CHamoru elite and Filipinos in the Philippines used race as the criterion for determining political representation and rights. As written in the AP telegram, Mercaido's resolution suggested that incorporating Guåhan into the Philippines would advance Guåhan's political representation within the US empire, something that CHamorus themselves had been advocating for since 1900. Yet the justifications for such a move were not solely based in political generosity. Mercaido argued that Guåhan was "intimately linked" to Philippine history via the exiled Filipino revolutionaries at the turn of the century as well as the island's being "inhabited by a people belonging to the same race" as Filipinos. The historical link between politics and race was, thus, promoted as justification for the Philippines annexing Guåhan. Although the AP reported that the resolution was not taken seriously by "considerably amused" Americans who had heard about it, the resolution launched a historic and serious debate among CHamoru leaders, who vehemently opposed the resolution, believing that it was antithetical to their long-held goal of further incorporation into US empire and their desire for US citizenship. One assemblyman of the Guam Congress declared, "The Chamorros are not, and never will be willing to sever their connection with the United States of America."[14]

The CHamoru elite's willingness to engage with the Naval Government's Americanization projects meant that they would be most affected by the possibility of Guåhan's integration with the Philippines. By the 1920s the elite saw, capitalized on, and benefited from the transformation of Hagåtña into what they may have considered a "modern" US military outpost as opposed to a neglected Spanish colony. Several government administrations, all of which attempted to carry out McKinley's orders to bring about a benevolent empire, established Progressive Era institutions and policies that catered to the "uplifting" of the CHamoru people. These included the Susana Hospital, where CHamorus were treated for illnesses with the latest research (or experiments) in tropical medicine. White American nurses and navy wives taught modern American medical practices to CHamoru *pattera* (women healers), who melded their traditional knowledge with newer health practices.[15] The Normal School was established to teach pedagogy to CHamoru teachers; these teachers were stationed in schools throughout the island to teach English and other trades.[16] The Navy also instituted the

Insular Force Guard, where CHamoru men and boys learned rudimentary military drills and strategy.[17] In Hagåtña one could walk down Hernan Cortez Street to the Butler Store, and sip on a bottle of Coca-Cola while shopping for household goods and the latest fashion from the continental United States and Manila.[18] The Gaiety Theater showed a few Hollywood films; and the island's ice plant made cold and frozen foods possible. Here the intimacies between the Hagåtña elite and Naval personal grew even closer, sometimes leading to interracial marriages. The US Navy seem to bring US "modernity" to Guåhan.

The Naval Government, nevertheless, relied on entrenched notions of race and civilization to establish its colonial governance in the first half of the twentieth century. Scholars of Guåhan, including Anne Hattori, James Viernes, Robert Underwood, Penelope Bordallo Hofschneider, Elyssa Santos, Keith Camacho, Vicente Diaz, and Christine Taitano DeLisle, have historicized how the Naval Government's policies, which were often unilaterally devised by the Naval governor himself through "General Orders," were attempts to acculturate and discipline the CHamoru people into US modernity in ways both expansive (an advisory Guam Congress) and subtle (Governor William Gilmer's no-whistling rule).[19] The Naval Government believed these rules and orders, which were predicated upon the dismissal and at times illegalizing of CHamoru culture and language, were justified because they were aligned with the "civilizing" and liberalizing mission to bring the CHamoru people toward eventual full inclusion in the United States.[20]

The population of Hagåtña, however, was not representative of the entire island. Despite several decades of US colonial rule, the rural villages retained much of their Spanish-era influence, where CHamorus lived and worked at their respective *lånchos* (ranches), returning to the villages only a few days a week, such as on Sundays for Catholic masses.[21] With the lack of reliable roads and bridges throughout the island, CHamorus living in the villages rarely traveled to Hagåtña, and likewise, Naval officers rarely traveled to the rural villages on the island. A notable exception were the CHamoru *pattera* (midwives); as historicized by DeLisle, they traversed between "Native places and naval spaces" when caring for women's health using both CHamoru traditional medicine and American medical practices.[22] Because of the distance between the rural villages and Hagåtña, village populations were more racially homogeneous than the *mestisu* CHamorus in Hagåtña.[23] While some of members of those villages participated in political affairs, their voices might have been outweighed by the Hagåtña elite. The Hagåtña elite constituted most of the members in the Guam Congress, which the Naval governor

A map of pre–World War II Hågatña drawn by James M. Grafsguard using Naval sources and the knowledge of Emilie G. Johnston, daughter of Agueda and William Johnston. From the collection of the Richard F. Taitano Micronesian Area Research Center.

had created to "teach" CHamorus US politics. As merely an advisory body, however, the Guam Congress was not allowed to pass legislation; the Naval governor had autocratic authority over military and civilian affairs. The members of the Congress, nonetheless, took their positions seriously and discussed issues and policies that most affected the island's population, including the crafting and sending of several petitions for US citizenship. Between 1900 and 1950, CHamorus had sent nine petitions to US Congress and the president, asking for greater political representation within the Naval Government on Guam and, importantly, US citizenship, which they believed was the pinnacle of political inclusion.[24] They often, however, followed their displays of discontent not with anticolonial rhetoric but with a limited discourse of liberalism that emphasized their eligibility for inclusion based upon US racial and cultural criteria.[25] In doing so, the Guam Congress laid the rhetorical foundation for a liberal script of discontent as the political discourse for the island as a whole.

The Guam Congress was tasked with outlining the opposition to Mercaido's resolution. In differentiating themselves from Filipinos, CHamorus used racial difference as an indicator of loyalty to the United States. "Regarding the statement that the inhabitants of Guam belong to the same race as the Filipinos," a CHamoru member declared after reiterating his loyalty, "I am more or less inclined to believe that this is not so." For CHamoru leaders, the task was to find evidence that CHamorus were of a different race and thus justify a political future for Guåhan that did not cut ties with the United States if the Philippines were to receive independence. In both Mercaido's resolution and the CHamoru assemblyman's response, the definitions of race and nation reinforced one another.

As it turns out, CHamorus were engaging a conversation on race that Filipino intellectuals had been debating for decades. Well before the United States annexed the Philippines, Filipino *ilustrados* saw that defining the Filipino race was a key component to the intellectual foundations of Filipino anticolonialism and, by extension, Filipino nationalism. Filipino *ilustrados* often engaged in robust global intellectual conversations about the origins of the different peoples that inhabit the Philippine archipelago.[26] Jose Rizal, for instance, had lengthy correspondence with Austro-Hungarian scholar Ferdinand Blumentritt to theorize the racial heterogeneity of the Philippines.[27] Rizal agreed with Blumentritt's theory of wave migration—that the Philippine archipelago was peopled by three distinct waves of migration, each wave bringing a phenotypically different people with various levels of civilization. The first wave of "*negritos*" of the mountainous region belonged to a primitive, uncivilized past, who were pushed into the interior when subsequent waves arrived into the archipelago. The theory suggested that the second wave was composed of Malayans, who first settled on the coasts of the archipelago and then mixed with the interior *negritos*. As Filipino scholar Filomeno Aguilar has analyzed, Blumentritt argued that the racial mixing of the first and second waves produced the "mountain tribes." Rizal believed that these "mountain tribes" were not the ancestors for modern Filipinos—"their backwardness was virtually inherent in their alleged nature as second wavers."[28] Instead, according to the wave theory, the ancestors of the modern Filipino arrived in the third wave, which was believed to be a second set of Malay people, who became the "Tagalogs, Pamapanguinios, Visayans, Bicolanos, Ilocanos, Pagansinanons and Cagayanons." This third wave evolved to become new Filipinos, who were thought to be more civilized in customs and behavior. Filipino *ilustrados* couched their direct ancestry and genealogy in this third wave due to the supposed inherent civilization of those people. This racialization was a political move as much as it was one of scientific inquiry. They argued that they had pedigree proven by science, which meant that they were modern Filipinos who were racially superior enough to warrant colonial recognition and political rights within the Spanish Empire.[29] This race science continued to serve as proof for Filipino nationhood.

When the United States took hold of the Philippines, the wave theory of migration was used against Filipinos. Rather than agreeing with the *ilustrados'* ancestral claims to the "civilized" third wave, US colonial officials often emphasized the heterogeneity of the archipelago as a whole as a hindrance to the creation of a nation. One CHamoru woman's response to a newspaper essay prompt "Should the Philippines be granted Independence?" demonstrates how this race science, which circulated throughout empire, became useful for defining CHamoru race in the face of potential Philippine annexation. The essay was written by Agueda Johnston (née Iglesias), who is a famed figure in the historiography of Guåhan for her outspoken advocacy for US education and CHamoru identity in the middle of the twentieth century. Historian DeLisle describes Johnston as "not just a leader under U.S. naval tutelage but an important interlocuter and intermediary, whose direction and *giniha* [guiding] in modern education and other ostensibly American spheres would extend a longer story of CHamoru cultural survival through a new colonial order."[30] Johnston's early works, including her response to the essay prompt in which she argued that Filipinos were not ready for independence, are sites to explore the tensions of the racial ideologies circulating within the empire.

Johnston's work was a reiteration of racial science for CHamoru political purposes. Her writing reveals a keen understanding of how racial ideologies were used to define an ideal nation—an assertion that filtered into how CHamoru leaders articulated their sense of peoplehood. "When we speak of the people of any country, as the American people, the English people or the French people," Johnston wrote in her essay, "the idea conveyed is that the people of that country are a homogenous race with the same habits, tastes, ideals, and, to a lesser extent, religion."[31] In contrast, Johnston described Filipinos as a heterogeneous people—"The pagans, such as the Negritos and the Igorotes [*sic*] in the Northern islands comprise approximately one-fourth of the inhabitants, but in Mindanao and in Sulu in the south, the Moros who are Mohammedans, form practically the entire population. On top of the twelve million polyg[l]ot and largely helpless people, is a small but powerful and influential educated upper class, mostly of Spanish or Chinese mixture."[32] Strikingly, Johnson employed some of the same criteria for nationhood eligibility that Rizal had theorized half a century before, including notions of civilization rooted in religion, literacy, and knowledge of democratic government. Yet Johnston interpreted this racial and civilizational science in stern contradiction to Rizal's politically beneficial conclusions. Combined with the idea that Filipinos had been "agitating for independence" and the evidentially poor governance by "the high chiefs of the Filipinos, Manuel Quezon and Sergio Osmena," Johnston argued that rather than prepare for independence, Filipinos should respect the authority of the United States because "fitness for the performance of such important duties must first be fairly demonstrated." After all, she noted, "what more could a people want than to have a junior partnership with the mightiest, wealthiest, and most powerful nation on earth today?"

Johnston's strategic use of flattery reveals a critical consciousness of the diplomacy required and the criteria needed for CHamorus and Guåhan's full recognition by the United States. If these were the lessons learned—that racial homogeneity, docility to colonial policies, and staunch loyalty to the US flag were necessary to attain recognition from US colonial government—then CHamorus knew how to distinguish themselves from Filipinos. CHamorus were to prove their eligibility for liberal self-governance through a demonstration of civilization via the acceptance of a US-styled modernity and the assertion of a homogeneous racial heritage distinct from Filipinos. As seen in the response to the 1926 Philippine resolution, an American interpretation of Rizal and Blumetritt's wave migration theory became embedded in how CHamorus in Guåhan perceived the Filipino race, and became the basis of how CHamorus defined themselves as separate from Filipinos. They couched their arguments in articulations of race because that was the rhetorical terrain the US empire used to justify colonization and, oppositely, to determine eligibility for liberal self-governance.

There is, though, another way to think about race that breaks from the Western genealogy that US colonial officials, Rizal, and Johnston wrote about—namely, in terms of the kinship practices rooted in CHamoru genealogy and ontology. Although the historical record from which this chapter is derived does not show whether CHamoru elite appealed to CHamoru kinship to craft their understanding of race, it is nevertheless important to see CHamoru relationality as a backdrop for the conversations on race. Cross-imperial interactions did not prevent a continuity in CHamoru indigeneity, language, and culture through generations. CHamorus, for the most part, accepted "mixture" and *mestisu*-ness.[33] This acceptance was because for them "belonging" had less to do with racial purity and homogeneity than it did with family and kinship. As anthropologist Laurel Monnig describes, "Chamorros have narratives that consistently expand relatedness beyond 'blood' and 'biology'—such as through *kompaire*, friendship, and *poksai*."[34] *Kompaire* links generations of families to each other, and *poksai* refers to the "parental responsibility to any child, including those brought into the family through other means than giving birth."[35] In this system, children are raised not just in their immediate and extended families, but also in the children's community. *Kompaire* and *poksai* are intimately intertwined with the concept of *inafa'maolek*, or "to make good." *Inafa'maolek* is central to CHamoru culture and refers to the reciprocal social relations and responsibilities that a person and family have to other families to ensure mutual harmony within the community.[36] Kinship networks included those beyond the immediate family and were maintained through *inafa'maolek* throughout several generations.

Such an expansive nature of CHamoru kinship and belonging provided some space for non-CHamorus to integrate. For example, even though Filipino men were brought into Guåhan by the Spanish Empire to intermarry with local women and to "restock" the island, which had been decimated by centuries of colonialism, their marriages to CHamoru women were often predicated upon their obligations to her family and community. Put simply, she was not necessarily integrated into his family—as patriarchal Western norms assume—but he was integrated into hers. At the behest of CHamoru women who were "makers and shapers" of CHamoru culture, Filipino men were assimilated into CHamoru society and customs abiding by the matrilineal and matriarchal character of CHamoru genealogy and culture. Their mixed-race children were considered to be CHamoru as they more than likely were born into and raised by CHamoru families.[37] The cultural norms around marriage reveal how CHamoru kinship and belonging did not necessarily focus on racial similarities or differences. Rather, they depended upon whether outsiders such as Filipinos integrated and assimilated themselves into CHamoru society by abiding by and fulfilling *inafa'maolek*. Thus, racial science was not the only terrain upon which race, nation, and belonging could be articulated in Guåhan.

CHamorus were not just operating with abstract liberal concepts of race to bolster rhetoric for political gain. They were grappling with the foundations of the CHamoru people: their culture, their identity, their community, and their ontological ties to the island of Guåhan. Defining race was not merely a scientific project; it was a project of articulating nation and peoplehood. These ideologies had material consequences for the political futures. So when confronted by the 1926 resolution that called for annexing Guåhan to the Philippines, CHamoru leaders were forced to differentiate themselves from Filipinos in order to legitimize their political goals, to reaffirm their aspirations to become US citizens, and to protect their sovereignty.

Articulating Racial Difference

The CHamoru desire to become more integrated within the United States is perhaps an unlikely form of anticolonialism. US colonialism brought with it symbols of modernity such as paved roads, telecommunications, and consistent trade at the port, and these were seen as improvements to the island's way of life. As Agueda Johnston wrote in another essay published in *The Guam Recorder*, "thousands of dollars have been spent on public improvements and utilities such as water systems, sewers, roads, hospitals, and public works of a similar character which are of but little, if any, military value."[38] Yet these public works *were* of value to the Naval station; the Navy also needed these services to sustain its presence. But Johnston's perception of the creation of public services as a derived from a "paternal and beneficent government" demonstrates how many CHamorus positively perceived US colonialism.

What the CHamoru elite did contest was the United States' continuing hypocrisy when it came to notions of democracy and self-government in Guåhan. The CHamoru elites' discourse of protest, however, was through reiterations of desires for further inclusion through US citizenship. A congressmen at the Guam Congress's inaugural meeting in 1916 believed that the Congress would allow the CHamoru people to "enjoy through their representatives the privilege of advocating their lawful rights as *citizens* of a nation so highly known through the civilized world for its liberty, republicanism and justice, which ignores and rejects any distinction between races and which embraces equality alone, not only in its social relations, but also in its laws."[39] Invoking liberty, republicanism, and racially equality, this CHamoru leader demonstrated the firm belief in US liberalism, or at least its rhetorical power, to garner a more advantageous platform for negotiating colonial policy. Yet several years later, CHamorus expressed discontent with how the Naval Government fell short of these expectations and did not allow binding political representation in the affairs of the island. They emphasized their desires for more political rights, such as a civilian government and US citizenship, and were terrified by the prospect of annexation into a Philippine government that they believed could not offer the same opportunities as the United States.

Given the racialized landscape upon which political claims were made in this period of imperialism, the CHamoru leaders of the Guam Congress couched their rhetoric in terms of race science and civilization, positioning them as more civilized than Filipinos, and thus more deserving of integration into the United States. After the initial shock of the Philippine resolution, the men of the Guam Congress took some time to investigate the claims set forth by Philippine representative Mercaido and met on October 2, 1926, to discuss their findings in Dorn Hall in Hagåtña. Mr. Calvo from Santa Cruz, Hagåtña, spoke in familial terms and declared without equivocation: "Gentlemen—Guam and its people to this date have deeply embedded in their hearts their love for the United States of America; America is their mother country; their best and most beloved guardian."[40] Other members of the Congress followed suit, another stating, "You cannot find a Chamorro who is not loyal to the American Flag." With this consensus, whatever evidence they would present was with the ultimate purpose to disentangle the political future of Guåhan from that of the Philippines.

Despite the centuries of racial mixing between Guåhan and the Philippines, some members of the Guam Congress rejected their Filipino ancestors and embraced their European or Spanish ancestors in order to claim whiteness. Jose M. Torres from Hagåtña referred to the racial science circulating the empire: "If we compare the two people [CHamorus and Filipinos] by their origin, or blood, many authors and scientists who study human races write in their books that the two races of people are not near alike."[41] Mr. Charfauros of Hågat agreed: "Guam is inhabited by a race different from

Filipinos. It could be noticed from their physical structure, means of subsistence, and language."[42] Jose M. Torres cited a former Naval governor of Guam, Roy Smith, who described phenotypic qualities that distinguished CHamorus from Filipinos: "The Chamorro is generally taller and more athletic than the Tagalog and of a lighter color."[43] More than likely, the CHamoru members of the Guam Congress, especially those from Hagåtña, knew of the history of Filipino and CHamoru relations under the Spanish Empire, and indeed of their personal genealogies, which may have included Filipino ancestors.[44] To acknowledge that they had Filipino blood, however, would have been detrimental to their claim. Because they sought to associate CHamorus with a different, more "civilized" race, one member, Mr. Lujan of Yoña, suggested that "the Hawaiians much more resemble the Chamorros than the Filipinos and the Chamorros." CHamorus sought out to prove that the white blood within their genealogies connoted a sense of racial superiority and civilization in comparison to Filipinos.

Furthermore, CHamorus capitalized on how racial science explained the relationship between race and civilization.[45] During the meeting, CHamorus used CHamoru-Filipino history to prove civilizational differences. Most notably, the recent memory of the Filipino deportados who wreaked havoc in Guåhan in the late nineteenth century were brought into the discussion. Mr. Taitano of Hagåtña told the Congress that "in almost every instance where there is what we will call cold-blooded murder, the Filipinos are responsible, or at least men who have a little Filipino blood. They are just as treacherous as dangerous. Habitual law-breakers on this island are mostly of Filipino descent."[46] Religion, too, played a role. Jose M. Torres said that "while the Chamorro cannot boast of a better academic training or more riches than the Filipino, because the condition of his country does not permit him, yet he can say that he is more docile, obedient, holds higher respect for his government than the Filipino, because he is a better Christian."[47] In their perspectives, CHamoru morality—and Filipino lack thereof—was proof of their racial difference.

The Congress also disputed Mercaido's claim that historical relations between CHamorus and Filipinos were always amicable. Mr. Calvo reinforced Taitano and Torres's argument about Filipino incivility by relaying an anecdote about a group of CHamorus working in a rice field in the southern village of Humåtak, when an argument developed into a full-on fight. One man pulled a gun and "shot one of the men, though not fatally." What happened next led Calvo to believe that CHamorus were more noble than Filipinos. He continued, "As soon as the blood from the wounded man started to flow freely, the man dropped the Mauser, and the rest of the men started to flee in despair." In Mr. Calvo's perspective, the CHamoru man's refusal to engage in further violence signified his higher morality and civilization when compared to Filipinos. Calvo concluded that this event was "evident proof of [the natives] high esteem for Christianity and loyalty which we will never find prevalent among Filipinos."[48]

Racial distinctiveness, civilizational superiority, and the tense historical relationships between the CHamoru elite and Filipino deportados became evidence for the national incompatibility between them. Mr. Lujan of Dédidu warned that if the 1926 resolution passed and Filipinos became independent from the United States, "the Filipinos will not look down upon the Chamorros as they do their own blood." He argued that there was no incentive for Filipinos to consider CHamorus political equals, and that they probably would replicate colonial hierarchies. As people who continuously sought further integration into the United States, Lujan argued, to be integrated into the Philippines would have Filipinos "stamping of their foot on the Chamorros' forehead."[49]

The congressmen argued that the racial and cultural difference between CHamorus and Filipinos were so staunch that it affected how mixed-race Filipino-CHamoru children related to each of their parents. Mr. Torres stated that "neither can a person truly begotten of Filipino from a Chamorro mother—get along smoothly with a proper Filipino because of their traits and habits [are] altogether different. The Chamorro has a heart that he is a better man than the Filipino."[50] Brought up in the community in Guåhan, mixed-raced children were usually perceived as culturally CHamoru due in part to how their CHamoru mothers inculcated CHamoru cultural practices. However, Torres effectively rendered these CHamoru-Filipino children as solely CHamoru and disavowed their Filipino ancestry to argue for CHamoru integration into the United States.

For most of the special session, the congressmen articulated a CHamoru identity that was scientifically defined in opposition to a racial other, whether it be Filipinos or a general whiteness. One man, though, briefly affirmed a CHamoru identity based on ties to the island. He asked the crowd, "Why can't the Filipinos claim the Chamorros as Filipino descendants when, as they say, they are apparently of the same race?" In response, Mr. Taitano—a surname that is distinctively Indigenous CHamoru—exclaimed, "We are Chamorros, natives of Guam and not Filipinos, and we will always be Chamorros as long as we exist!"[51] Applause followed his remarks. Taitano's clarification—"as long as we exist"—pushed back against the oft-repeated trope that CHamorus had died out during the Spanish era, a common narrative among native and Indigenous peoples that served as a justification for genocide and settler colonialism.[52] Mr. Taitano defied this narrative of erasure. For him, the CHamoru race was not some nebulous racial category created in opposition to other races. It was a definitive native race rooted in the island of Guåhan.[53]

With evidence rooted in racial science, CHamorus amassed a portfolio of arguments that distinguished them from Filipinos, refuted Mercaido's resolution, and further proved their worthiness for integration into the United States. At the end of the meeting, Mr. Lujan of Dédidu proposed four points to include in the Guam Congress resolution. The fourth asked "to recognize the rights of the Chamorros as a tribe of loyal, law-abiding citizens of Guam separate from the rest of the so-called Asiatic race, and this will include a repetition of our request for naturalization laws for Chamorros." Subsequently, the Guam Congress published and sent a resolution to the US Congress conveying their loyalty to "OLD GLORY" and reiterated their peaceful acceptance of US colonialism. The sixth point was about race—"The Chamorro may have in ages past been of the same race as the Filipino, they have been so long apart that they are now so widely separated in thought, language, and customs, etc., that there is little in common between the two peoples."[54] Because of this, the resolution continued, they urged the president and the US Congress to ignore Mercaido's resolution. "Resolved," the last line read, "that we do most earnest petition the Congress of the United States of America to take such action as may be necessary to bestow the blessings of full citizenship upon the people of Guam."[55]

The writings of Agueda Johnston and the Guam Congress's responses to the 1926 Philippine resolution give insight into the racial dynamics of the US empire in the Pacific, where colonial subjects were required to show markers of civilization, modernity, and US culture to be considered civilized colonial subjects worthy of the promises of liberalism. CHamorus had used the US racial discourse that suggested that the Philippines was an archipelago riddled with problems stemming from its inherent contradictions with US racial logics and order. The Guam Congress articulated a CHamoru identity using racial science that was universally understood as preconditions for political rights and nationhood. In doing so, they argued that they had a strong connection to Guåhan; they had a distinct culture; they stood in close proximity to whiteness and civilization; and, most importantly, they were not Filipinos. By proving difference and articulating their own CHamoru identity, they hoped they would be recognized by the US officials as loyal colonial subjects deserving of greater integration into the United States.

Guam Citizenship, Alien Land Laws, and the Definition of "Native"

By the early 1930s, the political landscape of the US empire in the Pacific looked a little different. On the continent, the widespread anti-Chinese sentiment of the late nineteenth century merged with the rising fear of potential Japanese invasion of the American West. From 1882 to the 1940s, US politicians had passed and renewed several iterations of the Chinese Exclusion Act, which barred, and in some cases limited, laborers and migrants from the vast majority of Asia, the Pacific, and the Middle East, a region referred to as the Asiatic Barred Zone.[56] Japan and the Philippines were exempt from this barred region, due to a gentlemen's agreement with Japan and the colonial status of the Philippines. With the increased migration of Japanese and Filipino agricultural workers to the West Coast, white nativists who harbored anti-Asian sentiment sought to dispossess and disenfranchise Asians in their respective communities. With regard to the Pacific, the Hare-Hawes-Cutting Act in 1933 stipulated 1944 as the first projected date for Philippine independence. The following year the Tydings-McDuffie Act sealed the deal. The Philippines was slated to become independent, and Filipinos would no longer be US nationals. In this process, Filipinos became "aliens" to the United States.

Although exclusion was the legal norm for nonwhite peoples from the Asia-Pacific region, the CHamoru drive for US citizenship was in full swing. Several CHamoru leaders, such as Baltazar Bordallo and Frank B. Leon Guerrero, cultivated diplomatic networks to shore up support for their political aims. While many Naval governors dismissed their efforts, Naval Governor Willis Bradley exercised his unilateral power in 1930 to create a status called "Guam citizen," which was seen as the next half-step forward in political education for the CHamoru people. Guam citizenship was not legally binding in the US legal system or international law, but it was a catalyst for CHamorus to more strongly advocate for political rights both on the island and across the North American continent.

Guam citizenship followed the US criteria for citizenship, which emphasized traditional patriarchal norms, such as US-style families characterized as heterosexual, racially homogeneous, and religious, and where the women were subservient to their husbands.[57] Governor Bradley declared that Guam citizens included those who were born or naturalized in Guåhan, including (1) "every person residing on Guam on 1 February 1899" who did not have any allegiance to any foreign power; (2) every woman who, prior to

Governor William Bradley, seated, signs a Guam Congress Proclamation in 1931. *Left to right*: Antonio Perez, Judge Camacho, and José Roberto. From the collection of the Richard F. Taitano Micronesian Area Research Center.

September 22, 1922, had married a citizen of Guam; (3) every future child who was born in Guåhan whose father held Guam citizenship; and (4) every child under the age of twenty-one whose father qualified with the above rules.[58] Imbued with US gender ideologies, Guam citizenship was passed down through the father's citizenship status; women were given Guam citizenship by way of their husbands.[59] This US style of family, however, contrasted with CHamoru kinship traditions in which matrilineal lines dictated a person's place within society.

Although Guam citizenship was a boon for CHamoru leaders who worked hard to demonstrate Americanization for political aims, it was not clear if it also applied to the several dozen Filipino and other foreign men who lived on the island. By the 1920s there was a small yet thriving Filipino community in Guåhan, and the 1940 census counted 365 Filipinos.[60] Two of the community's most prominent members were former Filipino revolutionary exiles, Leon Flores and Pancrasio Palting, mentioned in chapter 1. After opting to stay in Guåhan when they were released from prison in 1902, they had established large, influential families, earned reputations through employment in the Naval Government, and positioned themselves at the center of the Filipino community in Guåhan. According to a speech Leon Flores had delivered during a memorial dedication to commemorate Filipino revolutionary exiles who had died on the island, he and Palting "remained in Guam at the request of Governor Seaton Schroeder to serve under his administration."[61] Palting remembered that it was immediately after he pledged allegiance to the United States in 1902, that Governor Seaton Schroeder "prevailed upon me [Palting] to continue in Guam, and become an official of the Government under his administration."[62] Flores and Palting secured positions within the Naval Government in various capacities, providing support to the US colonial officials, who had little formal knowledge of the Spanish language and legal system, which remained in place in Guåhan well into the twentieth century. Flores and Palting worked as island attorneys, judges of first instance, and registrars of lands, deeds, and titles.

As elaborated upon in chapter 1, both Flores and Palting married into the Dungca family of Hagåtña shortly after their release from exile.[63] The patriarch of the Dungca family, Justo Dungca, was a descendent of a Spanish-era Filipino deportado. His wife, Marcela, was born in the Philippines according to the 1920 US census.[64] During the Spanish period, the Dungca family gained fluency in CHamoru culture and customs. They were examples of the type of Filipino family that integrated into the Hagåtña elite. Dungca frequently attended to political matters that impacted the island in the early years of the US presence. Palting married Soledad Dungca; Flores married Felicita Dungca. By 1920 Palting had two children—Margarito (later known as Paul) and Florencia—and lived next to Justo Dungca on Herman Cortez Street in Hagåtña.[65] After the untimely death of his first wife, Felicita, Flores married Ana Camacho; their son Felixberto Camacho Flores, born in 1921, would become the first CHamoru bishop of Guam in 1970.[66]

The Flores and Palting families had distinctively CHamoru-influenced Filipino identities. They all spoke the CHamoru language and were integrated into the networks of the Hagåtña elite and community obligations that were the basis of *inafa'maolek* relations on the island. According to James McDonald, a descendant and great grandson of Flores, the CHamoru language was the primary language of the household for generations. Juan Flores said that his grandfather, Nieves Flores (a nephew of Leon Flores who also settled in Guåhan to work for the Naval Government), had "assimilated into Chamorro society" but "never claimed to be anything else than Filipino."[67] Their Filipino heritage was something to be celebrated. Nieves frequently referred to his birthplace in Ilocos Norte as "the homestead," never forgetting his province in the Philippines.[68] Both James and Juan remember their Filipino great grandparents and grandparents as "old-fashioned," always well-dressed, indicative of upper-class education and training that was also practiced by the women in their families. James and Juan also remember that their Filipino ancestors living in Guåhan only spoke CHamoru, and when they did speak English, it was with Filipino accents.[69] Frequently members of their families traveled back and forth to the Philippines for education or to visit relatives. The Dungca house in Hagåtña was a social and familial center for the Filipino elite in Guåhan in the pre–World War II period.[70]

CHamoru relationality operated outside the bounds of racial science's neat categories. Western conceptions of race, belonging, and nation—those used by Rizal, Blumentritt, and Johnston—did not align with how CHamoru relationality and *inafa'maolek* mediated familial relations between Filipinos and CHamorus in Guåhan. Despite their lack of CHamoru blood, these Filipino families were considered "one of our own" (to use a phrase written by CHamoru genealogist and Catholic priest Påle' Eric Forbes) by both CHamorus in Guåhan who saw Filipinos contributing to the island's community and by the US officials who took a more legal definition of "native" to mean any inhabitant of Guåhan when the United States annexed the island in 1898.[71] At the time when politics relied on the sometimes vague and continuously shifting definitions of race, nation, and citizenship, there was also the possibility for Filipinos to become "native" by practicing *inafa'maolek* within the villages and kinship networks in Guåhan.

Although Flores and Palting held positions within the Naval Government, this did not mean they were not critical of US empire. They were quite the opposite. Both Flores and Palting were known for being abrasive toward hypocritical, autocratic Naval governors and the implementation of US federals laws that did not take into consideration Guåhan's colonial context. Palting was a vocal advocate for Guåhan rights, often lambasting the Naval Government, through petitions as well as under the guise of "prayers," for ill treatment of Guåhan residents. One prayer included the following—"We close our prayer to thee [God] for thy mercy and help, the first toward the people of Guam in general, and to the poor class in particular, and the second for our actual governor, to remedy for the terrible effects of the policy of the just gone administration of 'not plenty and low cost' but 'high prices and scarcity.'" He continued his prayer with several other examples of the negative effects of the administration's policy.[72] This resistance toward the US Naval Government would be exacerbated when they received a notice declaring that they had to turn over their properties to the government.

Despite the integration of Flores, Palting, and other Filipinos into CHamoru society, and perhaps due to their criticism of US colonialism, the Naval Government questioned their citizenship status. The issue was whether Filipinos living in Guåhan and their families were eligible for Guam citizenship as stipulated by Governor Bradley's 1930 executive order, or whether they were considered Filipino nationals, and thus "alien"—rather than native—to Guåhan. If they were ineligible for Guam citizenship, this would pose problems for Filipino men and their families, because the US Navy sought to enforce alien land laws, which meant that those without Guam or US citizenship could not own land in Guåhan. As migrants within the US empire, these Filipinos fell between the cracks of ambiguous laws that presumed the immobility of colonial peoples.[73] With the passage of the Hare-Hawes-Cutting Act in January 1933 which created the process and set the date for Philippine independence, Filipinos living in Guåhan held a liminal position in which they were neither foreign citizens, nor Guam citizens, nor fully fledged US citizens.

On September 18, 1933, a few Filipino and non-CHamoru men received a notice from the Naval Government of Guam requiring them to transfer their land to the authorities because the "acquisition of land by purchase, gift or inheritance by aliens in Guam is prohibited by law."[74] Pancrasio Palting, along with his daughter Florencia and his son Margarito, who was attending law school in Washington, DC, received this notice with a stipulation saying, "[You must] convey your title to said lands otherwise they shall be forfeited and escheated to the Naval Government of Guam in accordance with law" within ninety days. Although Florencia and Margarito had been born in Guåhan and their mother was understood to be native according to Bradley's "Guam citizenship" proclamation, they did not have the right to hold on to their land because their father was Filipino. The family were set to lose several properties, including a lot in the capital village of Hagåtña.

In sending out this notice, the Naval Government attempted to implement and enforce alien land laws that were prominent throughout the American West in the early twentieth century. These alien land laws, most notably the California Alien Land Laws of 1913 and 1920, forbade those who were not US citizens, or were not eligible to become US citizens, from owning property, in order to protect access to land for those who were "native born."[75] Because the Chinese Exclusion Act of 1882 and the 1917 Immigration Act limited non-European migration and citizenship, a large percentage of these "native-born" citizens were white, or proto-white in the case of Irish, Italian, and German peoples. Asians such as Japanese and Chinese immigrants faced increasing antagonism from working-class, nativists whites who sought economic opportunity. Here, the word "native" has relatively little to do with Native Americans or Indigenous peoples. Instead "native" referred to a person who was a "native-born" citizen of the United States, who had special rights over naturalized citizens and noncitizens. These Asian exclusion acts and alien land laws would not be repealed until World War II.

In the context of the predominantly mixed-race unincorporated territories of empire, the term "native" took on several contradictory, yet overlapping, definitions, all with different material consequences. "Native" retained the "native-born" definition that also applied to white nativists on the continent. Because the population of Guåhan in the 1930s was almost exclusively CHamoru, "native" also became synonymous with the CHamoru people. If the term "native" can become simultaneous with CHamoru, however, what happens when CHamoru-ness has a capacious definition? As I argued in the early section of this chapter, CHamoru identity was not solely based in race, but emphasized notions of kinship and practices of *inafa'maolek* that tied people to one another and the land itself. In the context of 1930s Guåhan and the "native" wives of the Filipino men, "native" did not necessarily mean CHamoru blood; it was their active participation in CHamoru society well as the fact that they had been born in Guåhan. To be "native" in Guåhan in the 1930s was to be simultaneously "native-born" in Guåhan, while participating in CHamoru society even though one did not have CHamoru blood.

The attempt by US Naval officials to enforce alien land laws shows how US notions of race and citizenship were rigid and limiting and informed by patriarchal norms in heterosexual relations based in the US continental context. A woman who would be considered native in both the CHamoru and the US sense could not be native if married to a Filipino man. According to the Tydings-McDuffie Act of 1933, the term "Filipino" no longer signified just a racial group, but a nationality, one with an alien status in the US empire. The slippery definition of the term "native" in Guåhan is one historical example of what Lenape scholar Joanne Barker notes: "What the Native means will change over time and place as various political constituencies lay claim on determining its significance."[76]

The ambiguous definition of "native" is indicative of how race, citizenship, and nation were unstable categories within the islands of the US empire. In Guåhan, even census takers were often confused by their dynamics.[77] In 1920 the US Navy conducted a census of the island in line with the Fourteenth Census of the United States. In Hagåtña, Vicente Tydingco—a last name recognized as Chinese-CHamoru—recorded the family of Leon Flores. By this time, Leon had married Ana Camacho, whose race was clearly noted as CHamoru. In the boxes for Leon and his sons Leon Jr. and Sergio, however, the "color of race" boxes are jumbled scribbles, a result of Tydingco writing over the abbreviation of "Cha" with "Fil."[78] To make it explicitly clear, Tydingco spelled out "Filipino" in the left-hand margins of the census page. It is possible that he first believed the Flores family to be "native" to Guåhan, their fluency in the CHamoru language and their position in Guåhan society demonstrating a special familiarity with the island.

In the same census year, another instance of racial confusion may have occurred in the recording of the family of Tomas A. Calvo. Calvo was described as "white."[79] His wife Regina and his children were also listed as white. The census enumerator, Arthur W. Jackson, may have recognized the European heritage of the Calvo family despite even Calvo's birthplace in the Philippines. His father was a Spanish colonial official who traveled between Guåhan and the Philippines. His mother was an Anderson, whose father was a Scottish sailor. This family, who by all intents and purposes would be considered CHamoru, was seen as white, and the census enumerator noted as such. Ten years later, for the 1930 census, the Calvo family was described as "Chamorro," a simple census change that may have shielded them from the alien land laws implemented just three years later.[80] The confusion captured by the census of Flores and Calvo families hints at both the fungibility and inadequacy of race categories when attempting to describe the islands of the empire, especially ones that were Spanish colonies for three hundred years.

In response to the Navy's notice, the Filipino men began a campaign to obtain Guam citizenship to save their land from Navy annexation. They wrote multiple petitions and letters over a period of several months to shore up support within the island and across the US empire. The first of these letters was sent on September 30, 1933, when some Filipinos filed a "petition for Guam Citizenship" with the Naval Government of Guam Judiciary Department; that petition was denied two months later. In addition, Leon Flores, along with Filipinos Daniel L. Perez, Bernardo T. Punzalan, and Geronimo P. Santos (all but Flores were US military veterans), sent a letter to the secretary of the Navy and the president of the United States, in the care of the Filipino resident commissioners of the Philippine Islands, to ask for Guam citizenship. Underscoring their loyalty to the US government as shown through their service to the US Navy, they "looked for protection of us in the possession and ownership of real estate of which we came into possession of during our long residence in this Island," all of which were previously certified by previous Naval governors and governments.[81]

The Filipino men were well aware of how their citizenship affected their wives' and families' ability to hold land. In another attempt to gain allies in their struggle for Guam citizenship, Filipinos reached out to the governor general of the Philippine Islands, the speaker of the House of Representatives and the Senate of the Philippine Congress, former governor of Guam Willis Bradley, and Filipino resident commissioners based in Washington, DC. Their letter dated October 16, 1933, stated that "those who came into the Island of Guam, at any time after the occupation thereof, by the military forces of the United States of North America, and the *native* girls whom they had married, and the children born to those marital unions, and their widows, are now considered by Governor Alexander's administration, Aliens to the United States in Guam."[82] Because citizenship and nationhood followed a family's patriarch, their "native" wives were considered to be Filipinos, despite their birth, livelihood, and families residing in Guåhan. Their children also became Filipino, as seen in the 1920 census with the Flores family.

When advocating for Guam citizenship, the Filipino men never claimed to be natives of Guåhan, but they did emphasize their wives and children's nativeness to tie them to the island. Besides Leon Flores and Pancrasio Palting, there were other Filipinos and foreigners who were affected by the Guam citizenship law. In letters to shore up support, the men are noted as those "who have resided in Guam a considerable length of time, who have married *native* women, have large families, and who it is believed would make loyal citizens." Flores was described as an "Attorney. Resident of Guam for 32 years. Citizen of the Philippines. Married to *Native*. Four (4) children." The others include Pascual Artero, who was noted as a "businessman. Citizen of Spain. Resident of Guam for 32 years. Married to *Native*. Seven (7) children"; Geronimo Pongo Santos, who was described as a "Barber. Resident of Guam for 19 years. Married to *Native*. Nine (9) children. Citizen of the Philippines"; and lastly, Adriano Maria Cristobal, "Federal Employee. Resident of Guam for 23 years. Married to *Native*. Five (5) children. Citizen of the Philippines."[83] In the 1920 and 1930 US census, some or all of Artero, Cristobal, and Santos wives and children were listed as CHamoru.[84] They asked for Guam citizenship, citing their connections to Guåhan via their relations with their native wives and children.

For the writers, their exclusion was an anathema to the US liberal rhetoric that supposedly emphasized the equality of people. Although they were not native to Guåhan, the men argued that they should not be considered "alien" either. They asked how, for the peoples of the Philippines, Guåhan, Hawai'i, American Sāmoa, and Puerto Rico, "all of which countries are still at present time held by it, as its possessions, territories, or like, as shown by the American Flag, which is flying in each of those countries, is any one of those people considered, reasonably, an Alien to it, the United States of North America?"[85] They exploited US liberal rhetoric of equality to justify further inclusion, rather than alienation, of US colonies and territories.

Furthermore, the writers of the letter used the irony of US liberal colonialism to show various instances of how colonial policy in Guåhan was improvised often at the whims of Naval governors. They argued that this autocratic style of government had applied to how they acquired land in the first place, and thus it was entirely possible for them to receive Guam citizenship if the governor simply pronounced them citizens. They wrote, "Former incumbents as Governors of Guam, *whose will were the 'LAW,'* whether manifested or expressed VERBATIM or in any style of writing, had sanctioned and approved the acquisition, the possession, the owning, the documentation—including registration, survey, payment of real estate taxes, and securing of Guaranteed Claim Title of Certificate of Title, and the laws of Guam call them indistinctly, signed by Notaries Public, Court Clerk, Courts Judges, etc. and Governors of Guam, on the part of those Filipinos, who now keep them in their possessions and controls."[86]

They argued that their land titles were valid not only due to the approval from the Naval governor, but because they were approved at various levels of the Naval Government's bureaucracy. Then, the writers pointed to the US Constitution and demonstrated their command of US law, using it as arguments against the arbitrary nature of Naval governance in Guåhan. They wrote, "The Constitutional law of the United States prohibits the promulgation of law, to have its retroactive effects, where that law is prejudicial to certain entities." They argued that their properties were exempted from the alien land laws because they came into ownership of them before the implementation of both Guam citizenship and the alien land laws.

And as a final statement, they mentioned how their families through no fault of their own would be negatively affected by the decision to deny Guam citizenship to Filipinos. In the Great Depression, they could not sell the land for profit, causing them to lose all wealth and subjecting them to poverty. They wrote that "transferring the said properties [to the Naval Government], for no consideration, to friends, or to relatives of their wives, is equivalent to throw them into the sea, and lose, forever, the fruits of honest struggles for life, during the long period of time of residences, as faithful subjects of the

United States, in Guam."[87] The enforcement of the alien land laws, thus, would deprive their families of their land and push them into poverty.

In their quest to keep their lands, the Filipino residents of Guåhan exposed the inadequacies and inconsistencies of US colonial governance across the Pacific.[88] The undefined territorial status of Guåhan and the ambiguous racial and citizenship status of the island's people made it difficult to understand how citizenship applied to Guåhan. Furthermore, the United States did not have clear regulations for colonial subjects like Filipinos moving between territorial spaces. On October 24, the Judiciary Department of the Naval Government of Guam sent a sympathetic letter to the governor about the Filipinos' petitions to have Guam citizenship apply to them.[89] It explained that because there were no naturalization laws and procedures for Guåhan at any period before this order, Filipinos had no opportunity to transfer citizenship. Furthermore, the only way noncitizens and children could receive citizenship was if the Court and the governor of Guam had "approved the decree, which should have the effect of making it legal." The writer suggested that immigration laws be created for the island patterned after the continental United States, "taking into consideration the immigration laws of Guam."

As predominately upper class, Filipinos claimed that their having Guam citizenship would help promote the island's development. In their perspective, the Filipino elites in Guåhan—particularly those who had worked for the Naval Government, businessmen, teachers, and landowners—were well respected, productive members of island society and deserved Guam citizenship.[90] Citing the fact that attaining residency within the continent only took five years, they wrote that "it is in the interest of the state [and] the individual to grant citizenship if it is clear that the petitioner desires in good faith to become a citizen and if he is industrious, in good health, and of good moral character." Thus, they argued there was economic incentive to ensure that law-abiding Filipinos remain in Guåhan. They would earn and spend their wealth within the local community and would be inclined to properly develop their land for economic growth. They warned also that "if an alien is not permitted to become a citizen there is always a tendency for him to move away and take his personal wealth to the land he can call his home."[91] In other words, their work for empire made them invaluable assets for the US empire and thus worthy of greater legal inclusion into Guam citizenship and the United States.

Two days later, on October 26, Pancrasio Palting received a suspension of the land claim issued by the Naval Government. Ion Pursell, a Navy official whom Palting in a letter to former Governor Bradley described as "Rasputin" and "disliked by all," wrote to Palting that the ninety-day notice to turn over land to the government was "hereby held in abeyance for the time being and until further notice."[92] The notice was also sent to Palting's daughter Florencia Dungca Palting and to his son Margarito Dungca Palting (later known as Paul). Included in the letter was the list of six properties that were to be handed over. One lot in particular, "Lot No. 37-New, situated between General Terrero Street and Hernan-Cortes Street, City of Agana, Guam," was divided twenty times, with Palting holding eight-twentieths, Florencia holding three-twentieths, and Margarito holding another three-twentieths.[93] This one property alone shows not only how the confiscation of property could affect a whole family, but how the family themselves understood communal property ownership. Nevertheless, the letter provided a short reprieve that allowed the government and the court to read the many letters and petitions sent by the Filipinos and their allies to decide whether or not to grant Guam citizenship to Filipinos and other foreigners living on the island.

On November 10, the senior island judge V. P. Camacho declared that the "petition of Leon Flores for Guam citizenship . . . is hereby denied." The summary to the proceedings said, "The petitioner is not one of those classes enumerated in the proclamation of the Governor of Guam, namely, that petitioner was not born in Guam; he is not a Chamorro, and was not in Guam on 1 February 1899."[94] Despite his "medal of service" for twenty years of service to the US Naval Government from Governor Bradley, Flores could not obtain Guam citizenship because he was Filipino. Other "aliens" in Guåhan received similar notes, including Adriano Cristobal and Geronimo Santos.[95] All of them had children with CHamoru wives. As a result of this decision, they were told to sell their land or risk having it taken by the government. A note written later atop of the document wrote, "All Filipinos-applicants for Guam citizenship were denied, thereby losing the stronghold from which to defend the forfeiture and escheat of their real properties, into the Naval Government of Guam, now held in Abeyance until further notice."

Palting, however, did not give up. He appealed his case on November 13, 1933, by sending a brief to the Chief of Naval Operations arguing against the legal basis of the two decisions made by the Naval Government of Guam. The first question was whether as a Filipino-born Guåhan resident, he would be considered "alien" to the United States, and the second, if the land under his name was legally obtained prior to the implementation of the alien land law of 1918, and thus not subject to the new order implemented in 1933.[96] Perhaps aware of the political moves to prepare the Philippines for national independence, Palting found it absolutely necessary to clarify the legal positions of Filipinos living in Guåhan. His intracolonial migration defied legal categorizations of citizenship and belonging for both colonial subjects as well as the territorial possessions.

In this brief, Palting provided an autobiography explaining his worthiness of inclusion in Guåhan citizenship because of his demonstrated loyalty to the United States.[97] Palting explained why he was in Guåhan in the first place. "It was in the midst of the Filipino revolution against the authority of the United States implantation therein," he wrote, "when in the year 1900, I with others had been removed by Army forces of the United States, from my natal province [Laoag, Ilocos Norte], against our will, to Manila, P.I."[98] Naming a few of his contemporaries—Apolinario Mabini, Artemio Ricarte, Pablo Ocampo—Palting wrote about how they were "ejected from the Philippine Islands, and brought as political prisoners into a place now known as the municipality of Asan, of this Island of Guam" in December 1901. They were "kept isolated from the rest of the World as obstructive elements" because "of the pacification for which the American military forces were working throughout the Philippine Islands."[99] Palting emphasized that his migration to Guåhan was not his personal choice, but a decision made by the US military.

In 1902, however, in exchange for his release from exile, Palting emphasized that he took an oath of allegiance to the United States, and recognized "without reservation, the supremacy of its authority to the Philippine islands." Although he was released, he "did not return to [his] native country" because the naval governor of the island, Seaton Schroeder, asked if Palting would be willing to "become an official of the Government under his administration." Palting agreed, and for several years after he had multiple positions within the Naval Government of Guam "swearing, in each and all cases of appointments, to my allegiance to the United States . . . without mental reservation." In all cases, Palting emphasized he proclaimed allegiance to the United States witnessed by military governors and officials, and thus, he argued that he should not be considered an "alien" of the United States and Guåhan. If military colonialism was the cause of Palting's exile from the Philippines, it was also the reason for his employment in Guåhan, and because of this, he argued that he should be considered a US citizen. If Palting's relationship with his Guåhan-born wife and children and his contributions to Guåhan society were not enough to support his claims for inclusion into the United States, perhaps it was his outright and recorded loyalty to the Naval Government of Guam that would convince colonial officials otherwise.

In a last-ditch effort to use US law to bolster his arguments, Palting quoted from the case *Fourteen Diamond Ring v. United States*, which decided that the

Philippines was not to be considered a foreign country—therefore, by birth he was not an "alien." He then reiterated his and his family's loyalty. He wrote, "The country Philippine Islands, to which I belong by birth, and the country Guam, to which I belong by residence, are under the control and sovereignty of the United States, to which their inhabitants and people, among whom I, my children, and my wife, are, owe allegiance and obedience as its subjects up to present time."[100] Loyalty to the United States would be the last piece of evidence for his claim.

Although the Filipino men used multiple reasons to protect their lands and property, they never claimed to be Indigenous or native to Guåhan in order to be recognized by the United States or the US Naval Government. Instead they took on the responsibility to uphold their obligations by claiming their relationships—their kinship relationships—to their native wives and children. In doing so, they sought to convey how they belonged to Guåhan and the United States, despite their Filipino race and nationality that came with it. Essentially, they found and tested the criteria for US citizenship—race, patriarchal responsibility, economic productivity, imperial geography, Americanization, and loyalty—showing that even if they did not satisfy racial criteria, they excelled at the rest. And because of this, they were not "alien" to the United States.

According to a letter from Atanasio T. Perez to Governor Bradley, as of March 1934 the foreigners who owned land in Guåhan did not have to give lands to the Navy. Perez, who had previously denied the Filipinos Guam citizenship, wrote, "Upon my arrival, I found what you already known from Mr. Palting that the Japanese, Spaniard, and Filipino residents had to sell their real estate properties within 3 months. However, this order was not carried out due to the cablegrams sent by the above named residents to Washington and coded radiogram was received from the Department [Navy] to hold the order in abeyance."[101] Somehow, Palting's arguments were heard by the Navy Department, and he did not need to transfer his land. Despite the favorable outcome for Palting, the legal battle for land demonstrates the difficulty with which Palting, Flores, and other men married to "native" women negotiated—legally, socially, and culturally—through the different articulations of race, citizenship, and belonging in the local CHamoru society that was ruled by the US Naval Government. Their lives demonstrate the precarity with which colonial subjects moved and migrated within the US empire.

WHILE THE PHILIPPINES' political future grew distant from the United States, CHamorus in Guåhan remained staunchly loyal to the United States flag. In December 1933, in the midst of deliberations within US Congress and the Philippine Legislature to discuss the future independence of the Philippine archipelago, the Guam Congress drafted another petition to the US Congress and the president, demanding US citizenship. Two thousand people signed the petition, and the Guam Congress garnered the support of previous Naval governors of Guam.[102] While the Philippines eventually garnered the Tydings-McDuffie Act, CHamorus in Guåhan were not given what they hoped for. When Guåhan and the Philippines were invaded by Japanese forces in December 1941, their separate paths toward inclusion and independence were put on hold.

Race, citizenship, and belonging and were continuously redefined in Guåhan in the 1920s and 1930s. The 1926 Philippine resolution and the Guam citizenship conundrum in the 1930s reflect how the overlapping and sometimes conflicting schemas of race had the potential for material consequences that spurred CHamorus and Filipinos to articulate their racial identities in terms that were recognizable to US colonial state. In this period of undefined political status and the growing desire to become US citizens, their essays, speeches, debates, and legal cases demonstrate the CHamoru and Filipino ability to understand, use, and critique the US empire's racialized colonial governance to their own advantage. Although Guåhan was not annexed to the Philippines and Filipino-native families were able to keep their land, the course of these two events reflect the racial complexities of the twentieth-century transformation of Guåhan's social relations under US empire. Relations grounded in CHamoru kinship networks and *inafa'maolek* became increasingly articulated in terms of race, nation, and citizenship.

Part II

Post–World War II Militarism (1944–1950s)

CHAPTER THREE

Natives and Aliens

CHamoru Land Dispossession, Filipino Migrant Labor, and Settler Militarism in Guåhan

In November 1949, Assemblyman A. C. Cruz, from the central village of Barigåda, testified in support of an organic act for Guåhan before a visiting commission of the Public Lands Committee of the US House of Representatives. Despite his support, Cruz was angered by the US Navy Department's inefficiency when dealing with land. He emphasized that during the reoccupation and rebuilding of Guåhan in the years after World War II, "abuses by the Government have been committed which will certainly astound Americans like you," and that due to the US military's "taking of private properties under the color and scheme of National Security, many a Guamanian property owner has been violently and grossly invaded in his rights of privacy and quiet possession of his property."[1] He lamented to the committee, "The land question on Guam is of primary importance." Although they were liberated from Japanese colonial occupation, the CHamoru people—many of them called themselves "Guamanians" to distinguish themselves from Chamorros of the Northern Mariana Islands, a former Japanese colony—faced unprecedented military land dispossession by the very country that purported to deliver freedom and democracy to the rest of the world.[2]

Meanwhile these CHamoru lands were transformed into a US military fortress by Filipino migrant workers. "Almost everything on Guam was built by the Filipinos," Pilar P. Malilay recounted in the documentary *Under the American Sun*.[3] She emphasized, "Roads, buildings, everything in the military was built by Filipinos." In 1952, Malilay was one of the few women recruited to work as registered nurses at Camp Roxas, one of several labor camps that housed migrant workers from the Philippines. She and five other nurses took care of anywhere from five thousand to ten thousand Filipino men. Usually only reported as statistics or seen in anonymous photos in the archives, roughly twenty thousand Filipino migrant workers toiled in the tropical Guåhan heat to build infrastructure, including airstrips, roads, and buildings, to support the US military's strategic realignment in the Pacific.[4] They were welders, electricians, stevedores, truck drivers, accountants, bakers, mailmen, commissary shopkeepers, and busboys. They could not move freely without permission from military personnel and were often paid low wages despite the backbreaking work they performed for their employers. Filipino labor built the military infrastructure upon the CHamoru land that the United States annexed for national defense and to project its power in the Pacific.

In World War II and the Cold War era, the US military transformed Guåhan into a military fortress to protect and project US liberal values abroad. In doing so, US military strategy took precedence over CHamoru land ownership and livelihoods. The US military commenced a process of land expropriation that denied CHamoru claims to land, reconfigured land ownership, displaced CHamoru people from their ancestral lands, and attempted to replace CHamorus with the settler institution of the US military. Militarism forced CHamorus to rely on military institutions for their livelihoods, pushing CHamorus from a primarily subsistence culture rooted at the *låncho* (ranch) toward one embedded in capital and labor. Moreover, the military transformation of the island was possible because the United States and the Philippines negotiated the establishment of international migrant labor circuits that recruited and transported Filipino workers to construct bases in Guåhan. These diplomatic agreements ensured that military contractors had access to a stable, cheap labor force, while also providing the Philippines with a postwar, postindependence economy built upon the exportation and remittances of Filipino workers abroad.

In other words, Guåhan became a settler-militarized island.[5] As CHamoru historian Alfred P. Flores argues, this pivotal moment in Guåhan's history demonstrates how US militarization of Guåhan was dependent on the "co-constitutive process that included CHamoru land dispossession, discursive justifications for remaking of the island, the racialization of civilian military labor, and the military's policing of interracial intimacies."[6] Flores connected this history of Guåhan to scholar Juliet Nebolon's observation of how, in World War II Hawai'i, regimes of militarism and settler colonialism mutually occluded, legitimized, and justified their manifestations. She called this convergence of colonialisms, "settler militarism."[7]

By placing this episode into a longer history of CHamoru-Filipino relations, I expand on Flores's and Nebolon's lucid arguments to historicize the impact of postwar settler militarism on the ideological and rhetorical terrain upon which CHamorus and Filipinos navigated and negotiated the growth of the US military empire in the Pacific. In chapter 4 I will historicize how US citizenship legitimized settler militarism in Guåhan. In this chapter I detail the struggles over land and labor to demonstrate how settler militarism transformed the island's physical landscape and, importantly, how CHamorus and Filipinos rearticulated their relationships to their land, nation, and each other. To resist US military land-takings and argue for US citizenship and a civilian government, CHamorus articulated the importance of land in terms of settler economies of Western land value rather than in terms rooted in CHamoru culture. For those from the Philippines, the experience of working abroad for the US military in the name of the Philippine nation-state had the effect of coalescing their strongly held regional identities, such Ilonggos and Ilokanos, into the broader term "Filipinos." To push back on the inequities of US empire, CHamorus and Filipinos held tight to these new relationalities to vie for better political and economic positions within empire. Yet, as I will argue, CHamoru and Filipino reiterations of these colonial logics in their negotiations *with* empire foreclosed potential CHamoru-Filipino solidarities *against* empire, and further entrenched, rather than overturned, US military imperialism in the Pacific.

Guamanian Land in Militarized Hands

Land is an integral component of CHamoru life. Michael Philips, grandson of CHamoru leader Baltazar J. Bordallo, wrote in a 1996 article, "Land is the soul of our culture; it, together with the sea, gives life to the Chamorro."[8] CHamoru society and cultural values remain interwoven with place; the land maps kinship networks and deep genealogy across time and space.[9] The land provides sustenance through farming and agriculture, especially at the *låncho*, which is also a space to learn *kostumbren CHamoru* (CHamoru culture).[10] There, families grow their own food, planting and harvesting by hand, and follow traditional knowledge that underscores the relationships between seasonal weather patterns, celestial temporality, and the land itself.[11] Traditionally, CHamorus farm just enough to feed themselves and fulfill community obligations through *chenchule'*, acts of giving and receiving. Food from the *låncho* has been essential to the *inafa'maolek* relationships that families have built with each other.[12]

During the Naval era before World War II, CHamoru conceptions of land as genealogy, ontology, and kin clashed with US notions of land as property to be developed for economic gain. While *lånchos* provided most of CHamorus' needs, Naval governors consistently spoke about the lack of food for naval personnel stationed on the island. They hoped that the locally grown food could supplement Naval shipments and ensure that the US Navy remained functional in Guåhan.[13] Thus, the Navy sought to educate CHamorus on the "proper ways" of land management by instituting a series of modernization practices to encourage CHamorus to participate in commercial farming. These programs and practices emphasized productivity in terms of "sustained labor and time discipline" and included publishing agricultural information in the *Guam Recorder*, creating farmers' markets, hosting special agricultural weeks, teaching farming in schools, and establishing an agricultural research station in Guåhan.

The Navy's emphasis on commercial farming as a sign of modernity became ingrained in how some enterprising CHamorus from elite families with large landholdings couched their worthiness for US citizenship and land rights. Many CHamorus, however, felt that working beyond kinship and family responsibilities for commercial gain was not a good use of time, and they did not consistently bring their produce to commercial market, much to the chagrin of Naval officials. As CHamoru historian Elyssa Santos argues, CHamorus had "an indigenous worldview that privileged familial obligations, called for a particular relationship with the island's ecology, and understood that supernatural forces also influenced one's time."[14] This worldview reveals and depends on the strong connection that CHamorus have had with their land.

The CHamoru relationship to land was challenged during and after World War II. From December 1941 to August 1944, the CHamoru people in Guåhan were subjected to Japanese imperialism that included forced changes in language, culture, and life.[15] CHamoru people were made to work for Japanese military operations, planting crops, building pillboxes for Japanese guns, and digging tunnels into the limestone cliffs.[16] The wartime experiences of abuse, such as rape, murder, and massacres of the CHamoru people, remain in the general consciousness of the people of Guåhan.[17] In reaction to the abuses, many CHamorus evacuated their village homes to seek safety in their secluded *lånchos*.[18] In the last months of Japanese occupation of Guåhan in the summer of 1944, the Japanese military forced CHamorus to leave their villages and *lånchos* and move into the inner valleys and dense jungles of the island to prevent them from reaching and communicating with US ships and planes that sailed past or flew over the island.[19] This forced relocation moved them away from their *lånchos*. Some families would not be able to see their land again.

When the US military invaded Guåhan in July 1944 as part of its island-hopping strategy across the Pacific, they used indiscriminate bombing that destroyed many of the structures on the island. According to historian Robert Rogers, "the American bombardment of Guam had gathered momentum from 18 July on to become by the morning of 21 July, the most intense crescendo of conventional firepower ever inflicted on any locality in the Pacific War."[20] The action weakened the Japanese forces but also destroyed much of the land that CHamoru people depended on to live. Villages no longer existed. *Lånchos* were destroyed. CHamoru historian Pedro C. Sanchez wrote, "the city of Agaña was in rubbles," leveled in order to "prevent Japanese troops from using buildings as cover against advancing Marines."[21] By the end of the invasion, Guåhan was a military wasteland, with broken-down tanks, unexploded bombs, and bullet casings scattered all over the island.

Guåhan and the Northern Mariana Islands played a crucial role in the US military mission to secure the Pacific Theater in the remaining months of World War II. After the Battle of Guam, the US military converted the island into "the nerve center of the final thrust against Japan."[22] Two-thirds of the island were condemned for military purposes, including spaces for soldiers to recuperate from the front lines, stations to house troops, and warehouses to store matériel. The military commenced a large-scale infrastructure project deploying thirty-seven thousand construction troops from the Naval Construction Battalion—better known as the Seabees—to dredge harbors, build breakwaters, and pave 103 miles of road "for access to airfields, ammunition dumps, camps, and other facilities."[23] The Seabees also expanded the water system to supply the large demand of military personnel. Because Guåhan was central to the US attack on Japan, they also built warehouses for "a large store of supplies, spare parts, equipment, fuels, and refrigerated foods be on hand at all times for the Fleet and for military forces on the island."[24] The island of Tini'an, north of Guåhan, stored the two atomic bombs that were dropped on Hiroshima and Nagasaki in 1945.

Even after the island was reoccupied by US military forces, the next months continued to be as destructive and uncertain for CHamorus. The population and landscape of the island underwent drastic transformations. At the height of the buildup, over two hundred thousand military personnel, contractors, and workers were stationed in Guåhan, compared to the roughly twenty-two thousand local CHamorus who had survived the war.[25] "Native labor" was not used for these large-scale projects because they "were needed in the reconstruction of their own homes and on Federal Economic Administration farming projects aimed at producing fresh foods for natives and garrison forces." The US Navy built temporary housing described as "primitive" for "15,000 natives [who] had to be housed, and three camps were set up in Agaña, Agat, and near the Ylig River."[26] World War II had mapped the island, previously understood in terms of CHamoru kinship and ecological relations, into one that was suitable for war.[27]

The United States' prevailing fear of communist aggression in the post–World War II period pushed US leaders to increase US involvement in the

A post–World War II Guåhan village with traditional prewar architecture. From the Jurlina Collection of the Richard F. Taitano Micronesian Area Research Center.

Pacific. For national security policymakers such as George Kennan and James Forrestal, Guåhan and the United Nations Trust Territories of the Pacific Islands would provide enough land mass and oceanic expanse to make the US presence in the Pacific felt by potential enemies.[28] This strategic shift meant that the small islands in the Pacific and their peoples bore the brunt of Cold War militarization. Guåhan was not built up to bring modernity to residents;

instead the island was transformed into "a great Army air base as well as the principal naval base in the western Pacific" for the future decades.[29] As a result, CHamorus found it difficult to recognize their island due to land annexation and rampant militarization. Their attempts to rebuild their lives after the war were halted by gates and fences that sealed off the military's "restricted zones" where no civilian could enter, let alone farm or forage for food. It is in this period that the US military became a settler institution in Guåhan, its presence made evident by the concrete roads, the chain-link fences, and the reinforced harbor that was built on annexed CHamoru land and sea.

In order to resolve land issues, in April 1945 the US Navy created the Guam Lands Claims Commission (GLCC), which was tasked with surveying, appraising, condemning, and subdividing lands in order to sell these lands back to the CHamoru people who had been displaced.[30] The GLCC became controversial among CHamorus, who had witnessed the hasty, unorganized, and coercive tactics the commission had used to obtain and redistribute land.[31] The commission also conducted its policies using land values based in Western liberalism that did not consider CHamoru relations to land.[32] The GLCC, similar to those historicized by Nebolon in wartime Hawai'i, depended upon "regimes of eminent domain and land leasing [that] wielded the commodity logic of abstraction, Lockean notions of improvement, and the ruse of the abstract individual property owner" which masked racial hierarchies inherent in settler militarism.[33] Furthermore, the GLCC was administered by the Naval Government rather than a civilian agency, a conflict of interest pointed out by many critics in the late 1940s. For instance, if a CHamoru landowner disagreed with a GLCC appraisal, they could only appeal to local courts controlled by the Navy; no further appeals process existed.[34] And if at first the GLCC found it difficult to account for land ownership due to the lack of historical land records and incomplete prewar cadastral surveys, the commission eventually used a simple phrase—"military purposes"—justify annexation.[35] The GLCC was the settler institution by which the US military sought to make its presence permanent on the island.

Early on, the US military annexed sites and built infrastructure that suggested that they fully intended to stay. The port town of Sumai became Naval Station Guam. The seaside area of Hagåtña was paved over for a road that connected the Airforce Base in the north to Naval station at Sumai. The farmlands in Barigåda were transformed into runways, a radio installation, and by the end of 1946, an eighteen-hole golf course named Admiral Nimitz Golf Course after Navy Pacific Fleet Commander Chester W. Nimitz. Indeed, military officials were obsessed with transforming Guåhan into a tropical US

Almost immediately after the US military recaptured Guåhan, the US commenced a military buildup to transform the island for military purposes at the end of World War II. United States Coast Guard. Public Domain.

leisure destination that met the expectations of white military personnel. In 1947 Laura Thompson, an anthropologist and advocate for CHamoru people since the prewar period, criticized how the US military took advantage of the war-torn island and loyal islanders.[36] She uncovered a Naval Government proposal to build a park in Hagåtña, which she believed was another ploy for the military government to control the most important asset of CHamoru life in the postwar period—land. The military planned to rebuild the capital village of Hagåtña "into a 'Santa Monica of the Pacific,' a city of which the Guamanians might be 'justly proud.'"[37] In order to do so, the Navy devised a plan to buy land at exorbitantly low prices and sell it back to CHamoru owners "to clear the title." The Naval Government, however, would also require the prospective landowners, "who have lost most of their assets," to "buy up and immediately pay for the new large lots as they are offered for sale and also build houses, according to Naval Government specifications, at a cost of several thousand dollars on the lots thus acquired."[38] Only islanders who already were cash-rich or who were connected to off-island investors could afford such a transaction. And even then, the investments to develop properties would be paid to military-associated businesses, because few non-military construction companies existed on the island.

The US military's desire to transform Guåhan into tropical paradise did not end with Hagåtña. Citing "defense purposes" in 1948, the military annexed sixty hectares at Tomhom (Tumon Bay) for their own private beach on prime beachfront property. Tomhom was culturally important to CHamorus and had already been in the possession of CHamoru families. The bay provided fishing areas and breadfruit and coconut trees that provided sustenance for local families. There were also cultural markers dotting Tomhom, including latte stones (ancient and sacred CHamoru stone pillars) and the shrine of Påle San Vitores, a Spanish-era missionary who brought Catholicism to Guåhan.[39] For CHamorus, the annexation of this land for the purposes of recreation for military personnel was excessive and outright disrespectful.[40] Even though they protested by sending petitions and letters to Secretary of Defense James V. Forrestal, CHamoru resistance to military land-taking was met with apathy from military leaders, who insisted that CHamorus and military personnel could share the land. The commanding general of the Marianas-Bonin area, Francis H. Griswold, commented that "combined Army–Air force requirement in Tumon area involves only a small portion of total land and approximately one-half of beach" and that he believed "all requirements can be met without undue hardship on Guam or local organizations."[41] The Tomhom Controversy and the "Santa Monica of the Pacific" park proposal demonstrate how military prioritized the needs of the US military—no matter how vague or inconsequential—over the sustenance, culture, and lives of the CHamoru people.[42]

Land matters fueled CHamorus' discontent against the Naval Government. As I described in the prologue, Jose M. Torres testified before the Hopkins Committee in 1947 about the ways the US military had continuously displaced

CHamoru people, so much so they could not rebuild their homes, forage or farm for food, or acquire property.[43] He couched his discontent by emphasizing the hypocritical inconsistency between US values of freedom and democracy and the US Navy's land policies in Guåhan. He reiterated his desire for US citizenship for all island residents in the hopes that a definitive legal status would enable CHamorus to have a greater say in the government affairs.

Similarly, CHamoru Catholic priest Father Oscar Calvo endorsed the possibility of a civilian government and US citizenship for Guåhan at the Hopkins Committee meeting. He also criticized the Navy's land policies, educating the visiting committee on just how important land was to the CHamoru people and why they were so adamant that the land issues be resolved quickly and justly. Calvo was disturbed by how the US military not only displaced CHamorus from their land but destroyed mangoes and tangerine trees that had sustained people throughout war. He told the committee, "The people are an agricultural people. Our backbone is the soil, we are working, it is true, for the government in the pre-war days, but these people, at the same time would have their ranches 3 to 4 miles out of Agana and we used to go out there in the evenings to feed the chickens, the hogs and carabao which would help support them together with the pay which was received from the government."[44] Calvo described CHamorus as an "agricultural people," referring to the subsistence culture and ingrained connections to the land. He also referenced the *låncho*, a CHamoru space described by CHamoru scholar Christine Taitano DeLisle as a site for "disciplining and cultivating Indigenous sensibilities" where families could grow food for themselves.[45] Wages earned from work for the Naval Government merely supplemented the abundance gathered from the *låncho*. The *låncho*, furthermore, had the power to protect and sustain CHamorus during the Japanese occupation. Calvo declared, "We were able to survive because we worked the soil from the sweat of our brows." He ended his comment, "As I said before, our backbone is the soil—needless to say that is our life here on the island."[46] Connecting CHamoru bodies to land, Calvo referenced a deeply understood—"needless to say"—CHamoru relationality to land beyond the commodified goods that the land provided. For Torres and Calvo, the US military's actions in Guåhan disrespected the essential relationship between the people and land.

Yet two years later, in November 1949, CHamorus began to describe land in terms of Western land values. Representative William Lemke of North Dakota led the US Congress Public Lands Committee to the island to inquire whether Guåhan residents desired an Organic Act that could "organize" the territory with a civilian government and bestow US citizenship. Several dozen testimonials, including ones from Frank B. Leon Guerrero and Baltazar J. Bordallo, reiterated their desire for an Organic Act. Some also used the hearings to express their discontent about just how destructive land annexation was for the CHamoru people. CHamorus spoke about the lowballed appraisals Naval officials had given them.[47] They commented on the environmental destruction from the bombings during the war as well as how the US military fenced off areas where they could no longer forage for breadfruit and other food. They also talked about the coercive nature of the GLCC.

Vicente T. Cruz's pithy exchange with Representative Lemke reveals the Naval officials' coercive tactics that led CHamorus to sign their lands away. Cruz had owned fourteen acres in the village of Assan where he and his father grew corn, watermelons, copra, and sweet potatoes before the war.[48] However, Cruz was living with his cousins in a different village, unable to build a home for himself after the US military annexed his land. Lemke asked about the land transfer process and if Cruz had been afraid of military officials. Cruz replied "Well, they made me sign it" and further clarified, "The Navy had more power in Guam than anyone else—more power than you have."[49] Historian Anne Hattori argues that the exchange between Cruz and Lemke speaks succinctly to the coercion CHamorus experienced when dealing with the Navy—an entity they had trusted but that had ultimately treated them unjustly. Cruz's situation was one of many that demonstrated to CHamorus the hypocrisy of US rhetoric of equality and fairness as it applied to Guåhan. CHamoru leaders frequently pointed to this hypocrisy to further advocate for a civilian government and US citizenship.[50] Indeed, Cruz testified, "about the Organic Act, I am 100% for it."[51]

Read in another way, Cruz's exchange with Lemke also demonstrates how the GLCC's use of Western land laws and appraisals limited the rhetorical terrain upon which CHamorus could resist military land annexation. To protest land annexation, CHamorus had to articulate land value according to Western forms of land commodification abstracted from its cultural significance and the CHamoru people's reliance on the land for livelihood. This articulation stood in stark contrast to how Father Calvo had talked about land two years earlier. For Cruz, the central problem was not the military's presence on the island or the US empire in general, but the US military's inability to make right their land transactions with CHamorus. Cruz had told the Committee that Naval appraisers did not consult him on his land's value and quoted him only $14.10. Even after he signed away his land, he continued to wait for the money.[52] His land had been developed into the admiral's house and guest house at

Marianas Command, which Cruz described was "the most valuable residence today." Throughout their testimonies, CHamorus like Cruz gave monetary figures, always higher than the Navy appraised, to convey just how important land was to them. This is not to suggest that CHamorus did not understand how land appraisals worked, but to emphasize how land had become commodified in the political rhetoric of CHamorus.

CHamoru commercial farmers also argued that the US military stymied their ability to establish a local Guåhan economy in the US entrepreneurial tradition. For example, Frank Perez, an assemblyman in the Guam Congress from the village of Barigåda, relayed the struggles he had in reestablishing his commercial farm. Before the war, Perez had owned 160 acres of land where he raised thousands of chickens, producing eggs for local consumption and export. He also raised hogs, which required farm infrastructure, including buildings and fencing. After the war, Perez attempted to rebuild his commercial farm on his land, but the commanding officer of the nearby hospital ordered him to move fences, whole chicken flocks, and passels of hogs on multiple occasions, making his enterprise more labor intensive and unsustainable. For Perez, this dynamic was frustrating. He told the committee, "It is a known fact that about half or more of the area of the most arable land on the Island of Guam, suitable for agriculture and raising of livestock, is in the hands of the military." While he understood that the US military needed land to end World War II, he exclaimed that "the time has come for the responsible agency to draw the line, that this area be permanently acquired for defense purposes and, that other areas are not needed, be returned to the Guamanians for their farming use and otherwise."[53]

Perez's testimony fell short of criticizing the outright presence of the US military in Guåhan. As a war survivor, he believed there was a need for the US military in Guåhan, and he reiterated his loyalty to the United States. He subsequently followed his expressions of discontent by demonstrating his understanding that Western land value was rooted in agricultural productivity. Perez said, "You can have seen, gentlemen, by this time, flourishing livestock farms on the Island all over, had any action been taken to protect the farmers and deed them land or assign them the land until such time as everything is set."[54] He and another assemblyman from Barigåda, Joaquin Guerrero, reiterated to the visiting congressional committee that not all farmers wanted to commit labor and capital into farming, especially when low-level military officials could arbitrarily dictate CHamoru movement and demand CHamoru land. They felt that agriculture—what Guerrero described as the "backbone of the country"—was no longer a possibility in Guåhan without secure access to land that the US military had annexed.[55] If to be American was to be self-sufficient, the US military presence, ironically, prevented CHamorus in Guåhan from fulfilling the requirements for US economic enterprise.

The testimonies from Cruz and Perez reveal CHamorus' belief that an organic act with a civilian government and US citizenship could shield them from the arbitrary military land policies. They are also examples of how CHamorus articulated their discontent by describing their relationship with land, utilizing US definitions of land value and citing their loyalty in war and their Americanness.[56] And it worked. By the end of the three-day hearing on the Guam Organic Act, CHamorus and the congressional committee agreed that the Naval Government's total control over the island's administration was an anathema to US values of democracy. Lemke agreed with the CHamorus, saying, "To me it seems very unfortunate that everybody connected with fixing the value of this land is more directly interested in the Government," and characterized them as "always over-zealous to find facts favorably for the government and submit them as just."[57] Furthermore, the government apparatus that should protect US citizens in the states did not exist in Guåhan's Naval Government. "In our Nation," Lemke clarified, land disputes were "determined by a jury of twelve men. Here, unfortunately, the only appeal is to the Secretary of the Navy. It is a question of whether he is a disinterested party. In my opinion, he is not."[58] Representative Lemke witnessed how the US military in Guåhan was not upholding liberal values of equality but acted as a colonizing force that affected loyal CHamorus who had proved their worthiness of full inclusion into the United States. They all, however, never questioned the US military's continued presence in Guåhan for the foreseeable future.

Land annexation was the first piece of a two-part process of US settler militarism in Guåhan—a integral component of how the United States built its postwar empire in the Pacific. As a result of military land takings, CHamorus became dependent on military and other off-island businesses for their livelihoods. Although the land continues to have cultural resonance among CHamoru people, CHamorus deemphasized a CHamoru relationality to land in their struggles against the US military and the GLCC, and spoke instead with liberal rhetoric of land as property and as a potential site for commodification. US settler militarism not only transformed the physical landscape but constrained the rhetorical terrain upon which CHamorus could resist military policies that took away their land.

Filipino Labor Migration and the "Rebuilding" of Guåhan

Jose Bello and Manuel Bello were born in the US colonial Philippines in the province of Ilocos Sur. They were the oldest sons of Blas Bello and Alejandra Bello, who owned and farmed small parcels land in the *barangays* of Santa and Dammay. Blas and Alejandra could not afford to send Jose and Manuel to school. As the eldest, Jose worked to support his six siblings. Manuel farmed their family's land and had dreams of attending agricultural school at Lagangilang National Agricultural School, now the University of Abra. In 1928, at seventeen, Jose left the Philippines, embarking on a ship to work on the plantations in Hawai'i. After years of hard labor with little pay, he decided to upskill, becoming a welder for more lucrative opportunities. He eventually found a job on the docks of Pearl Harbor shortly before the Japanese forces bombed Hawai'i, launching the United States into World War II in the Pacific. Meanwhile, his brother Manuel joined the Philippine Scouts fighting guerilla warfare in the mountains of Luzon, Philippines. Toward the end of the war, in October 1944, Jose was recruited by the US military to build infrastructure in the newly captured Northern Mariana Islands, where he searched for water sources and dug water wells to support the US advance across the Pacific. Although his stint in the island of Tini'an was cut short, Jose found himself in Guåhan searching for water sources a year later. While living at Camp Edusa, located near the northern village of Dédidu, he met Dolores Benavente, his future CHamoru wife. By February 26, 1946, they were married.[59]

Jose told his younger brother Manuel about the possibilities of jobs in Guåhan, where he could work to support his young family in Ilocos Sur. The air force base, where Jose worked as a welder, did not use recruitment companies to find workers.[60] Filipinos, especially Ilokanos, took advantage of this, and often recommended their relatives to their employers. So, in 1953 Manuel departed the Philippines and worked as an H-2 worker. Manuel wanted to save just enough money so that he and his family could live a comfortable life in the Philippines. He met his goal by the late 1950s, built a house in the *barangay* of Dammay, and purchased land to raise crops. Unfortunately, his son Maximo became extremely ill and needed expensive medical treatment, but ultimately passed away. The medical treatment ate into Manuel's savings, and with his daughter Marieta heading to college soon, Manuel decided to head back to Guåhan to earn more money for his family. Manuel, who was staunchly Ilokano, traveled only briefly to Manila, to embark on military transport ships. In Guåhan, his brother Jose used his connections to get Manuel a job as a busboy at the Andersen Air Force Base Officer's Club. Manuel lived in the barracks at Camp MARBO, another labor camp near the village of Mångilao. Meanwhile, Jose started the paperwork for his brother's permanent residency so that he could eventually gain US citizenship, which he did sometime in the 1960s.[61] The Bello brothers' migration stories were shaped by US colonial and military routes in the twentieth-century Pacific.

The story of the Bello brothers is a grounded example of how the US military used Filipino workers to transform annexed Hawaiian and CHamoru lands into usable spaces for US militarism. Historian Alfred Flores has cogently historicized how US military contractors recruited and employed Filipino workers to build US military infrastructure in Guåhan. He argues that "US settler militarism in Guåhan depended upon an exploitative hierarchical labor system that was predicated on race and nationality."[62] Building upon Flores's argument and the stories of Ilonggo and Ilokano workers such as the Bello Brothers, in this section I contextualize Guåhan as another locus to explore rise of racialization of the Filipino as migrant worker, and how the experiences of working abroad for individual economic freedom nevertheless collapsed strongly held regional identities for those from the Philippines into a singular Filipino national identity. In other words, the Bello Brothers left the Philippines as Ilokanos but worked and settled in Guåhan as Filipinos.

The proposed scale of the military rehabilitation and the subsequent military buildup required more labor than the local Guåhan population could provide.[63] After the initial buildup, the Seabees were not available because they were too expensive and difficult to deploy from the North American continent. Thus, the US Navy recruited skilled and unskilled workers "chiefly from the mainland United States and Hawai'i and in small numbers from the Philippines and other sections of the Pacific Ocean Area."[64] To fulfill demand, the United States and the newly independent Philippines crafted foreign policy agreements to mobilize "about 8,000 Filipino laborers to be employed directly by the United States outside the Philippines including Marianas-Bonins, Okinawa, and elsewhere in the Pacific."[65]

In 1947 the US Embassy and the Philippine secretary of state negotiated an Exchange of Notes, in which the Philippines allowed US military contractors to recruit Filipino laborers for US military bases throughout the Pacific.[66] The United States and the Philippines agreed that recruited Filipinos were to be hired on a short-term basis, "usually under contracts of one year in duration," and as nonimmigrant workers, they were "required to leave Guam and to return to the respective places or origin at the termination of their employment."[67] In addition, US military contractors were responsible for the workers' transportation via a US naval ship or commercial freighters and must abide by a regulated forty-hour work week. The workers also received "free laundry services, free medical and dental care, and other fringe benefits. Contract workers were additionally provided with free room and board."[68] Significantly, the Exchange of Notes also regulated Filipino workers' wages, which were generally higher than what they could earn in the Philippines. For Filipinos working abroad, the United States would pay "an increase in the current Philippine wages of 15 centavos per hour in lieu of free quarters and subsistence . . . plus a 25% overseas differential, then charge all employees for quarters and subsistence."[69] If the workers paid for their own housing and food, there was enough money to be "generally considered to be attractive," according to a 1948 US Navy report to the United Nations.[70] Their wages, however, were lower than wages paid to both workers from the States and Guamanian workers in the same military installations, which would later foment criticism from US labor unions and CHamoru leaders.

As a result of the Exchange of Notes, Filipino migrant workers became economic pawns in both the expansion of the US empire in the Pacific and Philippine nation-building in the postwar period. The Exchange of Notes gave the United States unilateral power to expedite the mass mobilization of Philippine citizens for US military projects throughout the Pacific. The US Embassy "requested to recruit Filipino employees as are necessary for duty outside the Philippines, and then process and ship such employees to the desired areas without further contact with Philippine authorities."[71] They required only the names and addresses for each of Filipino workers' next of kin.[72] Skipping the bureaucracy of the Philippine government allowed the US military "to avoid delays subsequent to processing caused by the submission of rosters for approval before shipment."[73] The seeming ease with which the Philippines allowed the US government to recruit Filipino workers is indicative of the United States' continued power in a postcolonial Philippines. In addition, the nascent Philippine nation-state also benefited from exporting labor, which not only relieved the labor surplus within the archipelago but also increased remittances back to the Philippines, a lucrative opportunity in the postwar Philippine economy.[74] This postwar Exchange of Notes demonstrates how, as scholar Robyn Rodriguez Magalit shows, "the Philippine state plays an active role in facilitating the placement of Filipino workers in the various sites where the US military and firms are located around the world."[75] The negotiations for Filipino labor were very much steeped in calculated foreign and economic policy for both the United States and the Philippines.

The US military's need for workers ultimately shaped immigration policy for Guåhan. Although not compliant with US immigration law, the Exchange of Notes governed US immigration policy in Guåhan until the 1952 Immigration Act.[76] Even then, the 1952 Immigration Act was administered in a way that incorporated the terms of the Exchange of Notes, as we will see in chapter 4.[77] The US military also influenced the implementation of the 1952 Immigration Act's H-2 program in Guåhan, which allowed companies to import temporary foreign workers if no local workers were available for a specific job. The US military justified its use of temporary H-2 workers by suggesting its mission to build military installations on the island was temporary in nature and, importantly, was "vital to national defense." As a result, in July 1953 the Immigration and Naturalization Services would "approve H-2 petitions filed by military contractors and by private businesses which 'substantially serve the Armed Forces or citizen or alien employees of the Armed Forces or contractors thereto within the Territory.'"[78] Beyond skilled workers such as engineers, electricians, welders, plumbers, roofers, and painters, the H-2 visa was also used to fill auxiliary jobs, such as "bakers, cooks, barbers and auto mechanics," that the Navy deemed "vital to the national defense."[79] Unskilled work consisted of stevedoring and transporting construction materials. Military labor encompassed not just construction work but also jobs that were needed to support, feed, and maintain the large group of migrant workers on the island.[80]

The US Navy worked with two main contractors to build military infrastructure in Guåhan, though other smaller companies existed. The first was Luzon Stevedoring Company (LUSTEVCO) and its subsidiary company Marianas Stevedoring and Development Company (MASDELCO). The company "was founded by US veterans of the [Spanish-American War of 1898] and became one of the leading cargo transportation companies in Southeast Asia."[81] The other large company was Brown-Pacific-Maxon, based in the continental United States in Texas, which was awarded contracts to complete construction at Andersen Air Force Base. Both companies recruited from the Philippines—mainly in the Iloilo and Ilocos regions, respectively, but also hired a few Filipino white-collar workers from Manila and white workers from the US South. Filipino white-collar workers were hired for auxiliary jobs that supported construction, including accountants, bakers, cooks, and doctors and nurses. The military contractors hired Filipinos for a wide array of trades that were necessary for the military projects, and did not hire local or US-based workers often. For all their work, Filipinos were placed at the bottom tier of a three-tier wage system, in which workers from the States were at the top and Guamanian (CHamoru) workers were in the middle.[82] As I will show in the last section of this chapter, this unequal pay scale would come under scrutiny from all sides.

The mobilization of Filipino workers throughout the postwar period was built upon a preexisting racialization that Filipinos were workers for empire.[83] The Bello brothers demonstrate this neatly. Like many Ilokano men experienced during the US colonial period in the Philippines, Jose had been recruited in 1928 as a *sakada* to work in the sugar plantations in Hawai'i.[84] Plantation capitalists in Hawai'i used Filipino labor to circumvent Asian Exclusion laws and break labor strikes. Moreover, they capitalized upon Ilokano familial ties and intimacies to encourage more men and their families to work for the plantations.[85] Though in a different context, the fact that Jose would aid his brother Manuel's migration to Guåhan in the 1950s, perhaps at the request of military recruiters at Andersen Air Force Base in Guåhan, also suggests the durability of the notion of "Filipinos as migrant workers" who could maintain military installations in Guåhan for the foreseeable future.[86] The brothers also demonstrate how Ilokanos (and perhaps others from the Philippines) used these racialized ideologies for their own gain even if the apparatus of empire generalized their identity to the more capacious group "Filipinos."

While in Guåhan, Filipino workers were segregated from the CHamoru community that lived just beyond their labor camp gates. Military contractors owned and operated the camps, allowing them to control their workers. According to historian Bruce Campbell, "BPM employed more than 17,000 laborers in the mid-1950s in makeshift camps, which later became cities, then disappeared upon completion of the contract."[87] Each camp was self-contained and self-sufficient; Filipino workers did not have to enter the civilian community for essentials. The camps consisted of Quonset huts—cost-effective prefabricated structures of galvanized steel shaped like a half cylinder that could house sleeping quarters for the workers as well as other offices.[88] Labor camps, some named after Philippine presidents, were located throughout the island, included Camp Edusa near Dédidu, Camp Quezon in Mangilao, Camp Magsaysay also known as Camp MARBO in Yigu.[89] Manuel Bello lived at Camp MARBO. The local population rarely visited the camps.[90] The most remembered and well-known was Camp Roxas, a labor camp for LUSTEVCO, located in the village of Hågat adjacent to Navy Base Guam in the southern half of the island.[91] Camp Roxas had "miles of barracks, a 15-acre beach, an open-air movie theatre, post office and sports facilities."[92] The camp also had its own clinic and hospital with recruited Filipino nurses. In 1950 there were seven thousand men and one woman in Camp Roxas. Because of the nature of MASDELCO's recruitment practices in the Philippines, most of the workers were from Iloilo Province.

In Guåhan, the labor camp became a paradoxical space of Filipino racialization. On the one hand, Filipinos retained strong regional identities, sustained partly because of military contractors' reliance on specific regions in the Philippines for workers. Regions and provinces in the Philippines have their own ethnic identity, often rooted in their own languages and dialects, with traditions, foods, and customs specific to that region. Each camp had a predominant regional language, and its workers were inclined to form friendships and bonds with those from the same region or province.[93] Historian Alfred N. Munoz observed that "the Filipinos in [Guam] were divided sharply into two groups: those from the Visayan islands stayed at Camp Roxas named after the first President of the Philippine Republic, Manuel Roxas, a favorite son of the Visayas; those from Northern Luzon stayed in Camp Quezon, so named after the Commonwealth President Manuel L. Quezon."[94] Furthermore, Don Marshall, general manager for LUSTEVECO spoke about Camp Busanda, which housed "Tagalog" workers from Manila who had specialized training.[95] The proliferation of mutual support groups that arose among Filipino workers who became permanent residents in the 1960s to the present maintained this regionalism. To this day, there is a general assumption that postwar Filipinos in Guåhan who are from the southern villages of Hågat and Sånta Rita are originally from the Iloilo provinces, and those who are from the central and northern villages are from the many provinces of Luzon, such as Ilocos region or Manila.[96] Coincidentally, the geographic locations of these Filipino groups parallel the geographic locations of their originating provinces. Northern provinces to northern Guåhan; southern provinces to southern Guåhan.

On the other hand, a cohesive Filipino identity emerged among different regional groups because of strict segregation from the local Guåhan and CHamoru community, as well as the repeated use of the national descriptor "Filipinos" by military construction companies, the Philippine officials, and eventually the Filipino workers themselves. Take, for instance, what can be seen in a photo of the MASDELCO Roxas Village float that may have appeared in a Guam Liberation Day Parade.[97] As Vicente Diaz historicized, the Guam Liberation Day Parade was first created to commemorate and memorialize the CHamoru lives lost in World War II; but it slowly evolved into a celebration of US liberation of Guåhan.[98] The Roxas Village float conveyed a clear message to the potentially thousands of people who lined the streets of Hagåtña to watch the parade. The Filipino workers at Roxas Village were "a supporting arm to the military." The float was decorated with the flags of the United States and the Philippines; the Guam flag was nowhere to be found. Filipinos on the float dressed as different types of workers. There were

Filipino healthcare workers caring for a sick or injured person laid out on a stretcher, a welder wearing a welding mask, a stevedore holding onto a dolly with a construction helmet, an artist with an easel, a surveyor with a telescope, and a white-collar worker with what looked like a desk with a typewriter. If the performances of the float's actors did not fully convey the "work" Filipino workers were doing, the float's sideboards literally had "shipbuilders," "stevedores," and "accountants" painted across them. The back end of the float, though cut out of the photo's frame, could possibly be made out to say, "for international defense." This image makes visible what historian Alfred Flores observed: that "the post–World War II militarization of the island resulted in the creation of a Filipino labor class that became synonymous with military employment."[99] The appearance of a Camp Roxas float laden with symbols of Filipino work for the US empire bolstered the progressive and modernization narrative of US military development that pervaded and justified US militarization.[100] It also cemented the idea that "Filipinos rebuilt Guåhan."

Beyond work, labor camps had opportunities for recreational and cultural activities for workers, including sports, arts, gardening, and religious services.[101] Recreational activities were strategies to contain potential worker discontent. These activities had the effect of coalescing disparate regional groups into a cohesive Filipino community for both CHamoru and white residents as well as the Philippine nation-state. A general manager of LUSTEVECO, Don Marshall, recalled that the company's baseball team, which had both Ilonggos and Tagalogs, won the Island Championship three years in a row. "We built the only lighted baseball field on Guam and the first electric scoreboard for basketball," Marshall remembered. "Our guys were so proud to be playing for their company and the Philippines, and they were good sportsmen."[102] Basketball was a popular pastime, with different departments of the company competing against one another and against white and CHamoru teams from other villages in tournaments.[103] In 1948 Jesus Puentebella, physical director for Camp Roxas, on behalf of "the Filipino Community in Guam numbering about sixteen thousand males," asked Philippine President Elpidio Quirino to purchase "a silver trophy for our Basketball league to be held in a short time to all people in Guam regardless of race as a gesture of friendship." Within a few days, the Philippine president agreed and sent a trophy to Guåhan a week later on a Pan American flight. In a gesture of gratitude, Puenteblla wrote a letter "to our beloved 'Apo'" stating, "Not only do we appreciate the simple trophy that he dearly gave us for the betterment of our youths, but also of his everlasting remembrance to his subjects in this

Camp Roxas float in the Guam Liberation Day Parade. Courtesy of Humanities Guåhan.

far away island in the Pacific."[104] Though seemingly inconsequential, sports were a retreat from the work Filipinos performed for their company, a way to bond with the camp mates, and a distraction from the fact that they were far from home. Sports were also a way to practice, perform, and represent the Philippine nation-state away from the archipelago.

With excess construction materials, Filipino workers built and decorated the Catholic church in Camp Roxas to conduct religious services on weekends and religious holidays, organize fiestas for patron saints, and receive Catholic sacraments.[105] In an interview with Patrick Luces, a Camp Roxas descendant, Luces noted that his father, Johnny Luces, participated in religious services at Camp Roxas every day and found community in church services. These nonwork activities provided some simulacrum of ordinary life, despite the carceral nature of the camps themselves. "Given that workers spent years, in some cases decades, away from the Philippines," wrote the Guam Humanities Council in a public exhibition about Camp Roxas, "the relationships they established with each other as well as with the local population laid the foundation for many life-long friendships and community support."[106]

This historicization of recreational activities at the labor camps throughout the island is not say that Filipinos did not share their discontent with military contractors. The labor camp was, after all, a labor camp. Military contractors were often accused of abusing their workers, paying them less than contracted, or facilitating unhealthy or violent living conditions in the camps.[107] In addition, military contractors took advantage of the surplus labor market in the Philippines and the foreign policy agreements made between the United States and the Philippines to render misbehaving and underperforming Filipinos as disposable and replaceable. If a worker's discontent brewed, contractors simply did not renew the worker's contract, and the worker was forced to leave the island. The number of grievances emerging from the labor camps was enough to warrant the establishment of a Philippine Consulate General in Guåhan in 1952 "to support their workers and to protect remittances."[108] The workers needed protection not only from contractors but also for the money they sent home to their families that ultimately bolstered the Philippine economy. While Filipinos previously had an unofficial representative associated with LUSTEVECO, the arrival of the Philippine consulate in Guåhan marked "the first official representation for the thousands of Filipino residents of the island."[109] Thus, any difficulty that occurred regarding Filipino workers in Guåhan became a matter of international affairs. Through their work in Guåhan, Ilokano and Ilonggo workers were thus recognized as "Filipinos" by Guåhan residents, United States, the Philippines, and eventually each other.

The military labor recruitment policies, the establishment of a Philippine Consulate, and the social dynamics within the camps made it possible for migrant workers from different parts of the Philippine archipelago to conceive of themselves collectively as Filipinos. In September 1954 the Filipino Community of Guam (FCG) was founded "with some 500 representatives from the three major labor camps and various business firms on island," to organize the large presence of Filipino workers in Guåhan.[110] It had five objectives, the first of which was to ensure the "welfare of Filipinos in Guam." As a mutual aid society, members of the FCG would be connected to a network of Filipinos who supported each other. The second goal was to "promote unity among all the Filipinos on the island," a way for Filipinos to connect despite regional differences and under a singular national identity. It was also, third, an advocacy group that could "provide a common and ready agency which could undertake projects that affect Filipinos here." The fourth objective was to "promote wholesome and friendly relations between Filipinos and local citizens and to create an atmosphere of good will and mutual trust," and fifth, to "seek more means for the improvement of Filipino relations with their employers especially with the US Armed forces agencies like the Navy and Air Force as well as private business firms." The FCG was a social and cultural organization that, nonetheless, had political goals to ensure that Filipinos in Guåhan were represented as a cohesive force in Guåhan's community. In later decades, the FCG configured itself as an "umbrella organization" that brought together smaller Filipino clubs and organizations that were organized by provinces, regions, or institutional affiliations. Ilonggos and Ilokanos, as well as other Filipinos, created their own groups to maintain specific ties to the home archipelago. In their later years, Jose and Manuel Bello were members and leaders of the small Ilocos Sur Families Association of Guam; their children participated in the organization as well. These organizations demonstrate how despite the moves toward coalescing all Filipinos into a singular group, they still recognized regional ties in the home archipelago.

The recruitment of Filipino workers for the military buildup continued beyond the transfer of Guåhan from the US Navy to the US Department of the Interior in 1950. By the time Camp Roxas closed its gates in 1972, "tens of thousands of Filipino workers" had made their way to Guåhan "to work and find a better life."[111] Most of their temporary contracts expired, and they were repatriated. Some settled on the island. Through their work for the US empire, Filipinos coalesced into a racialized labor force that contributed to settler militarism in Guåhan. This work—"Filipinos built Guam"—later became proof of their worthiness for liberal inclusion through US citizenship and justified their participation in discussions about Guåhan's political future.

Native Versus Alien Labor

By 1950 the prominence of Filipinos in military construction began to elicit criticism from CHamorus and white US settlers who worked on the bases. In the US congressional hearings on the Organic Act of Guam, where CHamorus presented their grievances about the US Navy's land policies, several speakers complained that Filipino laborers were "taking jobs away from American men—also the Guamanians."[112] F. L. Davis, the spokesperson for the Construction Man's Association of Guam, told the Public Lands Committee that military contractors prioritized the hiring of "alien" workers over US-based and Guamanian labor, despite the fact that there was increasing unemployment in both the US continent and in Guåhan. In Davis's experience, military contractors hired skilled workers from the States to teach Filipino workers skills and then subsequently replaced those US workers with cheaper

Filipino workers: "They surplused the men who taught them and kept the Philipino in his place."[113] Furthermore, Davis complained that the thousands of Filipino "alien" workers were being paid with US taxpayer dollars. "Why can't that money be spent on American people who are out of work?" Davis asked the committee. In Davis's view, military contractors, specifically Brown-Pacific-Maxon, used foreign labor for company profit, ignoring the needs of the US-based and CHamoru workforce.

The CHamoru struggle over land and the Filipino experience with military labor converged after the Organic Act of Guam in 1950. By this point, CHamorus had become US citizens with a civilian government. Becoming US citizens, however, had no effect on their disadvantaged position within the racialized wage economy in Guåhan. As historian Alfred Flores argues, "US settler militarism in Guåhan produced and depended on an exploitative hierarchical labor system that was predicated upon race and nationality."[114] Military contractors instituted a racialized, hierarchical pay scale determined by the cost of living in the workers' place of origin. White US workers, sometimes referred to as "statesiders," earned more than Guamanians, with wages based on the standard of living in West Coast cities plus an additional 25 percent overseas bonus.[115] Local Guamanians were paid the "prevailing wage rate in Guam set by the Government of Guam," which was "one-half the total of non-local hired employees [US settlers]."[116] Contractors believed that Guamanians did not require as much compensation as US settlers because they were local to Guåhan. Guamanians earned more than "alien" workers from the Philippines, who were paid according to the stipulations agreed in the 1947 Exchange of Notes—25 percent more than the wage in the Philippines plus free transport, housing, and other essential services.[117] Not coincidentally, both white workers and Guamanians believed this three-tiered pay scale mapped onto a racial hierarchy that was anti-American.

The racialized wage scale reflects how a person's national origin determined the value of their labor.[118] While military contractors could hire and train a local workforce, the pay scale ultimately made it more profitable for military contractors to hire Filipinos, which, historian Colleen Woods argues, "deepened an existing transpacific migration pattern whereby state and capital interest collaborated to control, and ultimately exploit the labor of Filipinos."[119] In addition, the Department of Defense was reluctant to train Guamanians "for fear that people would leave Guam for better wage incentives elsewhere."[120] Thus, not only were Filipinos cheaper to pay, but they were a more controllable workforce that were at the whims of military contractors, which were attributes deemed necessary to ensure efficient and profitable labor for their businesses. With US Cold War militarization as justification, the US military and military contractors capitalized on surplus Filipino labor to solidify US military presence in the Pacific.

In 1956, increased labor competition and the racialized pay scale took center stage during a series of congressional hearings about the applicability of the Fair Labor Standards Act of 1938 to the US territories and possessions.[121] Held in February and March 1956, the hearings revealed various perspectives on the complicated entanglement of Filipino labor in Guåhan in relation to US settler and Guamanian labor and the United States military. The primary concern was whether local businesses could afford to pay their workers the federal minimum wage. If not, the Fair Labor Standards Act could jeopardize economic growth for small businesses. Members of the US Congress, US Navy officials, labor union representatives, US territorial residents, and Philippine officials advocated for their respective constituents and how they would be affected by the regulations stipulated in the Fair Labor Standards Act.

The context of the rise of communism in the Asia-Pacific region permeated the testimonies. Many of the speakers used an anticommunist, prodemocratic rhetoric to appeal to the US Congress and advocate for their constituents. The military justified their arguments by leveraging their role in safeguarding freedom and democracy in the region from the expansion of communist powers. Labor unions argued that the United States' support for unequal wages for different races and nationalities was undemocratic and played into the perception that the United States was a hypocrisy of racial equality. Philippine government officials also argued that the low wages paid to Filipino citizens in US military installations counted as discrimination and was ultimately ineffective in garnering the respect of allied countries in their region. And for CHamoru representatives, they appropriated the rhetoric that Guåhan was a "'show place' of democracy within the reaches of Communist influence," as CHamoru leader Antonio B. Won Pat exclaimed, to advocate for higher wages and equal pay for local Guamanians, who were US citizens.[122] The lack of representation of the Filipino workers themselves, however, was unsurprising. Filipinos were abstracted into a cohesive labor population—"coolie" workers specifically—whose individual motivations to work were spoken in terms of national and geopolitical policy.

The US military was the largest employer in Guåhan, and it was clear that its contractors did not abide by the Fair Labor Standards Act, especially when it came to "alien" labor. At the time the US military was exempt from paying Filipino migrant workers according to the Fair Labor Standards Act because the 1947 Exchange of Notes outlined the process and payment by which recruited Filipino workers were brought to Guåhan. The question at hand was whether "alien" Filipino workers who were employed on US military bases in Guåhan should be paid the US minimum wage, a potentially expensive proposition, considering the low wages Filipinos earned in the first place. Admiral Joel D. Parks, the deputy chief of the Bureau of Supplies and Accounts of the US Navy, noted in his testimony that "if the act were held to apply to the imported Filipinos on Guam, the Department of Defense contractors and eventually the United States would be liable for wages and penalties in excess of $3 million for retroactive wage payments alone." Furthermore, Admiral Parks testified that if the act were to apply to military contractors in Guåhan, it would "increase contract costs of more than $9 million per year at the present operating level."[123] From Admiral Parks's testimony, it appears that the military as a whole—not just military contractors—was dependent on cheap, migrant Filipino workers to decrease the cost of building its fortress in the Pacific.

Similar to the justification for how the US military arbitrarily condemned CHamoru land after World War II, the US military justified the low wages paid to Filipinos and other "alien" workers by citing "national defense." The military wanted to increase its presence in the Pacific but was constrained by congressional budget cuts to defense spending. If there was an increase in minimum wage, Admiral Parks argued, then "we would have two alternatives. One is to drastically cut back the [military] operation at the expense of building up Guåhan as a defense bastion in the Pacific, and deport hundreds of these Filipinos back to the Philippines because we would not have the money to pay them." Filipino labor was necessary to "give the taxpayer the maximum value for his defense dollar."[124] Chief of Naval Operations Arleigh Burke concurred with Parks, emphasizing that Filipino workers in Guåhan were essential and that "substantial salary increases, without a corresponding increase in work performed or appropriations received, will cause a curtailment in the support to the fleet at the affected bases." Burke further emphasized that the cost of building bases could not be any lower, and that a further "reduction of these levels will inevitably weaken that defense and imperil our national security."[125] Put simply, Parks and Burke argued that the projection of the US military power in the Pacific was dependent on the low wages paid to Filipino migrant workers.

In addition, Admiral Parks used racist assumptions to imply that Filipino labor was not as valuable as white labor. He testified that that "though some of these wages are below the Fair Labor Standards Act minimum, they are considered fair and in proportion to productivity." He cited the need for US contractors to teach English to Filipinos and "instruction in American building and administrative techniques." He subtly implied that because "they have been paid a wage substantially higher than they could have learned in the Philippines, have lived under better conditions, and have learned new skills," Filipino laborers did not need a US minimum wage for their work.[126] In other words, Admiral Parks characterized the military employment of Filipino workers as a humanitarian act. His testimony demonstrates how the US military capitalized on the postcolonial economy of the Philippines, the country's surplus labor, and a sense of racial and cultural superiority to justify lower wages to Filipino workers in order to build its empire.

The pay scales did not go unnoticed in the Philippines. The Philippine ambassador to the United States, Carlos P. Romulo, believed that Filipino laborers faced work discrimination. In a letter to US Secretary of State John Foster Dulles, Romulo argued that the exemption of Guåhan from the Fair Labor Standards Act "would be interpreted in the Philippines as an act of discrimination against Filipino laborers in those American possessions." In addition, he argued that the disparity in wages could be used "to misrepresent and exploit divisions and prejudices in the most sensitive sectors of the world." Romulo also argued that the US military's treatment of Filipino migrant workers was antithetical to the US mission to spread liberalism in the region: "We must not give the enemies of *democracy and freedom* an opportunity to distort America's motives and magnify the amendment as a desire of the United States to perpetuate what they will undoubtedly brand as coolie labor."[127] By labeling the exploitation of Filipino workers as "coolie labor," Romulo made it clear that although the United States purports to use only free labor, the country was facilitating unequal labor regimes to profit from expanded militarism.

Labor unions also weighed in. Walter J. Mason, of the American Federation of Labor and Congress of Industrial Organizations (AFL-CIO), argued that the racialized pay scale and low wages hurt US Cold War foreign policy in the Pacific. He said, "Where you have natives on these bases working alongside one another or doing comparable work and receiving wages, say, one third or one-half of what is received by American workers, naturally I do not think it is helping our international relations."[128] The AFL-CIO had received a letter from Jose J. Hernandez on behalf of the Philippines-based labor union, Philippine Trade Unions Council (PTUC), whose mission was to "help in the realization our objective of fostering the solidarity of free world labor on the basis of justice and equality." PTUC asked the AFL-CIO to oppose the current iteration of the Fair Labor Standards Act because of its exemption of Guåhan, Wake, and Samoa from the US minimum wage law. In the letter, Hernandez wrote that "the PTUC strongly denounces this class legislation which is evidently aimed mainly against Filipino workers who constituted the great bulk of the working population [of Guåhan, Wake, and Sāmoa]." Hernandez argued that low wages paid to Filipinos "would certainly be to the great benefit of our enemies should any kind of discrimination based on color be committed by any democracies."[129] Essentially, labor unions argued that the implementation of minimum wage for military workers would convince people throughout the Asia-Pacific region of the promises of US liberal ideals vis-à-vis a communist alternative.

The contradictory testimonies from Burke, Romulo, and AFL-CIO representatives demonstrate how Filipino workers exemplified the uncomfortable convergence of the two sides of the US Cold War foreign policy: military expansion *and* humanitarian desire to spread US liberalism in the region.[130] While US military leaders cited "national defense" to justify racialized wage scales, Filipino statesmen and labor unions politicized the figure of the Filipino military worker to demonstrate the inconsistencies in the US actions abroad and its purported policy to protect liberal democracy and racial equality in the face of communism. Ultimately, Filipino workers in Guåhan were not just subjects of US immigration, military, or foreign policy; they, in and of themselves, collectively embodied the paradox of US liberal militarism.

At the hearings, CHamoru leaders were furious that the US military prioritized financial bottom lines over economic opportunities for CHamorus who were, by then, US citizens. In February 1956 the Guam Legislature passed a resolution that the US Congress should apply the Fair Labor Standards Act to Guåhan. The resolution stated, "There appears to be over 3,000 American citizens over 18 years of age who are not now gainfully employed," and that "there had been some laxity in giving such American citizens priority over alien labor." To be sure, the Guam Legislature emphasized the US citizenship of their CHamoru constituents to highlight how US military contractors prioritized the employment of foreign Filipino migrant labor over local labor.[131] As the US military condemned a considerable portion of CHamoru lands, displaced their families, and now prioritized "alien" workers, CHamorus saw that US citizenship did not necessarily give them rights or privileges in the US empire.

The Guam Legislature sent two representatives, Antonio B. Won Pat and Cynthia Torres, to plead Guåhan's case.[132] Before they started their testimonies, however, Won Pat wanted to ensure that the congressional representatives knew exactly who they were advocating for. Won Pat told the committee, "We want to make it very clear that when we speak of the people of Guam we are referring to the permanent residents of Guam. We are referring to American citizens who live and earn their livelihood in Guam."[133] Won Pat added,

"We want to make it equally clear that when we speak of the 'people of Guam' we are not including 'imported labor' whose employment is justified only when the supply of local labor is not equal to the current demand."[134] Won Pat emphasized the distinction between "native" Guamanians (mostly CHamoru) and perpetually foreign Filipinos, while reiterating Guamanians' US citizenship. In doing so, Won Pat made CHamorus strange bedfellows with white workers who participated in and benefited from the settler militarization of Guåhan, another symptom of how liberal rhetoric limits interracial solidarities against the inequalities of empire.

The stakes for CHamorus were high. Cynthia Torres argued that without access to their ranches because of the military's land takings, CHamorus were forced to transition into a cash economy they were not prepared for. The prewar education system was rudimentary and rarely taught the vocational and trade skills the military buildup demanded. Furthermore, the destruction wrought on the island in World War II hindered infrastructural and economic development that CHamorus could achieve on the civilian side of the island. CHamorus focused on resettling their lands, which military land annexation made difficult. Torres also mentioned that the land "owned or controlled by the military is a majority of the finest prewar farms."[135] Thus, it was impossible for CHamorus to cultivate a local agricultural economy.

Despite a construction boom, CHamorus faced an unemployment problem exacerbated by military contractors' preference for Filipino workers. As required by the H-2 temporary visa law in 1956, the military and its contractors were supposed survey whether there was local labor available to fill the job vacancies.[136] Contractors usually concluded that there were not enough local Guamanian and CHamoru workers to cover the demand for jobs. According to statistics presented by Won Pat and Torres, however, roughly thirty-seven hundred people in Guåhan were unemployed and could be hired for unskilled work. Yet the military continued to recruit Filipino workers for unskilled labor as well.

The preference for Filipino alien labor over CHamoru labor had ramifications for the development of a local Guamanian economy. As stated in a 1973 congressional study, "without question, the lower wages paid to the Filipinos, who were so prevalent in construction work, was a major factor in the domination of the construction industry during the 1950s, and in the failure of the native population to develop the necessary skills to compete effectively."[137] The relative ease with which military contractors could recruit Filipino labor stymied the growth of a skilled local CHamoru construction labor force. Military contractors also did relatively little to develop construction skills in the local population. These practices led to a cycle of US military contractors justifying the recruitment of temporary "alien" workers by arguing that there were not enough local skilled workers to perform the job, thus effectively making the recruitment of "temporary" Filipino H-2 workers, in practice, an ongoing, perpetual necessity.

Aside from the civilian Government of Guam, which maintained a preferential hire for "Guamanians" as written in the Organic Act of Guam, there were relatively few job opportunities for Guamanians outside of military work. This dynamic was exacerbated by the fact that the military often had more political and financial power over the territorial and federal government. Military contractors in Guåhan took advantage of this imbalance of power, often ignoring federal and local government officials. Won Pat lamented that it was "difficult for us to create some kind of economy other than the military because everything there is controlled largely by the military."[138] Military contractors often refused to negotiate with the Guam Legislature and Government, adding to the difficult political and economic situation. Torres testified that military contractors, especially Brown-Pacific-Maxon (BPM), discriminated against Guamanian workers and violated the "unavailable workers" requirement for the H-2 visa by offering incorrect or incomplete information about the availability local workers. Torres complained, "We have sent them resolutions inviting them to come and discuss the problem of hiring local residents. We have done everything we could about it, but they have always ignored our petitions and requests because they felt they were in the military area and we had no jurisdiction over them." Torres also referenced another military contractor that "refused all of these years to employ any local Guamanian citizens."[139]

Won Pat and Torres believed that the US military was reluctant to hire Guamanians because racialized pay scales simply made it more profitable and efficient to hire Filipino workers, transport them, house them, and discipline them. Won Pat noted, "The very fact that the Filipinos are paid a lower wage than the Guamanians . . . tends to deprive the Guamanian the same opportunity of earning, of obtaining a job."[140] In an exchange with Senator Carl Elliot of Alabama, Won Pat associated Filipino military work with forms of coerced labor:

> MR. ELLIOT: Why in your mind—if it be a fact that these two contractors prefer Philippine labor—why do you think that is true?
>
> MR. WON PAT: Well, it is easy to understand. *These aliens are paid what we call in common terminology coolie wages or slave wages.*

MR. ELLIOT: You contend that Guamanians could *perform the same work* that the aliens from the Philippines perform, at least insofar as some of the jobs are concerned?

MR. WON PAT: Yes, sir. I will say some of these jobs could be performed by local *citizens*.

MR. ELLIOT: But you say the contractors prefer to bring in the Philippine labor because they can get that labor considerably cheaper than they can get the Guamanian labor?

MR. WON PAT: That is correct, and in addition *I will say that since they are aliens they will be more submissive to the employer's wishes*.[141]

Won Pat had recognized a serious flaw in the supposedly helpful wage scales that paid Guamanian workers more than foreign labors. Filipino workers were more profitable for military contractors because they were paid "coolie wages or slave wages." And because Filipinos could be repatriated at the whim of their employers, they were "submissive," less prone to striking and subsequently halting the military buildup. Won Pat harkened back to nineteenth-century coolie labor regimes that exploited Asian migrant workers for capitalist gain, while ignoring the needs of white nativists.[142] He compared that history with Guåhan, where Guamanians—who were native CHamoru and US citizens—were cast aside and struggled in the face of land condemnation and limited economic opportunities. In racializing the Filipino migrant worker in Guåhan as a "coolie" and "slave" labor, Won Pat rendered CHamorus as "free" liberal subjects who were better positioned to display the United States' liberal values of democracy and equality in the Cold War Asia-Pacific region. In doing so, however, Won Pat excluded Filipinos from the US nation-state, and perhaps unwittingly argued that CHamorus were better "workers" who could "perform the same work" of transforming Guåhan's annexed CHamoru lands into spaces for the US military empire.

Other CHamorus and Guamanians, such as James T. Sablan, a member of the Guam Legislature, criticized how integral racism was to US military labor. He argued that BPM's racist policies in Guåhan were a result of the company's historical experience with Southern US labor regimes that justified paying little to no money for labor provided by nonwhite peoples. Sablan tied the legacies of the African American experience of slavery to the exploitation of Filipino workers in Guåhan to point out the flagrant racial preferences of military construction companies that hindered the possibility of Guamanian hires. He testified at the hearings, "Now as proof I don't think there is a single Negro in that Unit."[143] Sablan asked that US Congress reprimand BPM and the military for not hiring local Guamanians who could perform unskilled labor that many Filipinos were hired for. Sablan argued for CHamorus to receive "white" wages rather than critiquing racialized wage scales or arguing for equal pay for Filipino migrant workers, and seeking solidarity with Filipinos, former colonial siblings.

In short, CHamorus agreed that Filipinos were paid too little, but not as a form of solidarity with Filipino migrant workers. CHamorus wanted to participate in the military's wage economy, which was dominated by Filipino workers. Historian Alfred Flores writes that Filipinos and CHamorus had the shared objective of protecting their respective wages and labor rights in the Guam Wage Bill, but that "[there] was not a coordinated effort among CHamorus, Filipinos and others on the island to halt the militarization of Guåhan; instead, CHamorus and Filipinos had parallel movements, and each used their own set of strategies to oppose the bill."[144] The separate strategies toward a similar objective are a symptom of how liberal empire and settler militarism can both obscure and reinforce interwoven forms of colonialism: CHamoru land expropriation and Filipino racialized labor. To convince the US Congress, CHamorus relied on stereotypical tropes of Filipinos as "coolies" to exclude Filipinos from Guåhan and the US empire and doubled down on CHamorus' US citizenship to position them as liberal subjects. Filipinos, likewise, considered Guåhan as US territory, a place to seek liberal freedom through economic prosperity, rather than Indigenous CHamoru land. Neither CHamorus nor Filipinos questioned the nature of the US empire itself—the same empire that expropriated CHamoru land for "defense purposes" and "national security," pushed CHamorus into a wage economy, and fostered a neocolonial relationship in an independent Philippines. CHamoru and Filipino negotiations through and within the empire reveals the contradictions and limitations that emerge when liberal freedom is called for by Indigenous peoples and labor migrants in the Cold War US empire.

Settler Militarism Made Concrete

By the mid-1950s, US military infrastructure was etched into the island's landscape. Despite a short-lived military de-escalation in the late 1940s, the burgeoning Cold War tensions perpetuated Guåhan's status as a crucial node in military strategy. The US military continued to construct more infrastructure as military strategy evolved. As much as two-thirds of the island was military property, hosting close to a dozen military installations, including Naval Base Guam, Naval Magazine, Naval Station, Naval Air Station, Andersen Air Force Base, and many smaller ones. They dredged Micronesia's only deep-water

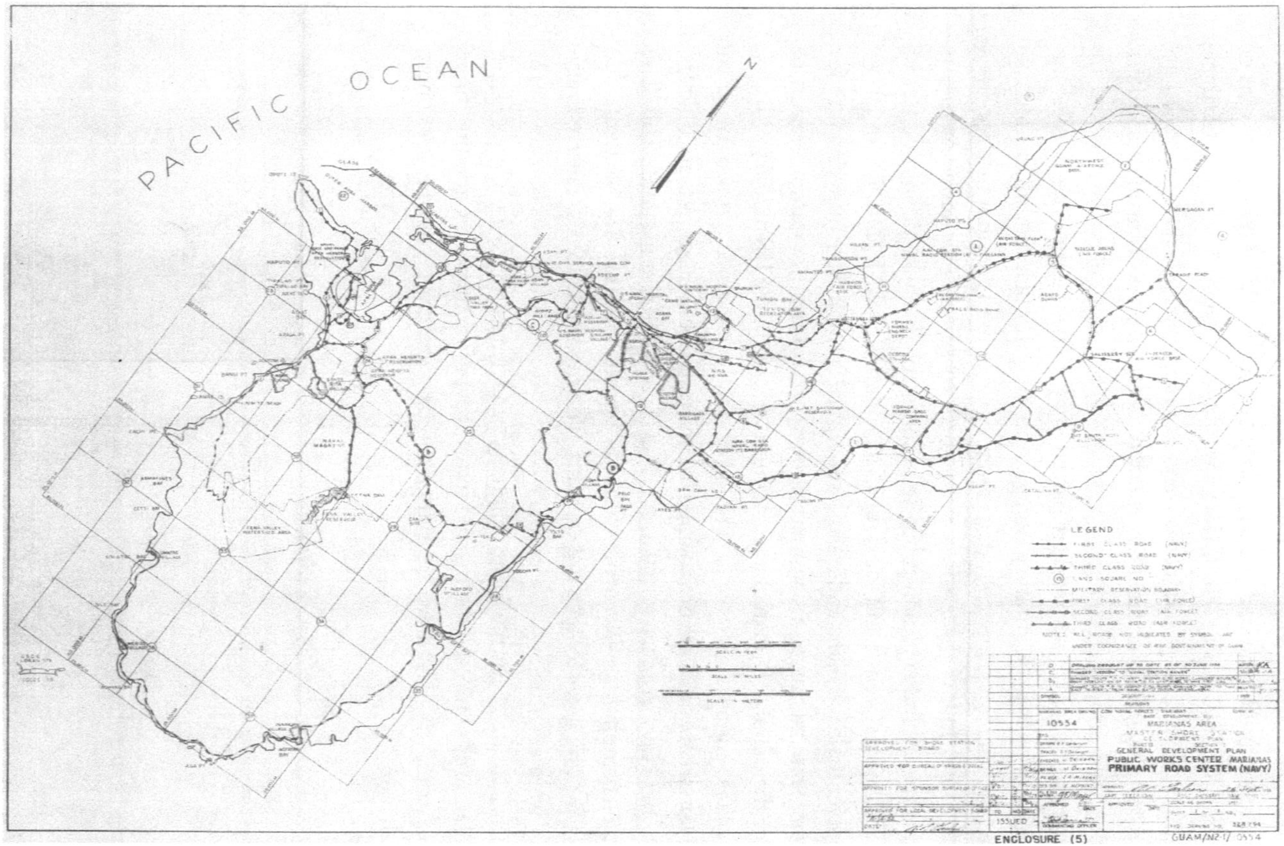

A 1952 military map shows the "Primary Road System" envisioned by the US Navy to connect military installations in Guåhan. Courtesy of the National Archives and Records Administration.

harbor, tapped into freshwater aquifers, and collected water in natural reservoirs enclosed behind military fences. These installations had communications centers that listened to the Asia-Pacific world, ammunition depots with tactical weapons including a nuclear arsenal ready to engage communist foes, power plants to electrify the bases, and runways that launched B-52 bombers and other military aircraft. A Naval hospital was erected to service the tens of thousands of military personnel who would make their way through Guåhan. Behind military gates and fences were—or rather, *are*—acres and acres of office buildings, training facilities, enlisted barracks, officer housing and officer clubs, and shopping centers. These bases and stations are delineated by fences and guard towers and are patrolled by military police cars. Limestone roads connect these military nodes, traversing through mountains and following beachlines. Power, water, sewer, and telephone communication lines and cables follow these roads from north to south. This infrastructure is earthquake- and typhoon-proof to account for the tectonic instabilities of the Marianas Trench and the ferocious typhoons of the Pacific Ocean.[145]

Eventually civilians and businesses tapped into military infrastructure for their personal use and commercial enterprise—another demonstration of how the people of Guåhan became more reliant on the US military. Villages, beaches, mountains, rivers, and lakes that were once known by their CHamoru names were now named for military acronyms or military officials, like Big Navy, Andersen, NCS, NCTAMS, MARBO, and Nimitz Hill. The once-cosmopolitan village of Sumai was transformed into Big Navy, guarded by towering gates to keep out civilians. The roads that locals traverse everyday were eventually given military names: Route 1 became Marine Corps Drive; Route 8, Purple Heart Highway; and Route 16, Army Corps Drive. CHamorus witnessed their island transform before their eyes into the "tip of the spear," an island whose settler military structure became ever more concrete.

CHAPTER FOUR

Newly American

US Citizenship as Settler Militarism

On August 1, 1950, Carlos P. Taitano, dressed in his best white suit, gazed excitedly over the right shoulder of Harry S. Truman. The president was signing into law H.R. 7273—The Organic Act of Guam—which declared Guåhan an organized unincorporated territory of the United States and ended nearly fifty years of the island's undefined political status.[1] The Organic Act also provided US citizenship for the people of Guåhan, a status that CHamoru leaders had advocated for since the turn of the twentieth century. For Taitano, a CHamoru retired US Army captain who was now a law student at Georgetown University, this moment signified the apex of CHamoru activism, symbolized the close of a chapter of American colonialism, and beaconed a renewed potential for a more *American* Guåhan.[2]

US citizenship, however, was conditional under the Organic Act of Guam. It was determined by US Congress's plenary power rather than the US Constitution.[3] This distinction meant that US citizens living in Guåhan, born or naturalized, could not vote for president, did not have voting representation in Congress, and were not guaranteed all of the rights and privileges outlined in the US Constitution. The Organic Act also stipulated that the responsibilities of the new civilian Government of Guåhan remained under the purview of the executive branch of the US government through the Department of the Interior. Less apparent, but more insidious, was that the US military heavily influenced the creation of the Organic Act in order to facilitate the continued militarization of Guåhan, which depended on CHamoru land dispossession and Filipino migrant labor.

The Organic Act of Guam did not directly affect the immigration or citizenship status of the thousands of recruited Filipino migrant workers employed at military installations and civilian establishments throughout the island. As described in chapter 3, the US military recruited Filipino workers through the Exchange of Notes which sat outside of federal immigration law and beyond the oversight of the Immigration and Naturalization Services (INS). Because of the exceptional character of the Exchange of Notes, there was some confusion about how to implement federal immigration policies in Guåhan during the transition between the Naval Government and the

President Harry S. Truman signs The Organic Act of Guam in 1950. Carlos Taitano, third from left, watches as Guåhan residents become citizens of the United States. From the Harry S. Truman Library.

civilian government. Federal officials had been inundated with thousands of Filipino migrant workers who did not have official immigration documentation. Instead of mass deportations, however, the US military persuaded the INS to grant immigration exemptions and waivers that incorporated undocumented Filipino foreign workers into the federal immigration laws. Some Filipino migrants became eligible for permanent residency, a crucial step in the pathway to US citizenship.

In Guåhan, US citizenship operated as a tool of empire: to placate CHamoru discontent and to recruit Filipino workers with the aim of solidifying Guåhan as the strategic military base at the dawn of the Cold War. In chapter 3 we saw that CHamoru land and Filipino labor were the foundations upon which the US military expanded its presence; in this chapter I argue that US citizenship, bestowed through the Organic Act and the INS, led to the legalization, obfuscation, and justification of US settler militarism in Guåhan. From the perspective of colonial officials, CHamorus with US citizenship were no longer colonial subjects, despite the fact that Guåhan's actual status as a colony was hidden behind the euphemistic phrase "unincorporated territory." The pathway for citizenship for Filipino migrant workers, moreover, ensured that the US military had a stable workforce to continue its operations in Guåhan and throughout the Pacific.

By analyzing how US citizenship as a tool of empire affected CHamorus and Filipinos differently, in this chapter I examine how inclusion for one group, in this case Filipinos, was predicated upon the continued colonization of the other, CHamorus. For Filipinos, US citizenship was based upon their work for empire, a way to individually rectify the social and economic turmoil caused by the legacies of US imperialism, militarization, and neocolonialism in the Philippines. CHamorus, on the other hand, learned early on that US citizenship did not protect them from military land annexation and came with the solidification of Guåhan's status as a militarized colonial possession. This chapter highlights how the CHamoru and Filipino desires for the liberal promises of inclusion through citizenship were premised upon the continuation of military empire in Guåhan and across the Pacific.

CHamorus and the Promise of US Citizenship

In the early movement for US citizenship before World War II, CHamorus used all the tools available to them. They sent petitions and letters, and they conferenced with federal officials, Naval officials, and members of the US Congress who visited Guåhan on their way to other destinations in the Pacific.[4] They created a continental-based network of academic scholars, lawyers, and businessmen who supported the CHamoru movement for citizenship. They used various rhetorical arguments, including exhibitions of loyalty to the United States and knowledge of US culture and language, and leveraged domestic US racial politics, regional geopolitics, and the threat of communism to persuade Congress and federal officials. The apex of prewar activism occurred in 1937, when Baltazar Bordallo and Francisco B. Leon Guerrero traveled across the globe to Washington, DC, on a diplomatic mission to lobby federal officials, testify before Congress, and eventually meet President Franklin D. Roosevelt.[5] As Bordallo mentioned at a 1937 congressional hearing, "The founders of this great Republic made no provision, because they never intended that this country should maintain two forms of government, one for its citizens, and another a different form, for its subjects."[6] Pointing to the contradictions of the US imperial project, Bordallo argued that the inequality of peoples within the US empire was hypocritical and contradicted US liberal ideals. Their solution to this inequality was simple. CHamorus believed that inclusion through US citizenship would fulfill the promises of political rights, equality, and self-government.

Bordallo and Leon Guerrero, however, were negotiating with a pre–World War II Naval Government that was reluctant to bestow citizenship on CHamorus. For example, Navy representative Claude Swanson testified in 1937 that the "Navy department is of the opinion that the enactment of this measure [US citizenship] would be prejudicial to the best interests of both the United States and the native population of Guam." He cited the recent geopolitical developments in the region, including the rise of the Japanese Empire and the planned independence of the Philippines as reasons to deny CHamorus citizenship. This sentiment was shared by members of Congress, including Senator Robert R. Reynolds of North Carolina, who saw that Guåhan was destined to be a pawn in an eventual war with the "Empire for the East." Swanson and Reynolds believed that bestowing citizenship to CHamorus would mean the United States was obligated to protect Guåhan, something that neither colonial official was willing to risk. Ultimately this did not matter because leaders in Washington also believed that the CHamoru people had not reached a sufficient degree of modernity and civilization to deserve US citizenship. "They have not yet reached a state of development commensurate with personal independence, obligations, and responsibilities of United States citizenship," Swanson wrote in his testimony.[7]

Refuting these claims, Bordallo and Leon Guerrero argued that the CHamoru people had achieved a sufficient level of Americanization through culture, education, language, and military loyalty. Bordallo testified before Congress: "We are now subjects of America through no choice of ours, and ever since American occupation we submitted peacefully and cooperated whole-heartedly with the American officials sent to our island to assume American sovereignty." Unlike other US territories, he reiterated, there had not been any uprising against the US colonial authorities, and further, CHamorus "have learned to respect and love the American flag."[8] Furthermore, to counter the racialized language of Naval officials, Leon Guerrero testified, "I still maintain that even under our present status as neither aliens nor citizens of the United States our attitude toward the Navy Department has been very friendly and will continue to be so." Bordallo and Leon Guerrero believed that their loyalty to the United States should be repaid with US citizenship. Perhaps harkening to CHamoru *inafa'maolek* relations, Leon Guerrero said further, "My people have been loyal, and they will continue to be so, but there should be some return for that loyalty from the Nation."[9]

Despite the warnings from members of Congress, CHamoru leaders believed that the United States would protect its colony in the Pacific. Margarito "Paul" Palting, son of Pancrasio Palting, testified at the hearing that "Uncle Sam will have to protect his investment in the Far East, and the fact that CHamorus may be granted American citizenship does not reduce nor increase the responsibility of the United States."[10] Unfortunately for Palting and his CHamoru co-testifiers, their presumption that the United States would protect Guåhan was wishful thinking. The CHamoru citizenship movement was sidelined in World War II.

The US military evacuated non-CHamoru US military dependents from Guåhan in the months leading up to the December 8 Japanese attack on and occupation of Guåhan.[11] A skeleton crew of Naval personnel worked with the lightly armed Insular Force Guard, consisting of young CHamoru men, to defend the island during the Japanese military invasion.[12] Throughout the war several CHamoru families, including the Bordallo family, the family of Agueda Johnston, and the Artero family, hid US Navy Radioman First Class George Tweed in the jungles of Guåhan, putting their lives in danger.[13] Japanese forces killed CHamoru priest Jesus Baza Dueñas for allegedly keeping secret the locations of six other US military personnel who escaped Japanese capture.[14] In resistance, CHamoru people sang songs wishing and hoping that Uncle Sam would save them from the Japanese occupation.[15] In southern Guåhan toward the end of the war, Japanese forces met stern resistance from young men from the villages of Malesso' who had heard their families were being massacred in caves. They rose up against and killed the small Japanese military presence in their villages, in an incident known as the massacre at Atåtte. They then swam toward one of the US warships surrounding the island to provide vital information to the US forces that were planning their invasion of Guåhan.[16] When the US soldiers arrived on the island, CHamorus waved their makeshift US flags.[17] The experiences of World War II in the Pacific proved to CHamorus that the United States protected its citizens, but not its colonial subjects.

If the island was a liability before the war, Guåhan suddenly became essential to US military operations in the Asia-Pacific region after US reoccupation. Although the US Navy attempted to facilitate the rebuilding of civilian life, they prioritized the remaining battles in the Pacific and pivoted to transform Guåhan into a large military fortress. As discussed in greater detail in chapter 3, the war and subsequent militarization resulted in the dispossession and displacement of nearly all CHamoru families in Guåhan. The capital, Hagåtña, was destroyed. Housing, medical care, and agriculture needed to be rebuilt from the ground up. Everyone on the island was coping with war trauma and the sheer loss of life. Military land annexation prevented CHamorus from resettling and rebuilding their homes.[18] The US military relied on and took advantage of CHamoru loyalty to retain Guåhan for military purposes. The Navy's policies frustrated CHamorus who could no longer return to their lands to support their families. The CHamoru men who transitioned to work for the military encountered a tiered racialized wage scale that paid them less than workers from the States. This growing discontent with Navy rule posed a threat to naval operations and security in Guåhan and the rest of the Pacific.

In all of this, CHamoru leaders believed their concerns were unheard by military officials. The experience of postwar rehabilitation pushed them to question the relationship between the US Naval Government and the people of Guåhan.[19] On the one hand, many CHamorus believed that the US military "liberated" CHamorus from Japanese occupation and brought modernity to the island. In return, CHamorus reciprocated with unabashed loyalty to the United States.[20] In return for this loyalty, CHamoru leaders believed, the least the United States could do was to bestow on the people of Guåhan US citizenship and liberal democratic rights. As Leon Guerrero told the Hopkins Committee session in Guåhan in 1947, "We feel that we are not asking too much for the privileges of Citizenship and civil rights, and an organic Law being passed, as it will give us more say."[21] Citizenship, they believed, would politically empower CHamorus in the postwar development of their island. As a result of its visit to Guåhan, the Hopkins Committee recommended that both Guåhan and American Sāmoa receive US citizenship, a boon for the CHamoru citizenship movement.[22]

CHamorus advocated for citizenship consistently before the US Congress, the secretary of the Navy, and the secretary of the interior. They used all the resources and networks they had cultivated over the decades to shore up support. This network included the Institute of Ethnic Affairs (IEA), an internationally minded nonprofit organization "whose purpose was 'to search for solutions to problems within and between white and colored races, cultural minority groups, and dependent peoples at home and abroad.'"[23] The Institute was founded in 1945 by John Collier, former commissioner of the Bureau of Indian Affairs and a historic figure in twentieth-century federal Indian policy, and Laura Thompson, an anthropologist who studied CHamoru culture in Guåhan.[24] As a US colony with an disenfranchised Indigenous population, Guåhan became a central project in their global anticolonial mission. In addition to providing updates about anticolonial and decolonial movements, the

IEA's monthly newsletter and eventually the *Guam Echo* reported about the quarrels between the US Navy and the Department of the Interior on the topic of Guåhan's political status. These publications and the IEA office in Washington provided an institutional foundation that helped CHamorus develop strategies for their citizenship movement in a global anticolonial context.[25]

At the IEA, CHamorus may have learned to use notions of racial equality—rather than racial proximity to whiteness as seen in the Naval era—to advocate for US citizenship. A letter that accompanied the donations to IEA from CHamorus stated, "We are now living in a new era with many rapid changes but with great hope that the present regime will be forever benevolent, fair, just and without any discrimination to race, color, nationality, or social standing."[26] CHamorus were articulating the tenets of racial liberalism, the view that colorblind racial equality and democracy were necessary to rectify the inequalities in US society both on the continent and in the empire.[27] Understanding the island's role in military affairs in the Asia-Pacific region, they argued that bestowing US citizenship and an Organic Act for Guamanians would conform to the racial liberalism that the United States promoted in the early Cold War.

Meanwhile in Guåhan, CHamorus became increasingly fed up with the Naval Government. In March 1949 the Guam Congress went head-to-head with Naval Governor Pownall over the legal powers of the Guam Congress. The Guam Congress was an elected CHamoru legislative body that was conditionally empowered by the Naval Government in 1947 to create laws for the civilian population of the island.[28] When the Guam Congress attempted to subpoena a white businessman to testify for an investigation, he refused to appear, arguing that the Guam Congress had no legal powers. Governor Pownall sided with the businessman, effectively making him "immune to the laws of Guam."[29] This was the final straw. CHamoru leaders saw that they were secondary to military affairs and the whims of Naval governors. The trust CHamorus held in the Naval Government was lost.

To protest the arbitrary rule of the Naval governor, the Guam Congress walked out to object to their limited legislative powers and criticize the unwillingness of the Naval Government to take seriously the concerns of the CHamoru people. The Guam Congress sent a letter to Governor Pownall four days after the walkout, emphasizing that "the Assembly's action was not based upon any single incident, but upon a series of actions which have occurred with increasing frequency." The Congress could not "determine when it is performing its mission and when it is not, when it is being repudiated and when it is not, and when it is being circumvented when it is not."[30] As a result of the Guam Congress walkout, CHamorus believed the only way any of the local problems could be solved was through national legislation that defined the territorial status of Guåhan, created a civilian government, and gave US citizenship to CHamorus.

Carlos Taitano, who was present at the walkout, knew that this was an important, unprecedented act of CHamoru defiance against Naval rule. To avoid Navy censorship, he secretly sent a telegram to two news correspondents. As a result of Taitano's actions, the *Washington Post*, the *New York Times*, and the *Honolulu Star Bulletin* characterized the Guam Congress walkout as a civil rights movement that exposed the un-American and arbitrary nature of military rule in the US territories. According to CHamoru historian Anne Hattori, "Taitano and the newsmen agreed that if the CHamoru people's desire for self-government was to be heard, an incident of substantial magnitude must occur, great enough to warrant major coverage in newspapers."[31] Taitano's quick thinking worked. Shortly after the news syndication, several commentaries—including one by John Collier—argued that the political situation in Guåhan was fodder for communist propaganda. As a colony with a people who demonstrated keen knowledge of US liberal ideals, who survived and aided the US forces during World War II, and who, yet, did not have US citizenship and were governed by a military government, Guåhan presented an antithesis to the United States' post–World War II self-image as protectors of democracy and leaders in racial equality.[32] The Naval Government in Guåhan became a liability in the US military's strategic interest in the Pacific region. The walkout pushed those in Washington over the edge, forcing the secretary of the interior, President Truman, and all others to put US rhetoric into action and deliver a civilian government to CHamorus and grant them US citizenship.[33]

Understanding this significant shift, CHamorus lobbied Washington officials as much as they could. On May 5, 1949, Concepcion "Connie" Barret visited Washington and testified before Congress.[34] On May 21, Truman called Secretary of Interior Henry Krug to plan the transfer of Guåhan from the Navy to the Department of the Interior, which eventually happened in August 1949. This transfer ended the US Naval Government in Guåhan and paved the way for the establishment of a civilian government through the Organic Act. In September, Carlton Skinner arrived on the island to become the first civilian governor appointed by the president. In November, Agueda Johnston attended the IEA conference advocating for US citizenship for CHamorus. The congressional hearings for the Organic Act of Guam were held in Guåhan in November 1949 with over one hundred testimonies.[35] In May 1950, Frank B. Leon Guerrero once again traveled to Washington, this time with Antonio B. Won Pat to present a petition with seventeen hundred CHamoru signatures in favor of an Organic Act.[36] On August 1, 1950, Carlos Taitano stood behind President Truman as he signed the Organic Act of Guam.

The Organic Act of Guam as Military Policy

Although CHamorus saw citizenship and a civilian government as tools to advocate for political rights, federal and military officials saw them as strategies to solidify the US military presence on the island. After World War II, the White House, the Department of the Navy, and the Department of the Interior debated about which departments should administer the US Pacific territories and the United Nations Trust Territories of the Pacific Islands.[37] The problem was how to balance US military strategic interests in the Pacific region with the foreign policy aim of displaying acts of democracy. In 1948 the United Nations designated Guåhan as a non-self-governing territory, a political status that marked the island as a "colony," which meant that the United States was required to report on and aid the island's decolonization process.[38] US military interest in the Asia-Pacific region, however, precluded any possibility that Guåhan could become independent.

The Navy and the Interior fought to gain control of Guåhan. Navy Secretary James Forrestal believed that Guåhan needed to remain under the jurisdiction of the US military to ensure security in the Western Pacific. Like in the prewar period, the Navy believed that granting rights to the civilians in Guåhan, especially in regard to land policy, might impede military actions on the island.[39] This argument held in the short run, but it became increasingly clear that military governments themselves were antithetical to US anticolonial and anti-imperial rhetoric, as observed by the Hopkins Committee in 1947.[40] To project the appearance of liberal democratic governance at the dawn of the Cold War, the United States needed to alter its colonial governance within its territories.

The Department of the Interior offered a seemingly less militaristic alternative. Secretary of the Interior Harold Ickes believed the Naval Government in Guåhan was not just a contradiction but an embarrassment to the United States. In an August 1946 article for *Collier's Magazine,* Ickes wrote that "the way these islands are governed will constitute a tablet of imperishable brass from which the other nations of the world can read just what the United

States of America and its protestations for democracy really mean."[41] Ickes argued instead that a civilian government for Guamanians was more aligned with US values "of representative government, of justice under law, and of fundamental rights and human freedoms for everyone everywhere."[42] Ickes' successor Julius Albert Krug later argued that Interior was better experienced to administer Guåhan's government because it had administered US territories before World War II, including Alaska, Hawai'i, and Puerto Rico, and it had worked with Native Americans and other Indigenous peoples across the empire.[43] Throughout these debates, the US military presence in Guåhan was never challenged.

By placing jurisdiction of Guåhan away from the military and into a federal department with an innocuous sounding name, the Interior Department argued that the United States could demonstrate to the world its intention to promote equality for all people while maintaining US sovereignty and military presence in Guåhan. "In Guam, a bastion of defense in the Pacific," Krug testified, "measures taken to satisfy the legitimate aspirations of the Guamanians would actually enhance our national security by binding these people more closely to the rest of the United States."[44] In Krug's reasoning, Guamanians would not resist the military if their grievances were heard, and if some semblance of a civilian and democratic local government was created. Thus, US citizenship and a civilian government were tools of settler militarism that at once were fulfilments of liberal "equality" and an entrenchment of militarism in Guåhan.

John Collier joined the debate between the Navy and the Interior Department on behalf of the people of Guåhan. As a founder of IEA, he expressed dismay at US Naval governance in Guåhan in a letter to the editor of the *New York Times* in April 1947.[45] Collier reiterated Guamanian desire for "self-rule" and further explained the injustices in Naval governance, including the Navy's reluctance to pay war claims for injuries and deaths, the annexation of land without compensation to landowners, the high cost of living due to the importation of food, the refusal to help islanders rebuild infrastructure, and the Navy's overreliance on foreign labor. Yet, like Ickes and Krug, Collier did not challenge the premise of the US military presence in Guåhan. He believed that CHamorus had proved their loyalty to the United States and that "the records give no reason to believe their [CHamoru] action would interfere with the Navy in the matter of United States defense."[46] CHamoru calls for a civilian government did not necessarily mean demilitarization. Collier finished his letter by pointing out that it was a blatant contradiction of US foreign policy to support postwar recovery of European countries but not to extend the same support to its own territories. If the loyalty of CHamorus was not enough to convince the Congress and the president, then maybe, Collier thought, the un-Americanness of Naval rule in the territories would persuade them.

Even though CHamorus saw the Organic Act of Guam and US citizenship as the result of hard-fought advocacy and unfettered loyalty to the United States, Washington prioritized US strategic military interests in the Pacific before considering the desires and needs of CHamoru people. In November 1949, congressional hearings were held in Guåhan to ascertain exactly what the CHamoru people envisioned for the Organic Act.[47] But the Organic Act of Guam was written without any input from CHamorus. The conversations between Interior, the Navy, and even the Institute of Ethnic Affairs reveal how Guåhan's colonial status and US citizenship for CHamorus always assumed that the island's future remained tied to US militarism and Cold War foreign policy. By transferring Guåhan from the Navy to the Interior Department, the United States justified its complete control over the island in a way that was acceptable in the new postwar world order. As historian Megan Black has argued, the Department of the Interior "was a key mechanism for ensuring *and* obscuring the projection of American power in the world, from U.S. settler colonialism to its global hegemony during and after the Cold War."[48] The Interior Department, with the heavy influence from the Navy, hoped to do exactly that—to obscure US settler militarism in Guåhan.

The Organic Act itself reflects this military strategy. Interior and the Navy worked together to craft legislation for a civilian government that would allow the president, as the commander in chief, and the US military to have critical say in how the island would be governed, while maintaining an image of democracy. The sections regarding the civilian government for Guåhan and US citizenship for Guamanians were toward the beginning of the Organic Act. Section 3 of the Act clarified Guåhan's status as a US "unincorporated territory." Though simple in its phrasing, this section represented the end of over fifty years of military rule of Guåhan, but also ensured that Guåhan had no path to statehood as ruled by the Insular Cases. The island's civilian government would have three branches—executive, legislative, and judicial—though the US president would appoint the island's civilian governor. Section 4 amended the National Act of 1940 to include residents of Guåhan as US citizens. The Organic Act also outlined the Bill of Rights and the duties of each branch of government.[49]

After the sections on US citizenship and civilian government in the Organic Act, the United States stipulated that Guåhan's legal existence remained tied to US foreign and military policy in the Pacific. Two other sections buried within the Organic Act of Guam—Sections 28 and 33—codified into law the US military's postwar land annexation. Section 28 transferred some US federal property and Naval Government departments to the civilian Government of Guåhan, which was under the purview of the Department of the Interior, "to be administered for the benefit of the people of Guam." In addition to land, facilities and infrastructure necessary for civilian affairs, such as bus lines, buildings, reservoirs, and sewage facilities, were transferred to the Government of Guam. This land transfer from Navy to Interior seemed to benefit the CHamorus people, who wanted more control over their island's affairs. Instead, however, it created the parameters for the legitimization of US military landholdings in Guåhan.

Furthermore, as an island under executive jurisdiction through the Department of the Interior, the Organic Act contained provisions that gave the US president the wherewithal to singlehandedly determine the future of Guåhan. Section 33 states, "Nothing contained herein shall be construed as limiting the authority of the President to designate parts of Guam as naval or military reservations, not to restrict his authority as a closed port with respect to the vessels and aircraft of foreign nations."[50] The commander in chief—not Congress—has the ultimate power in the affairs of the island. Paired with Section 28 of the Organic Act, which outlines "title transfers to all property, real or personal, owned by the United States," the Organic Act reserved the right for the president to revert Guåhan back into a military government.[51] Guåhan's civilian government was legally constructed to be subservient to military policy.

These sections were not created with hypothetical future scenarios. Around the time of the signing of the Organic Act, Truman, the Navy, and the Interior Department employed Sections 28 and 33 to retain control of annexed land for military strategic purposes. According to historian Robert Rogers, "To make retention of Guåhan's land by the military legal, Skinner [appointed civilian governor of Guam] was instructed to sign a quitclaim deed on 31 July 1950—the day before the Organic Act was signed—whereby GovGuam transferred all condemned properties to the United States of America 'for its own use.'" Later in October, Truman issued Executive Order 10178, which returned all the property in the quitclaim deed to the Navy to be divided among military services by need. Rogers notes, "These steps were taken without consulting CHamoru officials or owners of leased properties."[52] In other words, the presidentially appointed governor of Guam, Carlton Skinner, transferred land meant for the civilian government to the US

Navy *before* the Organic Act was signed. With the Organic Act becoming effective, not on August 1, but on July 21—an homage to the "Liberation of Guam" from Japanese occupation during World War II—the president, Interior, and the Navy ensured that the CHamoru land dispossession was legally codified and obscured by US citizenship and the rhetoric of freedom. As a result of these actions, Rogers notes, 33 percent of the island became permanently military property.

By examining the "fine print" in the Organic Act of Guam, Guåhan becomes another locus to explore how the post–World War II "decolonization" of the US territories of the Philippines, Hawai'i, and Alaska was geopolitical strategy for the United States to maintain power in the Pacific, while asserting narratives of democracy and decolonization. The Organic Act was a military document as much as it was a civilian one; the inclusion of CHamorus in the nation-state was predicated upon Guåhan being used for military affairs. The CHamoru people were left out of the loop and believed that US citizenship and a civilian government could help protect their land, but military and federal officials crafted the Organic Act of Guam to legalize and justify settler militarism. Furthermore, the shift from colony to an organized unincorporated territory was a rhetorical tool to allay fears and dispel assertions that the United States continued colonizing in the age of decolonization. As CHamoru scholar Kenneth Gofigan Kuper argues, Guåhan's "political status as a strategically located unincorporated territory, a.k.a. colony, is the grounds by which the United States can gamble with Guåhan for the pursuit of their national interest in the Asia-Pacific region." As Kuper succinctly writes, "It is in U.S. interests for Guåhan to remain a colony."[53] The creation and implementation of the Organic Act of Guam did not hinder or stall US settler militarism in Guåhan. Settler militarism was instead justified through what was seen as fulfillment of US liberalism via inclusion of CHamoru people who now had US citizenship.[54] Thus, Guåhan's history reveals the co-constituted nature of US settler militarism and liberalism.

The Case of Radio Barrigada

If at first CHamorus believed that US citizenship and the Organic Act would protect them from the unilateral, nonconsensual actions of the US Navy and aid their rehabilitation, the Case of Radio Barrigada demonstrated clearly that the United States continued to prioritize military strategic interests over the fundamental needs of the people of Guåhan. The Organic Act gave the Navy and the Air Force legal justification for their control over CHamoru lands, livelihoods, and civilian government. Employing Section 28 of the Organic Act, Truman signed Executive Order 10178 on October 31, 1950; this order specified the transfer of the land area of Barigåda, among other land lots, from the civilian government to the US military.[55] In 1951 the US military acted upon this executive order and condemned 2,930 acres for a radio communications in the center of Barigåda *after* CHamorus received citizenship. The Guam Legislature sprang into action, sending a resolution to the US Congress to question the priorities of the military and advocate for the 129 families who lived on and farmed the thriving agricultural area that was central to Guåhan's postwar food supply.[56] The resolution requested that the US federal government and military-affiliated cabinet members recognize that there were vast spaces of unused land already in the possession of the US Navy that could serve as a radio station, and it admonished the Navy for its inadequate compensation and the removal of people from their land. The Guam Legislature saw the Case of Radio Barrigada as the epitome of the ongoing battle against the US military's excessive land annexation that alienated CHamorus from their land and prevented their self-sufficiency.[57] Although the resolution was sent to Congress, nothing was done to prevent the military's land annexation in Barigåda

Three years later, in 1954, the Case of Radio Barrigada once again became an example of the US military's inconsiderate land annexation when member of the US Congress conducted hearings on the transition to a civilian government.[58] CHamorus were offended that on the land taken in Barigåda, the Navy had built not only had a telecommunications center but also a recreation center with a military-only golf course. CHamoru families, who had cultivated the land to sustain themselves, testified about the land they once held. Vicente Leon Guerrero and Tomasa Santos Rios had owned three hectares of land that were "well cultivated and contained large numbers of fruit bearing trees, yielding an income more than sufficient for the needs of our large family." Dolores T. Rosario had been able "to support [her] children from her farm and where [she] raised livestock."[59] Jose I. Franquez had owned eight acres that were "so fertile that [he] was able to grow anything that could grow on Guam," including "1,000 coconut trees, 33 citrus-fruit trees, 96 banana trees, 34 breadfruits, 10 dogdog [indigenous breadfruit], 2 carabao mangos, and 4 kapok trees besides the vegetables [he] planted for [their] daily use." He also had "a considerable number of livestock."[60] Jose Borja Flores had eight and a half acres of fertile farmland in addition to three buildings. They were just a few of the 129 families who were forced to leave the Radio Barrigada area, severed from land that had sustained them.

These families also became examples of how military-facilitated land annexation trapped CHamorus into a cycle of dependency on the US military for jobs and food security. The four families mentioned above were moved from their Barigåda properties to new suburban villages like New Dededo (Dédidu) in small compact lots that were, to them, overpriced and unsuitable for farming. Vicente Leon Guerrero and Tomas Santos Rios were given a total of $1,100 for their Barigåda property that was a little larger than three hectares. They were told to move away from land that fed them and were forced to purchase an "unimproved lot" of 95 by 100 feet which the government of Guam sold to them for $518. Due to problems with land deeds, Dolores Rosario was not paid for her property and, as a result, could no longer support her family. She had "found it necessary to ask the Helping Hands of Guam Organization for help."[61] Jose Borja Flores was offered $1,800 for his eight and a half acres, and moved to New Dededo on a 95 by 103 foot lot. Because he could no longer farm, he took up a job at the Naval air station, but his "earnings are not sufficient to meet the needs of my family and myself."[62] The Barigåda residents believed that they were not adequately compensated for their properties, especially given the amount of sustenance the land had provided for them. And as a result, they became dependent on charities and the military to live.

The "celebrated case" of Radio Barrigada demonstrates how land dispossession for "military purposes" hit at the heart of CHamoru livelihoods. A. C. Cruz testified, "To us, the people of Guam, there is no possession as dear as the land on which we live in, the land which we cultivate our daily food, the land which holds for us the abundant quantity of wild foods, the land without which most of our people cannot feel secure in their daily existence." This was the terrifying triviality of settler militarism in Guåhan. When Jose Franquez was offered $1,465 for his eight productive acres, he refused to accept the offer. He was subsequently "evicted by Federal marshal and was told to leave immediately." Franquez commented that "once in a while I have passed around that area only to see people having fun playing golf on my old neighbors' properties and to see a concessionaire making thousands of dollars at the expense of our misery." His land sat idle. In one question, Franquez revealed the cruel reality of US military land takings in Guåhan: "I question, 'Why was I evicted?' The answer, 'the land is needed for a military purpose such as a golf course.'"[63]

The response of the civilian government of Guam to the land problems at Radio Barrigada supported and reaffirmed the US military's intentions with Guåhan. The acting civilian governor of Guam, R. S. Herman, outright dismissed CHamoru discontent, calling the land annexation an "accomplished fact" and implying that the process was irreversible. He further explained that CHamorus would remain loyal despite the land annexation. Even though he acknowledged that Radio Barrigada lands were fertile and productive, he also argued that the golf course benefited the island in a similar way. He wrote, "Regardless of the purpose of the original land taking, it's felt that the presence of the golf course has contributed materially to the welfare and comfort of personnel by whom it is utilized." He further reiterated that "the government is well aware of the fact that the economy of Guam and the general welfare of its people depend in great measure upon the presence of the armed forces of the United States and their civilian employees." Guåhan, he wrote, was an established "outpost of great strength for the protection of the rest of the United States."[64] In this way, the golf course represented more than military misuse of CHamoru land. The Case of Radio Barrigada demonstrates how the US military's codified land annexation in Guåhan, legitimized CHamoru dispossession through "national security," and obscured its violence by couching the military's presence as fundamental to the "general welfare" of the island.

The Organic Act of Guam of 1950 is a military document disguised as a civilian document. While CHamorus saw civilian government and US citizenship as the fulfillment of liberal inclusion, federal and military agencies saw US citizenship and civilian government as the best solutions to execute Cold War foreign policy, stymie CHamoru discontent, and justify land annexations. The CHamoru experience with US citizenship is not unlike that of other Indigenous peoples who advocated for more rights within the US empire, yet whose US citizenship delegitimized their claims to land, self-determination, and sovereignty. As scholar Lana Tatour writes about the relationship between citizenship and settler colonialism, "citizenship becomes visible as a (liberal) technology of governance through which settler states control, manage, and contain indigenous peoples and their claim to sovereignty and self-determination."[65] The Organic Act of Guam of 1950 demonstrates precisely how citizenship operates as legal tool of settler militarism. Yes, as US citizens CHamorus were included into the nation-state, but their newly gained political rights would not alleviate the problems associated with the US settler militarism in Guåhan.

Filipinos, Permanent Residency, and US Citizenship

As CHamorus garnered the Organic Act, limited though it may be, Filipino migrant workers continued to work for US military contractors to build military infrastructure throughout the island. The provision for US citizenship in the Organic Act did not apply to these postwar Filipino workers. It applied specifically to those who were present or were descendants of those present in Guåhan during the transfer of the island from Spain to the United States on April 11, 1899. This accounted for all the CHamorus in Guåhan, and for non-CHamoru peoples, like the former Filipino revolutionary exiles, who were residents of Guåhan.[66] What did affect Filipino workers, however, was how the Organic Act's provision for a civilian government affected the application of federal immigration policy. In the transition between the Navy and the Interior Department, federal immigration law needed to be reconciled with how the US military had conducted their Filipino migrant labor recruitment since World War II.

As explained in chapter 3, immediately following World War II the US Navy commenced a large-scale military buildup in which the military condemned two-thirds of the island, paved hundreds of miles of road, built thousands of buildings both temporary and permanent, laid runways and airstrips, and dredged and fortified harbors.[67] The United States and the Philippines negotiated the Exchange of Notes of 1947, which allowed the US military and its contractors to recruit Filipino workers for both skilled and unskilled jobs.[68] This diplomatic agreement also stood in for US immigration policy as it applied to Guåhan.[69] Lyle H. Turner, an attorney who dedicated himself to the legal entanglements caused by the implementation of the Organic Act, estimated that in 1953, "there were 17,000 alien contract laborers in Guam all of which came from the Philippines. Of those 17,000 about 3,000 are in local businesses and private labor markets, so that even the Federal Government itself found it necessary to import 14,000 alien laborers from the Philippines."[70] This is compared to the roughly 27,000 CHamorus living in Guåhan in 1950.[71]

The US military's dependence on cheap imported Filipino labor to build this infrastructure was undeniable. Military and civilian enterprises relied on the steady importation of Filipino migrant labor to staff their operations and businesses. The number of military-adjacent businesses, such as bakeries, barbershops, clothing shops, restaurants, and commissaries, increased significantly to sell goods or provide services to the thousands of people on the island who worked on the military buildup. Many of these civilian businesses were owned by a cross section of the island's people (white US settlers, CHamorus, and Filipinos) who also depended on Filipino migrant labor, which the Naval Government of Guam allowed before 1950.[72] Furthermore, the civilian Government of Guam recruited Filipino professionals to fill the gap in several sectors of Guåhan's economy including the medicine, public health, and engineering. In March 1951, the Government of Guam employment services manager, Sabino Flores, traveled to the Philippines on behalf of the Government of Guam "to investigate recruiting possibilities in the Philippines for certain types of labor not available on Guam."[73] When Flores met with Philippine Secretary of Labor Jose Figueroa over dinner in Manila, Figueroa gave his "whole hearted assurance that the Philippines can meet all demands for practically all types of labor."[74] Flores recognized the labor surplus in the Philippines and urged the civilian Government of Guam to take advantage of the Philippine postwar economy, which depended on labor export and remittances.

Filipinos took advantage of Guåhan as a US territory to obtain better economic opportunities while simultaneously seeking pathways to citizenship that were otherwise unavailable. Alongside blue-collar workers, Filipino professionals such as healthcare workers, teachers, and accountants participated in the development of the Guåhan economy throughout the postwar period. The Government of Guam recruited Filipino doctors and nurses who graduated from US accredited universities in the Philippines, such as the University of the Philippines, and completed their medical residencies in the continental United States. After passing the examinations for US medical credentials, Filipino doctors worked at Guam Memorial Hospital, the island's only civilian hospital. These doctors were of some of first Filipino professionals to settle in Guåhan. They include Ben and Ofelia Sison, Sinforoso Tolentino, Marciano Santos, Rodolfo Silan, Tom Veloria, and Ernesto Espaldon.[75] As medical professionals, many of them and their families became well-known figures in Guåhan society. This labor migration history was a continuation of imperial labor routes of migration that characterized US colonialism in the Philippines.[76]

Guåhan's reliance on Filipino workers for all sectors of the island's workforce, both military and civilian, compelled those in charge of the island's immigration laws to consistently advocate for policies that kept Guåhan open to Filipino labor. In the transition between military and civilian governments, it became apparent that the 1947 Exchange of Notes operated outside the jurisdiction of US federal immigration laws. The presence of these Filipino migrant workers—many without passports and immigration papers, and some with expired military contracts—confounded the INS. They found themselves "faced with the problem that we had all of the alien contract laborers in Guam illegally."[77] Rather than deporting the Filipino workers, the INS, the US military, and the Government of Guam formed a coalition to work together to "regularize" Filipinos' immigration statuses by finding loopholes in federal immigration law, deciding court cases, and creating exceptions and waivers for Guåhan to ensure that the island could retain the thousands of Filipino workers. As a result, the INS constructed mechanisms for establishing a settled and stable working class by incorporating US military policies into federal immigration policy.

During the years 1950–52, the INS worked to make Guåhan's military labor recruitment practices retroactively comply with Section 3 of the 1917 Immigration Act, the prevailing federal immigration law at the time.[78] The complexity and diversity of Filipino workers' immigration cases required different solutions to "regularize" their statuses. The outcome of a Filipino's immigration status could fall into one of two categories. In the first category, a person who had a current contract with a company would be regularized as a "temporary contract worker." Federal immigration law prohibited the admission of temporary contract workers, but the coalition skillfully maneuvered the ninth provision of Section 3 of the 1917 Immigration Act to enable the US military to request and receive waivers to retroactively legally admit the nearly fourteen thousand temporary Filipino military contract workers.[79] Approximately three thousand Filipinos working in civilian companies were also given these waivers.[80] As temporary contract workers, they were required to leave the island before the third anniversary of their arrival. In one stroke of a pen, the INS aligned Filipino workers' status to federal immigration law, changing their status from illegal to legal in an instant.

In the second category, for Filipino workers employed in skilled or managerial work, who were often recruited without contracts, the INS determined that the workers were brought to the island under the "presumption of lawful admission." These jobs included bookkeepers and trained bakers, positions that could not easily be filled by the local population. To regularize their status, the Code of Federal Regulations (CFR) was updated to include a special circumstance of recruited workers who were admitted to Guåhan before December 24, 1952, without a contract. They were presumed to have been admitted into the United States legally—"presumption of lawful admission"—and thus eligible for US permanent residency.[81] As a result of this amendment and a subsequent set of Board of Immigration Appeals Cases in the late 1950s, the INS found approximately fifteen hundred Filipino white-collar workers who fell into this category.[82] Once the workers passed their medical and immigration inspections, the INS approved their immigration status as permanent residents, a necessary step toward US citizenship.[83] For the US military, this revision to the US CFR created a more permanent, skilled workforce and aided the smooth continuation of US militarism in Guåhan.

How the INS interpreted the 1917 Immigration Act to alleviate the perceived shortage in Guåhan's labor force ironically contradicts the intention of the Act itself. The 1917 Immigration Act was relatively exclusionary, making it difficult for races classified within the Asiatic Barred Zone from entering the United States.[84] The Philippines was not part of this zone in 1917 because of its colonial status, but post-Philippine independence immigration legislation sought to stop the free flow of Filipinos to the United States, exemplified by the 1946 Luce-Celler Act, which limited Filipino immigration into the States to one hundred Filipinos per year. Nevertheless, the US military's demand for Filipino workers for military construction provided just enough justification to admit Filipino workers permanently at the beginning of the Cold War.

The military and civilian economic development in Guåhan would have been in jeopardy without these small, yet significant, revisions to federal immigration law in its application to Guåhan. Instead of deporting Filipino workers, the INS simply accommodated their presence, influenced by the US military's need for labor in Guåhan. In a testimony, Lyle Turner remarked, "I'm sure the Congressmen will be able to appreciate the problem private businesses faced in 1952. If you had a similar situation in the United States where you suddenly found out about 90 percent of your employees would necessarily be terminated and you couldn't replace them."[85] The loss of 90 percent of the workforce would wreck both the civilian economy and the military buildup in Guåhan.

In December 1952, federal immigration laws changed with the Walter-McCarran Act. This federal change warranted a reassessment of immigration policies in Guåhan. Unlike the 1917 Immigration Act, the Walter-McCarran Act allowed temporary alien contract workers under the highly regulated and stringent H-2 visa. Employers could apply for foreign workers' H-2 visas *after* proving that local labor was unavailable and that the open positions were temporary in nature. Both requirements posed serious problems for Guåhan. The US Labor Department and the US employment service, in this case the Government of Guam, determined the availability of local workers.[86] In order to prove the lack of local workers, however, companies were required to advertise and recruit local workers before applying for H-2 visas. Many companies cited the unskilled local labor population and the difficulty recruiting potential workers from the continent who were often deterred by island's distance from the continental United States and reputation for poor working and living conditions. As Admiral Joel D. Parks testified in Congress in 1956, "There is no housing in Guam, no family housing for these . . . 8,000 people

Filipinos at a US naturalization ceremony in Guåhan. Courtesy of the Humanities Guåhan.

which would have to come there."[87] In addition, businesses believed that the local population did not have the specialized training required. In the early 1950s there were no established construction training programs and US contractors did not create any. So instead, military contractors and civilian businesses continued to recruit readily available foreign workers from the Philippines.

The second requirement of H-2 visas—that open job positions were temporary in nature—was trickier, given that the island's military presence was seen to be a long-term project. To become eligible for H-2 workers for its operations in Guåhan, the US military petitioned for an exemption to the 1952 Immigration Act in a similar fashion to the exemptions made with the 1917 Immigration Act. According to a congressional report, "The Navy argued in 1953 that the aliens employed in connection with its mission on Guam were temporary in the sense that the mission itself was a temporary one, and that they were vital to the national defense." On July 27, 1953, the INS "would approve H-2 petitions filed by military contractors and by private businesses which 'substantially serve the Armed Forces or contractors thereto within the Territory.'" Like the justification for annexing CHamoru land, US military strategic interests, once again, heavily influenced the enforcement of federal immigration law to subsequently fulfill the demand for a cheap, easily accessible labor force from the Philippines.[88]

Even though the US military argued that its postwar military buildup was a temporary project, its presence, nonetheless, was the opposite. US interventions in the Asia-Pacific region throughout the Cold War only reified and justified the presence of US military bases in Guåhan, effectively making them long-term installations in need of a consistent migrant and immigrant labor force. So even though the recruited workers were temporary on an individual basis—they were allowed to stay in Guåhan for stints of a maximum of three years, the H-2 program and the US military's waiver meant that Guåhan saw a revolving door of Filipino foreign workers throughout the rest of twentieth century.[89] When the blanket H-2 program ceased in 1959, the US military then lobbied for a Defense Parole System, which again allowed the military to continue recruiting foreign workers for its projects and missions. This time the US military argued that Guåhan's bases provided crucial reinforcements for the Vietnam War, and that thus there was a sufficient need for a large, imported labor force, which could not be filled by local labor.[90]

The INS was not as welcoming to local civilian businesses when it came to their H-2 visa applications. While military contractors directly associated with military operations were considered "temporary" and thus eligible for

H-2 workers, civilian businesses without military contracts had difficulty proving that their need was also temporary. Many Filipino migrant workers, such as "bakers, barbers, auto repairmen, service station attendants, radio repairmen, and soft drink bottlers," were employed by businesses that were recruited to support Guåhan's military presence, but were not tied to specific temporary construction contracts.[91] While local civilian businesses once garnered general support from the military, INS administrator Turner witnessed a change: "As I now understand it the military very properly feels that unless they have a direct connection with the business, and are able to evaluate that it does render a substantial service to the Armed Forces, it is not their duty or their position to make a certification."[92] By not supporting these local businesses through advocating for much-needed labor, local business owners argued, immigration law and the military stymied the development of a local civilian economy exclusive of the military.

The inconsistency in the application of federal immigration law to the US military in Guåhan versus its application to the civilian population continued to be a contentious issue throughout the latter half of the twentieth century. While the military persuaded federal agencies to create the Defense Parole Act in the early 1960s, civilian companies in Guåhan could not attain the same waiver.[93] Perhaps persuaded by CHamoru criticism of racialized wage scales, as explored in chapter 3, federal agencies believed that allowing foreign workers in the civilian side of Guåhan was detrimental to the development of a local labor force. By March 1960 the INS required any civilian company without ties to the military to repatriate one-third of their foreign workforce, approximately eight hundred workers in total.[94] This decision backfired. The civilian economy was left without enough skilled workers to create civilian infrastructure, train local workers, or develop other sectors of the island's economy, such as tourism. The INS created the Parole Act for Guam only *after* the island was severely damaged by Typhoon Karen in 1962 and Typhoon Olive in 1963, and *after* President John F. Kennedy lifted the island's military security clearance.[95] To rebuild Guåhan, local civilian companies recruited foreign workers, and by 1964 nearly seven hundred Filipinos were admitted as temporary workers.[96]

The establishment of long-standing US military bases and the creation of a civilian economy relied not only on the annexation of CHamoru land, but also on the work of Filipino migrant and immigrant workers in Guåhan. Since the end of World War II, the US military manipulated federal immigration law to use the growing population of Filipino H-2 migrant workers, permanent residents, naturalized Filipino-Americans, and eventually their family members as a persisting labor force for US militarism in Guåhan. As a result, CHamorus were left out of a burgeoning economy, which further exacerbated their loss of land in the postwar era.

Guåhan as a Militarized Stepping Stone

The growth in the number of Filipino permanent residents signaled the rise of a large nonwhite, non-Indigenous population in Guåhan, one that was diverse in experience, yet held the common view that Guåhan was definitively a US territory. A Filipino seeking a better life in the United States could feasibly begin the journey eastward toward the North American continent by first landing a job in Guåhan with the help of relatives or friends who were already on the island. If their relatives were US citizens, these Filipinos could use familial relations to secure US permanent residency and eventually US citizenship. What makes Guåhan unique is how large a role the US military played in the establishment of a Filipino community in Guåhan compared to the Filipino diaspora in the continental United States or Hawaiʻi, where agriculture and plantation economies often paved the way for migration in the early part of the twentieth century. The US military influenced so many aspects of Guåhan's governance that nearly every Filipino who arrived in Guåhan in this postwar period had ties to the US military and empire.

The US military dictated the movement of peoples into and out of Guåhan, ensuring its settled presence on the island. Despite the establishment of a civilian government, Guåhan was deemed a special security zone for military operations. A few months after the Organic Act of Guam was signed in 1950, the Department of the Navy reinstated the security clearance first implemented by Executive Order No. 8683 by Franklin D. Roosevelt before World War II.[97] Doing so allowed the US military vast control over the movement of peoples and goods in and out of the island despite Guåhan's colonial administration under Department of the Interior jurisdiction. Thus, any person who entered Guåhan needed clearance from the secretary of the Navy, who determined that the person entered primarily for, and posed no threat to, military operations.[98] As such, Filipinos arriving in Guåhan were vetted by the authorities and their entrance was deemed necessary to military operations.

Business-minded Filipinos capitalized on Guåhan's postwar military buildup to establish businesses on their own.[99] Mark V. Pangilinan and Manual Jose, for instance, became two of Guåhan's first millionaires.[100] Immediately after World War II, Pangilinan owned a business transporting US troops back to the mainland from the Philippines. He took the opportunity to create connections when he stopped over in Guåhan. In 1948 he opened a tailor shop, and then a restaurant and a furniture store, and soon he expanded his conglomerate to include "construction, insurance, retailing, sporting goods, publishing, hardware, and car dealerships."[101] Pangilinan was remembered as a "remarkable man" because "he not only immigrated to Guam and established an expansive business enterprise benefiting thousands of local citizens, but also chose to marry a Chamorro woman, and established his home on the island."[102] Jose was a concessionaire brought to Guåhan by the US military, and soon expanded his humble business outside the military's fences to include real estate, movie theaters, a bookstore, and a newspaper.[103] Both Pangilinan and Jose became well-known Filipino figures in Guåhan's business circles; they played prominent roles in the Filipino Community of Guam, as did their wives in the Filipino Ladies Association of Guam.

Some Filipinos used their participation in the US military during or after World War II to find economic opportunities in other parts of the empire. Lorenzo Batangan was born to a farming family in the province of Nueva Ecija. At a young age he moved to Manila to live with his uncle's family and to take care of his cousin, until the Japanese military bombed Manila in 1941. Batangan's life changed dramatically, like the CHamorus in Guåhan, who were bombed by the Japanese on the same day. To escape the chaos in Manila, he and his family fled back to the province. He then enlisted as a Philippine Scout and fought alongside US soldiers in guerilla warfare against Japanese forces. In an interview with his granddaughter Chloe Babauta, Batangan recounted that "when the Japanese surrendered to General MacArthur, the very day after, the Philippine Scouts forced me to re-enlist in the U.S. Army, [where] we were retrained."[104] His military records show that he enlisted in the US military on June 7, 1946, shortly before the United States declared the Philippines an independent country, and for three years he worked as military police in Manila.

In June 1949 Batangan was recruited by the US Air Force to work in Guåhan. With a sense of adventure, Batangan embraced the opportunity and worked as an auto mechanic with the US Airforce maintenance and transportation division at Harmon Airfield. After the mechanic job ended, Batangan found various jobs with the military and military concessionaires from 1950 through the early 1960s. His resumé showed that he worked as a laundry worker, labor packer, house boy, a painter, a general maintenance man, and finally a mess attendant until his retirement in the 1990s.[105] His jobs were on the northern side of the island, around or near Camp MARBO. For

Batangan, the US military provided opportunities to improve his socioeconomic circumstances, giving him a much better life than the farm he was raised in the province of Nueva Ecija.

Reflecting upon his time working in and for the US military, he commented, "The U.S. government takes care of your family, you have all the benefits, and they protect your family." The US military gave him not only a pathway to increase his socioeconomic status, but also a sense of purpose in an international cause. With pride, Batangan told his granddaughter that he joined the military, even though he was not a US citizen, because he wanted "to serve under the United States to defend our people."[106] He saw Filipinos and Americans as international partners in achieving security and freedom in the Pacific. Batangan represents what historian Simeon Man calls the construction of "good" Asians whose work for US military made them representations of US democracy in the postwar age of decolonization.[107] The fact that Batangan received US citizenship in 1961 fits the narrative that the United States promised freedom through racial liberal inclusion, but nevertheless it was predicated upon his work for US militarism in Guåhan.

Military labor recruitment practices in the Philippines also shaped the waves of Filipinos migrating into Guåhan. US military contractors recruited workers in the Philippines through regionally based recruitment processes that frequently exploited family connections to encourage many to sign up to be foreign workers in Guåhan. Filipinos who arrived in Guåhan or their descendants often cite the presence of another family member on the island who guided them through the process of adjusting to life on the island. In an oral history with me, my grandmother, Florita, from Panay Island in the Iloilo region, remarked that my grandfather Vic had an uncle—specifically his father's first cousin—working for the US Navy before he arrived in 1950. It was through Uncle Tuting that Vic had first heard about Florita, who was a student at the time. They sent letters to each other, eventually meeting in the Philippines in the early 1960s when Vic took a vacation from his job as an electrician. They were married in a quickly planned wedding in Iloilo. Florita then moved with Vic to Guåhan and settled in a village not too far from Camp Roxas, where Vic had worked for LUSTEVECO and MASDELCO. Although Florita does not recall how or when Vic received US citizenship, she nonetheless received her citizenship as a result of their marriage. They settled in Guåhan, bought land, built a house, and raised their family of five children, including my father Ramon, in the village of Sånta Rita. While the military provided the routes of empire for many Filipinos, family members provided support for Filipino migrant workers, giving them guidance on how to deal with their employers and how to live in Guåhan.[108]

Because some Filipinos in Guåhan had received US citizenship, they could petition their relatives to come to the United States. H-2 workers sometimes used their Filipino-American family members to petition for their permanent residency. A provision of the 1924 Immigration Act "allowed citizen to welcome their immediate relatives" without impacting national quotas.[109] By working in Guåhan, a temporary H-2 worker could work and seek permanent employment, while waiting for their relative to process immigration papers under the family reunification clause of the Immigration Act. This was the case for Jose Bello and Manuel Bello, from the Philippine province of Ilocos Sur, described in chapter 3. In Guåhan, Jose used his connections to get Manuel an H-2 job as a busboy at the Andersen Air Force Base Officer's Club. During this time, Jose started the paperwork to have his brother become a permanent resident so that he could gain US citizenship, which he eventually did sometime in the 1960s. Manuel then petitioned his daughter Marieta to work in Guåhan, and she became a US citizen in 1975. She quickly petitioned her mother and two younger sisters, including my mother Marlyn. They moved to Guåhan in 1976, and stayed with their Filipino-CHamoru cousins in Dédidu. They eventually moved to the new suburban neighborhood of Barrigada Heights. Marieta moved to Los Angeles in the late 1970s. While Manuel used Guåhan as an opportunity for economic gain to support his family in the Philippines, his daughter Marieta saw the potential in US citizenship to strike out on her own in the continent United States, when she moved to Los Angeles.[110] For the Bello brothers and their families, their migration stories were shaped by the routes of US militarism of the twentieth-century Pacific.

Filipinos, who no longer were US nationals after Philippine Independence, saw Guåhan as an island of opportunity, a stepping stone toward economic freedom, US citizenship, and further migration to the continental United States. Unlike for CHamorus, for whom US citizenship came with loss of their land to military land annexation, for Filipinos US citizenship was a way to individually rectify the social and economic turmoil caused by the legacies of war, imperialism, and militarization in the Philippines. World War II and the US military shaped the routes of migration for Filipinos throughout the Pacific, and especially to Guåhan. While some Filipino men saw the work abroad as temporary, and eventually returned to the Philippines, others settled in Guåhan. Some of them who were single when they first arrived in Guåhan traveled back to the Philippines to marry, eventually bringing their wives to settle in what they saw as a happy medium between the Philippines and the United States. Others married CHamoru women. Their families provided a sense of permanence and settlement. Other Filipino families used the island as their first location with the US empire, with the intention to move on to the continental United States. US citizenship made migration and settling easier. Yet, as the Filipino stories in this chapter show, attaining citizenship imbricated Filipinos and their families into a settler militarism, in which they embodied a non-Indigenous community who were both workers and settlers.

A CLOSE EXAMINATION of the Organic Act of Guam and the postwar immigration laws in Guåhan reveals how the liberal narratives of citizenship are more complicated than one of moving from exclusion to inclusion. By examining how exactly CHamorus and Filipinos obtained US citizenship in Guåhan, we see how US citizenship became a tool to further settler militarism, at once maintaining and legitimizing military presence. This history shows how the US military created exceptions and exemptions in the Organic Act of Guam and the application of US immigration laws that obscure the injustices of settler militarism, while simultaneously projecting liberalism in the Pacific. This is indicative of a form of "metapolitical authority," as described by Jodi Kim, where the US military in Guåhan executed "the power to not simply create these temporal and spatial exceptions but to discursively obfuscate and render these exceptions as precisely their opposite, as unexceptional."[111] Although citizenship symbolized liberal rights and economic opportunities for CHamorus and Filipinos, this desire for US citizenship also cemented imperial power in Guåhan.

Part III

Multicultural Guåhan (1960s–1990s)

CHAPTER FIVE

The Paradox of Paradise

The Rise of Multiculturalism and CHamoru–Filipino Tensions

In August 1970 the *Pacific Daily News* published a magazine about Guåhan's economic progress since the Organic Act of Guam of 1950. In a section titled "Guam USA: Land of Sunshine, Swaying Palms, and Friendly Smiles," the newspaper highlighted the economic and cultural transformation brought on by the island's nascent tourism industry. The cover depicted a welcoming local man with a big smile, a silhouette of a single coconut branch, and six men racing carabaos. The magazine was adorned with photos of brown-skinned men blowing conch shells, "island-shirt and muumuu clad" Japanese tourists at the Guam International Airport, an "old Chamorro woman" in *mestisa* dress carrying a baby described as a "Guamanian of the future," and local fishermen holding up their three-hundred-pound groupers caught fresh from the reef. The magazine also featured a collage that exhibited "A Real Tourist Attraction—Guam's Beautiful Girls" of a "variety" of ethnicities, and advertisements for new hotels and shipping companies promised "the paradise island of your dreams."[1]

The magazine signaled Guåhan's economic development, playing into the Cold War desire for an ideal, peaceful, and multicultural paradise. Indeed, the market for tourists from Asia—a mere three to four hours away by plane—was seen as the answer to the civilian economic growth the island needed. Rather than fly to Hawai'i, which could be more expensive, some Japanese tourists wanted a more affordable tropical destination that still had the feel of visiting the United States. As one representative of a Japanese-based tourism company said in 1968, "'Guam is another Hawaii,' only, 'unspoiled.'"[2] Embedded in this appeal of paradise were the gendered and racialized locals who brought a tropical exoticism to the Japanese tourists' experience.[3] In an era of racial unrest on the US continent and violence across the Third World, the *Pacific Daily News*, tourism boosters, foreign investors, local civilian companies, and the US military in Guåhan all emphasized that the island's multiculturalism presented "very little, if any, outward signs of racial tensions."[4] Guåhan capitalized on this image to become the island where Japanese tourists could "return with happy memories of their tropical honeymoon and

A Real Tourist Attraction

Guam's Beautiful Girls

A TOURIST ATTRACTION? Of course, of course. Guam's lovely girls, a heady variety of Chamorro, Filipina, Stateside, Chinese, Korean, Micronesian, and a mixture thereof are something else. Whether clad in minis or muumuus, whether serving as waitresses, clerks, or attending school the gals of the island are a sight to behold, beauty personified. They add the proper touch to a charming, friendly, beautiful island in the midst of the Pacific.

Mixed-race women in Guåhan became symbols of the island's multicultural modernity. Courtesy of the *Pacific Daily News*.

vacationers take back pleasant thoughts of their first visit to part of the United States."[5] Guåhan was the United States' newest peaceful multicultural tropical paradise in the Western Pacific.

Yet multiculturalism was the illusive façade that blunted the edge of different forms of US colonialism and militarism in Guåhan and the rest of the Pacific. Throughout the 1970s and into the 1980s, conflicts between Filipinos and CHamorus broke out among teenagers in Guåhan's public schools. Fifteen years after the *Pacific Daily News* lauded the peacefulness of the multicultural society, a CHamoru student from John F. Kennedy High School—coincidentally, the school that sits on a cliff overlooking the island's tourism district—ended up in the hospital with a concussion and "four large head lacerations after he was hit with a lug wrench and a belt buckle." The fight had occurred after he "made ethnic slurs against a Filipino student and another Filipino boy" and the Filipinos fought back. While students like the class president, who was Korean, did not notice racial tensions, one high school student commented after the fight, "'Kids are influenced by adults . . . they (some CHamoru students) know that this is their island and if Filipino boys become outspoken, they feel the Filipino students are trying to take over.'"[6]

If the Organic Act of Guam symbolized the island's racial liberal inclusion into the US nation-state, as chapter 4 shows, the 1960s and 1970s reflect Guåhan's liberal multicultural transformation.[7] In this chapter I historicize the cacophony of perspectives during Guåhan's rapid transformation to reveal the underbelly of liberal multiculturalism and show how it legitimated and reproduced settler militarism in Guåhan. As a militarized territory in the Pacific, Guåhan continued to be a strategic node of the United States' anticommunist mission to assert liberal and capitalist dominance in the Asia-Pacific region.[8] Tourism merely merged with militarism as a cohesive economic development project that depended on Guåhan's territorial—read "colonial"—status. Meanwhile, white US settlers shaped the island's institutions to US standards and culture, using the rhetoric of US multiculturalism as a "feel good" moral and humanitarian premise to assert themselves on island. Filipino immigrants used Guåhan as a US territory to escape martial law in the Philippines and seek economic opportunity, eventually influencing the island's economy and politics. The establishment of a robust and successful Filipino immigrant community helped to prove the "moral good" of multiculturalism and the US immigrant liberal narrative of inclusion.

Amid the transformation of the island, CHamorus struggled to maintain strong connections to their Indigenous language, culture, kinship, and stories of place. CHamorus saw how the practices of liberal multiculturalism, most notably cultural pluralism in public education, relegated them to being just another racialized group in the island's diverse community. CHamorus grew skeptical of this "equalizing" ideology, which ultimately privileged white US settler culture as the norm, and their critiques subsequently revealed how liberal multiculturalism worked in tandem with settler militarism. In its proclivity to embrace all races, liberal multiculturalism solidified Guåhan as a racially "modern" US unincorporated territory, made palatable US military presence, obscured CHamoru Indigeneity to Guåhan, and legitimized the settlement of a racially diverse set of non-CHamoru people in Guåhan. In this chapter I focus on how Filipinos, CHamorus, and white US settlers came to experience and perceive the transformation of Guåhan's social and cultural landscape. In chapter 6, I will demonstrate how contradicting perceptions of Guåhan as a place permeated the political debates around CHamoru self-determination and the possibilities of a renewed political status within the US empire in the 1970s through the 1990s.

The Economic Prospects of a Militarized Paradise

On November 11, 1962, Typhoon Karen slammed Guåhan with 175-miles-per-hour sustained winds and gusts up to 200 miles per hour. The typhoon sat over the island for nearly two days straight. Although fatalities were low, the island's infrastructure, which was built with temporary materials, was blown away, ripped apart, or otherwise unusable. The damage was so severe that President John F. Kennedy immediately sent recovery teams and aid packages to rebuild the island. Just a couple months before, President Kennedy had lifted the seventeen-year-old security clearance requirement that effectively held the island under the US military's control.[9] For the first time since 1938, a person leaving or arriving in Guåhan did not need to request permission from the US military to do so.[10] Guåhan's political and economic leaders sought to take advantage of the confluence of the end of security clearance requirement, the need to rebuild after Typhoon Karen and Typhoon Olive in April 1963, and the influx of millions of dollars in recovery aid to develop a modern Guåhan. Guamanians needed an industry that could diversify the island's economy beyond military spending but was not land intensive like agriculture, given that so much of the land had been taken by the military. Guåhan did have beautiful beaches, a tropical climate, and close proximity to the booming economic markets in Asia. And so tourism became the industry of opportunity.

In 1962 the presidentially appointed CHamoru governor of Guåhan, Manuel Flores, created the Guam Tourist Commission—later the Guam Visitors Bureau—to plan the island's economic development around tourism from Japan and other Asian countries.[11] A 1966 US congressional report on economic development in Guam noted that "a direct potential for Guam exists in the Japanese and Australian tourist markets" and can include travelers from "Hong Kong, Taiwan, Singapore, and Thailand" who could stop over in Guåhan on their way to the US continent.[12] With this market within reach, CHamorus, Filipino immigrants, US settlers, and other foreign investors capitalized on this potential. In 1967 the Guam International Airport opened, sharing the airstrip with the US Naval Air Station at the center of the island in Tiyan.[13] When the first commercial tour group from Japan arrived and stayed at the settler-owned Cliff Hotel, another US-based company, Continental Airlines, announced plans to build a hotel in Tomhom.[14] By 1969 it was reported that fifty-eight thousand tourists had visited Guåhan.[15] The prospects for a tourist economy seemed bright.

The irony was not lost on a few observers that Japan, which had held Guåhan captive for thirty-two months during World War II, was now the prime audience for Guåhan's civilian economic development, both as tourists partaking in getaways and as investors erecting skyrise hotels. At the invitation of Filipino immigrant and entrepreneur Alfred "Al" Ysrael, the Fujita Tourist Enterprise from Japan planned to build its first international hotel in Guåhan.[16] The Fujita Hotel was the first foreign-owned and -operated hotel built in Guåhan, and "paved the way for increased commercial confidence in Guåhan's potential as a world premiere, international visitor destination in the Western Pacific."[17] By 1973, 70 percent of Guåhan's quarter of a million tourists came from Japan, many of them honeymooners looking to stretch their dollars.[18] In Guåhan they could spend time at the beaches, shop tax-free in luxury shops such as Duty Free Shoppers, and take in "the casual atmosphere on the island."[19] If they wanted a historical tour, they could visit the parks that commemorated World War II in Guåhan. It seemed to many that Japanese tourists embodied not only the transformation of the island's economy, but also the shift of Guåhan as an island of war to one of peace. As one writer noted, "the sorrow and animosities of war are all but forgotten today by visitors and islanders alike."[20]

In Guåhan, however, militarism was not history; it was ongoing reality. Together, US militarism and the burgeoning tourism economy fortified the perception that Guåhan needed to remain a US territory for economic stability. Guåhan's economy was envisioned as servicing exports, the military, and tourists, and not necessarily the local community. The 1966 congressional report recommended that Guåhan focus its civilian economic development on (1) exporting goods manufactured in Guåhan, (2) increasing agricultural production to replace imported goods, (3) "tourism based on the United States, Japanese, Australian, and local military markets," (4) "other service exports, mainly based on further supplying the local military market," and (5) providing vocational training in public education.[21] To do their part in the island's economic development, the military would contribute jobs, concessionaires, and other secondary services that "provide grounds for confidence that the military will continue to assist Guåhan's development whenever it can do so without interference to its own missions."[22] In addition, "Guam's economic development will yield benefits to the military also, by making certain goods and services increasingly available, thereby relieving the military of the need to provide them for itself (often at considerable cost)."[23] In other words, settler militarism secured the possibility of a strong civilian economy and, vice versa, a strong civilian economy benefited settler militarism. Guåhan's economy reflects an example of "militourism," a phenomenon theorized by Teresia Teaiwa, Vernadette Gonzalez, and others, where militarism and tourism "illustrate the sometimes brutal and sometimes supple work of US domination . . . they demonstrate the manifold and overlapping circuits and modes of administrative control, ideological frameworks, and territorial occupations that are part of an American project of domination."[24]

Indeed, the US military was in Guåhan not to provide economic development to a US territory, but because of its larger mission to project military power and contain communism in the Asia-Pacific region. Important US military and geopolitical decisions and missions—including the Guam Conference in 1967, the Guam Doctrine in 1969, and Operation Linebacker in 1972, as historicized by scholar Evyn Lê Espiritu Gandhi—demonstrate how Guåhan remained central to the US military's interventions in Southeast Asia.[25] The Guam Conference led by President Lyndon B. Johnson in 1967 signaled an escalation and aggressive approach to Vietnam War policy. In the Guam Doctrine in 1969, President Richard Nixon declared what would become the policy of "Vietnamization," where the United States would retreat from the war and gradually hand over power to South Vietnamese forces. Lastly, in Operation Linebacker II in December 1972, Nixon called for the "Christmas bombing" campaign in Vietnam, using the United States' 165 B-52 long-range bombers stationed at Andersen Air Force Base in Guåhan.[26] The *New York Times* reported that at Naval Air Base Agaña (Hagåtña)—whose runways also served commercial tourism flights from Asia—"flights of three

The Guam Visitors Bureau started to advertise Guåhan as "Where America's Day Begins" to attract tourists from Asia who wanted an American experience close to their home countries. Courtesy of the Guam Visitors Bureau.

[B-52s] took off from here every 30 or 40 minutes, in staggering patterns on round-the-clock missions so that about 72 planes were in the air every 24 hours." The B-52s dropped bombs in what one military official called "the greatest air defense system in history."[27]

Paradoxically, the US military bases in Guåhan that served as launching points for bombs, troops, and supplies headed to battlefields in Vietnam, Cambodia, and Laos were also the stage for US humanitarianism in Operation New Life in April through November 1975.[28] Guåhan became the haven for approximately 110,000 Vietnamese refugees who fled the country after the fall of Saigon and sought safety in the United States.[29] The US military rescued, organized, and processed paperwork for Vietnamese refugees, setting the stage for "narratives of humanitarian rescue" that, Gandhi argues, "provided moral justification for [the] US military outpost in Guåhan."[30] Despite the lack of agency and mutual consent for US military affairs on the island, the people of Guåhan were generally welcoming to Vietnamese refugees, some even volunteering to house refugees if necessary.[31] Many CHamorus and Guåhan residents heralded the generosity of this military mission as evidence of Guåhan's character as a hospitable and welcoming place for all peoples of the world; this was perhaps a form of *inafa'maolek* toward Vietnamese people whose wartime experiences reminded CHamorus of their own experiences during World War II. The humanitarian aid in Operation New Life and CHamoru participation solidified the perception of some observers that Guåhan was a paradisical haven in the context of Cold War violence. In doing so, these humanitarian acts legitimized US settler militarism in Guåhan.

Due to the ongoing wars in Asia, the US military in Guåhan was seen as a steady customer base for a potential tourism industry, creating investment possibilities and job opportunities for settlers and immigrants. White US settlers, some of whom had strong ties to the US military, saw an opportunity to build businesses that catered to the burgeoning tourism industry. World War II veteran Earl Edward Kloppenberg, for instance, capitalized on military personnel and the new market of foreign tourist by establishing Kloppenberg Enterprises in 1947; his businesses included in-flight kitchen caterers, Turtle Tours, Turtle Cove (a beachside campsite), Paradise Pier, River Boat Cruises, and Dolphin Watching Adventures, in addition to other tourist-oriented activities that highlighted Guåhan's tropicality.[32] Likewise, Gordon Mailloux, another World War II veteran and white US settler, took it upon himself to boost Guåhan's tourism economy around the world. Mailloux first arrived in Guåhan as an intelligence officer for the Army. With a love for performance and theater, Mailloux contributed to the entertainment industry, eventually and problematically, legally changing his identity to "Johnny Guam."[33] In 1980 Mailloux used his self-given name to travel the world on a self-funded mission to boost Guåhan as a tourist destination.[34] His efforts landed him a position on the Guam Legislature later in the decade. Kloppenberg's businesses and Mailloux's performance came to represent how white US settlers boosted Guåhan's economy through the promotion of Guåhan as a multicultural paradise.

Meanwhile, Filipino immigrant investors and workers provided capital and labor for the growing tourism industry. For example, Al Ysrael and Manuel Jose became millionaire entrepreneurs by investing in real estate in and beyond Tomhom. For Ysrael, the settler population boom and the rise of tourism created the perfect opportunity to build housing. "In no time," according to a "who's who" book, Ysrael "became Guam's ranking landlord with the highest number of housing rental units, available to local and off-island residents."[35] Introduced in chapter 4, Manuel Jose began his business as a military concessionaire after World War II and expanded his enterprises to include real estate, department stores, movie theaters, and a newspaper, the *Guam Times Weekly*, where he voiced his opinions about Guåhan politics.[36] Likewise, Mark Pangilinan, another postwar Filipino immigrant, invested in the consumer and entertainment industry in Guåhan, providing American fashion, goods, and products that Japanese tourists purchased as *omiyage* (souvenirs). These Filipino immigrants, whose businesses started in the US military buildup in Guåhan, took advantage of the new tourism economy.

Furthermore, Filipino migrant and immigrant blue-collar workers transitioned from working for the US military to the tourism industry. According to *Filipiniana*, a newspaper published by the Filipino Community of Guam, "most of these new 'contractors' were really former individual wage earners employed by the bigger contractor firms before [Typhoon] 'Karen.'"[37] These workers found opportunities with the "multiplication of construction enterprises" and "found a new kind of freedom under the post-Karen era."[38] In addition, Filipinos with US citizenship in Guåhan took advantage of the family reunification clause of the 1965 Immigration Act to petition their relatives for permanent residency. This wave of Filipino immigrants could work in the burgeoning tourism industry as construction or hospitality workers.[39] After his contract with military contractors ended, Vic Oberiano, whom we met in chapter 4, transitioned to working with contractors who built skyrise hotels in the Tomhom area. In addition, Marieta Bello worked her second job as a restaurant hostess in a Tomhom hotel. Filipinos took advantage of the hospitality industry to earn money for remittances or to save up for further migration to the continent. With a diverse set of people building and working in this new economy, many believed that tourism signaled a new prosperous era in Guåhan's history.

The Paradox of a Multicultural Paradise

Both tourism and militarism relied on the perception that Guåhan was and would continue to be a multicultural paradise where investors could commodify the land, culture, and people; and where the US military could continue to obscure its land annexation and legitimize its continued military presence. In the Naval era, as described in chapter 2, the racialization of CHamoru people with *mestisu* heritage made them uncategorizable in US racial logics. Their mixed-race heritage was taken to justify both US military colonialism and CHamoru exclusion from US citizenship. In the era of Cold War multiculturalism, however, mixed race became a political and cultural asset in which Guåhan demonstrated the "beautiful" possibilities of a diverse *American* population.[40] In their tourism edition, the *Pacific Daily News* published a collage of women dressed in pageant attire, Miss Guam Universe sashes, women dressed in traditional Filipiniana, miniskirts, and tiaras. The women were "a real tourist attraction," "Guam's beautiful girls" who "whether clad in minis or mumus, whether serving as waitresses, clerks, or attending school, the gals of the island are a sight to behold, beauty personified."[41] They were, the newspaper added, "the proper touch to the charming, friendly, beautiful island in the midst of the Pacific."[42] Mixed-race women were a beacon of multiculturalism to be desired and consumed. They came to represent a feminized, multiracial Pacific in contrast to the masculine soldiers who transited through Guåhan.[43]

Even if it was a territory, Guåhan was an island in the far reaches of the Pacific where US multiculturalism was "already" realized. In a 1963 article "Guam: Pacific's New Melting Pot," Genevieve Ploke suggested that because there was "no Chamorro of pure blood living," Guåhan was "perhaps the original melting pot, [antedating] the first Irish lad to land in America and the first Oriental to reach Waikiki." The island's mixed-race women symbolized Guåhan's forward-thinking attitudes toward race and proved the island's modernity in age of Cold War liberal multiculturalism. Ploke wrote, "When you look around today, you become aware that intermarriages between island residents and off-islanders have produced a cosmopolitan atmosphere." She emphasized Guåhan's racial mixture in the stories of mixed-race couples finding love in travels "aboard a schooner enroute to the Orient," exiles in Guåhan after national revolutions, and metaphorical "international marital sweepstakes."[44] These stories were bolstered by photos of their daughters, whose names underlined their ethnicities. The daughters included Irene Ploke Sgambelluri, a "German-Polish-Guamanian," and Ellen Won Pat Chargualaf, a "Chinese-Guamanian-Puerto Rican." Nevertheless, Ploke's racial descriptions "whitened" these CHamoru women, especially in how she compared them to Polynesians, and made Guåhan's diverse and mixed-race population palatable to a US audience.[45] Implicitly, mixed-race Guamanian people simultaneously proved the "good" in US liberal multiculturalism and legitimized the United States' hold in Guåhan.

In this same article, Ploke also wrote about Dr. Pedro C. Sanchez, who "lost his bachelorhood in California when he met and married Florida Gailu [*sic*] of American Samoa."[46] Sanchez was the son of Guåhan-born Filipino Simon A. Sanchez and CHamoru Antonia Cruz from the village of Hagåtña. After growing up in Guåhan and surviving World War II, Pedro was one of the first few CHamoru boys who were sent to college in the continental United States, where he earned degrees at St. Thomas University in Minnesota, Columbia University in New York, and Stanford University in California.[47] After receiving his doctorate in education at Stanford, Sanchez served as the director of education in the US Virgin Islands, the director of the Peace Corps in the Philippines, and in various federal jobs across the North American continent. Sanchez returned to Guåhan to serve his island community as an educator as his father Simon A. Sanchez had done since the early 1920s. From 1970 to 1994, he served as president of the University of Guam.[48] A man with mixed-raced heritage and with international and imperial experience, the transformation he saw in Guåhan after the twenty-five years he had been abroad would have been certainly astounding.

Sanchez, however, would not have necessarily agreed with Ploke's uncritical perspective of US multiculturalism in Guåhan. In 1972 Sanchez was brave enough to articulate CHamoru fears of the island's rapid economic, demographic and social transformations at the Third Economic Conference in Guåhan. Sanchez saw that while business leaders, investors, and workers from all over the world capitalized on Guåhan's tourism development, "Guam's bewildered native-residents . . . are caught in the throes of a territory in rapid transition." He observed that Guåhan was a "kind of paradoxical paradise," in which the island was "rich and getting richer in some respects but also poor and getting poorer in other respects." He criticized the "preoccupation" and applause for what he believed was unwieldy, unplanned development that ultimately created a society where there was an "unconscious relegation of the social and other human aspects of development to a lower priority of attention and action." In other words, he argued that the Guåhan community was too focused on economic development, to the point where the island's civilian infrastructure, institutions, and services were falling behind and the people of Guåhan were being negatively affected.[49] He argued that this rapid transformation, especially in regards to land and demographics, threatened the livelihoods of the CHamoru people on their home island.

Sanchez observed that the US military and foreign tourism investors were working hand in hand to continue dispossessing the CHamoru people of their land. Sanchez noted that "the private ownership of land is shifting dangerously into the foreign hands." The onslaught of foreign, US settler, and Filipino immigrant investors who bought land near potential tourist hot spots did not bode well for the CHamorus, who had limited access to land and capital to develop and reap the benefits of the economic boom. The lack of outrage was incredibly ironic to Sanchez because "those who cry to high heaven and do everything within their power to keep Uncle Sam's Forces from acquiring land" were to him "awfully quiet, or even encourag[ing] private landowners to sell their land to foreigners!" Sanchez asked why tourism land dispossession seemed to be more palatable than militarized dispossession, and remarked that Guamanians should be more skeptical about who is taking advantage of Guåhan.[50]

Sanchez also warned about the rapid influx of immigrants, settlers, and foreign investors who threatened CHamoru livelihoods, culture, their ability to determine their future, and even their existence. The island's demographics had changed significantly, to the point where CHamorus had become a minority of the total population. This change was "making many of us jittery," Sanchez said, because "the new and dominant majority will no doubt change the character and lifestyle of the island." In an era of multiculturalism and the embrace of diversity, Sanchez's fears may have been misconstrued as conservative xenophobia, but his fears stemmed from his experiences in other spaces within US empire. He foresaw "clearly a second Hawaii developing here where the unsophisticated, untrained and generally unprepared native islanders would be swamped by the new, aggressive majority and relegated to the lower, economic and social strata of the new Guamanian society as native Hawaiians found themselves in the new Hawaiian society." In other words, this new settler population and settler economy jeopardized CHamoru control of the island's future.[51]

Sanchez also saw how the economic boom disproportionately benefited non-CHamorus. With this economic transformation, Guåhan became not an island of abundance, rich with family relations, traditional CHamoru culture and sovereignty, but instead one of scarcity of opportunities exacerbated by lack of infrastructural development for locals. Sanchez was worried by the rising numbers of CHamorus who had to depend on welfare programs despite the island's dynamic economic growth. He called the situation "downright disgraceful, indeed deplorable." The unbalanced benefits of economic growth, Sanchez noted, "will push ripples of changes, not necessarily for the better, in our people's social and cultural behavior in order to absorb the shock and the frustration." He added, "[We] may be shortchanging ourselves and the future generations for the sake of a handy and expedient way to make money." Sanchez pleaded with the audience, "For God's sake and for our people's sake, I implore you: *don't let this happen to Guam!*"[52]

Sanchez witnessed how tourism, militarism, and capitalism fundamentally changed the way the people of Guåhan related to each other, seeing money and wealth as something to be individually attained and kept, and not necessarily for the benefit of the entire community. As a result, these economic institutions and industries threatened CHamoru control over their economic and social lives, and moreover made CHamorus dependent on outside forces for their livelihoods and well-being. Although he would not use the term, Sanchez was articulating the process of settler militarism that included both the US military and tourism as the co-facilitators of land annexation and immigration that negatively affected the CHamoru people.

Standing before an audience of Guåhan politicians, business leaders, and investors, Sanchez boldly argued for a more concerted effort to manage the island's economic growth so that the people of Guåhan could adequately reap the benefits. Sanchez's solutions, however, challenged the capitalist propensity to see growth as the only symbol of success. Sanchez suggested the island should "slow down, even reduce the rate of growth," in order to ensure that Guåhan did not become "one big moral, spiritual, social, cultural and environmental disaster area!" For Sanchez, there was possibility in envisioning sound economic development rooted in the traditional CHamoru culture and *inafa'maolek*, where "society was at peace with itself and with the island." He said that CHamorus "were not rich, but no one was poor nor neglected either. They cared for one another, and they shared in the work and the wealth of islands." In his perspective, CHamorus had fostered, and could continue to foster, "a society where status and prestige came by sharing each other's wealth—not by accumulating it."[53]

Tourism, militarism, capitalism, and multiculturalism were intertwined in the development of modern *liberal* Guåhan. Sure enough, the Government of Guåhan's Department of Commerce announced that "the decade of the sixties saw Guam emerge from a 'military-base-plus-quonset-huts' economy to a bustling crossroads of the Pacific."[54] By the late 1970s it seemed that Guåhan was not just advertising the promise of a diverse and exotic population, but actually becoming a multicultural island. The Filipino population grew in the postwar military buildup to become 13 percent of the population in 1960 and 21 percent in 1980. The white US settler population saw the most dramatic increase in these years, from 3.5 percent in 1940 to a high of 38.5 percent in 1950 and remaining around 25 percent in 1980.[55] The growth of these settler populations meant that the CHamoru proportion of the island's population decreased. In 1940, before World War II and the postwar transformations, 90.5 percent of the island's population was CHamoru. Between 1950 and 1980, CHamorus were 45 to 50 percent of the island's total population. Essentially, CHamorus became a minority in their home island after just a few intense decades of settler immigration into Guåhan. For CHamorus, this was the paradox of paradise.

Formations of *Ang Mga Kababayan* in Guåhan

Social and cultural transformations also took place in the villages. Urbanization led to villages looking less like Spanish villages with dirt roads and family compounds, and more like US suburban subdivisions built with prefabricated houses and paved streets. Liguan Terrace and Kaiser subdivisions in Dédidu, Barrigada Heights in Barigåda, Latte Heights Estate in Mangilao, and Jonestown in Tamuneng among others came to define what a modern Guåhan village could look like. While CHamorus began to move into these new neighborhoods, the rise in typhoon-proof, concrete housing also meant there was space for a larger immigrant and settler population. As explained in depth in chapters 3 and 4, the US military and federal government created exceptional immigration laws that provided a consistent supply of labor for military installations in Guåhan. These laws and regulations led to the establishment of a large Filipino community that thrived on the island and added to its multicultural population. In these villages post–World War II Filipino immigrants and their families built community and their own enclaves throughout the island.

The Filipino population was substantial enough that a December 1963 issue of *Filipiniana* ran an article titled "How Many Filipinos Are There in

Guam?"[56] The anonymous writer observed that "it looks like every plane flight from Manila nowadays disgorges its own batch of immigrants to Guam, USA."[57] After accounting for the history of the rise of Filipinos living on the island due to the wealth of opportunities in the post–Typhoon Karen boom, the anonymous writer wondered what the boundaries of Filipino identity were in Guåhan:

> From the "Filipinos" naturalized since 1940 when the U.S. nationality act was passed? Since 1920 or 1930, when Filipino labor was allowed free entry into Hawaii? How about the children of Filipino exiles at the turn of the century and of those who, seeking mental refuge from the anguish of colonial domination, chose to live in the island? Or, should we also include the children of those who had come even before the end of Spanish rule over the island? How about the forebears of those who were here during the Manila Acapulco days? During the early Spanish days? Pre Spanish Era? Or, should we move forward to a later date in 1945 when some in the employ of the U.S. armed services remained here? How about the PINOYS who had filtered from the mainland U.S.A.? Where does one find these records now? All of them? How about 1954? 1956? It's a mess![58]

The writer found the boundaries of Filipino identity to be vague, especially considering Guåhan's long historical connection to the Philippines and the number of CHamorus who also had Filipino ancestry. The term "Filipino" could describe a racial or ethnic category, a nationality that denoted Philippine citizenship after Philippine Independence, a Filipino-American immigrant, or a descendent of a person from the Philippines, or in some cases it could be a marker of "outsider" in island society. Waves of Filipino migration also had significance. The "old timers" of the immediate postwar period were different from those who came during the martial law period in the Philippines in the 1970s; and the "old timers" were distinct from the arguably "older" Filipinos who could trace their genealogy to the US Naval era or the Spanish period. The further back in time Filipinos could trace their personal or family origins in Guåhan, the more "local" or assimilated they were perceived to be. And vice versa, the more recent their migration history, the more foreign they were. What is clear is that the Filipino community was diverse, rather than a homogeneous community with a singular history of migration.

Despite how US militarism shaped almost all generations of Filipino migration to Guåhan in the twentieth century, Filipino migrants who arrived from the 1970s waves had significant differences from those who came earlier.[59] For the small group of people I interviewed, the uncertainty of martial law featured prominently in their stories about emigrating from the Philippines and settling in Guåhan. Philippine President Ferdinand Marcos declared martial law in 1972, arguing that "the Philippines was in an emergency state as a result of a burgeoning Communist insurgency, and that he should remain in power," according to historian Mark John Sanchez.[60] Marcos suspended the writ of habeas corpus, imposed curfews, and deployed the Philippine military and the Philippine constabulary. This martial law period also saw the quelling of activists and political opposition through violence, murder, and mass arrests. When martial law began, many Filipinos who had the means and the connections in Guåhan took the opportunity to settle on the island. Even though the 1965 Immigration Act played a part in some of their stories, what was more crucial in their retelling was the uncertainty of martial law in the Philippines and what it meant for their future well-being.

This was the case for Sabina Tamondong and her husband Lawrence. Lawrence had been part of a student committee at the University of the Philippines, and he had to "denounce" student activism to be eligible for the US immigration process.[61] Sabina had taken a second job to supplement her low salary as an educator in the Philippine public school system; at that time, taking a second job was prohibited. Afraid that she and her husband might be found out, they attempted to leave the Philippines, and the United States seemed like the best bet. Sabina started the application process for US immigrant status as a professional; her master's degree from the University of the Philippines made her eligible. She and her husband departed the Philippines, leaving her two children behind, hoping that they could secure jobs and housing before bringing their children to the United States. When they discovered that Guåhan was considered a port of entry for US immigration—meaning that their years on the island would count toward their permanent residency requirement—they opted to settle in Guåhan because it was geographically closer to the Philippines and their children.[62] For them, Guåhan was a US island that could bring them freedom from martial law.

There was also a wave of Filipino immigrants in the 1960s and 1970s who were the children of Filipino workers who had worked in Guåhan in the 1950s. These children grew up in between two worlds: the Philippines and Guåhan. This upbringing shaped how they saw themselves as Filipinos in Guåhan. For some, martial law in the Philippines spurred them to settle more permanently in Guåhan. For instance, Edna Rebanal is the youngest child born to Juan Rebanal from the Bicol region of Philippines. Juan worked as an accountant for Koster and Wythe, a US construction company in Guåhan. He brought his children to Guåhan in 1960, and Edna attended school at Cathedral School in Hagåtña. She remembers being the "exotic" classmate who could only speak Tagalog among a classroom filled with CHamoru students. She learned a little bit of CHamoru from her friends and fondly recalls learning Filipino folk dances, such as the *tinikling* and coconut dances, at the Guam Academy of Music and Arts.

Edna moved back to the Philippines for high school, attending the all-girls school associated with Far Eastern University. She eventually graduated from the University of the Philippines in the early 1970s. During that time she visited Guåhan every summer to stay with family and friends. The early 1970s in the Philippines, Edna remarked, was when "the whole country was on shaky grounds with Marcos as President," and "that was the time when student activism was at its peak." As a student majoring in political science, she was all too aware of the government's disdain for student activists at the University of the Philippines. She remembers watching Jose Maria Sison, a Filipino activist, galvanizing students to criticize the Marcos government. "Martial law was imminent," Rebanal said, "I was still there when he [Marcos] suspended the writ of habeas corpus. I was on campus and of course I was listening to all the student leaders." Observing from across the Philippine Sea, Edna's father "was not happy with the situation." Even if she did not feel personally policed by the government, she realized that "the peace I was looking forward to, or had known in the past, was no longer there." At that point she decided to move back to Guåhan because she "knew what life [there] was like" and believed that there were more opportunities to start a career in Guåhan. "So I had to come back," she said. "It was not a difficult decision after graduating from college."[63] Guåhan was an escape from martial law in the Philippines.

Another Filipino living between two worlds, Ariel Dimalanta, described himself as "manufactured on Guam and assembled in the Philippines." Ariel's father, Antonio Dimalanta, was an architect for the Perez Brothers Company in Guåhan, and brought his older children from the Philippines to Guåhan. Ariel had been born in Guåhan, but he moved back to the Philippines with his family in 1957. In 1970 the family left the Philippines because of their increasing skepticism of political circumstances during Marcos's presidency. In Guåhan, Dimalanta's father worked on major construction projects such as the Hagåtña Cathedral and housing complexes such as Perezville in Guåhan. As an adult, Ariel found a passion for advertising, eventually winning an account to work on the new Guam Reef Hotel's marketing. The Japanese ownership hired Ariel, who then hired his family members—including his siblings, who were an architect, a photographer, and an illustrator. Seeing the success of his small company, Ariel decided to attend the Academy of Arts College in San Francisco in 1978 to learn new and innovative techniques. "It was easy to position yourself and be recognized at that time because the island was small," Ariel said.[64] He continued to work for hotels and the tourism industry, including for Japanese businesses who published Japanese tour and guidebooks for the island. Ariel's artwork helped to promote a multicultural Guåhan in these transformational decades. Both Edna's and Ariel's stories point to the intertwined histories of the Philippines and Guåhan during the Cold War; their multiple migrations and eventual settlement were shaped by the militarism and anticommunism across the Pacific.

With the Filipino Community of Guam (FCG) and the Filipino Ladies Association of Guam (FLAG), new immigrants who arrived in Guåhan in the 1960s and 1970s could find themselves in a well-established Filipino community that supported and welcomed newcomers making their way to a new island, a new country, and a new diasporic community.[65] The FCG was founded in 1954 by Filipino men who worked as contract and noncontract workers for the US military buildup in the immediate post–World War II era.[66] The founding members felt they had "a deep sense of duty" to bring Filipinos and Americans (and presumably Guamanians) together in Guåhan.[67] This mission toward responsible civic engagement and contributions to Guåhan society continued into the 1960s and 1970s. While the early leadership consisted of middle-class Filipino workers, its leadership evolved to include some of the wealthiest Filipino men living in Guåhan, including Mark V. Pangelinan and Manuel Jose. FLAG was the sister association of the FCG and was founded in 1962 by the wives of the Filipino men who made names for themselves in the booming years of Guåhan's economic growth. FLAG was a women's civic and cultural organization dedicated to fostering mutual relations between Filipinos and the people of Guåhan through philanthropy, volunteer work, and cultural events.[68]

The FCG sponsored the construction of pavilions at Paseo Park in Hagåtña and the Ipao Beach Park in Tomhom, and it erected monuments throughout the island to historical figures, including Filipino revolutionary Apolinario Mabini, President John F. Kennedy, George Washington, and the first CHamoru archbishop Felixberto Camacho Flores—a son of Leon Flores, a Filipino revolutionary exile described in chapters 1 and 2. The FCG restored historic buildings, including Spanish-era structures, and sponsored the construction of public spaces such as tennis courts and parks.[69] It also donated hemodialysis machines to the Guam Memorial Hospital and

Members of the Filipino Ladies Association of Guam meet with Dr. Pedro Sanchez of the University of Guam to discuss scholarships for students. Courtesy of the *Pacific Daily News*.

provided scholarships for students at the University of Guam. Through these acts under the FCG, Filipinos wanted to "pursue that noble task of helping make Guam progressive, and to offer gratitude to an island that has been a generous home to many of them."[70] Like the FGC, FLAG donated funds and materials to aid many organizations, events, and monuments, including medical equipment to Guam Memorial Hospital and typhoon-relief programs in the Philippines. Adding to the narrative that "Filipinos built Guam" as explored in chapter 3, the FCG and FLAG believed that their civic contributions to Guåhan helped modernize the island and thus justified their belief that Guåhan was "home."

The FCG eventually became the large umbrella organization for Filipino organizations on the island (FLAG did not participate in FCG), in which dozens of province-based, region-based, and even university-based organizations became the foundation for Filipino social life in Guåhan. They included groups such as the Samareños Association, the Batangas Association, the

Bicol Club of Guam, the Cavite Association of Guam, the Visayan Association of Guam, the Ilocano Association of Guam, the Aklan Association of Guam, the Circulo Pampagueño, the Alumni of University of the Philippines, among so many others.[71] These organizations celebrated the specificity of each region or institution, highlighting the diversity of the Philippines even in diaspora.[72] Filipinos throughout the island gathered together in events on the weeknights and weekends, for prayer groups, big religious holidays, pageants, civic organization events, and especially for the annual Philippine Independence Ball hosted by the FCG.

Each organization held monthly meetings and hosted one or two large annual events that celebrated a significant holiday specific to their province, town, or barangay in the Philippines. For instance, the Aklan Association of Guam, founded in 1965 by families from Panay Island who were employed as contract workers for the US Naval Station and at Camp Roxas, held their annual Ati-Atihan Festival starting in the mid-1970s. Widely celebrated in Iloilo Province, the festival honored the feast of Santo Niño. According to Patrick Luces—a descendent of Johnny and Aida Luces of the Iloilo Province in the Philippines and Hågat in Guåhan, the members of the Aklan Association practiced their drum patterns every Sunday for weeks before the festival and spent time making costumes that depicted "native" Ilonggo tribes customary among the celebrations in the Philippines.[73] Annual traditions such as the Ati-Atihan Festival, festivals for patron saints, and even Philippine Independence provided opportunities for the Filipino community to socialize and form bonds across generations in Guåhan. These groups fostered a sense of cultural continuity of their barangays and provinces in the Philippines through the forging of community in diaspora in Guåhan.

From Yigu, to Dédidu, to Tamuneng, to Sånta Rita and Hågat, Filipinos throughout the island were building an alternative social landscape of the island, in which their relations with other Filipino groups and families mapped their knowledge of Guåhan. Regional and provincial identities were preserved and passed down through formal organizations and especially in family groups who formed intergenerational friendships.[74] Arriving in Guåhan in the 1950s, Nerissa Bretania Underwood recalls how her family, the Bretanias, were close friends with the Luces, Delfin, Salas, and Malilay families.[75] Their friendships were fostered around their activities with the Camp Roxas Church. They were also forged on the mahjong tables that started early Saturday afternoons, played through the night and early morning hours before church services on Sunday morning, only to start yet again after church ended. Some Filipino families drove down to Hågat from the central village of Tamuneng to join them on the weekends. In addition, there were the families who lived in the R. R. Cruz subdivision, who were different from the family group who lived in the Bordallo subdivision, from those who lived in Hågat. The Oberiano family, which I am from, lived in the Bordallo subdivision, and were lifelong friends with the Sutacio, the Sotomil, and Doranilla families.[76] In other words, Filipinos saw Guåhan in relation to other Filipino groups and to US citizenship, not necessarily in relation to CHamorus. Guåhan became another space for Filipino identity formation in diaspora.

For Filipino immigrants to Guåhan in the 1960s through the 1980s, the formation of a Filipino identity beyond the Philippine archipelago was just as pertinent as finding a home and settling in Guåhan. The organizations and informal family groups preserved regional identities, rather than emphasizing a homogeneous Filipino identity among immigrants in Guåhan. This was especially true of the first few generations of postwar Filipino immigrants, who might have understood themselves, not in relation to Manila and the independent Philippine nation state, but in relation to their province. This identity was most evident in language politics. Originally from Iloilo Province, Nerissa Bretania Underwood recalled that her mother wanted her children to "maintain our Ilonggo language because she said when we did go back to visit, she did not want our cousins to be alienated from us, or us alienated from them."[77] For the Bretania family, language was central to their Ilonggo identity, and had to be preserved even in their migration to the United States.

Language politics also became a shorthand for Filipino class dynamics. Growing up in an Ilokano household in Barigåda, Marlyn Oberiano remembers how her mother Leonor Quimino Bello felt much more comfortable speaking to other Filipinos in English rather than Tagalog. Although some Filipinos thought she was "putting on airs" by displaying knowledge of the English language, Leonor was more proficient in English than Tagalog because of her elementary education in the rural province of Ilocos Sur during the US colonial period in the Philippines. Tagalog, which was the language of the provinces in and around Metro Manila and the basis for the country's postindependence national language, was a foreign language to Leonor. Filipinos who did not speak Tagalog were considered "provincial" with all the adjective's connotations. At the same time, however, Leonor's other daughter and Marlyn's sister, Eliza, spent time with her Filipino classmates at George Washington High School and learned Tagalog through conversations with them.[78]

The diversity of the Filipino community also included class distinctions. Organizations such as the FCG and FLAG were places where the Filipino elite mobilized other classes of Filipinos to carry out projects that were meaningful to them. For some Filipino women who participated in FLAG, the organization presented an opportunity to show wealth, elite connection, and proximity to both US and Metro Manila culture. Sabina Tamondong recalls that the elite ladies of the 1960s and 1970s, such as Edwina Jose—wife of real estate mogul Manuel Jose—called for sponsorships from banks, big businesses, and commerce, while the "working members" of the organization carried out the day-to-day activities of the organization, such as dropping off solicitation letters and picking up prizes and supplies. In addition, FLAG had strict regulations for formal gatherings, such as its annual Santa Cruzan celebration in which members were required to wear a Filipiniana mestiza dress, a traditional dress of the Philippines, crafted from rare materials such as piña thread, fine fabrics, and jeweled adornments imported from the Philippines.[79] According to Sabina, the Filipiniana mestiza dress distinguished the rich from the working-class poor, as the quality of the materials signified wealth. "They laughed at me during the time I joined," Tamondong recalled. "I had only two mestiza, the green and the brown." When the others pointed out that they recognized her dress from a previous event, Tamondong responded with a smile, "Oh no, it's a different shade."[80] Whatever the case may be, Filipiniana dresses for women and barong Tagalogs for men at large Filipino gatherings such as Santa Cruzan and the Philippine Independence Ball came to symbolize a cohesive Filipino identity in Guåhan.

The tensions around wealth and social mobility reflected the diverse class and occupational backgrounds of Guåhan's Filipino community. Whereas post-1965 Filipino migration to the continental United States skewed toward the educated classes—doctors, nurses, and teachers—who dominated the image of a middle-class Filipino America, Guåhan was different. Filipino labor migration to Guåhan in the late 1940s and 1950s and the use of family reunification immigration provisions meant that the newer waves of Filipino immigrants were more diverse in occupation and socioeconomic standing than their continental counterparts. As estimated by a former FCG president, Nita Baldovino, who arrived in Guåhan in 1972 as a young bride to an H-2 worker, "one percent of the thirty-three percent [of Guåhan's Filipino population] came rich. Most came as workers."[81] As an example, Nita remarked that five hours after her naturalization ceremony, she went straight to the immigration office to petition for her parents, who had received their US citizenship five years later. So, there were the upper-class millionaires who had business conglomerates; there were the professionals such as doctors and lawyers; there were the blue-collar workers who were electricians, carpenters, construction workers; and there were unskilled workers.

Despite the diversity in provincial identity and class background, the Filipino community became a cohesive and influential constituency in Guåhan politics. As a large voting bloc, Filipinos elected political candidates to represent the Filipino community in the Guam Legislature. In 1966 Oscar Delfin was the first Filipino immigrant to successfully run for the Guam Legislature. Nevertheless, it was still relatively difficult for Filipinos to be elected. Joe Dizon, a professor at the University of Guam, published a small survey of the 1970 Guåhan election showing that the rise of Filipino candidates in the 1970 election was spurred on by the increasing tensions around the anti-immigrant platforms of some electoral candidates. Six Filipino candidates made it past the primary elections for the Guam Legislature, but none of them won a seat. Ultimately, he argued, "the Filipino ethnic vote, which numbers 4,000 proves most inadequate by itself as a source of political strength." To ensure themselves a seat, they also "must seek wider support from the Guamanian and stateside voters," moving perhaps to "minimize ethnic origins" and speak the CHamoru language.[82] So although Filipinos came to represent a higher percentage of the island's population, their participation in the legislative process remained at the level of constituent and voter rather than leadership.

Nonetheless, because of this voting bloc, CHamorus and white US settlers began to see immigrants from the Philippines as a homogeneous "Filipino" community. Later in the 1970s, CHamoru politicians canvased for the Filipino vote in local elections and even played up their Filipino heritage from past generations.[83] For instance, in the 1978 gubernatorial election, Governor Ricardo Bordallo made a circuit of the induction ceremonies for Filipino regional organizations. Bordallo spoke at the FCG induction ceremony, and instead of offering a few short remarks on the accomplishments of the organization, he used the opportunity to talk about the successes of his own administration and his platform for the upcoming election. "My administration has endeavored to ensure that 1978 will be the beginning of a new era of balanced growth and prosperity for all," he announced.[84] To emphasize that his administration was meant for all people, not just CHamorus, he closed his speech by referring to his Filipino audience as his "fellow Guamanians," and "*Manetluhu* [*sic*]—*mgo* [*sic*] *kaibigan* at *kababayan*," ensuring that they understood that he believed that Filipinos were an integral part of the Guåhan community.[85] He shared his optimism that with Filipino "cooperation and support, our economy will continue to improve so that our children can live and work in a community with all the amenities and opportunities that we came to find on this promised land of Guam."[86] By including Filipinos in the island's future by using the inclusive "we" and appealing to notions of family, Bordallo sought to win the vote of the Filipino community.

For white US settlers, Filipinos exemplified the US immigrant narrative, a racial liberal narrative in which foreign people could become "included" into the nation-state through hard work, determination, and participation in civic activities. Filipinos were the "model minorities" that white US settlers touted as proof that Guåhan was a modern example of US liberal multiculturalism. By conditioning the acceptance of Filipinos in US society on their work for settler colonial institutions such as the military and tourism, white US settlers revealed the how liberal multiculturalism justified and perpetuated US settler militarism in Guåhan. For instance, the longtime editor of the *Pacific Daily News*, Joseph C. Murphy, wrote in a daily editorial in January 1976 about the "violent confrontations between Guamanians and Filipinos" and his belief that there was "some resentment by Guamanians for the rapid upward movement of the Filipino community." Challenging those who wanted to slow migration from the Philippines, Murphy believed that Filipinos were assets in Guåhan's long-term economic development. He wrote, "The Filipinos, through construction, through business, through the professions and through their rich cultural heritage have contributed a great deal to Guam." Citing the work of Lawrence Lawcock, another white US settler and a professor from the University of Guam, Murphy insisted that "the number of businessmen and professionals among the post–World War II immigrants who have achieved economic success provides an object lesson for newcomers in what good luck, perseverance or education can accomplish." Furthermore, Murphy believed that education about the Filipino immigrant experience in Guåhan, as opposed to CHamoru history, could settle CHamoru-Filipino tensions.[87] In emphasizing a narrative of immigrant inclusion over CHamoru history, Murphy implied that CHamorus were unnecessarily causing racial tensions in an otherwise idyllic, US multicultural island.

Some CHamoru politicians saw the rise of the Filipino community as a significant problem.[88] During the 1969 gubernatorial campaign, Joaquin C. Arriola ran on a platform of local control over immigration. In a thinly veiled criticism of the Filipino immigrant community in Guåhan, he said that "for every alien entering Guam there would be one less job, one less desk for American students, one less hospital bed, one less lot and house, and that much less in funds for a needy American family."[89] Arriola believed that greater local control over immigration policy—and, notably, the removal of

Guåhan as a port of entry for immigration processes—would curtail the immigrant population, which he saw was "mooching off" of the island's economic growth and limited resources. Many Filipinos, however, believed that Arriola had de-racialized his assertion by using "American" to refer to CHamorus and classified all Filipinos as "aliens." They believed that Arriola viewed Filipino immigrants as a monolithic group, stereotyping them as "cheap labor" and perpetually foreign. A Filipino commented on Arriola's proposed policies, "He's cutting his own throat. This guy is in trouble for belittling the force of the Filipinos on Guam."[90] Other anonymous Filipinos doubled down on their US citizenship, citing their contributions to the economic development of Guåhan, including paying taxes. With outright anti-immigrant sentiment as headline news in a gubernatorial election, Filipino-CHamoru relations were at an all-time low.

In the 1960s and 1970s, the Filipino community in Guåhan grew in population and in regional, occupational, socioeconomic, and political diversity. Those on the outside of the Filipino community, however, perceived them as a monolithic group that nonetheless had the capacity to influence the island's economic and political future. For Filipinos, the rhetoric of multiculturalism and the narrative of the "nation of immigrants" legitimized their presence and allowed them to thrive as US citizens in Guåhan. This narrative permeated other institutions in Guåhan, and many CHamorus feared that they were losing control over their island's future. If militarism and tourism became the political and economic settler institutions for Cold War Guåhan, then Filipinos were the demographic shift that threatened CHamoru influence by virtue of their sheer numbers.

Reclaiming *I ManCHamoru* in an American Classroom

While many CHamorus felt that they could simultaneously be CHamoru and American, embodied by the "Guamanian" identity, the demographic and economic transformations of the 1960s and 1970s disoriented CHamorus who were caught in the windstorm of change. CHamoru feminist scholar Laura Souder observed that the island's transformations created a sense of confusion among CHamorus regarding how to merge CHamoru culture with this new Americanized, multicultural, and globalized culture. In a 1977 article titled "Sifting Through Clues in Search of Identity," Souder detailed the real manifestations of Pedro Sanchez's paradox of paradise.[91] With rapid economic growth caused by tourism, Souder wrote, CHamorus were forced to rely on imports and migrant labor, which "leaves a bitter taste," as "the local person on the one hand, enjoys the comforts of change, but on the other hand, must depend on someone else to make it possible."[92] This sentiment was shared by Dr. Katherine B. Aguon, president of Department of CHamoru Affairs, who noted how the cultural transformation caused CHamoru youth, in particular, to feel insecure in their own island. She wrote that "they neither accept their heritage as being valuable nor as being truly their own. . . . The native islander is sinking slowly into a new world which has no meaning or room for him."[93] Despite US citizenship, the island's economic growth, and indeed the façade of peaceful multiculturalism, CHamorus no longer felt in control of their own destiny; and this discomfort trickled into other areas of their lives. This feeling of inadequacy, Souder observed, created "a growing resentment" between CHamorus, US settlers, Filipinos, and other Asians.[94]

Indeed, interracial tensions played out in Guåhan's public schools. Typhoon Karen, Typhoon Olive, and the subsequent federal rehabilitation funding allowed for the construction of multiple permanent concrete structures that housed the island's public school system. In the 1960s and 1970s, the public school system grew rapidly as the influx of Filipino immigrants and growth of the CHamoru population necessitated the opening of several elementary schools, junior high schools, and high schools throughout the island. At this time the children of military personnel as well as students from other islands in the Trust Territories of the Pacific Islands attended Guåhan's public schools, creating a diverse student population where Pacific Islanders, Asian, white, and Black students came together every day of the school year. Both local and federal government sources instituted teacher training programs as well as education administration programs at the College of Guam that could develop a strong local teacher base for the island. Other teachers, white US settlers and Filipinos alike, were recruited for the remaining open teaching positions. The curriculum broadly conformed to that of a "typical American system," which by the early 1960s highly prioritized English language for bilingual students.[95]

Due to the de facto segregation between CHamorus, Filipinos, white US settlers, and US military dependents in the villages of island, the public school became the multicultural arena where conflicts over Guåhan were fought out. Ariel Dimalanta remembers that when he returned to Guåhan in 1970 after living in the Philippines, he "saw violence. I saw kids fighting. I saw Filipinos cussing. Then I saw Chamorros cussing. Then that's when I learn that wow there is some racial clashes here."[96] Dimalanta did not quite feel this animosity in his younger years living on the island in the 1960s. Furthermore, the *Pacific Daily News* reported a slew of "race riots," including one at Dededo

Junior High School, in a village with a high proportion of Filipino students, where "a man brandishing a weapon outside its fence caused education officials to close the school at noon . . . and send the students home."[97] With rumors of an impending race riot between Filipinos and CHamorus due to an incident in which a student "had pushed one of them down during a break between classes," the assistant commissioner of Dédidu, Popoy Zamora, reported that "'a lot of the Filipino students didn't go to school (Friday) because of the bad rumors.'"[98] Zamora elaborated that the ethnic tensions were on the rise, including another instance where "11 Filipino girls were chased from the school grounds by a group of Guamanians."[99] After being chased, the Filipino girls had taken refuge in a house, and the CHamoru students tore down the screen door and throw rocks at the girls. The incident at Dededo Junior High School was not the only occasion that made the news, and it is likely that many racial tensions and incidents did not make the news at all.

The tensions between CHamorus and Filipinos also affected the teachers. As a teacher in the public school system, Sabina Tamondong experienced her fair share of ethnic aggressions from teachers from the US continent and from CHamoru students. As a teacher with a master's degree from the University of the Philippines, a US accredited institution, Sabina started as one of the highest-paid teachers at John F. Kennedy High School in Tomhom. Because of her credentials, she was able to choose the upper-level classes that other teachers wanted to teach, and she often felt that people underestimated her abilities because she was Filipino. Additionally, her students often criticized her accent. She relayed that the antagonism manifested outwardly in students saying "'go back to the Philippines,' right in my face." They also made fun of her accent saying, "'Mrs. Tamondong, that's not how you say it. Go teach in the Philippines.'" These incidents often shook her to her core; but realizing that she needed her job to support her two kids in the Philippines, she said to herself, "I'm going to swallow all those things. I'm going to prove you." She smiled, gritted her teeth, and continued teaching at JFK out of sheer will to provide for her children back in the Philippines.[100]

Meanwhile, CHamoru education leaders strongly believed that the careful curation of a public school curriculum was vital to the future of the CHamoru people. Souder argued that the identity crisis of the CHamoru people—she referred to them as "Guamanian" in this article—lay in "the existence of conflicting values created by a new education system and rapid economic development."[101] She believed the new curriculum deemphasized traditional CHamoru culture and customs based on family obligations and instead promoted a certain type of US experience based on liberal individualism and secularism. More insidiously, Samuel Betances, who had a doctorate in education and was Souder's husband, noted that US settlers and military families—he labeled them "Americans" in this article—molded the civilian educational system to match the desires of the US military. This desire for an Americanized education ran counter to what CHamoru teachers wanted for the island, which was an education rooted in the CHamoru culture and the social realities of the island. Betances asked rhetorically, "Should the Americans who have invaded Guam also control the institutions of Guam and insist that the Chamorro, in their homeland, be schooled to live as though they were going to live their lives in US suburbs they will never see, let alone inhabit? How practical is a white middle-class education for the brown Chamorro people of Guam?"[102] In other words, both Souder and Betances saw the school system in Guåhan as a settler military institution that served US settler and military dependents and assimilated CHamoru people into US culture.[103]

Not wanting to succumb to the negative effects of the island's transformation, Souder and Aguon, among many others, sought to recenter CHamoru identity, culture, and language in school curriculums to give students "a sense of belonging and identity."[104] CHamoru language experts Bernadita Dungca Camacho and Clotilde Gould, for instance, encouraged CHamoru youth to speak CHamoru by supporting bilingual education. Gould wrote that bilingual education was more than syntax and grammar, and that it had "to do with redesigning the child's entire outlook on life without destroying family ties, cultural identity, self-confidence or pride."[105] She saw how language was crucial for CHamoru students' identity formation and could ground them in the evolving island around them. In addition, a Guåhan-based education would incorporate CHamoru history and culture and teach students about Guåhan's environment in science classes. In other words, students would learn about how to be successful in Guåhan, rather than learn about snow and autumn, trains, "fireplace or a furnace," as Gould mentioned in her article, which were impositions of an educational system based on the continental United States.

To teach the CHamoru language and culture in Guåhan's public schools, CHamoru teachers applied for and received federal funding geared toward multiculturism and cultural pluralism in the US education system. Influenced by racial liberalism premised on the assumption that people of all races could be incorporated into the US nation-state, federally funded cultural pluralism programs in the 1970s sought to rectify racial and ethnic inequalities and interpersonal tensions by uplifting and embracing minority cultures within the curriculum.[106] In this cultural pluralism zeitgeist, social studies teachers and their students celebrated CHamoru identity by organizing the first "Chamorro Week" at George Washington High School in 1974 "to acknowledge the achievements of the Chamorro people and to foster a healthy interest in the language, customs, culture and history of Guam."[107] The week's festivities included the construction of a "Chamorro Village in the school's east courtyard," a theatrical production of "Juan Mala," a reenactment of a Spanish-CHamoru battle by the ROTC military science students, as well as various displays, entertainment, traditional activities such as weaving, as well as academic panels. The activities focused on the experiences and histories of Guåhan, rather than US presidents, US cultural activities around holidays, and other non-CHamoru traditions. The first Chamorro Week at George Washington was successful and became a hallmark for the island's schools for generations.

Ironically, Chamorro Week elicited much criticism from the non-CHamoru population in Guåhan. Even though "Chamorro week was really insignificant, without any real impact on the cultural continuity of the Chamorro people," Robert Underwood recalled, "the opponents of the week-long activity argued that since there was not going to be a Filipino week or a Micronesian week, that in the name of cultural equality, we shouldn't have Chamorro week." In an exercise of CHamoru culture, CHamorus were pitted against all other non-CHamoru groups on island. As one of the Chamorro teachers who organized the festivities, Underwood and other CHamoru educators fought back, arguing that schools were effective places for CHamoru elders to instill pride in CHamoru identity for the largest proportion of the island's population. Underwood felt such relegation of CHamoru culture as one of many "other" nonwhite cultures "was an injustice in the name of equality."[108] Thus, the use of cultural pluralism and multiculturalism in education inadvertently rendered CHamoru people—the Indigenous people of the island—into just another minoritized group.

The backlash against Chamorro Week proved to CHamoru educators that cultural pluralism and liberal multiculturalism continued to emphasize white US settler culture as the default culture even if it acknowledged the existence of other cultures. Even though Guåhan was CHamoru land and the plurality of the population was CHamoru, Aguon argued that in a cultural pluralism curriculum, "the island's history, language and traditions are 'add-ons' to an existing curriculum." She warned that it is in "this cultural pluralist rhetoric that the Pacific Islander in his homeland may be trapped." Instead, Aguon believed that CHamoru culture "should be the fundamental core to which

That Was A Chamorro Week That Was

Lifestyle

It was a week for reviving some traditional island pastimes: Above, stick fighting by Joe Chargualaf and Pete Perez at George Washington High School: At left, John Taitano and Anthony Rojas, fourth-grade students at Ordot-Chalan Pago Elementary, take a carabao ride. Below, San Miguel Elementary students take instruction in palm weaving from that school's Chamorro Week chairman, Felixberto Dungca.

It was a week for cultural exhibits. Cathedral Grade School in Agana displayed the above machete, made in 1891. Below, another exhibit shows, clockwise from left, an old metal pot, woven sleeping mats, bamboo containers for collecting tuba, a shrimp trap and a wooden coconut grater.

It was a week for Chamorritas, including Inarajan Junior High's Miss Chamorrita for 1975, Shirley Flores, shown as she was presented with a trophy yesterday afternoon by her parents, Mr. and Mrs. Vicente Flores of Inarajan. At GW, the Miss Chamorrita title went to Barbara Leonor, who represented the Filipino Students Association.

By 1975, schools on the island held a "Chamorro Week" to celebrate CHamoru culture, language, and history. Courtesy of the *Pacific Daily News*.

other areas of study are subsequently added. The people of Guam (those who live here as well as Chamorros) must be obliged to know Guam first before branching out to the world."[109]

These experiences of cultural pluralism in education evolved into a larger critique of US multiculturalism in Guåhan. Significantly, Robert Underwood published "Chamorro Challenge to Statesiders"—a scathing critique against white US settlers who lived in Guåhan. Tracing the history of cultural pluralism as a panacea to historical racial inequalities and exclusions in the continental United States, he challenged the assumption that multiculturalism and cultural pluralism were beneficial for Guåhan, an island in empire where the "dominant" Indigenous CHamoru culture was at danger of extinction. For Underwood, the Guåhan public school system was just one arena where white US settlers asserted themselves too confidently, saw Guåhan as solely as US territory, and disavowed their immigrant status in a CHamoru island with an Indigenous culture and society. Underwood wrote, "By the statesider's refusal to admit that he is an immigrant, he senses no special need to exert himself to become part of Chamorro society or even to understand it." Rather, Underwood wrote, the US settler "demands that island institutions be basically Americanized so he has equal access to them. In short, his demand for equality is a demand for institutions on his terms."[110] By suggesting that "equality" was underhanded rhetoric for white US settlers to impose their beliefs in Guåhan society, Underwood identified cultural pluralism, multiculturalism, and indeed racial liberalism as colonial tools that swept over the Indigenous relationship that CHamorus had to Guåhan. In other words, he saw that multiculturalism and white supremacy were not contradictory, but instead were, as scholar Dean Saranillio writes, "working in concert" to upend CHamoru people.[111]

Though not using the phrase at the time, Underwood articulated the dynamic process of settler militarism in which the term "settler" described not only the people who moved into a territory, but also the power to shape and mold institutions to a certain ideology—in this case liberal multiculturalism, which effectively dispossessed CHamorus of political and social power. Underwood underscored how white US settlers, many of whom had links to the military, "can be in virtual control of institutions, not because they are in positions of command, but because they set up the guidelines under which the system operates. They have instant access to its operations, can understand it fully to their benefit at any given moment. They benefit from the fact that the system exists in terms they understand, whether they choose to exploit it or not."[112] Even though white US settlers were a minority population in Guåhan,

Underwood argued, the Americanized system in Guåhan allowed them to take full advantage of the political, social, economic, news, and even educational institutions on the island. As a result, white US settler perspectives of Guåhan's politics and society heavily influenced the general population, often at the expense of the CHamoru people. He asked his readers, "Please never forget that Chamorros exist. They are everywhere. . . . Let us reaffirm Chamorro existence to counter the genocidal rumor that Chamorros no longer exist."[113] Forty-five years later, in an interview with Edward "Pulan" Leon Guerrero, Underwood admitted that his article "Chamorro Challenge to Statesiders" was his first articulation of "settler colonialism."[114] By linking liberal multiculturalism to settler militarism, Underwood underscored their co-constitutive power in maintaining and obscuring Guåhan's status as a US colony.

Even as the island became touted as a multicultural tourists' paradise in Tomhom, Filipino-CHamoru relations in Guåhan seemed to be getting worse in local villages during the 1970s. The tensions in schools warranted attention from public officials as well as concerned parents who wanted to ensure their children's safety. Eventually the racial and ethnic tensions in schools generated academic studies from the University of Guam and other researchers. This included Betances, who was hired by the College of Education at the University of Guam to create a series of "packets" that focused on cross-cultural education for Guåhan's public schools. His experiences revealed to him that even though cross-cultural education lauded cultural diversity, it did so at the expense of CHamoru people, whose connection to the land gave them "the most legitimate claim to Guam."[115] For Betances, cross-cultural education was not a panacea precisely because the tensions in schools were caused by US control over the island's politics and economy. He wrote, "Cross-cultural education cannot control US military policies or provide the Legislature with control of immigration policy."[116] In other words, Betances pointed to US colonialism as the root of the racial problems in school. Indeed, at that very moment the island's leaders attempted to reform the island's colonial status with the Guam Constitution Movement of the 1970s, explained further in chapter 6.

The CHamoru critique of cultural pluralism in the schools reflects how CHamorus responded to the economic and social transformations of the island. Many CHamorus feared that the available avenues for transmitting cultural knowledge to the next generation were being sidelined by white US settlers and immigrants who touted ideals of US liberal multiculturalism to impose a white settler culture. Furthermore, white US settlers heralded

Filipinos as exceptional students in contrast to CHamoru youth because they adapted well to Americanized education and conformed to the immigrant narrative of the United States. So, multiculturalism not only relegated the CHamoru people to a minority group—which they were not in Guåhan—but promoted Americanization and English as the baseline characteristics and educational goal for a successful young generation in Guåhan.[117]

The Recalibration of Race

In the 1960s, Filipino entrepreneur Manuel Jose established his own newspaper, the *Guam Times Weekly*, to compete against the predominantly white US settler-dominated *Pacific Daily News*. The newspaper was Jose's soapbox, where he commented on all aspects of the island's politics—gubernatorial races, immigration and labor laws, debates over Guåhan's territorial status, and so on. While his pieces in the *Guam Times Weekly* showed his support for Guåhan's political and economic development since the 1960s, Jose's reiteration of the theme that Guåhan was a "melting pot" frustrated CHamorus. In particular Jose depicted himself as a political cartoon character named "Taotao Guam," who was "native," bare-chested, and dressed in a grass skirt and interacted with other Westernized figures in suits and ties. Through "Taotao Guam," Jose criticized both US colonial policy and CHamoru leaders for ineffectiveness in business and politics. Jose's political cartoon character "Taotao Guam" demonstrated a Guamanian identity that was not necessarily tied to CHamoru heritage, but instead was multicultural and included Filipino perspectives.[118]

Jose was not afraid to voice his skepticism of CHamoru people's moves toward identifying as "Indigenous."[119] A few CHamorus students expressed their discontent by pointing out Jose's foreignness to Guåhan in a letter to the editor of the *Pacific Daily News*: "Since when do outsiders and non-CHamorus like yourself [Jose] have the right to define and to decide our identity as Chamorros and our rights to our island?"[120] They continued, "If you wish to denounce your Filipino heritage and call yourself Guamanian, feel free. However, in our definition you will always be a Tagalo, just like all the indigenous people of Guam and the Northern Marianas will always be Chamorro."[121] By calling Jose a "Tagalo," a derogatory term launched at Filipinos, the CHamoru students labeled Jose as perpetually foreign to Guåhan despite his contributions to the island.

As we have seen, then, liberal multiculturalism did not critique race as a category of difference arranged in a hierarchy of power. Instead it *emphasized* racial distinctions, which became a heuristic to define and divide CHamorus and Filipinos from each other. Furthermore, multiculturalism recalibrated colonial exclusionary racial logics into an apolitical, abstracted, yet celebrated way of marking difference, all the while obscuring the different historical legacies and material consequences of US colonialism. As a result, multiculturalism redirected the onus of the problem of interracial conflict to CHamorus and Filipinos themselves, pathologizing the tensions between them as flaws that could only be rectified through a better implementation and practice of US ideals and culture. Indeed, white US settlers continued to use race to differentiate good "Guamanians" from bad ones, demonstrating the enduringness of white supremacy within liberal multiculturalism itself.[122] Those who fulfilled the hardworking immigrant narrative (even if they were CHamoru) were heralded as the purveyors of the "good" of US liberalism. In this logic, CHamorus needed to learn from Filipinos, who came to represent the "ideal" racialized US citizen in Guåhan. CHamorus like Sanchez, Underwood, Aguon, and Souder observed that this rhetoric of racial equality rendered invisible the settler military logics that had colonized CHamorus. Thus, rather than creating cultural appreciation between CHamorus and Filipinos, liberal multiculturalism limited the possibilities for meaningful relations between the two communities that could be geared toward anticolonial ends. With the rise of multiculturalism, the opening of Guåhan to the rest of the world, the influx of immigrants from Asia, and the continued US military presence, Guåhan's culture shifted further away from being an island society based on CHamoru ethos of *inafa'maolek*—"making good"—into a culture that was a struggling unincorporated territory, the island paradise "Where America's Day Begins."

CHAPTER SIX

Commonwealth Now!

Envisioning Indigenous CHamoru Self-Determination in a Multicultural Guåhan

Responding to the whirlwind of the 1960s and 1970s in Guåhan and across the Pacific, the CHamoru people of Guåhan embarked on a movement to renegotiate the island's colonial status in the US empire. In the 1980s and into the 1990s, CHamoru political leaders, several Guåhan governors, senators from the Guam Legislature, and US congressional representatives were consumed by the Guam Commonwealth Movement. The movement was an island-wide endeavor that operated on multiple scales—the village community, the Government of Guam (GovGuam), within the halls of US Congress, and at the United Nations.[1] The ultimate goal was to draft a Commonwealth Act that devised a political status that combined the Guamanian desire to remain included in the United States, while also increasing local governance. It sought to rectify the limitations of the Organic Act of Guam and the problems caused by the continued presence of the US military and the rapid influx of settlers who threatened to displace and outnumber CHamorus in their home island.

Seeing an opportunity to shift the narrative of US colonialism in Guåhan, CHamoru activists launched the Indigenous CHamoru self-determination movement at a critical moment of island's political and social trajectory. For them, the Commonwealth Act had the potential to be the legal document through which CHamoru rights and self-determination could be ensured for the future. In a pivotal essay written in the early 1980s, Hope Alvarez Cristobal, a CHamoru activist and then chairperson of the Organization of People for Indigenous Rights (OPI-R), pointed out not only that the United States had failed to commence the decolonization process for Guåhan as stipulated by Chapter XI of the UN Charter, but also that "the inalienable right to self-determination" belonged specifically to the CHamoru people of Guåhan.[2] Along with other CHamoru rights activists, OPI-R had argued that the CHamoru people's genealogical and specific historical experience with colonialism in Guåhan made their rights inherently different from those of immigrants and settlers who arrived in Guåhan after World War II. If OPI-R and other CHamoru activists could have it their way, settlers in Guåhan would not be included in the "self" in "self-determination." As a result of their fervent advocacy during the Guam Commonwealth Movement, any debate over Guåhan's territorial status became almost inextricable from Indigenous CHamoru rights and self-determination.

Almost immediately the advocacy for Indigenous CHamoru rights in the Guam Commonwealth Act incited community and interracial tensions that surfaced in political meetings, schools, and in general island society. Opponents, many of whom were Filipinos and white US settlers, believed that CHamoru rights and self-determination violated US liberal values of equality and multiculturalism and discriminated against non-CHamorus within the legal system. They upheld US citizenship, immigrant narratives, and, indeed, their "inalienable right to vote" to decide the island's political future. These conflicts evolved into accusations of racial discrimination, descriptions of native inauthenticity, and epithets of colonial collaborators and perpetually "alien" immigrants. The movement for a Guam Commonwealth highlights how Indigenous self-determination was at odds with liberal multiculturalism, racial liberalism, and US civil rights.

In this chapter I historicize the Guam Commonwealth Movement of the 1980s in order to demonstrate how liberal multiculturalism and racial liberalism created cultural and structural impossibilities for Indigenous peoples who were attempting to exercise self-determination within the US settler military empire. The Guam Commonwealth Movement demonstrates how settler colonial regimes, as scholar Jodi Byrd has observed, "have created internally contradictory quagmires where human rights, equal rights, and recognitions are predicated on the very systems that propagate and maintain the dispossession of indigenous peoples for the common good of the world."[3] The contradictory draft of the Guam Commonwealth Act further reveals how CHamorus negotiated and challenged the rules of a liberal empire that did not conform to what they wanted for Guåhan's political future. Ultimately, the US federal government struck down the Guam Commonwealth Act's provisions on Indigenous CHamoru self-determination by protecting the voting rights of settlers and immigrants to "equally" determine the island's future. For CHamoru people, liberalism did nothing to correct the injustices of CHamoru experience of Guåhan's colonial past, and instead was used against them when they called for Indigenous rights. Their experiences demonstrate how liberalism only served to justify and reproduce US settler militarism in Guåhan.

An emergent Indigenous CHamoru consciousness, however, catalyzed a monumental shift in anticolonial and decolonial resistance that forms the bedrock of CHamoru activism and interracial solidarity in the twenty-first century. During the Commonwealth Movement, there was Filipino solidarity for CHamoru rights and CHamoru recognition of the shared histories of colonialism between Guåhan and the Philippines. CHamoru and Filipino's shared discontent with US empire signaled the possibilities of alternative relationalities beyond race, nation, and citizenship that at once proved the incompleteness of settler militarism and harnessed the potential to upend empire itself.

A Constitution and a Commonwealth

Rising discontent with US territorial rule in Guåhan sparked the CHamoru self-determination movement of the 1970s–1990s. The overwhelming presence of the US military, the rapid growth of an immigrant population, the limitations on local economic development due to the Organic Act of Guam, and the zeitgeist of Pacific decolonization propelled the island's leaders to ask whether they should negotiate a new political status for Guåhan. The island's demographics had changed significantly since World War II. What was a small population of roughly 22,000 before the war ballooned into 200,000 in 1947 and settled around 106,000 by 1980.[4] Most of the settler population boom was due to the growth of the Filipino community brought to Guåhan by military contractors and the tourism industry. In response, CHamoru leaders in the Guåhan Legislature articulated fears that CHamoru culture and "ways of life" would be lost and that CHamoru political influence would wane.[5] As we saw in chapter 5, this fear was exacerbated by the observation that settlers and immigrants promoted US multiculturalism and did not engage with CHamoru life and culture.

CHamoru leaders were also acutely aware of decolonization movements in the greater Pacific. Islands across the Pacific were becoming independent, starting with Western Samoa's decolonization from New Zealand in 1962. Closer to home, their CHamoru relatives in the Northern Mariana Islands, then part of the Trust Territory of the Pacific Islands, had begun negotiations with the United States on their future political status. Unlike for the Trust Territory and the Northern Marianas, the United States did not facilitate a decolonization process for Guåhan, citing the island's pre–World War II colonial status as a US possession. CHamoru leaders asked why this was so. As a former governor of Guåhan, Joseph F. Ada wrote retrospectively in 2002, "If we are unaware of these movements, it is because the US government has stepped up its policies to mold Guam in an American image and has averted our understanding of our rights as a people."[6] In Ada's view, the United States had transformed Guåhan into a US island in the Pacific, settled it with military bases, and promoted US multiculturalism to dissuade CHamorus in Guåhan from seeking self-determination. He wrote, "The worldwide movement toward independence and decolonization is still on-going, but Guam has continually been shielded from the excitement."

To confront the problems associated with US imperialism in Guåhan, coalitions of elected leaders as well as community organizations commenced a multipronged movement for territorial reform. Facilitated by GovGuam, the Guam Constitution Movement (1968–80), also known as ConCon, and the Guam Commonwealth Movement (1980–97) drafted legislation to solve the problems associated with Guåhan's territorial status. These movements, however, neither sought further incorporation into the United States as a state, nor declared Guåhan to be independent as its own nation-state. Rather, CHamorus and other Guåhan residents sought alternative renewed political statuses that allowed more local governance *within* the US empire.

In 1968, the Guåhan Legislature established a Constitutional Convention tasked to survey the limitations of the Organic Act. Forty-three delegates from around the island were elected to the first Guåhan Constitutional Convention in 1969. They established a Commission on Political Status (CPS) in 1973. A second Constitutional Convention began in 1975.[7] In both conventions, it became apparent that merely surveying and revising the Organic Act could not ameliorate the problems that Guåhan faced. In a 1975 report, the CPS criticized the way the US military "played an unduly large role in the life in Guåhan in areas not affecting the national security but of critical importance to Guåhan"; asserted that "immigration to Guåhan [was] threatening to change the way of life on the island"; and suggested that "a careful review of land ownership and land use in Guåhan [was] required." The CPS believed that their grievances about military land use and immigration could only be rectified by a complete transformation of the island's federal-territorial relationship. The CPS furthermore concluded that "Guåhan should be empowered to determine its future" and that "the relationship between the United States and Guåhan should be based on the principle of self-determination" and respect for the people of Guåhan.[8] In invoking "self-determination," the CPS elevated the issue of the island's colonial relationship with the United States to the realm of the international context and the United Nations. Thereafter, the Constitution Conventions shifted their purpose from merely revising the Organic Act of Guam to fundamentally transforming the island's political status.

Nonetheless, the CPS continued to draft a Guam Constitution, which they finalized in 1978. Most of the Constitution's articles were small revisions of the Organic Act of Guam, pertaining to eminent domain, control of natural resources and the environment, public education, and the organization of the three branches of government. Article XI, however, stood out. Titled "Chamorro Culture," Article XI acknowledged the significance of CHamoru culture to Guåhan and stipulated that "the evolutionary development of the Chamorro culture may not be abridged and no law may discontinue the Chamorro language, traditions, customs or other cultural components of Guam." The CPS also sought to preserve culturally and historically significant sites and establish a "Chamorro culture commission" to "study and promote the perpetuation of Chamorro culture and traditions and to have additional duties and powers provided by law."[9] Beginning with the Guam Constitution and Article XI, CHamoru culture became a central feature in any debate about Guåhan's political status.

The US federal government kept abreast of the developments of the Guam Constitution because it was a potential means to remove Guåhan from the United Nation's list of non-self-governing territories.[10] In 1960 the UN General Assembly passed Resolution 1514, which established the Committee of 24 (Special Commission on Decolonization). This committee monitored the decolonization progress of the remaining UN non-self-governing territories and required imperial powers to report on the territories' progress toward self-governance.[11] To comply with UN requirements, the Carter administration passed a bill in the US Congress in 1976 that allowed Guåhan and the US Virgin Islands to construct territorial constitutions. The administration also approved the Guam Constitution without changes in 1979.[12] If the Constitution was approved by voters in Guåhan, the United States could argue that the people of Guåhan had indeed practiced UN self-determination, and the United States would no longer be obligated to carry out the required decolonization process for Guåhan.

Despite the nods to the preservation of CHamoru culture, the Guam Constitution did not receive support from CHamoru activist groups. Robert Underwood, Anthony "Tony" Leon Guerrero, and Marilyn Manibusan formed PARA y PADA, an alliance of CHamorus who fought for the preservation of CHamoru culture in Guåhan society.[13] PARA y PADA was a conglomeration of two organizations: the People's Alliance for Responsible Alternatives (PARA) and the People's Alliance for Dignified Alternatives (PADA). PARA emerged in 1977 in response to a language policy instituted by the *Pacific Daily News* (*PDN*). When Lorraine Underwood attempted to place a "Happy

Birthday" advertisement for Robert Underwood that was written in Spanish and CHamoru, the editors of the *PDN* requested that she include an English translation. Describing himself as "part time faculty member; full time activist," Robert challenged the *PDN*, arguing that this request was reminiscent of the English-only policies instituted by the US Navy in the Naval era.[14] Underwood and some colleagues and friends carried out their first political demonstration, protesting at the *PDN* building in Hagåtña, where "people would go in there and cancel their subscription. . . . Someone burned a *PDN* out there in the middle of the street."[15] Eventually PARA also "invaded" a board meeting of the Guam International Airport Authority (GIAA), demanding that the airport include CHamoru language in its signage. The GIAA was sympathetic to PARA's cause and for a while was the only government agency that had CHamoru alongside English, perhaps due to the Pacific exoticism that the language added to Guåhan's touristic charm. PADA was organized by Senator Marilyn Manibusan of the Guam Legislature and Anthony "Tony" Leon Guerrero, president of the locally owned Bank of Guam. PADA began as "The Committee for a More Informed Vote on the Constitution," which attempted to delay any vote on the Guam Constitution, claiming that the island's voters were not properly informed of the drafted provisions of the Constitution.[16]

Together, their goal was to "Para y Pada I Constitution," or to "Stop and Slap the Constitution." They believed the Guam Constitution did not directly challenge the current political status of unincorporated territory and, in fact, avoided key issues such as immigration because "they were beyond the scope of the U.S. law that authorized the [Constitutional Convention]."[17] In addition, they believed the Constitution could prevent any future claims to increase Guåhan's self-governance, and thus make the CHamoru people and Guåhan "totally subservient to the federal government now in and the future."[18] Thus, PARA y PADA believed that deciding on a Constitution was to place the "carabao before the cart" when it came to Guåhan's political status.

The US government was so confident in the Guam Constitution that it invited the UN Committee on 24 to oversee the elections in 1979. During the election, an ambassador of a newly decolonized nation-state met with PARA y PADA to discuss the decolonization process. It was in this meeting that Underwood, Leon Guerrero, Manibusan, and other CHamoru activists understood that the fight for a renewed political status in Guåhan was connected to events around the world. Underwood later recalled that at the end of the meeting, "We started to say 'Wow there's a whole other world out there.'"[19]

They saw that the Guam Constitution was not just about Guåhan's relationship to the United States; it was about Guåhan's relationship to the rest of the world. With this international insight, PARA y PADA saw how the passage of the Guam Constitution could limit future possibilities for Guåhan's progress to self-government and indeed CHamoru self-determination.

Due to the fervent activism of PARA y PADA, the Guam Constitution received an unenthusiastic reception by both Guåhan political leaders and the people of Guåhan.[20] The Guåhan population voted to disapprove the Constitution on August 4, 1979, in an island-wide referendum. The Constitution ultimately failed because it was conservative in its aims, especially in regard to the protection of CHamoru people's right to self-determination. What emerged from the failed Constitution Movement, however, was a critical consciousness of how US colonial rule in Guåhan directly and specifically affected CHamoru people. Unlike the preceding generations of the 1930s or the late 1940s, whose political actions and diplomacy worked within the constructs of liberal ideals, this generation of CHamoru activists were not ashamed to explicitly criticize US imperialism and militarism in Guåhan from the CHamoru perspective. They believed that the most effective way to rectify the inequalities of US colonialism was to prioritize *CHamoru* self-determination, not just Guåhan's self-determination, in debates on political status. As a result of the Guam Constitution Movement, any conversation about Guåhan's political status became intrinsically tied to Indigenous CHamoru self-determination. In other words, what began as a movement to merely reform the federal-territorial relationship evolved into the movement for CHamoru self-determination.

Undeterred by the failure of the Guam Constitution, the Guam Legislature established the Commission on Self-Determination (CSD) in 1980. The transition from a reform-minded title "Commission on Political Status" to the "Commission on Self-Determination" in and of itself reflects Guåhan's reckoning with the UN Charter and how it can be leveraged in negotiations with the US empire. The CSD became the primary advocate for Guåhan in negotiations over the territorial-federal relationship in both the United States and the United Nations.[21] A task force was assigned to each of the seven potential political statuses as stipulated by the United Nations—statehood, independence, free association, status quo, territorial status with the United States, commonwealth with the United States, and "other." These task forces were charged with educating the island's population about the pros and cons of each of the statuses.[22] After an education campaign, GovGuam held a plebiscite to determine the island's desired political status in which all residents of Guåhan who were US citizens, regardless of race, were eligible to vote. In a September 1982 plebiscite, commonwealth status received the highest share of the votes, at 73 percent of the electorate.[23] According to Arnold Leibowitz, a lawyer advising the CSD, the Guåhan voting population knew that commonwealth status was vague in nature, "but it saw the status as embracing local self-government similar to that of a State, mutuality of action between the Federal government and Guam in key areas, similar to the CNMI, and, perhaps, some restriction on unilateral Federal military actions."[24] Compared to other political statuses, commonwealth seemed to offer the most room for negotiation, and was "promoted as a flexible status which could later lead to Statehood, or even Independence."[25]

The Activism of the Organization of People for Indigenous Rights

The CSD was influenced heavily by CHamoru activist organizations seeking to ensure that CHamoru rights remained a non-negotiable item in the drafting of the Guam Commonwealth Act. In particular, the Organization of People for Indigenous Rights (OPI-R) emerged out of PARA y PADA and continued advocating for CHamoru self-determination in the 1980s.[26] They described themselves as a diverse group of people whose "common bond is our belief that only Indigenous inhabitants of Guam, the Chamorro people, have the right to determine their political destiny by changing Guam's political status from a non-self-governing territory to a status considered as having a full measure of self-government."[27] OPI-R consisted of young CHamoru activists such as Robert Underwood and Ron Teehan, who led the Guam Landowner's Association, which in the 1970s and 1980s fought for the return of CHamoru lands from the US military. OPI-R also included Bernadita Camacho-Dungca and Clotilde Gould, two CHamoru women dedicated to the preservation CHamoru language and storytelling; Benjamin "BJ" Cruz, a lawyer; Chris Perez Howard, a writer; Laura Souder, a CHamoru feminist scholar; and Hope Cristobal, a community activist. A few Filipinos were also involved in OPI-R, including Nerissa Bretania, Maria Teehan, Marie Pablo, and William Hernandez.

Unlike previous generations whose CHamoru advocates held positions of power within the Guam Congress, the Guam Legislature, and the business community, the members of OPI-R were not government officials. They were mostly educators who chose to organize outside of official government roles. Some OPI-R members had spent part of their childhood or adulthood in the continental United States. Some attended higher education institutions for undergraduate, law, or doctorates, while others were veterans or spouses of veterans of the US military. Their imperial and international experiences shaped how they saw the CHamoru movement in relation to the rest of the world. In the tumultuous 1960s and 1970s, they learned from the civil rights movement on the US continent, protested US Cold War militarization of the Asia-Pacific, and witnessed Pacific decolonization. For instance, BJ Cruz attended Claremont McKenna College in California, where his roommate Ronald Ridenhour was a whistleblower for the My Lai Massacre during Vietnam War.[28] Ridenhour's act revealed to Cruz the deep harm the US military had committed in wars despite its rhetorical mission to spread democracy globally. Together with their experience protesting the Guam Constitution, these CHamoru activists understood that global movements for liberation, independence, and peace were connected to the CHamoru self-determination movement in Guåhan. Described as "intelligentsia of the Chamorro Movement" by CHamoru scholar Michael P. Perez, OPI-R went on to theorize the foundational principles of CHamoru self-determination that continue influence CHamoru movements into the twenty-first century.[29]

OPI-R advocated for CHamoru self-determination at multiple levels of governance: the local Guåhan government and community, the imperial government through testimonies in the halls of the US Congress, international society at the United Nations, and in their participation in movements for decolonization in the Pacific.[30] In Guåhan, they attended as many CSD meetings and public hearings as they possibly could, offering suggestions for how to include CHamoru rights in almost every article and draft. They also held public demonstrations, visited villages to educate the community, and published editorials, newsletters, and educational pamphlets. As educators in the public school and university system, they also reached younger generations. On the imperial level, when the Guam Commonwealth Act received its first congressional hearing in Hawai'i in 1989, OPI-R testified in support. They also attended smaller events when federal and UN officials visited to provide recommendations for the draft. And, significantly, in 1982 OPI-R made an appearance at the United Nations demanding that the United States recognize CHamoru self-determination. There, they made evident the empire that the United States attempted to hide. Throughout all their campaigns, they showed how different forms of colonialism had prevented CHamoru people from negotiating their territorial status and exercising self-determination. They also criticized the rhetoric of militarism and multiculturalism, which alongside their US citizenship obscured ongoing US colonialism. All the

Robert Underwood testified on behalf of Guåhan and the Organization of People for Indigenous Rights at the United Nations in 1982. UN Photo/ Miguel Jimenez.

while, they were still working against a general population and a US military that believed in the benevolence of US empire and the military in Guåhan.

Influenced by Pacific movements around them and Guåhan's unique position within US empire, OPI-R testified at the United Nations in New York in July 1982 before the Committee of 24. They were the first CHamoru generation to publicly and internationally criticize the United States for its colonialism in Guåhan, and specifically for how the United States used Guåhan as a military fortress in the Pacific. OPI-R was adamant that the US federal government did not take Guåhan's self-determination seriously because Guåhan was "tied up with the overwhelming reality of the presence of the U.S. military in large numbers." OPI-R pointed out that despite the UN's claim that "the presence of military bases should not be an impediment to self-determination on Guam," the way military and federal officials treated CHamoru claims to self-determination demonstrated otherwise. OPI-R saw how US security of the Asia-Pacific region in the Cold War was dependent on depriving CHamorus of self-determination.[31]

OPI-R's testimony at the UN situates them within an oceanic-wide movement for anticolonialism, decolonialization, and Indigenous rights in the Pacific.[32] Although Pacific decolonization came relatively late in the post–World War II age of decolonization, historian Tracey Banivanua Mar historicizes how Pacific Indigenous peoples in the 1970s and 1980s understood that colonialism and militarism were interlocking forms of imperialism that needed to be addressed simultaneously in decolonization and antinuclear movements. She argues that the Pohnpei Charter of 1978 and the creation of the Nuclear Free and Independent Pacific point to a "political sophistication, physical mobility and a cosmopolitan connectedness to international networks" that put the "Pacific, or Oceania, at the forefront . . . of the process of uncolonising peoples."[33] OPI-R had been taking notes from the greater Pacific to forge their critique of the US empire and strategize possibilities for CHamoru self-determination throughout the 1970s and 1980s. For instance, in November 1982 Guåhan hosted the Micronesian Educational Solidarity Conference, where CHamoru leaders and activists met delegates from Japan, Aotearoa (New Zealand), Hawai'i, New Caledonia, Tahiti, Kiribati, and Palau to devise island-specific strategies for decolonization and demilitarization.[34] Combining demilitarization, decolonization, and Indigenous CHamoru rights at the center of their activism, OPI-R and the Guam Commonwealth Movement was another node in the decolonizing Pacific that placed them at the forefront of global Indigenous intellectual thought.

Although they did not use the term settler militarism, OPI-R historicized the CHamoru experience of US colonialism in a way that criticized the interlocking colonial policies of militarism, land annexation, and immigration that displaced and dispossessed CHamoru people in Guåhan. They also challenged US liberal multiculturalism as the panacea for colonial injustices and argued that instead these ideologies facilitated setter militarism. Hope Cristobal wrote succinctly, "Huge camps of foreign workers and the application of US immigration laws to Guam has meant a continual stream of immigrants which threatens to make Chamorros strangers in their own land."[35] OPI-R executive director Leland Bettis, a white US settler who married a CHamoru woman, argued that this rapid "in-migration" was seen by as a "colonial tool" that "served to dilute the strength of the native people of a colonized area."[36] He suggested that immigrants, especially those who sought further migration to the US continent, were loyal to the United States, not Guåhan. By not making concerted efforts to contribute to the community, these transient US immigrants became imbricated in colonial structure and placed an undue burden on the CHamoru people of Guåhan. Thus, settlers did not necessarily refer to a "settled" population but also referred to the transient population of military personnel who left after short tours of duty and immigrants from the Philippines who used Guåhan as a stepping stone for further migration to the North American continent.[37] OPI-R did not see immigration and militarization as two separate issues. Instead they were integrated processes that made CHamorus a minority on their island.

With the immigration of non-Indigenous people into Guåhan and the emigration of Indigenous CHamoru people away from the island, CHamoru leaders and activists soon realized how immigrants were replacing CHamorus in their home island. Settler militarism not only manifested in the displacement of CHamoru people from their villages to other villages within Guåhan, but also in how CHamorus were pushed to find opportunities off the island, often relocating to the continental United States. Bettis wrote, "The out-migration of Chamorros was prompted in large part by the impact of military land-takings, the in-migration of thousands of outsiders, the development of an entirely new economy, the extension of US citizenship and new career opportunities in the military."[38] The CHamoru diaspora was quite large. In fact, Underwood noted, the Federation of Guamanian Associations of America estimated that there were fifty-five thousand CHamorus living in California in 1978. "This was startling," Underwood wrote, "for it indicated that more Chamorros resided in in California than on Guam itself."[39] Almost all CHamorus in California had some connection to the US military; many of them had enlisted into the armed services to earn a stable living.

OPI-R compared the CHamoru historical experience of dispossession and displacement to that of other Indigenous peoples within the US empire and across the globe. They observed that settler colonialism created systemic problems within Indigenous communities that included cultural preservation and self-determination, as well economic issues such as homelessness, incarceration, and fewer economic opportunities that affected the daily realities of Indigenous peoples within settler colonial societies. Underwood compared the experiences of CHamorus in Guåhan to the "painful lessons of the natives of Hawaii and the Maoris of New Zealand."[40] Because of this, Underwood wrote, Indigenous peoples "did not merely cease to maintain political control over their society, they began to disintegrate as a people, as a collective body."[41] Likewise, as Cristobal summarized to the US House Committee of Interior and Insular Affairs in 1986, "the situation of the Chamorro people is not new in the annals of American policy. It is similar to that of the American Indian, the Eskimo, and the native Hawaiian. The end result has unfortunately always been the same."[42] As a result, Cristobal lamented, the "Chamorro people are disintegrating under the pressures of social and economic change thrust upon them without their knowledge or control." Furthermore, land annexation and the rise of a settler population had led to Indigenous peoples who "eventually become displaced in their homeland and become the underclass, the disillusioned, the landless, the uneducated, the poor, and the jailed."[43] Both Underwood and Cristobal warned, "The future of the Chamorro people as a permanent underclass in the next century seems plausible."

OPI-R had solutions to the problems of settler militarism. To protect CHamoru rights in the Commonwealth Act, OPI-R sought the inclusion of CHamoru-centered policies and advocated for a voting process that limited any self-determination and political status plebiscite to those who could prove their Indigenous CHamoru identity. They influenced the CSD to devise practical legal policies that embedded CHamoru rights into the Guam Commonwealth Act, including the establishment of a Chamorro Land Trust as well as a provision for mutual consent between GovGuam and the US federal government. While these provisions were generally accepted, the provisions for a limited plebiscite faced tremendous opposition.

OPI-R believed that only the CHamoru people of Guåhan bore the right to self-determination as stipulated by UN Charter. As Chris Perez Howard wrote to Congressman Antonio B. Won Pat in Washington in May 1982, "By definition, on the island of Guam, only the Chamorro people, the 'indigenous inhabitants' of Guam have the right of self-determination. It is unjust for anyone other than the Chamorro people to vote in any plebiscite to determine their political destiny." To push US rhetoric into action, Howard cited the UN Charter and the US Constitution—specifically, that the United States was obligated to uphold treaties. Howard continued in his letter to Won Pat, "Any change in status from a non-self-governing territory to one considered as having a full measure of self-government would be considered as an act of self-determination."[44] OPI-R argued that the vote for Guam Commonwealth, as the status that would be closest in practice to self-determination, should solely be decided by CHamoru people.

In arguing for "CHamoru self-determination," OPI-R faced the problem of defining the boundaries of CHamoru identity for a limited plebiscite. To do so, OPI-R challenged the equalizing nature of US citizenship by outlining how CHamorus faced inherently different forms of colonialism due to their Indigenous relationship to Guåhan.[45] First, to contest assertions of the CHamoru extinction, OPI-R reaffirmed that "the Chamorro people are a readily identifiable ethnic, social and historical group." Secondly, while immigrants and settlers participated within the settler military structure, CHamorus had experienced US military land annexation, dispossession, and displacement since World War II. To specify who exactly experienced this form of colonialism in Guåhan, OPI-R suggested that people could verify the

CHamoru-ness through "historically reliable sources" such as the 1940 US census, the 1946 US Navy census, the 1950 census, and "those who obtained citizenship through the organic act." These censuses, they argued, could pinpoint specific people and ancestors who felt the acute experiences of post–World War II settler militarism.[46]

Anticipating opposition that would cite US liberal multiculturalism, OPI-R also wanted to make sure that the vote did not seem to discriminate against non-CHamorus. For example, CHamorus who did not live in Guåhan, including those in the CHamoru diaspora, were not eligible to vote, though they could reclaim "this right by establishing residence of Guam."[47] Furthermore, those of Filipino and other non-CHamoru heritage who were in Guåhan and received US citizenship through the Organic Act of 1950 were eligible to vote in a limited plebiscite according to OPI-R's criteria. Nonetheless, OPI-R left out the immigrant population who settled in Guåhan *after* 1950—more than a majority of the population. How OPI-R sought to define the boundaries of CHamoru identity shows how CHamorus once again had to prove their indigeneity through evolving sets of criteria, this time in relation to the specific history of postwar settler militarism that could be proven by colonial documentation. This reveals how settler militarism continued to change the terrain upon which CHamorus could define CHamoru identity and legitimately argue for liberal rights, including self-determination.

This emphasis on CHamoru indigeneity was in response to the shifting connotations of the term "Guamanian," which became an issue for CHamoru activists like OPI-R who attempted to assert Indigenous rights. CHamoru activist and OPI-R member Ronald Teehan emphasized that the United States "clearly defined who Guamanians were"—specifically "the inhabitants, natives, people of Guam, Guamanians"—in multiple laws concerning the governing of Guåhan, including the Organic Act of Guam of 1950.[48] The United States referred to the inhabitants of Guåhan as "Guamanians," surmised Underwood, "in order to distinguish Chamorros from one island to another, such as Guamanian, Saipanese and Rotanese."[49] The Organic Act of Guam also referred to "Guamanians" in two sections. First, US citizenship was bestowed upon "Guamanian persons and persons of Guamanian descent" and, secondly, preferential treatment for government jobs would be "given to qualified persons of Guamanian ancestry" in order to ensure "the fullest participation by Guamanians in government of Guam, opportunities for higher education and in-service training facilities."[50] It was apparent that federal and military officials were using "Guamanian" synonymously with

CHamorus who were from Guåhan. Underwood reiterated this point during a public hearing: "Without hesitation, it is clear that when they recognized the rights of Guamanians at the end of the war until the Organic Act, they were referring to the Chamorros."[51] Furthermore, CHamorus of the early postwar period happily took on this appellation, some believing that it sounded "American" and would thus demonstrate their loyalty to the United States.[52]

With the demographic transformation of Guåhan in the 1960s, however, the term "Guamanian" took a more capacious definition, referring to all people who lived in Guåhan, regardless of their ethnic origin.[53] Filipinos, white US settlers, as well as other Asians proudly identified as "Guamanians" despite having no CHamoru heritage. They adopted the term "Guamanian" in the same way that a resident of the state of California could call themselves "Californian." CHamoru leaders also began to use "Guamanian" referring to all residents of Guåhan. So, when the United States and some CHamoru leaders in Guåhan stated that the right to self-determination was inherent to "Guamanians," non-CHamorus—white US settlers and Filipinos alike—began to assert their right to determine the future for Guåhan as well. The history of the term "Guamanian," in and of itself, shows the evolution and connection between Guåhan's multiculturalism and racial liberalism.

If the term "Guamanian" equalized all residents of Guåhan in a US liberal multicultural narrative, CHamoru activists like OPI-R began to the word "Indigenous" to reclaim their special relationship to Guåhan and to distinguish themselves from immigrants and settlers. The consequences were substantial. Reflecting on this moment, Underwood wrote that "the use of the term 'indigenous' proved to be a watershed contribution because the comparisons to other 'indigenous' peoples became part of the political and social dialogue. This had not been the case in the past because of the complexity of identity and self-identification issues historically in Guam."[54] When OPI-R argued that self-determination for Guåhan was "a people's right," OPI-R defied international convention, specifically the UN's "Saltwater Thesis" that made decolonization a territorial process.[55] In other words, OPI-R placed the right to self-determination *within* the CHamoru *people* and not with the territory of Guam. In doing so, they became part of the global Indigenous movement of the Fourth World that used self-determination to vie for rights on the international stage. Yet, as soon as the members of OPI-R proclaimed Indigenous CHamoru self-determination, they fought backlash from Filipinos, white US settlers, and others who held tightly to US liberal multicultural ideals.

Unsettling the Opposition

OPI-R and the limited plebiscite—the "Chamorro-only vote" as it was negatively called by its opponents—received vitriolic criticism by those invested in the US empire in Guåhan. To many people, in particular white settlers and Filipinos, the question of Guåhan's political status was a separate issue from CHamoru rights or self-determination. From their perspective, "CHamoru-only voting" leveraged the power of Indigenous CHamoru heritage over US citizenship in all local matters pertaining to Guåhan. They found this antithetical to US multiculturalism and racial liberalism, and they believed that all people who lived within the territory had a say in the political future of the island. For instance, the mostly white editorial staff of the *Pacific Daily News* treated the question of Indigenous identity as a trivial topic among other questions of political status and equal elections. "What is an indigenous person?" one editorial read. "Is a person who was born on Guam, but whose parents immigrated from the mainland, indigenous? Is a person whose parents came from, say, the Philippines, but who was born and reared on Guam, indigenous?" For the *Pacific Daily News* and many opponents of OPI-R in the 1980s, Indigenous rights and self-determination were radical ideologies that violated the rights of non-CHamorus in Guåhan. The editorial continued, "Guam's political status is a vital question that affects all its residents, whether they have been five years or fifty, be the white, brown, black or yellow."[56]

Likewise, Shelby Shapiro, a representative of the Workman's Circle, an organization that catered to the working class and laborers on island, adamantly opposed CHamoru self-determination and rights in the Commonwealth Act. Shapiro argued that CHamoru self-determination may harm Guåhan's diverse population. In his submitted testimony, he wrote, "Guam is home to people of many cultures: Chamorros, 'Mainlanders,' Filipinos, Japanese, Chinese, Indians, Sikhs, Koreans, Vietnamese, Palauans, and the list goes on. What is unique about the island is that, given a population a bit less than that of a small city (around 100,00) in a relatively small land area (about 210 sq. miles), there is a generally cosmopolitan outlook. Why? Because of the island's multicultural aspects. Guam—if not a 'melting pot' is at the very least, a 'mixed salad.'"[57] Using familiar tropes of multiculturalism such as "melting pot" or "mixed salad," Shapiro argued that Guåhan's diverse population added to a certain internationalism that was indicative of a progressive and modern society. Shelby's testimony is indicative of the arguments used by proponents of US multiculturalism to undermine the CHamoru self-determination movement.

Appealing to US multiculturalism, Shapiro also said Guamanians should not have any say in US immigration policy. He believed that immigration made Guåhan a better place for everyone: "This island is home to the peoples of many cultures, and it is this variety, this diversity, this profusion of different ideas, attitudes, customs and modes of thought that makes our island an exciting place to live. This is also what has made America—the land of immigrants—great." Shapiro reaffirmed the perception that Guåhan was undoubtedly American and that CHamoru people were incorrect to claim they should have control over immigration. "There is no proof whatever," explained Shapiro, "that the people of this island have had 'hardships' 'imposed' upon them because of immigration. If anything, the immigrants have done the opposite." Shapiro continued, "This Article is a complete slap in the face to the frequently cited cultural tradition of Chamorro hospitality."[58] For Shapiro, multiculturalism and the presumption of unconditional CHamoru hospitality were assets to Guåhan. The propagation of these notions by settlers elided the CHamoru desire for self-determination.[59]

White settlers' oxymoronic emphasis on multiculturalism and the mixed-race heritage of CHamoru people served to delegitimize CHamoru claims to indigeneity and self-determination. White settlers used the perceived "inauthenticity" of the CHamoru identity against CHamoru rights activists. "There are no 'pure Chamorros,'" and "there is no such thing as a 'pure culture' anywhere," Shapiro wrote. At the same time, however, Shapiro also weaponized mixed-race Filipino-CHamorus against the CHamoru self-determination movement. Even though OPI-R received support from the Filipino-CHamoru archbishop, Felixberto Flores, Shapiro quoted the archbishop as saying "there are no Guamanians without Filipino blood in their veins."[60] In Shapiro's perspective, Indigenous identity required a purity of culture and blood, something that did not apply to CHamorus. Underwood also received ad hominem attacks from opponents. "They made fun of my name," Underwood testified at a public hearing, "they say that I'm racist, and many times they've asked me if my parents and I are full-blooded Chamorro. Maybe they are establishing that if they mock me or my peers then they will diminish the dignity of us who support the rights of Chamorros."[61] What Shapiro and other opponents failed to acknowledge was that CHamoru identity did not revolve around the purity of blood, but on genealogy, language, and culture. It also relied on the continuity of connections to the islands that the CHamoru people emphasized in their daily lives.

In addition, opponents of CHamoru self-determination and the limited plebiscite also weaponized CHamorus' US citizenship to argue that

CHamorus had relinquished any right to self-determination. Charles Troutman, a lawyer who resided in Guåhan, opposed CHamoru self-determination, stating, "These people, the Chamorros however defined, have made one critical choice of self-determination already. By making that choice, seeking U.S. citizenship, they became a part of a larger group—U.S. citizen residents of Guam."[62] Because Guåhan was an unincorporated territory and because the Organic Act had clauses on US citizenship, Troutman argued that self-determination was an unnecessary exercise. If a self-determination plebiscite were to happen, however, Troutman argued, self-determination would belong to the entire territory and any resident and citizen living within that territory should be eligible to vote. Troutman concluded that "as a non-self-governing territory, all inhabitants of Guam have the right to self-determination."[63]

When white settlers used the diversity of the island to deny CHamoru self-determination and justify continued US control over Guåhan, they demonstrated the enduring quality of white supremacy in liberal multiculturalism and racial liberalism that purportedly provide equality for all peoples.[64] US citizenship flattened the historical inequalities of empire. White settlers rendered invisible Indigenous CHamoru colonial experiences while emphasizing the injustice of Filipino migrant exclusion and the perceived lack of voting rights for white settlers in the decolonization process for Guåhan. Thus, liberal multiculturalism and racial liberalism operated as tools of settler militarism, in which racial hierarchies and diverse colonial experiences were conflated, flattened, or ignored all together in the service of dispossessing Indigenous CHamoru people of political power and sovereignty in Guåhan. Liberal multiculturalism and racial liberalism also reproduced settler militarism by legitimizing and justifying white and Filipino influence that were vital to military presence in Guåhan.

The Commonwealth Act and the CHamoru self-determination movement presented Filipinos and Filipino-Americans living in Guåhan with an uncomfortable situation. Filipino stories of migration and their desire to fulfill the promises of liberalism had both legitimized their presence in Guåhan and fueled the prevailing narrative of a multicultural United States. They navigated Guåhan society as immigrants in search of economic opportunities beyond their homeland, while simultaneously being racialized as disposable laborers and workers. Even so, many of them believed that equality and full inclusion in US society depended on their work for the empire and their contributions to island society. The CHamoru rights and self-determination movement directly challenged this liberal immigrant narrative. As a result,

Filipino immigrants' feelings and perspectives toward the Commonwealth and CHamoru self-determination were hostile. In describing the "asymmetrical relations" between Filipinos, CHamorus, and the US empire, Guåhan scholar Vicente Diaz writes that Filipinos were "not innocent bystanders, poor helpless immigrants, who want only to live a life of dignity often denied back home. Many Filipinos look down on CHamorus as not culturally rich as people in their mother country, even as they look to Guam as a wonderful place to have the best of both worlds."[65] Filipinos tended to laud Guåhan's relationship to the United States and subsequently ignored the importance of CHamoru culture in Guåhan. There were, however, some Filipinos who fully supported CHamoru self-determination.

The CHamoru self-determination movement unsettled Filipino identity in Guåhan. The shifting connotation of "Guamanian" and the relatively novel use of "Indigenous" to describe the CHamoru people sparked heated discussions. At a CSD public hearing in July 1985, Rogelio A. Sardea described himself as "Filipino by blood, American by citizenship, and a Guamanian by choice to reside in the island of Guam." He asked the CSD, including Governor Ricardo Bordallo, "Are we developing a Commonwealth Act for Guam or are we developing a Commonwealth Act for the Chamorros?"[66] In response, Paul Bordallo, a member of the CSD, attempted to reassure Sardea that the Commonwealth's provisions on Indigenous CHamoru rights would not create different categories of Guåhan residents and, in addition, CHamoru rights would eventually help all residents of Guåhan. Sardea found Bordallo's answer insufficient and subsequently questioned the very categories and names that the CSD and the general population employed. "If you mean that Chamorro means all the Guamanians who are citizens then I adhere to all what you said. But this has been a confusion. Am I a Chamorro or am I just a Guamanian? Am I a U.S. citizen and A Guamanian but never a Chamorro?," he asked.

Some Filipinos argued the term "Indigenous" was divisive and inherently discriminatory. In a public hearing in Hagåtña, Manfred Mortera, who described himself as a Filipino "born a United States citizen to two non-Chamorros in 1967" and a member of the Guam Youth Congress, thought the Commonwealth Act discriminated against Filipinos. He believed that the drafters of the Commonwealth used the term "Indigenous" to deny immigrants certain rights because of the presumption that they had already self-determined. Mortera argued against this interpretation of "self-determination." "My father immigrated to Guam," he announced. "My mother was born in Hawaii [. . .] I wasn't given a choice to where I was to be born." Despite being born and raised on Guåhan, Mortera complained the act denied him "rights," yet "the indigenous person will be given rights that I won't have simply because I was born after 1950."[67] Under the criteria set forth by OPI-R, Mortera would not be eligible to vote in the limited plebiscite.

Filipinos were fearful that CHamoru rights and self-determination would lead to harsh consequences for non-CHamorus who called Guåhan home. Because of this, they doubled down on their US citizenship and continued to support US governance of Guåhan to protect their interests. For instance, Sardea told the CSD, "The land [has] been a big concern. Many people here have acquired properties through legal means. They pay for it. They pay the market price, and many Filipinos are worried that after the Commonwealth the Chamorro will take our lands." From Sardea's perspective, CHamoru governance would mean the suspension of liberal rights such as land ownership. Because of this, Sardea told the Commission, "I can assure that my family and with other peoples in Guam they felt alienated. . . . Many Filipinos, and I will be frank, the Filipinos are saying, hey 'time to ship up,' otherwise we will be taken away or kicked out of this island."[68] Sardea's comments reveal how CHamoru self-determination, in and of itself, was seen as inherently contradictory to liberal freedom within empire.

Robert Underwood attempted to reframe the animosity of Filipino-CHamoru relations in Guåhan to persuade the Filipino population, who could potentially jeopardize the provisions on CHamoru self-determination. Underwood refocused the criticism away from individual Filipinos, stating that it was not about race or culture, but about the colonial mechanisms and sheer number of Filipinos who would prevent the CHamoru people from self-governing. Underwood did not deny the Filipino community's cultural and economic contributions. He wrote in an essay, "Both promoters of the Filipino contributions to Guam and their detractors fail to recognize that Filipinos are not being judge here. It is not the value of Filipinos, their economic potential, their eating habits, their customs, or their backgrounds that make a difference. It is merely the fact of numbers, the capacity of a society to absorb those numbers and the desirability of a society being able to plan its future."[69]

Underwood took it one step further by emphasizing the shared colonial histories of Guåhan and the Philippines. He saw how Guåhan and the Philippines have had an undeniably deep past and believed that CHamorus and Filipinos could draw from that history to rewrite and reinterpret the multicultural narrative for Guåhan. He wrote, "All Chamorros must recognize that there is at least one Filipino progenitor in each and every Chamorro family. The migration to the Mariana Islands from the Philippines in the 1800s is part of the island's history." Although many CHamorus had Filipino heritage, Underwood implied that their CHamoru genealogies connected them to Guåhan in a fundamentally different way. In addition, Underwood made a distinction between the generations of Filipinos migrants who made meaningful connections to the CHamoru people and Guåhan, and those Filipinos who took advantage of Guåhan's colonial status to attain economic gains or obtain US citizenship. He wrote, "The migrations of the 1800s took place over longer periods of time and the Filipinos were eventually assimilated into Chamorro life and culture. There is little evidence that this is occurring now except in rare, individual circumstances."[70] Here Underwood signaled a CHamoru-Filipino relationality beyond contemporary notions of race and nation by invoking Filipinos who "assimilate into Chamorro life and culture." There was room for Filipino solidarity within the CHamoru self-determination movement rooted in CHamoru relationality.

Filipino Solidarity

Despite the interracial tensions that were exacerbated by white settlers' use of Filipinos as pawns in the multicultural narrative of Guåhan, OPI-R's work attracted Filipina allies, including Nerissa Bretania, Marie Pablo, and Maria Teehan. Maria Teehan was married to Ron Teehan, another vocal CHamoru OPI-R leader, whereas Nerissa Bretania was, in her own words, "the token Filipino" and "the only legitimately independent Filipino that was involved."[71] Nerissa became involved with OPI-R in early 1980s, when her friend, Hope Cristobal, invited her a meeting. Nerissa was blown away by the intellectual language of Robert Underwood, Ron Teehan, and Benjamin Cruz. They way in which they spoke about imperialism and colonialism in Guåhan history reminded her of Paulo Freiere's call for liberatory education, which she learned about after taking an education course taught by Robert Underwood at the University of Guam. Quickly Nerissa became OPI-R's treasurer.

As Filipina women, Nerissa, Marie, and Maria were important players for OPI-R and the CHamoru self-determination movement in general. In an oral history interview, OPI-R member BJ Cruz said that Filipina women were strategic offsets to the hotheaded CHamoru men who often alienated would-be allies with their sharp tongues and incomprehensible theoretical language.[72] For example, in their most successful political action, Nerissa

Bretania and Marie Pablo convinced all but one of the island's village mayors to sign a petition to the United Nations to show that there was support for a change in political status.[73]

While their positionalities were strategic for political activism, Filipina women were also at the crossroads of different and contradictory perspectives that they needed to reconcile.[74] They wanted to stand in solidarity with CHamoru people who had experienced injustices of colonialism in Guåhan, without seeming as if they disregarded their Filipino heritage and disrespected their Filipino families' immigrant struggles. They grew up in a Filipino community that for the most part spent time among themselves and not with CHamorus, due in part to how US militarized labor regimes separated the communities and limited relations between Filipinos and the CHamoru communities on the island. This separation reified for Filipinos the perception that Guåhan was predominantly a US territory and not the land of the CHamoru people. Critics of the Filipina women activists' believed that they misunderstood the idea behind self-determination, were ungrateful for their US citizenship, were disrespectful of their family's immigrant experience, and denied their Filipino heritage. Filipino allies grappled with these contradictions that were microcosms of the inherent tension within settler colonial regimes where immigrants and their civil rights are often placed in opposition to Indigenous peoples and their rights.

When she began working with OPI-R, Nerissa was not sure how to articulate her support for the CHamoru self-determination movement. Nerissa's perspective changed after one transformative conversation with her mother, Rosalina Bretania. Rosalina was a history teacher, who lived in the Philippines during the US colonial period and World War II, and who moved overseas with her husband and young children to an unfamiliar island. She had a unique imperial perspective that enabled her to draw upon her personal experiences and her historical knowledge to find connections between what her daughter wanted to do without sacrificing her Filipino identity. Rosalina told Nerissa, "Every group of people have a right to [self] determine, especially if they have been colonized. They have a right to determine which political direction they want to take." Furthermore, Rosalina told Nerissa, "For the CHamorus, they also have to exercise that right. And for us, we already exercised it as a group and as individuals because we have closer ties to the United States." To Rosalina, CHamoru self-determination would be a fulfillment of the universal right for a people to determine and govern themselves. She emphasized that Filipinos had already exercised national self-determination when the Philippines obtained independence, and that as

Filipino immigrants in Guåhan, they had also exercised individual self-determination in their decision to migrate to the United States.[75] By evoking the related imperial histories of the Philippines and Guåhan, Rosalina gave Nerissa historical and moral reasons to articulate how and why Filipinos can and should stand in solidarity with CHamoru self-determination.

The generational lessons of the Filipino fight for independence sat in the minds of Filipinos in Guåhan who supported CHamoru self-determination. Another young Filipino from the village of Dédidu, Philip Sumang, differentiated the immigrant struggles of Filipinos living in Guåhan from the struggles of CHamorus who sought self-determination. He testified in a CSD public hearing in 1985, "Although I am an immigrant from the Philippines, the local Chamorro people have shown me respect and have treated me with dignity. . . . It is now my turn to show them my respect and permit the existence of their dignity as they permitted mine." His support for the CHamoru self-determination movement was an act of reciprocity toward the community who had given him much, a practice of *inafa'maolek*. Furthermore, Sumang linked his family's personal history with Philippine Independence to Guåhan's quest for self-determination. His grandfather taught him "to recognize this because everyone has the right to determine themselves. My grandfather was there [in the Philippines] fighting for their rights to have their independence, and finally they gained it."[76] In this reading of the history of US imperialism across the Philippine Sea, Sumang saw interconnected and related struggles of Filipino independence and CHamoru self-determination.

Filipinos in solidarity with CHamoru self-determination were primed to complicate the US liberal immigrant narrative by rooting their identity in the Philippine homelands and understanding their connection to Guåhan through the CHamoru people. They understood how US imperialism colonized different peoples differently and how those forms of colonialism intersected. As Filipino scholar who calls Guåhan home, Tabitha Espina writes, Filipino reflection, remembering, and resistance "can act as a starting place for decolonial epistemology on Guåhan that honors the sovereignty of the CHamoru people through acknowledging how we meet in the colonial matrix of power."[77] By identifying this "colonial matrix of power" and articulating an alternative narration of their presence on the island, Filipinos that stood in solidarity with CHamoru self-determination challenged the US racial liberalism, usurped the US settler colonial project of Indigenous erasure and immigrant assimilation, and chose instead to see themselves in relation to CHamorus. Doing so practices what Josephine Faith Ong and I call "*inafa'maolek* solidarity," where a deep acknowledgment of one's own genealogy and an understanding of different intersecting forms of colonialism become the foundation to critique ongoing settler colonialism in Guåhan and be in solidarity of CHamoru self-determination.[78]

"Commonwealth Now!"

After monthly meetings over a period of two years and with input from Guåhan government leaders, community advocates, CHamoru rights activists, and federal officials, the CSD had a draft of the Guam Commonwealth Act in 1986.[79] According to the CSD, the draft expressed "the consensual aspirations of the people of Guam to change the island's political status from that of an unincorporated territory to that of a self-governing Commonwealth, recognizing the sovereignty of the United States of America."[80] At first glance, the Commonwealth Act seemed to be an oxymoronic, contradictory document that contained ideas and concepts that did not necessarily fit together.[81] The Commonwealth Act was presented as an anticolonial document, but it did not request decolonization. It employed both US rhetoric of freedom and equality while also emphasizing special rights for Indigenous CHamoru people. It asked for more local control over systems and institutions that are usually reserved for federal powers, such as the US military and immigration policy. At the same time, however, Commonwealth was seen as an "intermediary step" for a potentially more "permanent" political status such as statehood or independence. The draft reflected how CHamoru leaders navigated through contradicting imperial and international policies and negotiated perspectives from all sides, liberal and radical, including UN and US conventions, visions of Indigenous CHamoru self-determination, and the diverse desires of residents of the island.

As a result, the Commonwealth Act was a conservative document when compared to other anticolonial movements around the Pacific that sought independence from their colonial metropoles. Historian Robert Rogers wrote, "Although radical by Guamanian standards, Chamorro activists are decidedly mild in their demands in comparison with indigenous-rights advocates in New Caledonia, Fiji, and Southeast Asia."[82] Indigenous CHamoru visions for Guåhan's political future did not match the independent nation-state model, nor did they conform to idealized US conceptions of racial liberalism, multiculturalism, and even representative governance. At the core of the Commonwealth Act, however, was the explicit assertion that CHamoru people should determine the future of the island of Guåhan—a concept that was revolutionary for an island that had been controlled unilaterally by colonial powers for nearly four hundred years.[83]

The draft Commonwealth Act began with a preamble that reflected the uncomfortable contradictions of practicing Indigenous CHamoru rights and self-determination within the liberal US empire.

> In recognition of the long-cherished aspiration of the people of Guam to direct the course of their own destiny, and with the belief that mutual respect, understanding, and compromise among people form a more perfect Union, the people of the United States of America, nurtured in the ideals of liberty and democracy, conscious of the obligations under the Treaty of Paris of 1898 and the Charter of the United Nations, do hereby embrace the establishment of the Commonwealth of Guam, ever mindful that the right to self-determination is the heritage of the Chamorro people of Guam, shall be protected.[84]

Adhering to both the US rhetoric of "liberty and democracy" and the UN rhetoric of "right to self-determination," the Act's preamble simultaneously, and perhaps uncomfortably, recognized a "compromise among people" and an assertion of CHamoru people's special relationship to Guåhan and their right to self-determination. The slippage between "the people of Guam" at the beginning of the preamble and "the Chamorro people of Guam" toward the end signaled the uncomfortable transformation of island society. On the one hand, the CSD wanted to assert CHamoru self-governance to protect the Indigenous claims to Guåhan, but on the other hand, they knew that the United States would not approve a document that was solely dedicated to CHamoru claims. They also represented the tensions during the public hearings of the Commonwealth Act in which the CSD sought to incorporate input from both CHamoru activist groups such as OPI-R and the Filipino community in anticipation for a future vote that would determine the act's submission to Congress.

Among other issues—such as the judicial system, trade, taxation, law enforcement, labor, transportation and telecommunications, airlines, land and natural resources, and US financial assistance—the Commonwealth Act sought to rectify the central problems associated with settler militarism.[85] Three provisions—CHamoru self-determination, mutual consent, and local control over immigration—were the most significant. In Article I, "Political Relationship," the Commonwealth Act stipulated that US Congress would recognize "that Commonwealth does not limit the pursuit by the Chamorro people of any ultimate status which they may seek in their progress toward fulfillment of their inherent right of self-determination as expressed in Article 73 of the Charter of the United Nations and in United Nations Resolution

1514."[86] Importantly, Article I also addressed and protected the rights of US citizens under the US Constitution, in particular the Fourteenth and Fifteenth Amendments. Here, the CSD hoped to distinguish Indigenous CHamoru self-determination as an international right defined by the United Nations from the rights of US citizenship bestowed by the US Constitution.

In Article III, the CSD wanted to ensure that the people of Guåhan had a seat at the proverbial table when it came to military activities in Guåhan. Article III, "Foreign Affairs and Defense," stipulated that the United States had to consult with the Government of Guam and receive "mutual consent" on treaties and international agreements that affected the island. Specifically, Article III stipulated that "no military security zones shall be established and no foreign military personnel shall be stationed on the Island of Guam without approval of the government of the Commonwealth except in time of declared war, and no military bases will be established without consultation with the Governor of the Commonwealth of Guam."[87] In addition, the CSD included provisions that allowed GovGuam to access and regain control over excess federal lands that lay vacant.[88]

Article VII on immigration policy created the oddest coalition of supporters. Local control over immigration policy was supported by both CHamoru activists who sought to limit immigration, and business leaders who criticized how US federal immigration policies affected the recruitment and retention of foreign migrant workers for civilian economic development. With local control, the Commonwealth would allow Guåhan to delist the island as a port of entry for US immigration and determine "the admission, exclusion, and expulsion of such aliens." The CSD reasoned that the "continuous and mounting immigration from Asian countries under the U.S. Immigration and Naturalization law has imposed hardships on the people of the island, and could submerge their Chamorro identity within a few decades."[89] Perhaps not wanting to appear anti-immigrant, as was the case with many CHamorus who held this perspective, the CSD argued that there was legal precedent in the Commonwealth of the Northern Mariana Islands and American Sāmoa for a US territory to control immigration policies.

The CSD commenced an educational campaign to shore up support from the Guåhan community. They had originally hoped to have a plebiscite in 1986, but it was postponed to August 1987 after the inauguration of a new governor, Joseph F. Ada, and a nine-week educational campaign.[90] In August, only 39 percent of the island's eligible electorate, all residents of Guåhan regardless of racial and ethnic origin, participated in the plebiscite. Officials believed the low voter turnout was due to unsuccessful education campaigns.

The ballot was organized so that a voter had to approve or disapprove each of the articles, and all except two articles were approved by the electorate. The two articles, perhaps unsurprisingly, were on the two most controversial topics: CHamoru self-determination and immigration. It was assumed that these two articles failed to garner support because "voter trends strongly indicated that relatively more Filipino voters turned out than Chamorro voters to ensure defeat of Articles 1 and 7."[91] Because of the articles' failure, the CSD rewrote the articles to create a more concrete process for CHamoru self-determination, and changed immigration policies from "delisting" to creating a two-year grace period for current residents to petition for their relatives' immigration to the United States. The CSD then conducted another educational campaign for another election that was held in November of the same year.[92] With the strong possibility that the Filipino voting bloc could reject the articles on CHamoru self-determination and immigration, OPI-R conducted their own educational campaign to get CHamoru people out to the polls with the apt slogan "*Hunggan!*"—CHamoru for "yes!"[93] They created pamphlets, wrote editorials and op-eds, held rallies in support of the Commonwealth Act, and created hype around the plebiscite to encourage people to vote.

Still, it seemed that white and Filipino residents of the island opposed the act, while CHamoru people supported it. Even with the revisions, the Commonwealth Act did not sit well with Filipinos. The day before the vote, Filipino medical doctor Eddie Del Rosario told the *Pacific Daily News*, "as far as indigenous rights like self-determination, we recognize that right. But what guarantees do we have that we are not going to be second-class citizens, for instance, in political representation and economic opportunities."[94] The fear of exclusion and inequality prevailed in the minds of Filipino voters. The Commonwealth Act was still perceived to be a document for CHamorus, not for everyone on island.

In the November 7, 1987, plebiscite, 57 percent of the island's electorate voted and the clauses on CHamoru self-determination and immigration both passed. The *Pacific Daily News* published unofficial results, including the breakdown of votes for the Commonwealth articles according to village.[95] In the highly suburbanized villages with high concentrations of immigrants, such as Dédidu, Yigo, and Tamuneng, a majority (50 to 59 percent) voted no on the articles. Southern rural villages with higher proportions CHamoru residents, such as Humåtak, Malesso,' and Inalåhan, voted "yes." With this approval from the Guåhan electorate, the CSD took the win and presented the act to Congress in February 1988.[96]

The Commission on Self-Determination in Washington, DC. From the collection of the Richard F. Taitano Micronesian Area Research Center.

The Unconstitutionality of the Guam Commonwealth Act

The CSD and the Guam congressional representative, Vicente "Ben" Blaz, secured a congressional hearing for the Commonwealth Act in December 1989 in Honolulu, Hawai'i. The CSD solicited as many testimonies as they could, and it was estimated that "over 200 people from Guam were in attendance, [and] many former political and community leaders, youth representatives and ordinary citizens joined Guam officials in presenting testimonies."[97] The commitment of these two hundred people from Guåhan to travel to Hawai'i—some of whom fundraised from the island's community—was a powerful demonstration of the overwhelming support for the Commonwealth. In all the testimonies delivered during the hearings, not one person from Guåhan opposed the Commonwealth Act. Even Gordon Mailloux ("Johnny Guam") a white senator who served the Guam Legislature and waxed lyrical about the benefits of US militarism and tourism in Guåhan, supported the Guam Commonwealth Act because of its provisions to stimulate a local, self-sustaining economy.[98]

Living in a country that promised liberty and self-governance and witnessing decolonization movements around the world, a former governor of Guam, Ricardo Bordallo—along with hundreds of CHamorus in Guåhan—envisioned a world in which the CHamoru people of Guåhan self-determined and self-governed. Bordallo offered his testimony: "We are few; we are distant; we are politically powerless, but we are Americans." He asserted that CHamorus "seek to become members of the American political family in our own separate house, far removed from yours. We seek autonomy and self-government in the form and manner best suited to our needs and situation."[99] In a paradoxical line of reasoning, Bordallo appealed to the liberal rights inherent in US citizenship to advocate for the Guam Commonwealth Act for all those living within the territory and to support the Indigenous CHamoru right to self-determination for Guåhan.

Among the sixty people who testified at the hearings, Ron Rivera took to the podium to deliver the testimony for OPI-R. Rivera pushed the congressional delegation to consider how the United States' reluctance to acknowledge CHamoru self-determination was cause for international embarrassment. "To undermine Chamorro self-determination," he testified, "is to give life to imperialism at a time when we are celebrating its demise in other parts of the world." Although OPI-R believed that the Commonwealth Act was not a true form of CHamoru self-determination because it was approved by CHamoru and non-CHamoru residents of Guåhan, Rivera said that OPI-R supported the Act because it had explicitly noted that CHamoru self-determination was a priority in this new territorial relationship. In CHamoru, Rivera declared, "I magahet na linibri siempre u fatto gi ya hita kumu gaige I destinu-ta gi kannai-ta"—"True freedom will come to us when our destiny is fully in our hands."[100] Subtly different from Bordallo's testimony, Rivera articulated "freedom" as the end of imperialism through CHamoru self-determination.

Despite the dozens of testimonies in support of the Commonwealth Act, one testimony had more power than all the others combined. Stella Guerra, an assistant secretary of the Office of Territorial and International Affairs, represented the Federal Interagency Task Force on the Guam Commonwealth Act. Sitting with her were representatives from the Department of the Interior and the Department of Justice, as well as a representative for the Commander in Chief Pacific of the US Navy. Guerra and the task force recognized "the desires for a new political relationship" and they understood that "the new relationship may require significant changes from the status quo." Although Guerra conveyed that "the Administration wholeheartedly endorses and supports commonwealth and increased self-government for Guam," the task force also strongly urged "the enactment of legislation, *permissible under the Constitution of the United States, acceptable to the Congress, the Administration, and the people of Guam* to achieve a commonwealth relationship which brings greater measure of self-government to the people of Guam."[101] The Commonwealth Act had to be approved by federal and imperial agencies, including the US Navy. The imperial government was not going down without a fight.

The Guam Commonwealth Act—a culmination of nearly a decade of public hearings in Guåhan, legal counsel who advised on constitutional law, and input from members of the US Congress and a UN ambassador—was torn apart by federal agencies who upended the most significant goals of the Commonwealth Act on the basis of US constitutionality.[102] Guerra emphasized that the "Federal-Guam relationship cannot be unilaterally determined by Guam."[103] Guerra pointed out several provisions that were of special concern to the interagency task force. The first was the Commonwealth Act's clause on "mutual consent" in regard to military affairs. Guerra noted that this provision would not hold constitutional muster because it placed Guåhan at the same legal level as the US federal government. It would also result in "legislative and regulatory chaos" and "make it impossible for Federal agencies to carry out their program and policy responsibilities in the Commonwealth." Mutual consent would especially constrain US military operations on the island and thus threaten national security. US national security, once again, justified the denial of CHamoru self-determination and the continued colonization of Guåhan. Furthermore, the Commonwealth Act's provisions on immigration were too stringent. While the task force was willing to create special exceptions to account for Guåhan's geographic location, they were not willing to give the Government of Guåhan complete control over immigration policy, especially naturalization. All in all, Guerra testified that the task force ultimately could not support a bill that would "infringe on, constrain, or impede the overall conduct of U.S. immigration policy, foreign relations, international defense commitments, and national defense."[104] In other words, the interagency task force found that the Commonwealth Act did too much to limit federal—"colonial"—operations in Guåhan, and thus local self-governance and CHamoru self-determination could not be possible.

The Commonwealth's keen attention to CHamoru self-determination came under special scrutiny because it contradicted the US racial liberalism. These sections stipulated that any future self-determination plebiscite would be limited to those of CHamoru descent. The task force believed that the Guam Commonwealth Bill "could be used to deny some U.S. citizens the right to vote based solely on their ethnic background." It was "unconstitutional." Guerra continued, the limited plebiscite "would violate the express language of the Fifteenth Amendment. It would also violate the Equal Protection clause of the Fourteenth Amendment, by impinging in a racially motivated manner, on the fundamental right to vote." The civil rights held within the Fourteenth and Fifteenth Amendments—post–Civil War amendments passed to protect the rights of formerly enslaved Black Americans during Reconstruction—were used to stymie the exercise of Indigenous CHamoru rights in Guåhan. In any iteration of the Guam Commonwealth Act or any iteration of CHamoru self-determination, CHamorus could not challenge the colonial policies that were the basis of their discontents. Guerra argued that provisions on CHamoru self-determination were "hopelessly flawed."[105]

Despite the successful show of support for the act from the Guåhan delegation, the Commonwealth Act was sent back to the drawing board for revisions. The CSD continued to work with the congressional leaders and the Bush administration Task Force on Guam to reconfigure the act and find compromises in 1990 through 1992.[106] Finding compromises was difficult, however, because the CSD was adamant about keeping the provisions on CHamoru self-determination and local control of immigration, and the Bush administration continued to operate through the lens of constitutionality. Even when Robert Underwood became the congressional representative for Guåhan in 1992, the CSD could not get the Guam Commonwealth Act through Congress. It received its final hearing in 1997.[107] By this point, support for Commonwealth status had waned. The Guam Commonwealth was not realized and the hopes for CHamoru self-determination were placed on hold.

THE CHAMORU SELF-DETERMINATION MOVEMENT, embodied by the strong support for the Guam Commonwealth Act of the 1980s and 1990s, represents the contradictions of US multiculturalism and racial liberalism. Guåhan's leaders attempted to revise a political relationship with the United States that would solve the problems that settler militarism introduced to the island and reassert CHamoru power and self-determination by claiming Indigenous identity. Even with support from Filipino allies who understood that CHamoru struggles were related to their homeland's struggle for independence, the fight for Indigenous CHamoru rights and self-determination came up against the multicultural narrative of the United States. By protecting the voting rights of "all" peoples and citing "national defense," the United States obstructed Indigenous self-determination and decolonization on CHamoru terms, demonstrating how US liberalism worked to render invisible setter militarism in Guåhan and constrain the rhetorical terrain upon which CHamorus could convey their discontent. In other words, US liberalism in its many forms is the mechanism by which settler militarism could reproduce and justify itself. Despite one hundred years of advocacy for more self-governance and self-determination, the CHamoru people remained discontent with US empire in the Pacific.

Conclusion

Toward Decolonization

By no means was the demise Guam Commonwealth Movement the end for CHamoru resistance against US settler militarism in Guåhan. CHamoru activists continued to express their discontent. In 1993 CHamoru activists from Nasion Chamoru defiantly scaled the fence at the Naval Air Station in an act of anticolonial resistance.[1] The armed military police arrested them, including Angel "Anghet" Leon Guerrero Santos, who was the radical face of the CHamoru independence movement at the turn of the twenty-first century.[2] When the military police charged them with trespassing on federal property, Nasion Chamoru argued that the US military had trespassed on their ancestral lands.[3] Anghet served a six-month sentence in a federal prison in California for physically attempting to reoccupy his land. Although the majority of the people of Guåhan perceived them as radicals who "jumped the fence," Nasion Chamoru redefined CHamoru discontent and outlined the stakes of why CHamoru self-determination was fundamentally important to the island of Guåhan.[4]

Other CHamoru activists ran for elected positions in the US Congress and within the Guam Legislature and worked to influence laws and created institutional foundations so that CHamoru self-determination would always be in public discourse. Robert Underwood, a member of the Organization of People for Indigenous Rights (OPI-R), was Guåhan's nonvoting representative to the US Congress from 1993 to 2003. He introduced several iterations of the Guam Commonwealth Act and held hearings before it eventually died in Congress. Hope A. Cristobal, another OPI-R member, was elected to the 23rd Guam Legislature in 1995. In 1997 she passed a bill in the Guam Legislature (after a veto by the governor) to establish the Commission on Decolonization, the successor to the Commission on Self-Determination (1980–97) and the Commission on Political Status (1969–80).[5] In line with the work of OPI-R, the act to create the Commission on Decolonization emphasized the "inalienable right of the Chamorro people to self-determination" and stipulated that the "Chamorro people" included "all inhabitants of Guam in 1898 and their descendants who have taken no affirmative steps to preserve or acquire foreign nationality." Even so, the act's legal and moral basis for

Al Lizama, a CHamoru activist with Naison CHamoru, holds sign protesting the US military occupation of CHamoru lands in the early 1990s. Courtesy of the *Pacific Daily News*.

self-determination was founded upon the liberal tenets embedded in the 1898 Treaty of Paris, the Charter of the United Nations, several UN resolutions, and the Organic Act of Guam. The act also created task forces that were charged with educating the public on three possible statuses: statehood, free association, and independence. Except for a short hiatus at the turn of the twenty-first century, the Commission on Decolonization has continued its work well into the 2020s. Despite valiant efforts of CHamorus expressing their discontent in the US Congress and at the United Nations, Guåhan continues to be a US colony—a seemingly anachronistic political formation in the twenty-first century.

In these chapters I have shown how throughout the twentieth century the US empire has strengthened its hold in Guåhan, fortifying the island with military bases and infrastructure meant to project US power in the Pacific. This development has had undeniable consequences for Indigenous CHamoru people and those who have come to call Guåhan home. As a result of settler militarism, Guåhan transformed from an island whose social relations were predicated upon one's participation in CHamoru social relations and *inafa'maolek* to an island where one's social belonging became based upon race, ethnicity, and citizenship. To slow this transformation and resist the efforts of the US military to displace them, CHamorus have had to redefine and reassert their indigeneity and their belonging to Guåhan in multiple, sometimes contradicting ways. Filipino migrants, immigrants, and their descendants have become imbricated in this project of settler militarism as both colonial and neocolonial subjects of the US empire. At the same time, Filipinos have created their own vibrant communities, which have, nonetheless, been used as pawns in the rhetoric of US liberal multiculturalism that bolstered the US settler military presence. This history of Guåhan has shown how liberalism and settler militarism have coalesced into the epitome of twenty-first-century imperialism, where the lack of self-governance and self-determination is shrouded in the seemingly agreeable rhetoric of national and global security and equality for all.

Yet these chapters also hold the building blocks for CHamoru-Filipino relationalities beyond those prescribed by empire. The friendships forged between Filipino revolutionaries and the CHamoru elite during the imperial transition between the Spanish and US empires point to a convergence of intellectual thought that criticized US colonialism. The Hagåtña elite of the 1920s and 1930s consisted of both CHamorus and Filipinos who fought against the arbitrary and autocratic US Naval rule in order to protect the future of their families in Guåhan. Though with historical hindsight we can critique their having worked for the US military, the Filipino community of Guåhan of the postwar period believed they contributed positively to the island's development and by extension aided the CHamoru people. We can see pro-CHamoru rights Governor Ricardo Bordallo in the 1970s and 1980s appreciating Filipino contributions to Guåhan, calling Filipinos brothers and sisters. And we see Filipino women standing in solidarity with the Organization of People for Indigenous Rights when they launched a global campaign for CHamoru self-determination. When CHamorus and Filipinos worked together to critique empire, they did so by grounding themselves in interpersonal relations beyond the liberal categories of race and nation. They partook in *inafa'maolek*, hoping to "make good" the relations between CHamorus and Filipinos despite the empire's propensity to divide them. Although US settler militarism has created structural antagonisms that pit CHamorus and Filipinos against each other in the service of empire, CHamorus and Filipinos on their own in Guåhan have been working side by side, if not together, against the injustices of the US empire.

US Settler Militarism for the Twenty-first Century

History seems to be repeating itself. In the early 2000s, the United States and Japan engaged in a series of discussions and negotiations called the Defense Police Review Initiative, which "focused on alliance transformation . . . with particular attention to the posture of U.S. and Japanese forces in Japan, as well as transforming the capabilities in the Western Pacific around the U.S. and Japanese alliance."[6] By 2006 the two countries came to the Alliance Transformation and Realignment Agreement (ATARA), which reiterated the US commitment to providing aid for Japan's defense, while initiating a "new phase in alliance cooperation" as outlined in the United States–Japan Roadmap for Realignment Implementation. According to this roadmap, this new phase would require relocating "approximately 8,000 III Marine Expeditionary Force personnel and their approximately 9,000 dependents" from Okinawa to Guam.[7] Doing so "would place them on the furthest forward element of *sovereign territory* in the Pacific capable of supporting such a presence," "position U.S. forces to defend the homeland including the U.S. Pacific territories," "provide powerful U.S. presence in the Pacific region," and "provide capabilities that enhance global mobility to meet contingencies around the world."[8] ATARA and the roadmap also indicated a "cost-sharing arrangement" in which Japan would foot $6.09 billion dollars of the $10.27 billion (in 2008 dollars) for "required construction [that] would include facilities and infrastructure for *maintaining a permanent presence on Guam.*"[9]

Even though the initial timeline of realignment has been delayed, the impact of this agreement has led to incredible transformation in the past two decades.[10] The details of the entire military buildup are too complex to consider in this conclusion, but among the various planned infrastructural projects to fulfill ATARA, two are noteworthy. They are the construction of Marine Corps Camp Blas and the Live-Fire Training Range Complex (LF-TRC) in Dédidu. These have caused the massive deforestation of a thousand acres of native limestone forest in Finagåyan and the periodic closing-off of the National Wildlife Refuge at the culturally significant area of Litekyan, also known as Ritidi'an. During the "clearing" of the limestone forest in Finagåyan, military contract construction companies came upon nearly a dozen ancient CHamoru burial sites, including artifacts of latte stone sites, which are archaeological indicators of a historically populated area. Historic preservationists temporarily halted smaller construction projects, but they had no power to deter the military buildup. Military construction continued as soon as the law allowed. In the establishment LFTRC, which sits atop a cliff that overlooks the National Wildlife Refuge, military training exercises are not only harmful to federal environmental conservation projects, but also endanger thousand-years-old CHamoru imprints that stain cave walls. They restrict peoples' access to CHamoru medicinal plants, and potentially pollute the island's primary water resource, the Northern Guam Aquifer.[11] Both these projects, the first to house the Marines and the second to train military personnel from all branches of the military, have placed the desires of the military and "national defense" before the CHamoru people.

It is not just the physical presence of the military installations that is expanding. There is once again another population increase of non-CHamoru people due to military contractors' reliance on foreign migrant labor, in addition to the expected eight thousand Marines and their dependents. The US military has contracted foreign and local construction companies, which employ foreign migrant workers on H-2B and H1-B visas. In August 2022 the governor of Guam announced the presence of three thousand H-2B workers, with expectations of seeing up to five thousand by the end of 2024.[12] Housed in workers' barracks and transported on company buses to worksites, these transient workers, mostly from the Philippines, seek economic gains in Guåhan without necessarily having knowledge of or engaging in networks with CHamorus and the local community. The island's population increased once again with the expected arrival of the US Marines from Okinawa in 2024.[13] Forebodingly, the US Marines had an infamous reputation in Okinawa for illicit activities, including sexual violence and traffic accidents surrounding the base, a major reason for fervent Okinawan anti-base activism since the 1990s.[14] Though each individual—migrant worker and soldier—may be transient in nature, the sheer number of them has pushed, and will continue to push, the limits of local Guåhan society.

Furthermore, with expenditures in military construction in the hundreds of millions of dollars every year since the commencement of the buildup, the local Guåhan economy has become increasingly reliant on the spending of military contractors on the island, especially those who employ locals and pay taxes to the Government of Guam. The report *Economic Outlook for Guam* published by Office of the Governor of Guam in 2023 notes that the rise island's economy is largely due to construction activity associated with ATARA, and that "Guam's location in the Pacific will continue to provide a fundamental advantage for defense and support the long-term trend of tourism expansion."[15] The Government of Guam acknowledges how much increased militarization has benefited the island's economy. In addition, the COVID-19 pandemic of 2020 and Typhoon Mawar in 2023 devastated the once booming tourism industry, the island's only substantial civilian industry.[16] In other words, Guåhan existence has become socially and economically more intertwined—even more so than in past history—with the presence of the military.

The Final Environmental Impact Statement (FEIS) for the military buildup, published by Naval Facilities Engineering Command, shows that the US military was aware of the environmental and social impact this would have, and has had, in Guåhan. The study suggested that the military buildup "may stress the Guam economy" and that this "would be felt more severely by low-income people, who often do not have the resources to buffer hard economic times." It also noted the adverse effects the buildup would have on public health and social services facilities, water supply, and "strains on government services and the social fabric."[17] As a result of the FEIS, thousands of people from Guåhan sent comments to convey their discontent with the military buildup, to which the military responded at best with mitigation efforts that would ease the burden of a population increase and at worst with nonchalance.

Even though the military buildup has been a boon for some, many low- and medium-income families have felt the financial burdens associated with the increased cost of living caused by militarization. With its rising population, the military encourages military personnel to find housing off-base, resulting in them seeking housing in local villages, using their Overseas Housing Allowance and their Veterans Affairs home loans to rent and buy property.[18] Some local landlords have raised their rents to meet the military stipend saturating the upper end of the rental market. Paired with the already high cost of living associated with food and low median annual earnings, local families—CHamoru and Filipino—have found it too expensive to live in

Guåhan. As a result there has been a growing exodus of families, young and old, leaving Guåhan to seek more economic opportunities and social welfare in the continental United States.[19] Many of them join the US military. This is yet another manifestation of settler militarism and the "logic of elimination"—diaspora; where another wave of settlers threatens to replace the CHamoru people because it has become too expensive for CHamorus to remain in Guåhan.

Toward Decolonial Futures

History is indeed repeating itself. Despite the military buildup, CHamoru activists and leaders, land and water protectors, cultural practitioners and educators, poets and scholars—too many to list in this conclusion—have transformed their discontent into Indigenous decolonial activism. In these organizations, younger CHamoru activists learned from elders who navigated different manifestations of US colonialism in the past to dream and work toward the island's decolonial future. They actively resist and refuse the erasure that US settler militarism continues to produce in the twenty-first century by grounding their practices in CHamoru relationship to land, the revival of CHamoru culture and language, and a remapping of Guåhan as a CHamoru place. Since the announcement of the US military's realignment, a massive movement for demilitarization has launched campaigns to halt the buildup. Involved organizations include We Are Guåhan, Save Pågat campaign, and the women's organization Fuetsan Famalao'an.[20] The direct-action group Prutehi Litekyan (Save Ritidian; now Hita Litekyan) has led efforts to organize a coalition of CHamoru and non-CHamoru allies to save the vital cultural and ecological site of Litekyan. Activists have protested at military gates, written letters to local Guåhan and congressional leaders, testified at every hearing possible, and launched lawsuits against the United States in both federal courts and in international forums.[21] They testified at the United Nations and crafted archipelagic solidarity movements across the Pacific. They stand in solidarity with other Indigenous movements throughout the world, including those in Hawai'i, Okinawa, and Palestine. It would require another book-length project to historicize and describe the incredible abundance of CHamoru activism and solidarity movements since the mid-2000s.

Others have continued to fight for a self-determination plebiscite for Guåhan according to the Charter of the United Nations. This includes Independent Guåhan, an official task force associated with the Government of Guam's Commission on Decolonization, which has been vocally educating the island's public about the possibility of an independent future for Guåhan. Not only do they engage in political work, but they also preserve and share the history of the island from various viewpoints, emphasizing CHamoru culture and language in a multitude of media from concerts to podcasts.[22] They have created a stunningly robust archive and educational resource for all things related to Guåhan's past, present, and potential futures.

There is a whole host of organizations, mutual aid groups, and individuals engaged in envisioning a Guåhan beyond settler militarism. The Government of Guam has supported Kumisión I Fino' CHamoru yan I Fina'nå'guen I Historia Yan I Lina'la' I Taotao Tåno (the Commission on CHamoru Language and the Teaching of the History and Culture of the Indigenous People of Guåhan), which creates programming to ensure that CHamoru culture never fades from public view.[23] The Chief Hurao Academy has been at the forefront of CHamoru language immersion for youth, providing a full curriculum in the CHamoru language. They also provide opportunities for the children's families to learn CHamoru to increase language use at home.[24] Sagan Kotturan CHamoru, another cultural and learning center, hosts CHamoru artisans and cultural practitioners, including *yo'amte* (traditional healers), musicians, farmers, and slingstone throwers. The cultural dance groups På'a' Taotao Tano' and Guma' Pålu Li'e'–I Fanlalai'an are using chants and dance to teach CHamoru language, history, legends, and cultures.[25] Nihi Indigenous Media is dedicated to Indigenous CHamoru storytelling in all forms of media.[26] Environmentally minded groups such as the Micronesian Climate Change Alliance work locally and throughout the Mariana Archipelago to advocate for environmental sustainability rooted in CHamoru connection to land and waters.[27] Participating in the global Land Back Movement, Guåhan Sustainable Culture, a nonprofit organization dedicated to food sovereignty through cultural revitalization, has transformed a fifty-acre former ecotourism business into a food resiliency hub in the village of Yoña, to educate the island's community on sustainable agriculture and aquaculture rooted in CHamoru and non-CHamoru relationships to Guåhan and each other.[28]

In solidarity with CHamoru self-determination and decolonization efforts, the organization Filipinos for Guåhan has worked to increase awareness about what a decolonized future means for Filipinos who call Guåhan home, and how they can ethically contribute to the cause. We believe that the right to self-determination belongs to the CHamoru people, and instead of advocating for a particular political status, we see our role as active supporters of CHamoru movements for self-determination, decolonization, and sovereignty as a whole. Our outreach is grounded in our own Filipino ancestors' struggles of migration, while being mindful of the CHamoru people on whose lands our ancestors settled. In doing so, we believe we can respectfully practice *inafa'maolek* for a people and an island that have given us and our families so much.[29]

It is not just organizations and groups dreaming up decolonial futures. Writers such as Craig Santos Perez and Julian Aguon share their literary work globally, increasing awareness of how CHamoru people are resilient in the face of US militarization.[30] CHamoru scholars such as Michael "Miget" Bevacqua, Kenneth Gofigan Kuper, and Victoria Lola-Leon Guerrero to name only a few are on the ground changing the narrative of Guåhan history in public discourse, making sure to include the revitalization of the CHamoru language at the core of their missions. There is a dynamic zeitgeist of CHamoru cultural pride, where individual poets, artists, designers, singers, songwriters, crafters, and so many others are defining for themselves what it means to be CHamoru.

In setting their sights on decolonization, the CHamoru people are doing more than resisting settler militarism political manifestations. They are, at once, engaged in a renaissance of CHamoru indigeneity both in Guåhan and in the CHamoru diaspora, proving to the world that they will not be easily subsumed by the US empire. Filipinos work in solidarity alongside them. They, CHamorus and Filipinos, practice a decolonial present and envision a decolonial future with *inafa'maolek* at the core. As CHamoru lawyer and activist Julian Aguon so eloquently wrote, "Guam may have to bear the burden of being a colony in a world suffering from decolonization fatigue, but—to be clear—her people mean to live."[31]

Notes

Prologue

1. The Hopkins Committee consisted of Dr. Ernest M. Hopkins, Mr. Maurice J. Tobin, and Dr. Knowles Ryerson, who were intellectuals and academics who were appointed by the Secretary of the Navy to research and recommend policies for the Naval Governments in Guåhan and American Sāmoa. United States, *Hopkins Committee Report.*

2. Hattori, "Guardians of Our Soil."

3. "Open Forum in the Halls of Guam Congress, Agana, Guam, 3 March 1947," folder 32, box 2, Governor Willis Winter Bradley Jr. Papers, MSS 960, Micronesian Area Research Center, University of Guam.

4. "Open Forum."

5. United States, *Hopkins Committee Report.*

6. "Memorial Dedication," *Guam Recorder*, May 1937, 27.

7. Tony Palomo, "52 Filipinos Exiled Here Included an Elite Group of Intellectuals," *Territorial Sun*, May 28, 1961, 10.

8. Ancestry.com, U.S., World War I Draft Registration Cards, 1917–1918 (online database).

9. "Adolfo Camacho Sgambelluri," in *Hale'ta I Manfåyi*, 147.

10. "Who's Who in Guam: Mr. Jose M. Flores," *Guam Recorder*, April 1937, 15.

11. "Memorial Dedication," 9.

12. "Memorial Dedication," 27.

Introduction

1. "Proclamation," folder 14, box 3, National Archives, RG 80, Annual Reports of the Governors of Guam., 1901–1940, MSS 930, Micronesian Area Research Center, University of Guam.

2. Lowe, *Intimacies of Four Continents*, 4.

3. "Proclamation."

4. Lowe, *Intimacies of Four Continents*, 3; Jung, *Menace to Empire*, 10–11; Stoler, *Duress*, 177, 188, 197; Goldstein, "Introduction"; Westad, *The Global Cold War*, 10.

5. Lowe, *Intimacies of Four Continents*, 3; Westad, *The Global Cold War*, 22.

6. Lowe, *Intimacies of Four Continents*, 16.

7. Lowe, *Intimacies of Four Continents*, 2–3; Westad, *The Global Cold War*, 10–11.

8. Flores, *Tip of the Spear*, 42.

9. Bevacqua, "Chamorros, Ghosts, Non-Voting Delegates"; Kuper, "Kontra I Peligru, Na'Fansåfo Ham."

10. Espiritu, Lowe, and Yoneyama, "Transpacific Entanglements," 176.

11. Bevacqua and Cruz, "Banality of American Empire," 141.

12. Bevacqua and Cruz, "Banality of American Empire," 141.

13. On military base studies with particular references to Guåhan, see Kim, *Settler Garrison*; Lutz, *The Bases of Empire*; Davis, *The Empires' Edge*; Vine, *Base Nation.*

14. Kauanui, *Paradoxes of Hawaiian Sovereignty*; Saranillio, *Unsustainable Empire*; Jung, *Menace to Empire*; Goodyear-Ka'ōpua, Hussey, and Kahunawaika'ala Wright, *A Nation Rising*; Fujikane, *Mapping Abundance.*

15. On Spanish colonialism in Guåhan and the Marianas, see Atienza, "Priests, Mayors and Indigenous Offices"; Madrid, *Beyond Distances.*

16. Sales, "#NeverAgainToMartialLaw."

17. Flores, *Tip of the Spear.*

18. The one significant exception is Flores, *Tip of the Spear.*

19. Lowe, *Intimacies of Four Continents*, 146–47.

20. Lowe, *Intimacies of Four Continents*, 2–3.

21. On CHamoru-Filipino relations, see Camacho, "Filipinos, Pacific Islanders, and the American Empire,"; Diaz, "Bye Bye Ms. American Pie"; Rondilla, "The Filipino Question"; Flores, "'Little Island'"; Ong, "Colonial Boundaries of Exilic Discourse."

22. Diaz, "Bye Bye Ms. American Pie," 157.

23. Oberiano, "Race and Empire," 243. I am heavily indebted to Molina, HoSang, and Gutiérrez, *Relational Formations of Race Practice*, for helping me articulate this methodology.

24. Saranillio, *Unsustainable Empire*, 24.

25. Kristin Oberiano, "What It Means to Identify as a Settler," *Guam Daily Post*, October 7, 2017; Espina, "Ali'e' and Asi'i," 104–5.

26. Espina, "Ali'e' and Asi'i," 116.

27. Diaz, "Bye Bye Ms. American Pie," 156.

28. Espiritu, *Home Bound*, 5–6.

29. A critique shared by Jung, *Menace to Empire*, 16; and Teves and Arvin, "Decolonizing API," 108.

30. Notable exceptions include Flores, *Tip of the Spear*; Espina, "Ali'e' and Asi'i," 115; Camacho, "Filipinos, Pacific Islanders and the American Empire," 17; Espiritu, Lowe, and Yoneyama, "Transpacific Entanglements," 187.

31. Ricardo J. Bordallo, "Is Guam for Sale? No." Paper delivered at 10th Island Conference on Public Administration (1989), quoted in Michael F. Philips, "Land," in *Hale'ta*, 2.

32. Brandon Cruz, *I Tinituhon: Rediscovering Fo'na & Pontan*, https://www.youtube.com/watch?v=yQPM1Iayq7s&ab_channel=BrandonLeeCruz.

33. Monnig, "Proving Chamorro,'" chap. 5 (221–78).

34. The definition of *inafa'maolek* can be discerned by its constitutive parts: *in-a-fa'-maolek*: "in" denotes a noun; "a" creates a reciprocal relation between two entities; "fa'" is "to make"; "maolek" means "good."

35. DeLisle, *Placental Politics*, 4.

36. DeLisle, *Placental Politics*, 4. Oberiano and Ong, "Envisioning *Inafa'maolek* Solidarity."

37. Camacho, *Sacred Men*, 23; Oberiano and Ong, "Envisioning *Inafa'maolek* Solidarity."

38. Wolfe, "Settler Colonialism," 388, 395.

39. Wolfe, "Settler Colonialism," 388, 395.

40. Nebolon, *Settler Militarism*, 5.

41. Nebolon, *Settler Militarism*, 5.

42. Nebolon, *Settler Militarism*, 13.

43. Flores, *Tip of the Spear*, 3.

44. On loyalty as a limited political language for CHamoru colonial resistance, see Diaz, "Deliberating Liberation Day," 165.

45. Kauanui, "False Dilemmas," 291.

46. The debate of whether to label immigrants and migrants as "settlers" within a settler colonial regime is a contentious one. For instance, Lorenzo Veracini makes a critical distinction between settlers—"[they are] founders of political orders and carry their sovereignty with them"—and migrants—who "can be coopted" but do not "enjoy inherent rights and are characterized by a lack of sovereign entitlement." Veracini, *Settler Colonialism*, 3.

47. Samuel Betances, "Limits of Cross-Cultural Education in Solving Ethnic Conflict in Guam," *Islander* by *Pacific Daily News*, October 23, 1977, 4.

48. Likewise argued by Gandhi, *Archipelago of Resettlement*, 133–34, 136.

49. Also argued in Flores, *Tip of the Spear*, 6.

50. Fujikane, *Mapping Abundance*, 14.

51. Rodriguez, *Migrants for Export*.

52. On Filipino migration to different geographies of US empire, see Poblete, *Islanders in the Empire*; Mabalon, *Little Manila Is in the Heart*; Baldoz, *Third Asiatic Invasion*; Labrador, *Building Filipino Hawai'i*; Espiritu, *Home Bound*; Manalansan and Espiritu, *Filipino Studies*; De Leon, "Sugarcane Sakadas"; De Leon, *Bundok*; Woods, "Building Empire's Archipelago."

53. Saranillio, "Colliding Histories," 259–60. On American education in the Philippines, Clutario, *Beauty Regimes*; Kramer, *The Blood of Government*.

54. Works such as Ikyo Day's *Alien Capital* and Manu Karuka's *Empire's Tracks* offer Marxist interpretations of Asians in settler colonial spaces. My work instead follows in the tradition of scholars of Asian settler colonialism, including Kanaka Maoli scholar Haunani Kay-Trask, settler aloha ʻaina Candace Fujikane, and Dean Saranillio, among many others. See Fujikane, "Introduction," in Fujikane and Okamura, *Asian Settler Colonialism*, 6; Fujikane, *Mapping Abundance*, 12. For more on Asian Settler Colonialism, see Saranillio, "Settler Colonialism"; Saranillio, "Why Asian Settler Colonialism Matters."

55. Joe Taitano II, "New Census Data Reveals More About Guam Residents," *Pacific Daily News*, November 14, 2022, https://www.guampdn.com/news/new-census-data-reveals-more-about-guam-residents/article_ea886778-5e64-11ed-a2fd-1b6252d2bdad.html.

56. Joe S. Dizon, "Filipinos in Guam's 1970 Elections," *Guam Recorder*, January–March 1970, 56–59.

57. Haidee Eugenio Gilbert, "Campaigns Discuss Impact of Filipino Voters," *Pacific Daily News*, August 20, 2018, https://www.guampdn.com/news/local/campaigns-discuss-impact-of-filipino-voters/article_670565cc-83e4-5674-87f4-e2027ce75516.html.

58. Monnig, "'Proving Chamorro.'"

59. Also argued by M. Cruz, "Identity and Self-Determination in Guam," 79.

60. Fujikane, "Introduction," 12. On Native identity defined through Indigenous genealogy versus liberal notions of race and colonial blood quantum policies, see Kauanui, *Hawaiian Blood*.

61. Espina, "Ali'e' and Asi'i," 105.

62. Oberiano and Ong, "Envisioning *Inafa'maolek* Solidarity."

Chapter One

1. Philippine Diary Project, "Diary of Apolinario Mabini 24 January 1901." http://philippinediaryproject.com/1901/01/24/thursday-24-january-1901/.

2. US Congress, *Letter from the Secretary of the Navy.*

3. Mabini, *La Revolución Filipina.* While there have been a few works that historicize Mabini's incarceration in Guam, few have historicized him and the relations he had with CHamoru people. One work stands out in historicizing the significance of this CHamoru-Filipino encounter: Ong, "Colonial Boundaries of Exilic Discourse." On Mabini's incarceration in Guåhan, see Navarro, "Philippines-Marianas Relations"; De Viana, *In the Far Islands.*

4. On carcerality and Filipino exiles in Guåhan, see Ong, "Sculpted Memories."

5. On US colonialism in the Philippines at the turn of the twentieth century, see Kramer, *The Blood of Government*; Hoganson, *Fighting for American Manhood*; Go, *American Empire.* On US colonialism on Guåhan at the turn of the twentieth century, see Diaz, "Pious Sites"; Hofschneider, *A Campaign for Political Rights.*

6. Rogers, *Destiny's Landfall*, 86; Madrid, *Beyond Distances*, 57.

7. CHamoru families on Guåhan, especially those with Spanish last names, can trace their ancestry to an imperial soldier who was stationed in Guam sometime during the Spanish era. Clement, "Bifurcating the Hagåtña Narrative," 167–94.

8. Clement spells Hagåtña as Agadña to conform to Spanish period orthography. Clement, "Bifurcating the Hagåtña Narrative," 176.

9. Clement, "Bifurcating the Hagåtña Narrative," 182.

10. Madrid, *Beyond Distances*, 9.

11. Clement, "Bifurcating the Hagåtña Narrative," 167.

12. Historian Michael Clement argues, rightly, that histories of *mestisu* CHamorus of Hagåtña have come to dominate CHamoru historiography, and that more research is necessary to historicize CHamorus outside of the capital city to better demonstrate the diversity of CHamoru indigeneity in the Spanish and US periods. Clement, "Bifurcating the Hagåtña Narrative," 167–69.

13. On Pacific peoples and mobility, see Chang, *World and All the Things upon It*; Diaz, "Voyaging for Anti-Colonial Recovery"; Underwood, "Excursions into Inauthenticity"; Droessler, *Coconut Colonialism.*

14. Bruce Campbell, "Luis de Torres," Guampedia, https://www.guampedia.com/luis-de-torres/.

15. Madrid, *Beyond Distances*, 10.

16. Audreya Taitano and Shannon Murphy, "Padre Jose Bernardo Palomo," Guampedia, n.d., https://www.guampedia.com/padre-jose-bernardo-palomo/; Madrid, *Beyond Distances*, 15.

17. Madrid, *Beyond Distances*, 15.

18. Aboitiz, "Philippine Asianist Thought."

19. Bankoff, *Crime, Society, and the State*, 185.

20. Bankoff, *Crime, Society, and the State*, 185.

21. *Noli Me Tangere* was originally published in 1886 and is widely hailed as the novel that spurred the Philippine Revolution. In this scene, a Catholic priest was referring to the Mar-

ianas as a penal colony for Filipinos who sought to join the revolution against the Spanish colonial government. Rizal, *Noli Me Tangere*, 307.

22. Madrid, *Beyond Distances*, 206.

23. Rogers, *Destiny's Landfall*, 95; De Viana, *In the Far Islands*, 155, 118.

24. Entry for October 17, 1851, under the title "Filipino Convicts on Guam." According to William Safford, a US lieutenant governor stationed in Guåhan in 1900, Spanish Governor de la Corte "anticipated no trouble in allowing the convicts to be scattered over the island as long as there were no ship in the harbor, as there was no possible means for them to escape from the island but it was his intention to have them divided into gangs, placed under surveillance of guards, and employed as far as possible from the port." Anticipating no trouble, the governor distributed the convicts "among the most respectable and industrious citizens of the island dedicated to agriculture and other useful pursuits." Safford, *History of the Marianas Islands*.

25. Safford, entry for November 8, 1851, *History of the Marianas Islands*.

26. Safford, entry for November 8, 1851, *A History of the Marianas Islands*.

27. This section on the Spanish period of deportados exiled to Guåhan as a result of the Cavite Mutiny is heavily reliant on and grateful for the research and guidance of Carlos Madrid. Madrid *Beyond Distances*.

28. Schumacher, "The Cavite Mutiny," 58.

29. Rogers, *Destiny's Landfall*, 96.

30. De Viana, *In the Far Islands*, 125.

31. Ibáñez del Carmen and Resano, *Chronicle of the Mariana Islands*, 69.

32. Ibáñez del Carmen and Resano, *Chronicle of the Mariana Islands*, 63, 64, 70, 71.

33. Ibáñez del Carmen and Resano, *Chronicle of the Mariana Islands*, 64.

34. Rogers, *Destiny's Landfall*, 96.

35. Rogers, *Destiny's Landfall*, 97.

36. De Viana, *In the Far Islands*, 120.

37. Madrid, *Beyond Distances*, 72.

38. Madrid, *Beyond Distances*, 213.

39. Madrid, *Beyond Distances*, 213.

40. Ibáñez del Carmen and Resano, *Chronicle of the Mariana Islands*, 105.

41. Father Ibáñez left the island sometime between 1878 and 1887. This is when Father Francisco Resano started to write his diaries about life in Guåhan. Resano continued to write about Guåhan until his death in 1892. Ibáñez del Carmen and Resano, *Chronicle of the Mariana Islands*, 106.

42. Ibáñez del Carmen and Resano, *Chronicle of the Mariana Islands*, 106.

43. Ibáñez del Carmen and Resano, *Chronicle of the Mariana Islands*, 106.

44. Quoted in Madrid, *Beyond Distances*, 200.

45. Aboitiz, "Philippine Asianist Thought," 20.

46. De Viana, "Development of the Philippine Foreign Service."

47. Kramer, *The Blood of Government*, 92–93.

48. Kramer, *The Blood of Government*, 97.

49. Kramer, *The Blood of Government*, 145.

50. Rogers, *Destiny's Landfall*, passim 103–6.

51. Rogers, *Destiny's Landfall*, 108.

52. For more details about the partition of the Marianas, see Farrell, "Partition of the Marianas."

53. Rogers, *Destiny's Landfall*, 110.

54. Safford, *A Year on the Island*, 22.

55. Safford, *A Year on the Island*, 29.

56. Safford, *A Year on the Island*, 148.

57. Safford, *A Year on the Island*, 150.

58. Safford, *A Year on the Island*, 151.

59. Safford, *A Year on the Island*, 151.

60. Kasperbauer, "The Chamorro Culture," 29. On *inafa'maolek*, see Cunningham, *Ancient Chamorro Society*, 86–89.

61. Safford, *A Year on the Island*, 6.

62. Hattori, "Navy Blues," 18–19.

63. Hattori, "Navy Blues," 18, 24.

64. Letter to the Secretary of the Navy (August 28, 1899), No.18-GS, Richard P. Leary Papers, MSS 2370, Micronesian Area Research Center (MARC), University of Guam (UOG).

65. Safford, *A Year on the Island*, 52.

66. Safford, *A Year on the Island*, 52.

67. Safford, *A Year on the Island*, 53.

68. Safford, *A Year on the Island*, 52.

69. Letter to the Secretary of the Navy.

70. Safford, *A Year on the Island*, 53.

71. Safford, *A Year on the Island*, 102.

72. Leon Guerrero, "Forzado System."

73. Mabini also mentions this unnamed woman during his stay on Guam. De Viana, *In the Far Islands*, 134.

74. "Proclamation," folder 14, box 3, National Archives, RG 80, Annual Reports of the Governors of Guam, MSS 930, MARC, UOG.

75. "Proclamation."

76. "Proclamation."

77. To my knowledge, this petition has not been historicized in previous histories of the period. Translation with help from ChatGPT. The original Spanish is as follows: "El pueblo chamorro, como antes queda dicho, abriga la esperanza de haber de entras, si es que ya insensiblemente no lo ha hecho, en la senda del progreso asi moral, como material, por venir siendo gobernado por una nación eminentemente libre por su forma de gobierno, y eminentemente comercial é industriosa y esa legítima esperanza le da títulos para que los altos Poderes, qun distrayendo un tanto su atención de los vastos asuntos, que la ocupan dediquen de élla un poco al adelantamiento de esta Isla, hay pobre y casi improductiva, pero que, mediante la dirección de una mano hábil, podría al cabo de algún tiempo enriquecerse, resarciéndose entonces del tiempo perdido y coadyuvando, en la medida de sus fuerzas, á lo que el Estado exija." "La Gobernador de isla de Guam," folder 12, box 3, National Archives, RG 80, Annual Reports of the Governors of Guam, MSS 930, MARC, UOG.

78. "La Gobernador de isla de Guam."

79. "La Gobernador de isla de Guam."

80. Rogers, *Destiny's Landfall*, 111.

81. Memoirs, William Edwin Safford Papers, 1899–1901, folder 2, MSS 980, MARC, UOG. After leaving Guam, Safford published several academic pieces on his experiences on Guåhan, scientific findings in botany from the island, as well as CHamoru-English dictionary he compiled with Påle' Palomo. He served as a botanist with the Department of Agriculture, and earned a PhD from George Washington University. He was a well-respected scientist who had genera of plants named after him. He passed away in 1924. Jillete Leon Guerrero, "Introduction to William Edwin Safford (1859–1926)," in *A Year on the Island of Guam*, 6–7.

82. Several folders in William Safford Papers, folder 1, MSS 980, MARC, UOG.

83. Atanasio Perez to William Safford, July 5, 1902, William Edwin Safford Papers, folder 1, MSS 980, MARC, UOG.

84. Safford, "Guam and Its People."

85. During the first forays into insular empire, "American colonizers initially defaulted to Spanish precedents or deferred to native aspirations." McCoy, Scarano, and Johnson, "On the Tropic of Cancer," 11.

86. William Safford's journal recorded: "Trouble in the village of Agaña, The *Gobernacillio* has arrested the Justice of the Peace and locked him up in a Calaboose. Investigation necessary. It is hard enough to preserve harmony between the natives and the enlisted men—its more difficult to regulate family quarrels." Safford, *A Year on the Island*, 154.

87. Gualhen I. Aguila, "Capture of Mabini," *Philippine Free Press*, January 4, 1941, 16–17.

88. Aguila, "Capture of Mabini."

89. Kalaw, *The Philippine Revolution*, 239; Reyno, *The Political, Social, and Moral Philosophy*, 38–39.

90. Mabini, *The True Decalogue*; *Mabini's Decalogue for Filipinos*, Project Gutenberg, 2005, https://www.gutenberg.org/files/14660/14660-h/14660-h.htm; Kalaw, *The Philippine Revolution*, 88–89; Reyno, *The Political, Social, and Moral Philosophy*, 50–57.

91. Kalaw, *The Philippine Revolution*, 3, 88, 106, 142, 144, 238–39, 242–43.

92. On the rise of the US security state in response to anticolonial actors such as Mabini, see Jung, *Menace to Empire*.

93. Veloso, *Testament and Political Letters of Apolinario Mabini*, 337.

94. Weber, "Fearing the Flood."

95. Elihu Root to Secretary of the Navy, December 26, 1900, folder 28, box 3, National Archives, RG 80, Annual Reports of the Governors of Guam, MSS 930, MARC, UOG. Also known as the "Mabini Folder," in National Archives, RG 80, General Records of the Department of the Navy, 1804–1983.

96. George C. Remey to Naval Governor of Guam, January 14, 1901, folder 28, box 3, National Archives, RG 80, Annual Reports of the Governors of Guam, MSS 930, MARC, UOG.

97. This dispatch was sent from the headquarters of the US Marine Corps to Governor Schroeder on April 9, 1901, four months after the arrival of the Filipino exiles. Folder 28, box 3, National Archives, RG 80, Annual Reports of the Governors of Guam, MSS 930, MARC, UOG.

98. Philippine Diary Project, "31 January, 1901," http://philippinediaryproject.com/1901/02/01/1st-of-february-1901/.

99. Philippine Diary Project, "31 January, 1901," http://philippinediaryproject.com/1901/02/01/1st-of-february-1901/.

100. "Letter to His Brother Alejandro, July 25, 1901," in Veloso, *Testament and Political Letters of Apolinario Mabini*, 339–40.

101. Veloso, *Testament and Political Letters of Apolinario Mabini*, 340.

102. Veloso, *Testament and Political Letters of Apolinario Mabini*, 340.

103. Veloso, *Testament and Political Letters of Apolinario Mabini*, 341.

104. Veloso, *Testament and Political Letters of Apolinario Mabini*, 342; Philippine Diary Project, "13 February 1901," 1/02/13/13th-of-february-1901, http://philippinediaryproject.com/1901st-few-days-of-december-1901/.

105. "Pio Del Pilar: 1865–1931."

106. Original Spanish is as follows: "Se nos ha dicho ademas que nuestra rigurosa incomunicacion es debida a la peticion de los naturales de la Isla, escarmentados de los filipinos confinados por delitos comunes en tiempo del Gobierno espanol, los cuales cometieron todo genero de abusos." Mabini, *La Revolución Filipina*, 2:229.

107. Seaton Schroeder to Assistant Secretary of the Navy, January 28, 1901, folder 28, box 3, National Archives, RG 80, Annual Reports of the Governors of Guam, MSS 930, MARC, UOG.

108. Philippine Diary Project, "24th of February 1901," http://philippinediaryproject.com/1901/02/24/24th-of-february-1901/.

109. Philippine Diary Project, "24th of February 1901."

110. Mabini, *La Revolucíon Filipina*, 2:236.

111. For instance, Pedro Paterno, who succeeded Mabini as prime minister after the Malolos Constitution, was the son of Maximo Paterno, whom Påle' Palomo had met in Guåhan in the 1870s.

112. Veloso, *Testament and Political Letters of Apolinario Mabini*, 344.

113. Philippine Diary Project, "13 February 1901," 1/ 02/13/13th-of-february-1901/"http://philippinediaryproject.com/1901/02/13/13th-of-february-1901/.

114. Mabini, *La Revolucíon Filipina*, 2:242–43.

115. Mabini, *La Revolucíon Filipina*, 2:241.

116. Mabini, *La Revolucíon Filipina*, 2:236.

117. Tony Palomo, "52 Filipinos Exiled Here Included an Elite Group of Intellectuals," *Territorial Sun*, May 28, 1961, 10.

118. Palomo, "52 Filipinos Exiled Here," 10.

119. Palomo, "52 Filipinos Exiled Here," 10.

120. US Congress, House Resolution 404, "Commemorating 100 Years of Relations Between the People of the United States and People of the Philippines," 105th Congress, June 9, 1998, *Congressional Record* 144, no. 73.

121. Veloso, *Testament and Political Letters of Apolinario Mabini*, 345.

122. Veloso, *Testament and Political Letters of Apolinario Mabini*, 346.

123. Veloso, *Testament and Political Letters of Apolinario Mabini*, 346.

124. Veloso, *Testament and Political Letters of Apolinario Mabini*, 351.

125. Veloso, *Testament and Political Letters of Apolinario Mabini*, 355.

126. Veloso, *Testament and Political Letters of Apolinario Mabini*, 356.

127. Veloso, *Testament and Political Letters of Apolinario Mabini*, 356.

128. Palomo, "52 Filipinos Exiled Here," 10.

129. Apolinario Mabini, "Introductory Manifesto," in *The Philippine Revolution*, trans. Leon Ma. Guerrero (1969), https://www.philippinen.at/aufi/history/mabinioc.htm.

130. Apolinario Mabini, "X: End and Fall of the Revolution," in *The Philippine Revolution*, https://www.philippinen.at/aufi/history/mabini10.htm.

131. Apolinario Mabini, "XI: Conclusion," in *The Philippine Revolution*, https://www.philippinen.at/aufi/history/mabini09.htm.

132. Apolinario Mabini, "XI: Conclusion," in *The Philippine Revolution*, https://www.philippinen.at/aufi/history/mabini09.htm.

133. Scholars and community members interested in Guåhan history have labeled this petition the "first Chamorro petition" of the long movement for CHamoru self-governance in the twentieth and twenty-first centuries. I refrain from labeling all the signers as only CHamoru. Upon researching the signers of the petition, some of them had *mestisu* heritage, including Filipino, Spanish, and Irish ancestors. One petitioner, Charles Stimpson, was a white Navy sailor assigned in Guåhan. My goal here is not to critique the historiography itself, but to suggest that the long movement for more rights, self-determination, and self-governance for the island of Guam has included a diverse set of supporters. CHamoru historian Anne Hattori has used the phrase "Guamanian petition" in her article "Navy Blues," and although the term "Guamanian" is anachronistic as well, I think it is a better descriptor of those who signed the petition. On Naval-era petitions from Guåhan, see Hofschneider, *Campaign for Political Rights*.

134. House of Representatives, Committee on Insular Affairs, *Petition*, 2.

135. Downes v. Bidwell, 182 US 244 (1901), https://supreme.justia.com/cases/federal/us/182/244/.

136. House of Representatives, Committee on Insular Affairs, *Petition*, 2.

137. House of Representatives, Committee on Insular Affairs, *Petition*, 2.

138. House of Representatives, Committee on Insular Affairs, *Petition*, 2.

139. House of Representatives, Committee on Insular Affairs, *Petition*, 2.

140. House of Representatives, Committee on Insular Affairs, *Petition*, 4.

141. General Orders, no. 69, folder 28, box 3, National Archives, RG 80, Annual Reports of the Governors of Guam, MSS 930, MARC, UOG.

142. "Mabini Folder," folder 28, box 3, MSS 930, MARC, UOG.

143. "Mabini Folder."

144. Veloso, *Testament and Political Letters of Apolinario Mabini*, 364.

145. Veloso, *Testament and Political Letters of Apolinario Mabini*, 368.

146. Veloso, *Testament and Political Letters of Apolinario Mabini*, 369.

147. Tony Palomo, "Among the Exiles, A Sublime Paralytic," *Territorial Sun*, May 7, 1961, 10.

148. Palomo, "Among the Exiles," 10.

149. Palomo, "Among the Exiles," 10.

150. Palomo, "Among the Exiles," 10. On employment of colonial elite, see Go, *American Empire*.

151. Often perceived as a form of tutelage, the new American colonial officials utilized preexisting colonial elite to manage their newly acquired colonies. See Go, *American Empire*.

152. Palomo, "Among the Exiles," 10.
153. Palomo, "Among the Exiles," 10.
154. Cook, "A Survey of Exiles," 72.
155. "Letter to William Safford from Justo Dungca, 21st March 1904," William Edwin Safford Papers, folder 11, MSS 980, MARC, UOG.

Chapter Two

1. Jose C. Torres, "Guam Congress Special Session, 25 September 1926," folder 22, box 1, Guam Naval Government Records, 1899–1950, MSS 870, Micronesian Area Research Center (MARC), University of Guam (UOG).
2. "Guam Congress Special Session."
3. "Proceedings of Guam Congress Meeting, October 2, 1926," folder 22, box 1, Guam Naval Government Records, 1899–1950, MSS 870, MARC, UOG.
4. While there were reasons to see differences, the 1926 petition was the first time CHamorus articulated differences through race. Robert Underwood, interview with the author, August 14, 2019.
5. This system continued into the 1930s, when the Philippine Commonwealth was established as a result of the Hawes-Cutting Act and the Tydings-McDuffie Act, which stipulated that the Philippines must have independence by 1945.
6. On race and liberalism, see Wolfe, *Traces of History*, 10; Lowe, *Intimacies of Four Continents*, 7; and Jung, *Menace to Empire*, 18–19.
7. Goldstein, "Introduction," 16.
8. Clement, "Bifurcating the Hagåtña Narrative," 176.
9. DeLisle, *Placental Politics*, 101–3.
10. "Proceedings of the Guam Congress Meeting," October 2, 1926. folder 22, box 1, Guam Naval Government Records.
11. Shah, *Stranger Intimacy*, 15; King, "Structural Sources of Ambiguity."
12. Arvin, *Possessing Polynesians*.
13. DeLisle, *Placental Politics*.
14. "Proceedings of the Guam Congress."
15. On health practices in prewar Guåhan, see Hattori, *Colonial Dis-Ease*; DeLisle, *Placental Politics*.
16. Underwood, "American Education."
17. Viernes, "Negotiating Manhood."
18. Leo Babauta, "Chester Carl Butler," Guampedia, https://www.guampedia.com/chester-carl-butler/.
19. On the US Naval era in Guåhan, see Hattori, *Colonial Dis-Ease*; Viernes, "Negotiating Manhood"; Camacho, *Cultures of Commemoration*; DeLisle, *Placental Politics*; Underwood, "American Education."
20. Goldstein, "Introduction," 16.
21. Flores, *Tip of the Spear*, 18–19.
22. DeLisle, *Placental Politics*, 43, 76.
23. Clement, "Bifurcating the Hagåtña Narrative."
24. Hofschneider, *A Campaign for Political Rights*.

25. DeLisle, *Placental Politics*, 155.

26. Aguilar, "Tracing Origins"; Thomas, *Orientalists, Propagandists, and Ilustrados*.

27. Aguilar, "Tracing Origins."

28. Aguilar, "Tracing Origins," 614.

29. Aguilar, "Tracing Origins," 606; Aboitiz, "Philippine Asianist Thought," 28.

30. Translation of *giniha* provided by glossary in DeLisle, *Placental Politics*, 157.

31. Agueda Iglesias, "Should the Philippine Islands Be Granted Independence?," *Guam Recorder*, December 1926, 239.

32. Iglesias, "Should the Philippine Islands Be Granted Independence?," 239.

33. Monnig, "'Proving Chamorro,'" 132.

34. Monnig, "'Proving Chamorro,'" 204.

35. Monnig, "'Proving Chamorro,'" 206.

36. Lilli Perez-Iyechad, "Inafa'maolek: Striving for Harmony," Guampedia, December 21, 2019, https://www.guampedia.com/inafamaolek/; Cunningham, *Ancient Chamorro Society*, 86.

37. Diaz, "Bye Bye Ms. American Pie," 151.

38. Iglesias, "Should the Philippine Islands Be Granted Independence?," 211.

39. As his name suggests, Tomas Anderson Calvo was of *mestisu* background, with ancestors from Scotland and Spain by way of the Philippines, and CHamorus. Calvo attended the University of Santo Tomas in Manila. Cited in P. Sanchez, *Guåhan, Guam*, 109. For Calvo's background, see Tony Palomo, "52 Filipinos Exiled Here Included an Elite Group of Intellectuals," *Territorial Sun*, May 28, 1961, 10.

40. "Proceedings of the Guam Congress."

41. "Proceedings of the Guam Congress," 3.

42. "Proceedings of the Guam Congress," 6.

43. "Proceedings of the Guam Congress," 3.

44. As described by historian Robert Rogers, "A Spanish census of 1727, for example, reported more than 4000 families of Spanish and Filipino soldiers and retirees, most of whom had Chamorro wives and children of mixed ethnicity." Rogers, *Destiny's Landfall*, 79.

45. Thomas, *Orientalists, Propagandists, and Ilustrados*, 57.

46. "Proceedings of the Guam Congress," 5.

47. "Proceedings of the Guam Congress," 3.

48. "Proceedings of the Guam Congress," 5.

49. "Proceedings of the Guam Congress," 2.

50. "Proceedings of the Guam Congress," 3.

51. "Proceedings of the Guam Congress," 6.

52. L. Thompson, *Guam and Its People*, 30.

53. Viernes, "Negotiating Manhood," 228.

54. "Resolution of Guam Congress," folder 22, box 1, Guam Naval Government Records, 1899–1950, MSS 870, MARC, UOG.

55. Guam Congress, "Resolution of Guam Congress," *Guam Recorder*, November 1926, 209.

56. On Asian exclusion, see Lew-Williams, *The Chinese Must Go*; Ngai, *Impossible Subjects*; Lee, *Making of Asian America*.

57. Miles, *Ties That Bind*, 3.

58. Folder 37, box 1, Governor Willis Winter Bradley Jr. Papers, MSS 960, MARC, UOG (hereafter cited as Bradley Papers). There are many caveats not included in the body of this paragraph. A more complete text of the proclamation is as follows: "Every person born or naturalized in Guam and subject to the jurisdiction thereof. Every person residing in Guam on 1 February, 1899, who at that time owed no allegiance to any foreign prince or power other than to the Crown of Spain, and that solely by virtue of allegiance to the Government of Guam. Every woman who, prior to 22 September, 1922, married a citizen of Guam; provided, that such women might, at the time of her marriage to said citizen of Guam, have been lawfully naturalized in the United States of America. Every child heretofore born or hereafter born out of the limits and jurisdiction of the Island of Guam, whose father was or may be a citizen of Guam at the time of such birth; provided, that the rights of citizenship shall not descend to a child whose father never resided in Guam. Every child under the age of twenty-one years at the time of the issue of a certificate of naturalization by the Government of Guam to the father of said child; provided, that the said child takes up actual residence in Guam within a period of two years from the date of naturalization of the father."

59. It is unclear whether the 1922 Cable Act—which allowed women with US citizenship to retain their citizenship status despite marrying a foreign man—also applied to those living in Guåhan.

60. Government of Guam, Interagency Committee on Population, *Guam's People*, 134.

61. "Memorial Dedication," *Guam Recorder*, May 1937, 27.

62. Pancrasio Palting to the Attorney-General of Guam, October 27, 1933, folder 5, box 9, MSS 930, National Archives, RG 80, Annual Reports of the Governors of Guam 1901–1941, MARC, UOG.

63. "Letter to William Safford from Justo Dungca, 21st March 1904," MSS 980, William Edwin Safford Papers, MARC, UOG.

64. "Justo B. Dungca [Agana, Guam]," 1920 United States Federal Census database, Ancestry.com, https://www.ancestrylibrary.com/search/collections/6061/records/114536889.

65. "Pancrasio Palting [Agana, Guam]," 1920 United States Federal Census database, Ancestry.com, https://www.ancestrylibrary.com/search/collections/6061/records/114536892.

66. Eric Forbes, "Archbishop Felixberto C. Flores," Guampedia, https://www.guampedia.com/archbishop-felixberto-c-flores/.

67. James McDonald, phone interview with the author, October 10, 2019.

68. Juan Flores, interview with the author, October 1, 2019.

69. McDonald, phone interview.

70. United States Department of the Interior, "National Register of Historic Places Inventory."

71. Påle' Eric Forbes writes in his online blog that though they were not considered CHamoru, they were considered "one of our own," connoting a notion of belonging that existed outside the criteria of race, nation, and citizenship. The US definition of "native" is derived from Thompson, *Guam and Its People*, 32. Påle' Eric Forbes, "First Pinoy Elected," blog post, Paleric, May 24, 2022), https://paleric.blogspot.com/2022/05/first-pinoy-elected.html.

72. Pancrasio Palting to Honorable President Franklin D. Roosevelt, April 7, 1936, folder 31, box 1, Bradley Papers.

73. On ambiguity in colonial governance, see King, "Structural Sources of Ambiguity."

74. Ion Pursell to P. R. Palting, Florencia Palting, and Margarito Palting, folder 28, box 1, Bradley Papers.

75. Almaguer, *Racial Fault Lines*, 186.

76. Barker, *Native Acts*, 19.

77. King, "Structural Sources of Ambiguity," 778.

78. "Leon Flores [Agana, Guam]," 1920 United States Federal Census database, Ancestry.com, https://www.ancestrylibrary.com/search/collections/6061/records/114535381.

79. "Tomas A. Calvo [Agana, Guam]," 1920 United States Federal Census database, Ancestry.com, https://www.ancestrylibrary.com/search/collections/6061/records/114536285.

80. "Tomas A. Calvo [Agana, Guam]," 1930 United States Federal Census database, Ancestry.com, https://www.ancestrylibrary.com/search/collections/6224/records/103911354.

81. Letter to the Governor of Guam, October 24, 1933, folder 28, box 1, Bradley Papers.

82. Letter, "The Filipinos in Guam," October 16, 1933, folder 28, box 1, Bradley Papers.

83. Letter to the Governor of Guam, October 24, 1933.

84. "Pascual S. Artero [Agana, Guam]," 1930 United States Federal Census, Ancestry.com, https://www.ancestrylibrary.com/search/collections/6224/records/103904933; "Adriano M. Cristobal [Agana, Guam]," 1920 United States Federal Census, Ancestry.com, https://www.ancestrylibrary.com/search/collections/6061/records/114537011; "Geronimo P. Santos [Agana, Guam]," 1920 United States Federal Census, Ancestry.com, https://www.ancestrylibrary.com/search/collections/6061/records/114532223; Geronimo P. Santos [Agana, Guam]," 1930 United States Federal Census, Ancestry.com, https://www.ancestrylibrary.com/search/collections/6224/records/103911300.

85. Letter, "Filipinos in Guam."

86. Letter, "Filipinos in Guam."

87. Letter, "Filipinos in Guam."

88. Letter to the Governor, October 24, 1933.

89. Due to the limited clarity of the document in the archive, the author of this report is unknown. Letter to the Governor, October 24, 1933.

90. Letter to the Governor, October 24, 1933.

91. Letter to the Governor, October 24 1933.

92. Rasputin comment in Palting to Captain Bradley, March 14 1934, folder 29, box 1, Bradley Papers; Ion Pursell to P. Palting, Florencia Dungca Palting, and Margarito Palting, October 26, 1933, folder 28, box 1, Bradley Papers.

93. This may refer to General Herrero Street, which is consistent with the 1920 Census.

94. Naval Government of Guam, Island Court Citizenship Proceedings for Leon Flores, folder 29, box 1, Bradley Papers.

95. Naval Government of Guam, Island Court Citizenship Proceedings for Geronimo Santos, folder 29, box 1, Bradley Papers.

96. The first query of the two is explored more deeply in the next paragraphs. The second argued that even if the court decides that Palting and his family were aliens, the United States has decided in previous cases that laws should not be enacted retroactively. Thus, the land that he acquired before 1918 should not be subject to the law of 1933.

97. Lisa Lowe writes that "commensurate with the political philosophy's affirmation of the individual's passage to freedom through economic industry and political emancipation, the *autobiography* served as a particularly powerful genre for the individual achievement of

liberty through ethical education and civilization. In a sense, the autobiography is the liberal genre par excellence." Lowe, *Intimacies of Four Continents*, 46.

98. Palting to Attorney General of Guam, National Archives, RG 80, Annual Reports of the Governors of Guam, folder 5, box 9, MSS 930, MARC, UOG.

99. Palting to Attorney General of Guam.

100. Palting to Attorney General of Guam.

101. A. T. Perez to Governor of Guam Willis Bradley, folder 29, box 1, Bradley Papers.

102. Hofschneider, *Campaign for Political Rights*.

Chapter Three

1. House of Representatives, "Public Hearings," 139.

2. The wartime experience led many CHamorus in Guåhan to adopt the appellation "Guamanian" as a way to distinguish themselves from Chamorros of the Northern Mariana Islands, who have a different orthography for the CHamoru language. Throughout this chapter and subsequent chapters, historical actors may use the term "Guamanian" to refer specifically to CHamoru people and at other times to refer to any person, regardless of race, who resided on the island. My own analysis and interpretation of primary sources will be more specific. I will use "CHamoru" when the historical actor was using "Guamanian" to refer specifically to the Indigenous people of the island, and I will use "Guamanian" when the historical actor was using "Guamanian" to refer all residents of the island regardless of race. On CHamoru versus Guamanian, see Gina E. Taitano, "Adoption of 'Guamanian,'" Guampedia, October 8, 2020, https://www.guampedia.com/adoption-of-guamanian/; further historicization of the term can be found in chapters 5 and 6. On the wartime experience of Guåhan, see Palomo, *Island in Agony*; Camacho, *Cultures of Commemoration*; Higuchi, "Japanisation Policy"; Higuchi, *Japanese Administration of Guam*. On immediate post–World War II Guåhan history, see Hattori, "Guardians of Our Soil"; Viernes, "Fanhasso I Taotao Sumay"; Camacho, *Sacred Men*.

3. *Under the American Sun* [film], directed by Burt Sardoma Jr., produced by Bernie Provido Schumann, 2014. The documentary's website is www.camproxas.com.

4. Rogers, *Destiny's Landfall*, 201; Campbell, "Filipino Community of Guam"; Flores, "'No Walk in the Park'"; Flores, *Tip of the Spear*.

5. Settler militarism happens differently in differently locales. Rather than "failing forward" into statehood, as Dean Saranillio argues was the case for Hawai'i, the granting of US citizenship to CHamorus in Guåhan ensured that the island remained a nebulous space of empire, always foreign in a domestic sense. Nebolon, "'Life Given Straight from the Heart,'" 25; Nebolon, *Settler Militarism*; Saranillio, *Unsustainable Empire*, 19.

6. Flores, *Tip of the Spear*, 3.

7. Nebolon, *Settler Militarism*, 5.

8. Philips, "Land," 3.

9. DeLisle, *Placental Politics*, xi–xii; Monnig, "'Proving Chamorro,'" 231.

10. Flores, *Tip of the Spear*, 17–18.

11. Santos, "'Practicing Economy,'" 36–38.

12. Hattori, "A Take on Taking," 8.

13. Viernes, "Chamorro Men in the Making."

14. Santos, "'Practicing Economy,'" 38.

15. Higuchi, "Japanisation Policy."

16. Palomo, *Island in Agony*; Flores, *Tip of the Spear*, 116–19.

17. On wartime memory, see Camacho, *Cultures of Commemoration*; Camacho, *Sacred Men*.

18. On World War II experience in Guåhan, see Howard, *Maraquita*; Onedera, *A Borrowed Land*.

19. Hattori, "Guardians of Our Soil," 189.

20. Rogers, *Destiny's Landfall*, 181.

21. P. Sanchez, *Guåhan, Guam*, 235. Also described in Stevens, *Guam, USA*, 107.

22. United States, *Building the Navy's Bases*, 341.

23. United States, *Building the Navy's Bases*, 351, 356; Coote, *A Report*, 14.

24. United States, *Building the Navy's Bases*, 351.

25. Hattori, "Guardians of Our Soil," 189.

26. United States, *Building the Navy's Bases*, 357, 355.

27. See Na'puti, "Archipelagic Rhetoric."

28. James Forrestal, letter to the Times, "Naval Government in Pacific: The Secretary of the Navy Points Out Policy in Administering Islands," *New York Times*, September 24, 1946; "The Director of the Policy Planning Staff (Kennan) to the Secretary of State," in Petersen et al., *Foreign Relations of the United States, 1948*, vol. 1, pt. 2, doc. 6.

29. United States, *Building the Navy's Bases*, 339.

30. Coote, *A Report*, 11.

31. On coercive tactics during military annexation, see Flores, *Tip of the Spear*; Hattori, "Guardians of Our Soil"; Monnig, "'Proving Chamorro'"; Viernes, "Fanhasso i Taotao Sumay."

32. Flores, *Tip of the Spear*, 25.

33. Nebolon, *Settler Militarism*, 23.

34. Thompson, "Guam's Bombed Out Capital," 68.

35. Coote, *A Report*, 4; Monnig, "'Proving Chamorro,'" 237.

36. Laura Thompson was a contributor and member of the Institute of Ethnic Affairs (IEA), a Washington, DC, based nonprofit organization dedicated to advocating for colonized peoples throughout the globe, but especially in Guåhan and the US territories. On the IEA, see Cogan, *We Fought the Navy*.

37. Thompson, "Guam's Bombed Out Capital," 67.

38. Thompson, "Guam's Bombed Out Capital," 68.

39. Hattori, "Guardians of Our Soil," 194; Hattori cites Simon Sanchez.

40. Tomhom Bay was also useful for CHamorus because of its potential as a tourism hotspot for the civilian economy. Francis Moylan, a former resident of Hawai'i, testified to the Public Lands Committee that returning Tomhom would allow for the development of a tourism economy, built and managed by local entrepreneurs. House of Representatives, "Public Hearings," 158.

41. "The Tumon Bay Controversy," *Guam Echo*, July 30, 1948, 4.

42. Monnig, "'Proving Chamorro,'" 223. On militarism extending beyond military functions, see Kim, *Settler Garrison*, 28.

43. "Open Forum in the Halls of Guam Congress, Agana, Guam, 3 March 1947," folder 32, box 2, Governor Willis Winter Bradley Jr. Papers, MSS 960, Micronesian Area Research Center, University of Guam.

44. "Open Forum," 20.

45. DeLisle, *Placental Politics*, 158.

46. "Open Forum," 20.

47. House of Representatives, "Public Hearings," 117.

48. In this testimony, Cruz revealed that he had lived in New York City and California in the early decades of the twentieth century. He applied for US citizenship in 1935 but was denied and sent back to Guåhan.

49. The transcripts of the proceedings included notations of "laughter" throughout Cruz's testimony. It is not clear if this was from the crowd or from Cruz himself. It makes me wonder if this was a nervous laughter, a laughter that suggests absurdity, a laughter that shows familiarity, or a response Cruz's performance in his testimony.

50. Hattori, "Guardians of Our Soil," 197–98.

51. House of Representatives, "Public Hearings," 180.

52. House of Representatives, "Public Hearings," 181.

53. House of Representatives, "Public Hearings," 51–52.

54. House of Representatives, "Public Hearings," 52.

55. House of Representatives, "Public Hearings," 64–65.

56. As Guåhan scholar Vicente Diaz noted, CHamorus saw how hyper-loyalty "was the only political language that could be heard and understood by the Americans." Diaz, "Deliberating Liberation Day," 165.

57. House of Representatives, "Public Hearings," 115, 117.

58. House of Representatives, "Public Hearings," 117.

59. The story of the Bello brothers is a culmination of family stories that have been told to me by my family over the years. Jose Bello, unpublished autobiography, in the possession of his daughters Carline B. Bukikosa and Bella B. Martinez in Guåhan; Marieta Bello, oral histories with author; Marlyn Oberiano, oral histories with author; Eliza Bello Salas, oral histories with author; Juliana Quimino Barnachea, oral histories with author.

60. Kenneth C. Robertson, "Survey of Alien Labor Policy for Guam, October 14–25, 1964," p. 14, folder 22, box 12, Governor Manuel F. L. Guerrero Papers, 1963–1969 (MSS 2480), Micronesian Area Research Center, University of Guam.

61. Jose Bello's family is unsure under what circumstances he was able to receive US citizenship. It is believed that Jose's first wife, whom he married while in Hawai'i before World War II, was a US citizen, and his family thought he could have received citizenship then. Alternatively, he could have been made a citizen through the post–World War II Luce-Celler Act, which allowed Filipinos who had settled in the United States to become permanent residents and US citizens. Lastly, Jose could have also received citizenship after marrying Dolores, who would have become a US citizen as a result of the 1950 Organic Act of Guam. Whatever the circumstances were, what does matter is that Jose was the first link in a chain of family members who settled in the United States.

62. Flores, *Tip of the Spear*, 61.

63. US Department of the Navy, "Guam: Information," 11.

64. US Department of the Navy, "Guam: Information," 11.

65. US Department of State, "Philippines: Recruitment of Filipino Laborers." On the relationship between immigration and foreign policy, see Gabaccia, *Foreign Relations.*

66. House of Representatives, *Use of Temporary Alien Labor*, 4; Flores, "'Little Island,'" 105–6. On global Filipino labor, see Rodriguez, "Toward a Critical Filipino Studies."

67. US Department of the Navy, "Guam: Information on Guam," 11.

68. House of Representatives, *Use of Temporary Alien Labor*, 4.

69. US Department of State, "Philippines: Recruitment of Filipino Laborers," 2540.

70. US Department of the Navy, "Guam: Information on Guam," 11.

71. US Department of State, "Philippines: Recruitment of Filipino Laborers," 2540.

72. US Department of State, "Philippines: Recruitment of Filipino Laborers," 2542.

73. US Department of State, "Philippines: Recruitment of Filipino Laborers," 2541.

74. Woods, "Building Empire's Archipelago," 138.

75. Rodriguez, "Toward a Critical Filipino Studies," 41.

76. Rogers, *Destiny's Landfall*, 217.

77. House of Representatives, *Use of Temporary Alien Labor*, 5.

78. House of Representatives, *Use of Temporary Alien Labor*, 10.

79. Campbell, "Filipino Community of Guam," 39; Guam Humanities Council, *A Journey Home*, panel 4.

80. In fact, throughout this postwar period, any and all migration to and from Guåhan was deemed necessary to US military operations. Guåhan was a secure military location, and any person on the island received a "security clearance" from the US Navy. Before World War II, President Franklin Delano Roosevelt had signed Executive Order No. 8683, which in 1941 established Guåhan as a secure location for US military operations. When the US military reoccupied the island, President Truman reinstated the security clearance for Guåhan, and it remained in place until President John F. Kennedy lifted the order in 1962. The security clearance ensured that any person leaving and going to Guåhan had an approved military reason. Filipinos who came in the period between 1946 and 1962 received a security clearance because of the essential labor they contributed to the military buildup. Filipino workers' intrinsic value was in their potential to be workers that could support Philippine economic and foreign policy. Stevens, *Guam, USA*, 94.

81. Flores, "'No Walk in the Park,'" 819.

82. Flores, "'No Walk in the Park,'" 823.

83. On Filipinos as racialized labor, see Poblete, *Islanders in Empire*; Clutario, *Beauty Regimes*; De Leon, *Bundok.*

84. Poblete, *Islanders in Empire*, 54–56; De Leon, *Bundok*, 147.

85. Poblete, *Islanders in Empire*, 49; De Leon, *Bundok*, 151.

86. In my oral history interviews with Filipino immigrants and their families, there was a trend where family relations often created the opportunity to move abroad. Ruben Payumo, oral history; Florita Oberiano, oral history.

87. Campbell, "Filipino Community in Guam," 41.

88. Flores, "'No Walk in the Park,'" 826.

89. Guam Humanities Council, *A Journey Home*, panel 2.

90. This does not mean the local population did not visit the camps at all. When talking to CHamoru people in Guåhan about my research, a handful of them recalled going to Camp Roxas to play basketball against Filipino teams.

91. Burt Sardoma, *Under the American Sun* (film), 2014.

92. Campbell, "Filipino Community of Guam," 41.

93. Flores, *Tip of the Spear*, 75.

94. Munoz, *Filipinos in America*, 123. This observation was also mentioned by Dr. Robert Underwood in interviews with the author.

95. Don Marshall transcript, *Under the American Sun*, http://www.camproxas.com/Transcript-DonMarshall.html.

96. With the post-2006 US military buildup in Guåhan, the dynamics of the Filipino community in Guåhan have changed.

97. Guam Humanities Council, *A Journey Home*.

98. Diaz, "Deliberating Liberation Day."

99. Flores, "'No Walk in the Park,'" 814.

100. On military and modernization rhetoric in postwar Guåhan, see Flores, *Tip of the Spear*, 41–42.

101. Guam Humanities Council, *A Journey Home*, panel 3. Alfred Flores suggests that this is a form of welfare capitalism in which companies utilize modes of recreation to appease and prevent worker discontent.

102. Don Marshall transcript, *Under the American Sun*, http://www.camproxas.com/Transcript-DonMarshall.html.

103. Flores, "'No Walk in the Park,'" 825.

104. Folder 5, box 27, Elpidio Quirino Papers, Filipinas Heritage Library, Ayala Museum, Manila, Philippines.

105. Patrick Luces, interview with author, Dédidu, Guam, December 11, 2019; Guam Humanities Council, *A Journey Home*, panel 3.

106. Guam Humanities Council, *A Journey Home*, panel 3.

107. Flores, "No Walk in the Park,'" 827.

108. Flores, "'No Walk in the Park,'" 829.

109. "Umayan Arrives Here; Will Open Consulate Today," *Guam Daily News*, August 4, 1952, 1.

110. Filipino Community of Guam, "Know the Philippines Exhibition: Carnival & Exposition," Filipino Community of Guam Vertical File, University of Guam, Micronesian Area Research Center, 38.

111. Guam Humanities Council, *A Journey Home*, panel 8.

112. House of Representatives, Committee on Public Lands, *Investigation of an Organic Act for Guam*, 166–68.

113. I am using the term "Guamanian" here because the law was not referring specifically to CHamoru people. House of Representatives, Committee on Public Lands, *Investigation of an Organic Act for Guam*, 166–68.

114. Flores, *Tip of the Spear*, 61.

115. As testified by Vance O. Smith, a representative of the Guam Chamber of Commerce. House of Representatives, Committee on Public Lands, *Investigation of an Organic Act for Guam*, 172–74.

116. Campbell, "Filipino Community in Guam," 31.

117. Campbell, "Filipino Community in Guam," 31; Flores, "'No Walk in the Park,'" 819.

118. Woods, "Building Empire's Archipelago," 136.

119. Woods, "Building Empire's, Archipelago," 132.

120. Campbell, "Filipino Community in Guam," 39, 30.

121. House of Representatives, Committee on Education and Labor, *Minimum Wages in Certain Territories*, part 1.

122. *Minimum Wages in Certain Territories*, part 2, 480.

123. *Minimum Wages in Certain Territories*, part 1, 116.

124. *Minimum Wages in Certain Territories*, part 1, 267.

125. *Minimum Wages in Certain Territories*, part 2, 475.

126. *Minimum Wages in Certain Territories*, part 1, 116.

127. *Minimum Wages in Certain Territories*, part 1, 146.

128. Mason used the word "native" to describe a person from the Asia-Pacific region as a whole, not necessarily CHamorus, thereby erasing Indigenous peoples whose land was expropriated for empire. *Minimum Wages in Certain Territories*, part 1, 146.

129. *Minimum Wages in Certain Territories*, part 1, 154.

130. On civilian military work, see Jackson, *Work of Empire*.

131. *Minimum Wages in Certain Territories*, part 1, 345.

132. In 1956, Guåhan and the other the territories did not have voting representation in the US Congress. Antonio Won Pat was a member of the Guam Congress since 1936 and was a senator in the Guam Legislature since the signing of the Guam Organic Act in 1950. Cynthia Torres was one of two women senators elected to the Third Guam Legislature in 1954. Cynthia Torres was the daughter of Agueda Johnston and earned her degree in education at the University of California in 1958. She was a businesswoman, teacher, and community leader serving at several government departments and educational institutions in Guåhan. *Hale'ta: I Manfåyi*, 171–72.

133. *Minimum Wages in Certain Territories*, 2:480.

134. *Minimum Wages in Certain Territories*, 2:480.

135. *Minimum Wages in Certain Territories*, 2:481.

136. House of Representatives, *Use of Temporary Alien Labor*.

137. House of Representatives, *Use of Temporary Alien Labor*, 13–14.

138. *Minimum Wages in Certain Territories*, 2:490.

139. *Minimum Wages in Certain Territories*, 2:499. Italicized for emphasis.

140. *Minimum Wages in Certain Territories*, 2:499. Italicized for emphasis.

141. Emphasis my own. *Minimum Wages in Certain Territories*, 2:487.

142. On coolie labor in nineteenth century United States, see Jung, *Coolies and Cane*.

143. House of Representatives, Committee on Interior and Insular Affairs, *Guam Mariana Islands*, 53.

144. Flores, *Tip of the Spear*, 82–83.

145. Information from Aaron, "Regional Cold War History."

Chapter Four

1. "Signing of the Guam Organic Act," 1950, Photograph. 7.5×9.5in, Black and White, Harry S. Truman Library and Museum, https://www.trumanlibrary.org/photographs/view.php?id=42091.

2. Hattori, "Righting Civil Wrongs"; Hofschneider, *Campaign for Political Rights*.

3. Blackhawk, “Foreword,” 55–56.

4. On the Guam Congress Walkout of 1949, see Hattori, “Righting Civil Wrongs.”

5. Hattori, “Righting Civil Wrongs”; Rogers, *Destiny's Landfall*, 145; Nicholas Yamashita Camacho and Tony Palomo, “Francisco B. Leon Guerrero,” Guampedia, October 15, 2019, guampedia.com/francisco-b-leon-guerrero/.

6. Senate, Committee on Territories and Insular Affairs, *Citizenship for Residents of Guam*, 97.

7. Senate, Committee on Territories and Insular Affairs, *Citizenship for Residents of Guam*, 2, 99.

8. Senate, Committee on Territories and Insular Affairs, *Citizenship for Residents of Guam*, 96.

9. Information on Francisco B. Leon Guerrero as Kiko Zoilo and “machete scientist” is from Michael Bevacqua, “F. B. Leon Guerrero Was a Fascinating Force in Guam Politics for Close to Half a Century,” *Pacific Daily News*, July 2, 2020, https://www.guampdn.com/story/opinion/2020/07/02/f-b-leon-guerrero-fascinating-force-guam-politics/5362268002/.

10. Senate, Committee on Territories and Insular Affairs, *Citizenship for Residents of Guam*, 71.

11. Most notably, Agueda Iglesias Johnston was married to Navy Lieutenant William Gautier Johnston and remained in Guåhan. William Johnston was captured by Japanese forces and exiled to Japan, where he died in captivity. Rogers, *Destiny's Landfall*, 151; Patricia Long Diego and Jillete Leon-Guerrero, “Agueda Iglesias Johnston,” Guampedia, https://www.guampedia.com/agueda-iglesias-johnston/.

12. Lazaro Quinata, “Guam Insular Guard,” Guampedia, July 31, 2019, https://www.guampedia.com/guam-insular-guard/.

13. More instances on CHamorus aiding American military men can be found in Rogers, *Destiny's Landfall*, 161–62.

14. Rogers, *Destiny's Landfall*, 166.

15. Paul J. Borja, “Song of Hope, Song of Faith,” Guampedia, July 12, 2020, https://www.guampedia.com/song-of-hope-song-of-faith/. Pete Seeger produced a cover of this song. Pete Seeger, “Uncle Sam, Won't You Please Come Home to Guam,” Smithsonian Folkways Collection, https://www.youtube.com/watch?v=lPrnaxtkiAg.

16. Torres, *Massacre at Atåte*.

17. This is an abbreviated list of CHamoru acts of resistance during World War II. There are countless examples written, told in oral history, and commemorated throughout the island in monuments, events, and in other forms. World War II is so central to the narrative of Guåhan history that World War II is referred to as “the war” and marks the major temporal divide for Guåhan's twentieth century. Diaz, “Deliberating Liberation Day”; Camacho, *Cultures of Commemoration*.

18. “Open Forum in the Halls of Guam Congress, Agana, Guam, 3 March 1947,” folder 32, box 2, Governor Willis Winter Bradley Jr. Papers, MSS 960, Micronesian Area Research Center (MARC), University of Guam (UOG).

19. Rogers, *Destiny's Landfall*, 195.

20. Diaz, “Deliberating Liberation Day.” Anne Hattori argues in *Colonial Dis-Ease* that the brutal occupation under the Japanese Empire skewed the CHamorus' view of prewar

Guåhan. Hattori critiques the commonly held view that prewar Naval governance was benevolent, good, and beneficial despite the racist and colonial measures that the US Naval Government had enforced on the CHamoru people. Robert Underwood also criticizes the postwar rhetoric of CHamoru loyalty when used to demand more equality in terms of federal-territorial relations. See also Underwood, "Uncle Sam."

21. "Open Forum," 3.

22. United States, *Hopkins Committee Report.*

23. John Collier, "Prospectus for the Institute of Ethnic Affairs" quoted in Cogan, *We Fought the Navy,* 31.

24. In 1947 Laura Thompson published *Guam and Its People,* a groundbreaking book about CHamoru culture.

25. *Newsletter of the Institute of Ethnic Affairs,* February 1946, 3.

26. "The Guamanians Speak," *Newsletter of the Institute of Ethnic Affairs,* September 1946, 10.

27. Man, *Soldiering Through Empire,* 4; Ngai, *Impossible Subjects,* 234.

28. In August 1947 the secretary of the Navy, John L. Sullivan, issued an interim Organic Act that gave the Guåhan Congress the power to make changes in existing laws. If the Naval governor and the Guåhan Congress disagreed with enacted policies, the decision was to be made by the secretary of the Navy. Carano and Sanchez, *Complete History of Guam,* 347; P. Sanchez, *Guåhan, Guam,* 297.

29. "News Notes: Guam," *Institute of Ethnic Affairs Newsletter,* March–April 1949, 6.

30. A. B. Won Pat, Speaker of Guam Congress, to the Governor of Guam, March 9, 1949, folder 60, box 2, Governor Carlton S. Skinner Papers, MSS 2850, MARC, UOG.

31. Hattori, "Righting Civil Wrongs," 2.

32. On civil rights movements and their connection to Cold War foreign policy, see Dudziak, *Cold War Civil Rights.*

33. Hattori, "Righting Civil Wrongs"; Cogan, *We Fought the Navy,* passim 135–42.

34. Cogan, *We Fought the Navy,* chap. 12.

35. House of Representatives, US Congress, "Public Hearings Conducted before a Subcommittee of the Public Lands Committee," Agana, Guam (hereafter cited as Guam Organic Act Hearings).

36. Rogers, *Destiny's Landfall,* 221.

37. Friedman, *Governing the American Lake,* 102–3; Harold Ickes, letter to the editor, "Naval Stand Questioned: Secretary Forrestal's Statements on Guam and American Samoa Are Questioned," *New York Times,* October 21, 1946, 23.

38. US Department of the Navy, "Guam: Information on Guam."

39. James Forrestal, "Naval Government in Pacific," letter to the Times, *New York Times,* September 24, 1946, 27.

40. United States, *Hopkins Committee Report.*

41. Harold Ickes, "The Navy at Its Worst," *Collier's Magazine,* August 31, 1946, 22.

42. House of Representatives, Committee on Public Lands. *Providing a Civil Government,* 3.

43. Friedman, *Governing the American Lake,* 183.

44. House of Representatives, Committee on Public Lands. *Providing a Civil Government,* 3.

45. John Collier, "Naval Rule in Guam: Hope Expressed That Congress Will Remedy Situation Soon," *New York Times,* April 12, 1947, E8.

46. Collier, "Naval Rule in Guam," *New York Times*, E8.

47. Guam Organic Act Hearings, November 22, 1949.

48. Black, *Global Interior*, 4.

49. Guam Legislature, P.L. 630, "The Organic Act of Guam." For this section, I used a digitized copy created by the Micronesian Area Research Center, University of Guam.

50. Guam Legislature, P.L. 630, "The Organic Act of Guam," 11.

51. Guam Legislature, P.L. 630, "The Organic Act of Guam,"11.

52. Rogers, *Destiny's Landfall*, 230; Executive Order 10178: Reserving Certain Real and Personal Property.

53. Kuper, "Kontra I Peligru, Na'Fansåfo' Ham," 59.

54. Simeon Man observes that "war was the terrain upon which racial liberalism unfolded and gained traction." Man, *Soldiering Through Empire*, 4.

55. Barigåda is the current CHamoru orthography for the village called Barrigada in English. Radio Barrigada is a proper noun used in official military and local government to identify this land area. Executive Order No. 10178, October 31, 1950, Reservation of Property in Guam for Use of the United States, box 279, Central Files, Records of Office of the Territories, RG 126, National Archives at College Park, MD.

56. "Resolution relative to memorializing the Congress of the United States, the President of the United States, the Secretary of National Defense, the Secretary of National Defense, the Secretary of the Interior, and the Governor of Guam to reconsider the taking of property in Radio Barrigada and review other land takings in Guam." Congressional Records—Senate, September 7, 1951, 11015 (hereafter cited as "Resolution").

57. "Resolution."

58. House of Representatives, Committee on Interior and Insular Affairs, *Guam Mariana Islands*.

59. House of Representatives, Committee on Interior and Insular Affairs, *Guam Mariana Islands*, 43.

60. House of Representatives, Committee on Interior and Insular Affairs, *Guam Mariana Islands*, 44.

61. House of Representatives, Committee on Interior and Insular Affairs, *Guam Mariana Islands*, 43.

62. House of Representatives, Committee on Interior and Insular Affairs, *Guam Mariana Islands*, 44.

63. House of Representatives, Committee on Interior and Insular Affairs, *Guam Mariana Islands*, 44.

64. R. S. Herman to James P. Davis, October 12, 1951, folder GU Lands 8–4 (part 2), Withdrawals-Reservations-Military, box 290, National Archives, Central Files, Naval, RG 126, National Archives, College Park, MD.

65. Tatour, "Citizenship as Domination," 14.

66. Guam Legislature. P.L. 630, "The Organic Act of Guam," sec. 4.

67. United States, *Building the Navy's Bases*, vol. 2, passim 341–57.

68. Flores, "'Little Island,'" 218; Woods, "Building Empire's Archipelago," 138.

69. US Department of State, "Philippines: Recruitment of Filipino Laborers," 2539.

70. House of Representatives, Committee on Interior and Insular Affairs, *Guam Mariana Islands*, 23.

71. Government of Guam, *Guam's People*, 134.

72. Stevens, *Guam, USA*, 130.

73. Sabino Flores is the son of Nieves Flores, whom we met in chapter 2. Memo of Sabino Flores, "Travel to Manila, P.I. in order to investigate recruiting possibilities—report of," folder 25, box 2, Carlton Skinner Papers, MSS 2850, MARC,UOG.

74. Memo of Sabino Flores, "Travel to Manila."

75. Guam Legislature, Resolution No. 130-31 "Relative to Honoring and Congratulating"; Guam Legislature, Resolution No. 560-31(COR) "Relative to Posthumously Recognizing."

76. On migration of Filipino medical professionals, see Choy, *Empire of Care*.

77. House of Representatives, Committee on Interior and Insular Affairs, *Guam Mariana Islands*, 23.

78. Court of Guam Case *Ex Parte Rogers* reinforced this decision. House of Representatives, Committee on Immigration, *Use of Temporary Alien Labor*, 7.

79. House of Representatives, Committee on Interior and Insular Affairs, *Guam Mariana Islands*, 23.

80. Stevens, *Guam, USA*, 130; House of Representatives, Committee on Interior and Insular Affairs, *Guam Mariana Islands*, 23.

81. The pertinent section of the CFR is as follows: "*Aliens admitted to Guam.* (1) An alien who establishes that he was admitted to Guam prior to December 24, 1952, by records, such as Service records subsequent to June 15, 1952, records of the Guamanian Immigration Service, records of the Navy or Air Force or records of contractors of those agencies, other than as a contract laborer, was not otherwise excludable under the Act of February 5, 1917, as amended, and who continued to reside in Guam until December 24, 1952, regardless of the period of time for which admitted." "Presumption of Lawful Admission, Aliens Admitted to Guam," *Code of Federal Regulations*, 8 CFR 1101.1(i), https://www.law.cornell.edu/cfr/text/8/1101.1.

82. Board of Immigration Appeals, "Matter of C-Y-L-," June 10, 1959, 372. C-Y-L was not Filipino, but "a 38-year-old married male alien, a native and citizens of China," but his case created precedent for other Filipinos to claim permanent residency in Guam.

83. House of Representatives, Committee on Immigration, *Use of Temporary Alien Labor*, 8.

84. Ngai, *Impossible Subjects*, 19.

85. House of Representatives, Committee on Interior and Insular Affairs, *Guam Mariana Islands*, 23.

86. House of Representatives, Committee on Immigration, *Use of Temporary Alien Labor*, 9.

87. House of Representatives, Committee on Education and Labor, *Minimum Wages in Certain Territories*, 268.

88. House of Representatives, Committee on Immigration, *Use of Temporary Alien Labor*, 10.

89. On "permanent transient temporality," see Gandhi, *Archipelago of Resettlement*, 111–15.

90. House of Representatives, Committee on Immigration, *Use of Temporary Alien Labor*, 20.

91. House of Representatives, Committee on Immigration, *Use of Temporary Alien Labor*, 10.

92. House of Representatives, Committee on Interior and Insular Affairs, *Guam Mariana Islands*, 24.

93. House of Representatives, Committee on Immigration, *Use of Temporary Alien Labor*, 16.

94. Kenneth C. Robertson, "Survey of Alien Labor Policy for Guam, October 14–25, 1964," p. 6, folder 22, box 12, Governor Manuel F. L. Guerrero Papers, MSS 2480, MARC, UOG.

95. US Naval Oceanography Command Center, "Tropical Cyclones Affecting Guam," 40.

96. Robertson, "Survey of Alien Labor Policy," 15.

97. Barrett and Ferenz, "Peacetime Martial Law in Guam"; Quimby, "Security Clearance on Guam," Guampedia, October 13, 2019, https://www.guampedia.com/security-clearance-on-guam/.

98. Barrett and Ferenz, "Peacetime Martial Law in Guam," 7.

99. Stevens, *Guam, USA*, 130.

100. Sanchez, *Guåhan, Guam*, 280.

101. US Congressional Record, "50th Anniversary."

102. "Marciano 'Mark' Vega Pangilinan, Sr.: Invincible Pioneer Entrepreneur," in *Hale'-ta I Manfåyi*, 3:201.

103. P. Sanchez, *Guåhan, Guam*, 280.

104. Chloe Babauta, "Filipino World War II Veteran Reflects on Service," *Pacific Daily News*, November 10, 2017, https://www.guampdn.com/story/news/local/bayanihan/2017/11/10/filipino-world-war-ii-veteran-reflects-service/843096001/?hootPostID=78b1477eb9c1b7b2552 ea174ad8f167b.

105. Chloe Babauta, oral history interview with the author, December 29, 2019.

106. Babauta, "Filipino World War II Veteran Reflects."

107. Man, *Soldiering Through Empire*, 3.

108. Florita Oberiano, oral history with author, December 25, 2019.

109. Mabalon, *Little Manila*, 246.

110. Jose Bello, unpublished autobiography, in the possession of his daughters Carline B. Bukikosa and Bella B. Martinez in Guåhan; Marieta Bello, oral histories with author; Marlyn Oberiano, oral histories with author; Eliza Bello Salas, oral histories with author; Juliana Quimino Barnachea, oral histories with author.

111. Kim, *Settler Garrison*, 18.

Chapter Five

1. "Guam USA: Land of Sunshine, Swaying Palms, and Friendly Smiles," Guam Progress Insert, *Pacific Daily News*, August 30, 1970, 1–45.

2. "Japanese Group May Take Over Hotel: $1,000,000 Business," *Guam Daily News*, September 3, 1968.

3. On the relationship between militarism and tourism, see Teaiwa, "Bikinis and Other s/Pacific n/Oceans"; Gonzalez, *Securing Paradise*; Camacho, "Enframing I Taotao Tano.'"

4. "A Hobglob of Ethnic Groups: A Mixture of the Old and the New," *Pacific Daily News*, Progress Edition, August 30, 1970, Tourism Section, 6. On the rise of US multiculturalism in the Cold War in the continental United States, see Brilliant, *Color of America Has Changed*; Espiritu, *Asian American Panethnicity*; Dudziak, *Cold War Civil Rights*.

5. Janet Go, "Guam—The Honeymoon Island: Return of the Japanese," *Pacific Daily News*, Progress Edition, August 30, 1970, Tourism Section, 4.

6. Victoria King, "School Settles After Race Incident," *Pacific Daily News*, January 15, 1985, 1.

7. On critiques of liberal multiculturalism from the Pacific perspective, read Trask, *From a Native Daughter*; Fujikane and Okamura, *Asian Settler Colonialism*; Saranillio, "Colliding Histories"; Saranillio, *Unsustainable Empire*.

8. Gandhi, *Archipelago of Resettlement*, 34–42.

9. In the 1950s, Governor Carlton Skinner attempted to promote tourism in Guåhan. Due to the security clearance, however, the Government of Guam found it extremely difficult to lure investors to the island. Government of Guam, *Guam 1970*, 20.

10. Rogers, *Destiny's Landfall*, 218–19.

11. "Guerrero Moves to Build Up Tourism—Creates Commission," *Guam Daily News*, June 27, 1973, 1.

12. House of Representatives, Committee on Interior and Insular Affairs, *Economic Development of the Territory of Guam*, 14.

13. "Tiyan" is the CHamoru word for stomach. The village is near the center of Guåhan and is only two miles away from the tourism district in the village of Tomhom. Today a person could see the tourism district with high-rise hotels upon stepping out of the front entrance of the Guam International Airport. Rogers, *Destiny's Landfall*, 222.

14. "First Tourist Group Arrives, 17 from Japan," *Guam Daily News*, August 1, 1967, 1; "Continental to Build Guam Hotel, 92 Rooms, Near Ipao Beach," *Guam Daily News*, August 1, 1967, 1.

15. Rogers, *Destiny's Landfall*, 222.

16. "Japanese Group May Take Over Hotel," 1.

17. "Alfred Curie Ysrael: Real Estate Developer Improving Guam's Quality of Life," in *Hale'-ta I Manfåyi*, 3:284.

18. Rogers, *Destiny's Landfall*, 228.

19. "Japanese Group May Take Over Hotel," 1.

20. Go, "Guam—The Honeymoon Island," 4.

21. US Congress, Committee on Interior and Insular Affairs *Economic Development of the Territory of Guam*, 20.

22. US Congress, Committee on Interior and Insular Affairs, *Economic Development of the Territory of Guam*, 12.

23. US Congress, Committee on Interior and Insular Affairs *Economic Development of the Territory of Guam*, 12.

24. Gonzalez, *Securing Paradise*, 5. See Teaiwa, "Reflections of Militourism."

25. Gandhi, *Archipelago of Resettlement*, 37–42.

26. Gandhi, *Archipelago of Resettlement*, 37–42.

27. Richard Halloran, "The War Is Suddenly Grim for the B-52 Fliers on Guam," *New York Times*, December 30, 1972, 1.

28. Gandhi, *Archipelago of Resettlement*, 79–101.

29. Rogers, *Destiny's Landfall*, 233. For a more detailed history of this moment in Guåhan's history, listen to Evyn Lê Espiritu Gandhi, "Operation New Life," *Memoirs Pasifika*, Podcast Audio, April 27, 2021, https://www.memoirspasifika.com/episodes/episode-03-operation-new-life-nfh9l-neafg?fbclid=IwAR3ir8tJCGPoiRAfrlEh-3i_G7jy-Lad_ESPaMi_fovyDtnoZr3L4P-vmbs.

30. Gandhi, *Archipelago of Resettlement*, 86.

31. James A. Herbert, "Job Center Finding Evacuees Homes," *Pacific Daily News*, April 24, 1975, 2A.

32. "Earl Edward Kloppenberg," in *Hale'-ta I Manfåyi*, 3:160–62.

33. Not to be confused with "Johnny Guam Jr.," a pet monkey that was brought into Guåhan illegally via an Air Force MAC flight by Gordon Mailloux and was forcibly repatriated back to the Philippines. Ron Ige, "Baby Monkey Saved from Destruction," *Pacific Daily News*, September 24, 1986, 4.

34. "Gordon Mailloux, 'Johnny Guam,'" in *Hale'-ta I Manfåyi*, 3:178, 180.

35. "Alfred Curie Ysrael," in *Hale'-ta I Manfåyi*, 3:287.

36. P. Sanchez, *Guåhan, Guam*, 280.

37. "How Many Filipinos Are There in Guam—The Better Query Seemed to Be: How Many Are Domiciled Here?," *Filipiniana*, December 1963, 3, 5, 7, 11, Societies & Associations Vertical File, Nieves Flores Memorial Library Hagåtña, Guam Public Library System.

38. "How Many Filipinos Are There in Guam," 3, 5, 7, 11.

39. The 1965 Immigration Act allowed US citizens to petition for their relatives through the family reunification clause. Many Filipinos took advantage of this, and often started a chain of migrants from the Philippines. For more reading on the 1965 Immigration Act, see Ngai, *Impossible Subjects*; Chin and Villazor, *Immigration and Nationality Act*; Choy, *Empire of Care*.

40. This is similar to what Dean Saranillio historicizes in the multiculturalism of Hawai'i Statehood. Saranillio, *Unsustainable Empire*, 182–83.

41. "A Real Tourist Attraction: Guam's Beautiful Girls," *Pacific Daily News*, Progress Edition, August 18, 2021, 10.

42. "Guam USA: Land of Sunshine, Swaying Palms, and Friendly Smiles," *Pacific Daily News*, August 30, 1970, 10.

43. On gender and militarization in Guåhan, see Frain, "Women's Resistance."

44. Genevieve Ploke, "Guam: Pacific's New Melting Pot," *Pacific Profile*, November 1963, 8–10.

45. *Pacific Profile* was a magazine highlighting events and issues relating to the American Pacific. Ploke, "Guam," 8–10. On whiteness and Polynesia, see Arvin, *Possessing Polynesia*. At this point in time, a person who was "Guamanian" was understood to be CHamoru. Ploke, "Guam," 9, 36.

46. Ploke, "Guam," 36. The correct spelling of Sanchez's wife's name is Florida Galea'i. Simon Sanchez interview with the author (November 11, 2019).

47. Samantha Marley Barnett, "Dr. Pedro Cruz Sanchez," Guampedia. https://www.guampedia.com/dr-pedro-sanchez/.

48. Samantha Marley Barnett, "Dr. Pedro Cruz Sanchez," Guampedia. https://www.guampedia.com/dr-pedro-sanchez/.

49. Pedro C. Sanchez, "Guam: Paradox of a Paradise," *Guam Recorder*, October–December 1972.

50. Sanchez, "Guam: Paradox of a Paradise," 60.

51. Sanchez, "Guam: Paradox of a Paradise," 60.

52. Sanchez, "Guam: Paradox of a Paradise," 60–61. Emphasis in the original.

53. Sanchez, "Guam: Paradox of a Paradise," 61–62. Some leaders, including Frank F. Blas, the director of Commerce for the Government of Guam, agreed with Sanchez's view that prospects were bleak for CHamorus in a world of unfettered economic growth. In a response to Sanchez's speech, Blas wrote that "Dr. Sanchez has not simply 'cried wolf.' In my opinion, he has correctly assessed the situation." Conrad Stinson, a former president of the Guam Federation of Teachers and a white US settler himself, wrote that Sanchez's speech was "perhaps the clearest commentary to date on the subject of Guåhan and the effects of the current economic boom on our society." See, Sanchez, "Guam: Paradox of a Paradise," 64.

54. Government of Guam, *Guam 1970*, 9. Copy found in folder 25, box 10, Governor Carlos G. Camacho Papers, MSS 2150, Micronesian Area Research Center (MARC), University of Guam (UOG).

55. Government of Guam, Interagency Committee on Population, *Guam's People*, 134, 138.

56. "How Many Filipinos Are There in Guam," 3, 5, 7, 11.

57. "How Many Filipinos Are There in Guam," 3.

58. "How Many Filipinos Are There in Guam," 7, 11.

59. Edna Rebanal, interview with the author, Tamuneng, Guam, January 2, 2020.

60. Sanchez, "Let the People Speak," 7.

61. Sabina Tamondong, interview with the author, Tamuneng, Guam, January 4, 2020.

62. Tamondong interview with the author.

63. Rebanal interview with the author.

64. Ariel Dimalanta, interview with the author.

65. For more readings of the Filipino community in Guåhan in the post–World War II period, see Campbell, "The Filipino Community of Guam"; Flores, "'Little Island'"; Pobutsky and Neri, "Patterns of Filipino Migration."

66. "Know the Philippines Exhibition: Carnival & Exposition," 38, Filipino Community of Guam, Vertical File, MARC, UOG, 38.

67. "Know the Philippines Exhibition," 8.

68. Filipino Ladies Association of Guam, "59th Induction and Christmas Ball," January 3, 2020, event booklet, private collection of the author. A copy of the booklet, as well as past booklets, may be found with the Filipino Ladies Association of Guam.

69. "25th Anniversary: Installation of Officers, January 26, 1980," Filipino Community of Guam Vertical File Collection of the Nieves Flores Library in Hagåtña, Guam Public Library System.

70. "25th Anniversary: Installation of Officers," 26.

71. "25th Anniversary: Installation of Officers," front cover.

72. On Filipino communities in Guåhan, see Campbell, "The Filipino Community on Guam"; Velasco, "The Ube ('Roots') Generation." On Filipino communities in Asian America, see Vo and Bonus eds., *Contemporary Asian American Communities*; Bonus, *Locating Filipino Americans*; Espiritu, *Home Bound*.

73. Patrick Luces, interview with the author, Dédidu, Guam, December 11, 2019.

74. Norman Analista, interview with the author, Mangilao, Guam, November 26, 2019.

75. Nerissa Bretania Underwood, interview with the author, Tamuneng, Guam, September 9, 2019.

76. Florita Oberiano, interview with the author, Santa Rita, Guam, December 24, 2019.

77. Underwood, interview with the author.

78. Marlyn Oberiano, oral history with author; Eliza Bello Salas, oral history with author.

79. Mina Roces has written about the symbolism of Filipiniana or mestiza dress in politics and society. See Roces, "Gender, Nation and the Politics of Dress."

80. Tamondong, interview with the author.

81. Baldovino was a former president of the Filipino Community in Guam. Nita Baldovino, interview with the author, Tumon, Guam, January 7, 2020.

82. Joe Dizon, "Filipinos in Guam's 1970 Elections," *Guam Recorder*, January–March 1972, 56–59.

83. Robert Underwood, interview with the author, Mangilao, Guam, January 14, 2018.

84. "Remarks at the Induction Ceremony, Filipino Community of Guam at the Marianas Ballroom, February 4, 1978," folder Speeches January–August 1976, box 56, First Term, the Papers of Governor Jerome Bordallo, MARC, UOG.

85. "Manetluhu" is CHamoru for "my siblings" in an outdated orthography for the CHamoru language. It would be spelled *mañelu-hu* today. "Kaibigan at Kababayan" is Filipino (Tagalog) for "friends" and "countrymen."

86. "Remarks at the Induction Ceremony."

87. Joseph C. Murphy, "The Filipino on Guam—Plus or Minus?," *Pacific Daily News*, January 15, 1976, 19.

88. The criticism of the lack of local control of immigration is not new to the 1970s. As shown in chapter 3, the preponderance for military and off-island businesses to hire temporary labor from the Philippines was criticized by CHamoru politicians in US Congress, most notably by Antonio B. Won Pat and Cecilia Bamba.

89. Montie Protasio, "Arriola Brings Out 'Alien' Issue," *Pacific Daily News*, August 19, 1970, 1. This quote has been interpreted in Diaz, "Bye Bye Ms. American Pie."

90. Protasio, "Arriola Brings Out 'Alien' Issue," 4.

91. Laura Souder, "Sifting Through Clues in Search of Identity," *Islander Magazine*, published by *Pacific Daily News*, January 16, 1977, 7.

92. Souder, "Sifting Through Clues," 8.

93. Aguon, "The Guam Dilemma," 90.

94. Souder, "Sifting Through Clues," 8.

95. Underwood, "American Education," 252, 275, 277, 287.

96. Dimalanta, interview with the author.

97. James A. Hebert, "Riot Talk Abbreviates School Day," *Pacific Daily News*, March 1, 1975, 1.

98. Guadalupe C. Borja, "Students Allowed Hearing," *Pacific Daily News*, March 6, 1975, 4.

99. Hebert, "Riot Talk," 5.

100. Tamondong, interview with the author.

101. Souder, "Sifting Through Clues," 7.

102. Samuel Betances, "Limits of Cross-Cultural Education in Solving Ethnic Conflict in Guam," *Islander Magazine* by *Pacific Daily News*, October 23, 1977, 4.

103. On education as settler militarism, Nebolon, *Settler Militarism*, 127.

104. Souder, "Sifting Through Clues," 8.

105. Clotilde Gould, "Uno Dos Tres Kuatro," *Islander Magazine* by *Pacific Daily News*, January 16, 1977, 9.

106. Banks, "Multicultural Education," 16–17.

107. Phill Mendel, "Chamorro Week: Catching Up on Culture," *Pacific Daily News*, February 24, 1974, C-2.

108. Robert Underwood, "'Chamorro' Challenge to 'Statesiders,'" *Islander Magazine* by *Pacific Daily News*, October 23, 1977, 12.

109. Aguon, "The Guam Dilemma," 98–101.

110. Underwood, "'Chamorro' Challenge to 'Statesiders,'" 10–11.

111. Saranillio, *Unsustainable Empire*, 13.

112. Underwood, "'Chamorro' Challenge to 'Statesiders,'" 10.

113. Underwood, "'Chamorro' Challenge to 'Statesiders,'" 12.

114. PulanSpeaks, "Robert Underwood—Reflections on CHamoru Activism," January 22, 2021, video, 1:05:49, https://www.youtube.com/watch?v=54A5SQTaZmo&t=23s&ab_channel=PulanSpeaks.

115. Betances, "Limits of Cross-Cultural Education," 3–7, 14.

116. Betances, "Limits of Cross-Cultural Education," 6.

117. Aguon, "The Guam Dilemma," 100.

118. A relatively complete set of the *Guam Times Weekly* can be found at the Micronesian Area Research Center at the University of Guam. On playing "native," see Deloria, *Playing Indian*.

119. Robert Underwood, interview with the author, Mangilao, Guam, January 14, 2018.

120. Marie A. Crisostomo, Laura I. Manglona, Josepha S. Igisomar, Antoinette Laguana, Barbara C. Millon, Wencesiao C. Leon Guerrero, Frank Aguaio, Frances M. Raguindin, Martha Palma, Goring Duenas, Ana C. Taitano, Teresita A. Salas, Manuel P. Duenas, Raymond A. Perez, letter to the editor, *Pacific Daily News*, July 30, 1977, 27.

121. Crisostomo et al., letter to the editor, 27.

122. Saranillio, *Unsustainable Empire*, 13.

Chapter Six

1. On the Guam Commonwealth Movement, see Stade, *Pacific Passages*; Rogers, *Destiny's Landfall*; M. P. Perez, "Chamorro Resistance and Prospects." On this period of Guåhan history, see *Hale'ta Kinalamten Pulitikåt*.

2. A version of this essay was delivered at the United Nations in 1982 by Robert Underwood, Ron Teehan, and Chris Perez Howard. Cristobal, "Organization of People for Indigenous Rights," 82. On self-determination in the international context, see Mar, *Decolonisation and the Pacific*; Simpson, *The First Right*; Getachew, *Worldmaking After Empire*.

3. Byrd, *Transit of Empire*, xix.

4. Government of Guam, Interagency Committee on Population, *Guam's People*, 134; Hattori, "Guardians of Our Soil," 189.

5. Dizon, "Filipinos in Guam's 1970 Election," 57.

6. Ada, "The Quest for Commonwealth," 130.

7. For more detailed information about the process of the Constitutional Conventions, read Ada, "The Quest for Commonwealth"; P. Sanchez, *Guåhan, Guam*, 418–39; Josh Tenorio and James Perez Viernes, "Guam Constitutional Conventions (ConCon)," Guampedia, https://www.guampedia.com/guam-constitutional-conventions-concon/. On Taitano's

political stance, read Dominica Tolentino, "Richard Flores Taitano," Guampedia, September 23, 2020, https://www.guampedia.com/richard-flores-taitano/.

8. Ada, "The Quest for Commonwealth," 138–39.

9. Government of Guam, "Draft Constitution of Guam Adopted by the Constitutional Convention, September 14, 1977," Micronesian Area Research Center (MARC), University of Guam (UOG), https://issuu.com/guampedia/docs/draft_constitution_of_guampft.

10. Ada, "The Quest for Commonwealth," 150; Rogers, *Destiny's Landfall*, 242; Underwood, "Dies Mit," 105.

11. Simpson, *The First Right*, 151.

12. In 1973 and 1974, the Nixon administration conducted a study in Guåhan, unknown to the Government of Guam, to ascertain how the territory would be managed. Known as "The Secret Guam Study," it suggested that Guam receive a renewed political status of Commonwealth similar to the Northern Mariana Islands. The study's recommendation was not taken up by the Carter administration. Rogers, *Destiny's Landfall*, 240, 242. On the "Secret Guam Study," see Willens, *The Secret Guam Study*.

13. Robert Underwood conducted an interview with Edward Leon Guerrero on the YouTube channel PulanSpeaks in which he discusses the CHamoru activist group "Para y Pada." PulanSpeaks, "Robert Underwood—Reflections on Chamorro Activism," January 22, 2021, video, 1:05:49, https://www.youtube.com/watch?v=54A5SQTaZmo&t=23s&ab_channel=PulanSpeaks.

14. Ada, "The Quest for Commonwealth," 152; PulanSpeaks, "Robert Underwood."

15. PulanSpeaks, "Robert Underwood."

16. Ada, "The Quest for Commonwealth," 151; Underwood, "Dies Mit," 103–4.

17. Ada, "The Quest for Commonwealth," 148.

18. Quoted in Ada, "The Quest for Commonwealth," 151.

19. PulanSpeaks, "Robert Underwood"; Underwood, "Dies Mit," 105.

20. Rogers, *Destiny's Landfall*, 264.

21. Guam Legislature, "P.L. 15-128: An Act to Create the Commission on Self-Determination for the People of Guam and Appropriate the Sum of One Hundred Fifty Thousand Dollars ($150,000.00) to Carry Out the Activities of the Commission," 2nd sess., 1980.

22. Ada, "The Quest for Commonwealth," 158. On the development of various UN-specified statuses, see Simpson, *The First Right*, 155–60.

23. The Commission on Self-Determination held two plebiscites in 1982. The first, which took place in January, was determined to be inconclusive because none of the status options obtained a simple majority of the votes.

24. Leibowitz, *Defining Status*, 338.

25. Ada, "The Quest for Commonwealth," 161.

26. Underwood, "Dies Mit," 106.

27. Organization of People for Indigenous Rights (OPI-R), "Self-Determination: A People's Right," folder 7, box 5, Papers of US Congressman Ben Blaz, 1984–1992, MSS 010, MARC, UOG.

28. Benjamin Cruz, interview with the author, January 13, 2017.

29. M. P. Perez, "Chamorro Resistance and Prospects," 177.

30. OPI-R, "Self-Determination." On CHamoru participation in Pacific-wide decolonization movements, see Oberiano, "Guam's Quest."
31. OPI-R, "Self-Determination."
32. Oberiano, "Guam's Quest."
33. Mar, *Decolonisation and the Pacific*, 3.
34. Oberiano, "Guam's Quest," 254.
35. Cristobal, "Organization of People for Indigenous Rights," 82.
36. Bettis, "Colonial Immigration in Guam," 111.
37. On permanent/transient temporality of settler militarism, see Gandhi, *Archipelago of Resettlement*.
38. Bettis, "Colonial Immigration in Guam," 115.
39. Underwood, "Excursions into Inauthenticity," 163.
40. Underwood, "Immigration and Guam's Future," 60.
41. Underwood, "Immigration and Guam's Future," 60.
42. House of Representatives, Committee on Interior and Insular Affairs, *United States–Guam Relationship*, 56.
43. House of Representatives, Committee on Interior and Insular Affairs, *United States–Guam Relationship*, 56.
44. Chris Perez Howard to Ricardo Bordallo and the Commission on Self-Determination, folder "Political Status" #9, box 60, Papers of Antonio Borja Won Pat, MSS 2930, MARC, UOG.
45. Ronald Teehan argued that "the U.S. Constitution was unilaterally thrust upon us by the U.S. Government so now we are conveniently trapped into including all Americans, and all people who come to Guåhan under unilaterally established American immigration law and the rights of the Chamorro people under this rationale are conveniently buried." Commission on Self-Determination Meeting Minutes (February 13, 1985), 23, folder February 20–28, 1985, box 58, Papers of Governor Jerome Bordallo, 2nd Term, MARC, UOG, 23.
46. OPI-R, "Self-Determination."
47. OPI-R, "Self-Determination."
48. OPI-R member Ronald Teehan made these arguments on behalf of OPI-R at a meeting for the CSD. Commission on Self-Determination Meeting Minutes, 23.
49. This was a testimony written in CHamoru submitted to the Commission on Self-Determination. Translation by Lawrence Lizama. "Public Hearing on the Draft Commonwealth Act Dededo Community Center, July 25, 1985," attachment D, 81, folder July 16–31, 1985, box 58, Papers of Governor Jerome Bordallo, 2nd Term, MARC, UOG (hereafter cited as "Public Hearing—Dededo").
50. The Organic Act of Guam as Amended (1950), 2, 4.
51. "Public Hearing—Dededo," attachment D.
52. "Public Hearing—Dededo," attachment D.
53. C. T. Perez, "Chamorro Re-telling of 'Liberation,'" 70.
54. Underwood, "Dies Mit," 107.
55. OPI-R, "Self-Determination"; Simpson, *The First Right*, 154.
56. "Defining Eligibility for Status Vote," *Pacific Daily News*, May 14, 1981, 8.
57. "Public Hearing—Dededo."

58. "Slap in the face" was a reference used by PARA-PADA, a prior iteration of the Organization of Peoples for Indigenous Rights. Para-Pada's name come from the CHamoru language to "stop slapping Chamorros." Shelby Shapiro, "Workman's Circle 'No!' to the Draft Commonwealth Act," folder July 16–31, 1985, box 58, Papers of Governor Jerome Bordallo, 2nd Term, ARC, UOG; Rogers, *Destiny's Landfall*, 241.

59. CHamoru scholars have critiqued how notions of CHamoru hospitality have been used to justify military claims to land. For example, Kuper, "Kontra I Peligru, Na'fansåfo' Ham," 175–76, 289–90.

60. Underwood, "Dies Mit," 103; Shapiro, "Workman's Circle 'No!'"

61. Robert Underwood submitted his testimony to the Commission on Self-Determination's public hearing in Dédidu. Robert's grandfather James H. Underwood was a white US Marine from North Carolina who arrived in Guåhan at the beginning of the twentieth century and married Ana Pangelinan Martinez. Born in 1948, Robert Underwood obtained citizenship *jus sanguinis*, rather than through Organic Act of Guam, because of his paternal grandfather's and father's US citizenship. His written testimony in CHamoru is as follows: "Annai in laknos este siha na puntu, meggai dumespresia i direchon I man-Chamorro yank on todu hami ni' sumopopotte este na direcho. Ma fa'chalek I na'an-hu, ma sangan na hu chatli'e' otro rason taotao yan meggai biahe di ma faisen yu' kao kabales na Chamorro I haga'-hu yan I mañaina-hu. Buente ma po'po'lu na yanggen ma despresia yu' pat sino otro siha gi mangga'chong-hu na ma ribaha I deknedad I direchon in Man-Chamorro." "Public Hearing—Dededo," attachment D.

62. Charles Troutman to the Commission on Self-Determination, July 30, 1985, folder August 1–14, 1985, box 58, Papers of Governor Jerome Bordallo, 2nd Term, MARC, UOG.

63. Troutman to the Commission on Self-Determination.

64. Saranillio, *Unsustainable Empire*, 13.

65. Diaz, "Bye Bye Ms. American Pie," 155.

66. "Public Hearing on Draft Commonwealth Act," 38, folder July 01–15, 1985, box 58, Papers of Governor Jerome Bordallo, 2nd Term, MARC, UOG, 38.

67. "Public Hearing on Draft Commonwealth Act," 8.

68. "Public Hearing on Draft Commonwealth Act," 39–40.

69. Underwood, "Immigration and Guam's Future," 63.

70. Underwood, "Immigration and Guam's Future," 63.

71. Nerissa Bretania and Nerissa Lee are both names for the person Nerissa Bretania Underwood described in chapter 5. Nerissa married Robert Underwood in 2009, and subsequently changed her name to Nerissa Bretania Underwood. Nerissa Bretania Underwood, interview with the author, Guam, September 9, 2019.

72. Benjamin Cruz, interview with the author, Guam, January 13, 2017.

73. A copy of this petition is in OPI-R, "Self-Determination."

74. Vivian Dames writes about how the positionality of being a Filipina woman "of" Guåhan creates a "conflicted position" in regards to activism and scholarship about Guåhan. Dames, "Rethinking the Circle of Belonging," xxi–xxii.

75. Nerissa Bretania Underwood, interview with the author, Guam, September 9, 2019.

76. "Public Hearing on Draft Commonwealth Act," 20.

77. Espina, "Ali'e' and Asi'i," 103.

78. Oberiano and Ong, "Envisioning *Inafa'maolek* Solidarity."

79. "Commonwealth Now!" was the slogan for the Commission on Self-Determination's educational campaign.

80. Commission on Self-Determination, "Guam's Quest for Commonwealth: A Draft Guam Commonwealth Act" (Mangilao: Micronesian Area Research Center University of Guam), https://issuu.com/guampedia/docs/the_draft_guam_commonwealth_act_pft. (Hereafter cited as "Draft Guam Commonwealth Act.")

81. The Guam Commonwealth Act went through several revisions during its seventeen-year life as a result of federal suggestions and changes, as well as CHamoru and Guamanian leaders' attempting to reinstate certain provisions. For the purposes of this book, I have chosen to focus on the first iteration of the Guam Commonwealth Act, which was published and disseminated to the Guåhan community in 1986. This version would be the document that spurred several debates over concepts of Indigenous rights and sovereignty in the 1980s.

82. Rogers, "Guam's Quest for Political Identity," 58.

83. Scholars of Indigenous politics have noted how state-based solutions did not necessarily fit the political goals of Indigenous peoples. The CHamoru people and the Commonwealth Act were no exception. On Indigenous visions of decolonization, see Mar, *Decolonisation and the Pacific*; Anaya, *Indigenous Peoples in International Law*; Simpson, *The First Right*.

84. "Draft Guam Commonwealth Act," 3.

85. The Papers of Governor Ricardo J. Bordallo (Second Term) at the Micronesian Area Research Center contain the minutes of these meetings and are rich with the discussions regarding the application of certain laws in Guåhan, and how Guamanians could argue for what they want in the Commonwealth Act.

86. "Draft Guam Commonwealth Act," 3.

87. "Draft Guam Commonwealth Act," 5.

88. "Draft Guam Commonwealth Act," 9.

89. "Draft Guam Commonwealth Act," 7.

90. Ada, "The Quest for Commonwealth," 167.

91. Sanchez, *Guåhan, Guam*, 450.

92. *Pacific Daily News* Voter's Guide insert. A copy of this was found at the Pacific Collection, University of Hawai'i at Mānoa.

93. Organization of People for Indigenous Rights, "Hunggan!, Chamorro Self-Determination and Local Control of Immigration for Commonwealth," Hamilton Library, Pacific Collection, University of Hawai'i at Mānoa.

94. "Where They Stand on the Draft Act Vote," *Pacific Daily News*, November 6, 1987, 4.

95. "Tabulated Breakdown of Village Vote," *Pacific Daily News*, November 9, 1987, 4.

96. By this point in time, various members of Congress, legal teams and counsels, federal officials, and UN officials had contributed their perspectives on how the Commonwealth Act should be written. The Commission on Self-Determination took these into consideration, but ultimately decided to work with the issues that mattered to them most. For more detail about these conversations and the politics behind the drafting of the Commonwealth Act and the subsequent plebiscite, read Ada, "The Quest for Commonwealth"; Rogers, "Guam's Quest for Political Identity."

97. Ada, "The Quest for Commonwealth," 175.

98. House of Representatives, Committee on Interior and Insular Affairs, *Guam Commonwealth*, 412–17.

99. *Guam Commonwealth*, part 2, 9.

100. *Guam Commonwealth*, part 2, 257, 260–61.

101. *Guam Commonwealth*, part 2, 271–72. My italics for emphasis.

102. The interagency task force did support some provisions of the Commonwealth Act, including those that dealt with federal laws that hampered economic development, guidelines around eminent domain, and access to excess federal lands. Furthermore, they did support provisions that helped CHamoru people. These included the establishment of the Chamorro Land Trust, and greater education programming "aimed at preserving and promoting their culture, and enhancing their social and economic well-being and advancement." House of Representatives, Committee on Interior and Insular Affairs, *Guam Commonwealth*, part 2, 273.

103. *Guam Commonwealth*, part 2, 271.

104. *Guam Commonwealth*, part 2, 275–76.

105. *Guam Commonwealth*, part 2, 275.

106. Ada, "The Quest for Commonwealth," 175–80.

107. House of Representatives, Committee on Resources, *Hearing on H.R. 100*.

Conclusion

1. Video footage of this event can be found in Chris Barnett, "Old Videos of Late Angel Santos Resurface, Shed Light on Current Events," kuamnews, YouTube Video. https://www.youtube.com/watch?v=yQkuBqvxcN8&ab_channel=kuamnews.

2. Dominica Tolentino, "Angel Leon Guerrero Santos," Guampedia, September 17, 2020, https://www.guampedia.com/angel-leon-guerrero-santos/.

3. Michael Lujan Bevacqua, "Angel L. G. Santos Interpretive Essay: Matatnga," Guampedia, https://www.guampedia.com/interpretive-essay-angel-l-g-santos/.

4. "Two Poems Written by Angel Santos in Federal Prison," *No Rest for the Awake—Minagahet Chamorro*, ed. Michael Lujan Bevacqua, published February 28, 2019, http://minagahet.blogspot.com/2019/02/two-poems-written-by-angel-santos-in.html.

5. Guam Legislature, "P.L. 23-147: An Act to Create the Commission on Decolonization for the Implementation and Exercise of Chamorro Self-Determination," 2nd sess., 1997.

6. Department of the Navy, Joint Guam Program Office, "Final Environmental Impact Statement," ES-4.

7. Rice et al., "United States–Japan Roadmap," 2.

8. The first direct quote is taken from Rice et al., "United States–Japan Roadmap," 2–3; the last three are from the "Final Environmental Impact Statement," ES-2.

9. Rice et al., "United States–Japan Roadmap," 3. Direct quotation from "Final Environmental Impact Statement," ES-6. Emphasis my own.

10. Rice et al., "United States–Japan Roadmap," first projected completion in 2014. At the time of writing, the expected completion year is 2025.

11. Na'puti, "Archipelagic Rhetoric," 11; Aguon, "No Country for Eight Spot Butterflies."

12. Office of the Governor of Guam, "Leon Guerrero-Tenorio Administration Welcomes Historic H-2B Milestone," Press Release, August 25, 2022.

13. Konstantin Toropin, "Marines Reopen Base on Guam as Part of a Shift from Okinawa," Military.com, January 26, 2023, https://www.military.com/daily-news/2023/01/26/marines-reopen-base-guam-part-of-shift-okinawa.html#:~:text=The%20Marine%20Corps%20said%20that,be%20added%22%20to%20the%20island.

14. Vine, "No Bases?"; Akibayashi, "Okinawa Women Act."

15. Gary Hiles, "Economic Outlook for Guam: Fiscal Year 2024," *2024 Executive Budget Request*, Governor of Guam, (2023), https://bls.guam.gov/economic-outlook-reports/.

16. Haidee Eugenio, "Guam Arrivals Drop 10% from 2024, Still 42% of Pre-pandemic Levels," *Pacific Daily News*, March 4, 2025, https://www.guampdn.com/news/guam-arrivals-drop-10-from-2024-still-42-of-pre-pandemic-levels/article_55f1a3c8-f7e5-11ef-92e6-bbdd871c53f3.html.

17. "Final Environmental Impact Statement," ES-52–54.

18. SMS Research & Marketing Services, Inc. "Guam Housing Study and Needs Assessment: RFP#-GHURA-5-6-2019-CPD—January 2020," Guam Housing and Urban Renewal Authority, 24. A copy of this report can be found at https://ghura.org/sites/default/files/ghura_housing_needs_assessment.pdf.

19. The Reason We Left Guam (Part 1)," Kandit News Group, September 19, 2023, https://kanditnews.com/the-reason-we-left-guam-part-1/; "Governor: The Struggle Is Real, but There Is Hope, and We're in a Better Place than We Were Before," Kandit News Group, September 19, 2023, https://kanditnews.com/governor-the-struggle-is-real-but-there-is-hope-and-were-in-a-better-place-than-we-were-before/; Andrew Van Dam, "People Are Fleeing Puerto Rico, Guam and Every Other U.S. Territory. What Gives?," *Washington Post*, September 23, 2022, https://www.washingtonpost.com/business/2022/09/23/american-territories-population-loss/.

20. "We Are Guåhan," Guampedia, https://www.guampedia.com/we-are-guahan/; Frain, "Women's Resistance."

21. Na'puti, "Archipelagic Rhetoric."

22. "Independent Guåhan," *Independent Guåhan*, https://independentguahan.org/.

23. "Kumisión I Fino' CHamoru yan I Fina'nå'guen I Historia Yan I Lina'la' I Taotao Tåno," Kumisión I Fino' CHamoru yan I Fina'nå'guen I Historia Yan I Lina'la' I Taotao Tåno, https://kumisionchamoru.guam.gov/.

24. "Chief Hurao Academy," Chief Hurao, Inc., https://www.huraoacademy.com/.

25. Faye Varias, "Frank Rabon," Guampedia, https://www.guampedia.com/frank-rabon/; Judy Flores, "Leonard Iriarte," Guampedia, https://www.guampedia.com/leonard-iriarte/.

26. "Our Mission," Nihi Indigenous Media, https://www.nihiguam.org/mission.

27. "We Are Micronesian Climate Change Alliance," Micronesian Climate Change Alliance, https://mccalliance.org/.

28. "Nurturing Food Sovereignty and Resilience," Guåhan Sustainable Culture, https://gusustainable.org/.

29. Oberiano and Ong, "Envisioning *Inafa'maolek* Solidarity"; "Filipinos for Guåhan," Filipinos for Guåhan, https://www.filipinosforguahan.org/; Espina and Ong, "Bonds of Island Activism."

30. "About," Craig Santos Perez, http://craigsantosperez.com/; "About," Julian Aguon, https://www.julianaguon.com/about.

31. Aguon, *The Properties of Perpetual Light*, 32.

Bibliography

Primary Sources

ARCHIVES

College Park, MD, United States
  National Archives and Records Administration
    Records of the Office of the Territories, Record Group 126
Hagåtña, Guam
  Nieves Flores Memorial Library
    Filipino Community of Guam, Vertical File
Honolulu, HI, United States
  Hamilton Library, University of Hawai'i at Mānoa
    Pacific Collection
Makati City, Philippines
  Filipinas Heritage Library, Ayala Museum
Manila, Philippines
  Lopez Museum and Library
Mangilao, Guam
  Micronesian Area Research Center, University of Guam
    Governor Carlos G. Camacho Papers (MSS 2150)
    Governor Carlton S. Skinner Papers (MSS 2850)
    Governor Edward John Dorn Papers (MSS 750)
    Governor Manuel F. L. Guerrero Papers, 1963–1969 (MSS 2480)
    Governor Willis Winter Bradley Jr. Papers (MSS 960)
    Guam Naval Government Records 1899–1956 (Executive Orders & Guam Congress) (MSS 870)
    National Archives, Record Group 80, Annual Reports of the Governors of Guam, 1901–1941 (MSS 930)
    Naval Operation Records AR-146-79, 1900–1918 (MSS 970)
    Papers of Agueda Iglesias Johnston
    Papers of Antonio Borja Won Pat, 1965–1984 (MSS 2390)
    Papers of Governor Ricardo Jerome Bordallo
    Papers of US Congressman Ben Blaz, 1984–1992 (MSS 010)
    Papers of US Congressman Robert A. Underwood (MSS 030)
    Reverend Father Jose Palomo y Torres Papers, 1836–1919 (MSS 2250)
    Richard P. Leary Papers, 1899 (MSS 2370)
    Roy James Papers (MSS 720)
    Thomas E. Mayhew Papers (MSS 690)
    William Edwin Safford Papers, 1899–1901 (MSS 980)

San Francisco, CA, United States
National Archives and Records Administration
Records of Naval Operating Forces, Record Group 313

NEWSPAPERS

Collier's Magazine
Filipiniana
Guam Daily News
Guam Daily Post
Guam Echo
Guam Recorder
Guam Recorder (1970s)
Guam Times Weekly
Harper's Weekly
Islander Magazine
Manila Times
Newsletter of the Institute of Ethnic Affairs
New York Times
Pacific Daily News
Pacific Profile
Philippine Free Press
Territorial Sun
Washington Post

ONLINE ARCHIVES AND DATABASES

Ancestry.com
US World War I Draft Registration Cards, 1917–1918
1920 United States Federal Census—The Island of Guam
1930 United States Federal Census—The Island of Guam
Foreign Relations of the United States
Guam Legislature Archives
https://archives.guamlegislature.gov/public-laws/
https://archives.guamlegislature.gov/resolutions/
Philippine Diary Project. http://philippinediaryproject.com/1901/01/24/thursday-24-january-1901/.

PUBLIC EXHIBITIONS, PODCASTS

Guam Humanities Council. *A Journey Home: Camp Roxas and Filipino American History on Guam* [Exhibition]. Hagatña: Guam Humanities Council, 2009.
Memoirs Pasifika. Podcast. https://www.memoirspasifika.com/.

PUBLISHED PRIMARY SOURCES

Coote, Robert K. *A Report on the Land-Use Conditions and Land Problems on Guam.* Bureau of Land Management, US Department of the Interior (August 1950).
Cristobal, Hope. "The Organization of People for Indigenous Rights: A Commitment Towards Self-Determination." In *Chamorro Self-Determination*, edited by Robert Underwood and Laura Souder. Mangilao, Guam: Micronesian Area Research Center, 1987.
Government of Guam, Department of Commerce. *Guam 1970: An Economy in Transition.* Hagåtña: Government of Guam, 1971.
Government of Guam, Interagency Committee on Population. *Guam's People, "A Continuing Heritage": A Statistical Profile of the Territory of Guam, 1920–1980*. Hagåtña, Guam, 1988.

Guam Legislature. P.L. 15-128. "An Act to Create the Commission on Self-Determination for the People of Guam and Appropriate the Sum of One Hundred Fifty Thousand Dollars ($150,000.00) to Carry Out the Activities of the Commission." 2nd sess., 1980.

Guam Legislature. P.L. 630. "The Organic Act of Guam." 81st Congress, Chapter 512. August 1, 1950.

Guam Legislature. Resolution No. 130-31. "Relative to Honoring and Congratulating Dr. and Mrs. Benjamin and Ofelia Sison on the Celebration of Their Fiftieth (50th) Wedding Anniversary." 31st Legislature, 1st sess., June 3, 2011.

Guam Legislature. Resolution No. 560-31(COR). "Relative to Posthumously Recognizing and Commending Dr. Sinforoso C. Tolentino; and to Further Extend a Warm Un Dångkolo Na Si Yu'us Ma'åse' to Him for His Commitment and Dedicated Work in Serving the People of Guam Throughout His Professional Years in the Healthcare Community." 31st Legislature, 2nd sess., October 18, 2012.

Howard, Chris Perez. *Maraquita: Revisited*. Mangilao: University of Guam Press, 2019.

Ibáñez del Carmen, Aniceto, and Francisco Resano del Corazón de Jesús. *Chronicle of the Mariana Islands: 1846–1899*. Translated and annotated by Marjorie G. Driver, Spanish text edited by Omaira Brunal-Perry. Mangilao, Guam: Micronesian Area Research Center, University of Guam, 1998.

Mabini, Apolinario. *La Revolución Filipina (con otros documentos de la época)*. 2 vols. Manila, Philippines: Bureau of Printing, 1931.

———. *Testament and Letters of Apolinario Mabini. [Letters and Documents in This Book Translated from "Cartas Politicas de Mabini."]* Edited by Alfredo S. Veloso. Quezon City, Philippines: Asvel, 1964.

———. *The True Decalogue*. Washington, DC: Philippine Press Bureau, 1922.

Onedera, Peter R. *A Borrowed Land*. Mangilao: University of Guam Press, 2024.

Petersen, Neal H., Ralph R. Goodwin, Marvin W. Kranz, and William Z. Slany, eds. *Foreign Relations of the United States, 1948, General; the United Nations*. Vol. 1, part 2. Washington, DC: Government Printing Office, 1976.

Safford, William. "Guam and Its People." Smithsonian Report, 1902.

———. *A History of the Marianas Islands*. Edited and transcribed by Jillette Leon Guerrero. Unpublished, Guam, 1901.

———. *A Year on the Island of Guam: Extracts from the Notebook of Naturalist William Edwin Safford*. Edited by Jillette Leon Guerrero. Agana Heights, Guam: Guamology, 2016.

Stevens, Russell. *Guam, USA: Birth of a Territory*. Honolulu: Tongg, 1953.

United Nations. *Chapter of the United Nations and Statute of the International Court of Justice*. San Francisco, 1945. https://treaties.un.org/doc/publication/ctc/uncharter.pdf.

OTHER FEDERAL DOCUMENTS

Congressional Record. "50th Anniversary of M. V. Pangilinan Enterprises." June 3, 1998, E991.

Department of the Navy, Joint Guam Program Office. "Final Environmental Impact Statement: Guam and CNMI Relocation: Relocating Marines from Okinawa, Visiting Aircraft Carrier Berthing, and Army Air and Missile Defense Task Force Executive Summary (July 2010)."

Executive Order 10178: Reserving Certain Real and Personal Property in Guam for the Use of the United States. October 30, 1950. https://www.trumanlibrary.gov/library/executive-orders/10178/executive-order-10178.

"Resolution Relative to Memorializing the Congress of the United States, the President of the United States, the Secretary of National Defense, the Secretary of National Defense, the Secretary of the Interior, and the Governor of Guam to Reconsider the Taking of Property in Radio Barrigada and Review Other Land Takings in Guam." Congressional Records—Senate, September 7, 1951, 11015.

Rice, Condoleezza, Donald Rumsfeld, Tarō Asō, Fukushiro Nukaga, and United States–Japan Security Consultative Committee (SCC). "United States–Japan Roadmap for Realignment Implementation." May 1, 2006. https://www.secnav.navy.mil/eie/ASN%20EIE%20Policy/Forms/DispForm.aspx?ID=19).

United States. *Building the Navy's Bases in World War II: History of the Bureau of Yards and Docs and the Civil Engineer Corps, 1940–1946*. Washington, DC: Government Printing Office, 1947.

———. *Hopkins Committee Report for the Secretary on the Civil Government of Guam and American Samoa*. 1947. Available at HathiTrust, https://hdl.handle.net/2027/umn.31951002668985h.

United States. Department of the Interior. "National Register of Historic Places Inventory—Nomination Form: Agana Houses Thematic Group." January 3, 1995. https://npgallery.nps.gov/GetAsset/5e69984e-ad36-43a7-8294-2de88a0cb247.

United States. Department of the Navy. "Guam: Information on Guam Transmitted by the United States to the Secretary-General of the United Nations, Pursuant to Article 73 (e) of the Charter." Washington, DC: Government of Guam, 1948.

United States. Department of State. "Philippines: Recruitment of Filipino Laborers and Employees, Agreement Effected by Exchange of Notes Signed at Manila May 13 and 16, 1947." In *U.S. Treaties and Other International Agreements*, vol. 7, part 3 (1956), 2539.

US Congress. House of Representatives. 57th Congress, 1st sess. *Letter from the Secretary of the Navy: A Petition from the Inhabitants of Guam Relating to a Permanent Government*. Washington, DC: Government Printing Office, 1902.

US Naval Oceanography Command Center. Joint Typhoon Warning Center (ComNavMarianas). "Tropical Cyclones Affecting Guam (1671–1990)." October 1991. https://apps.dtic.mil/sti/tr/pdf/ADA134016.pdf.

CONGRESSIONAL HEARINGS

House of Representatives. *Letter from the Secretary of the Navy: A Petition from the Inhabitants of Guam Relating to a Permanent Government*. 57th Congress, 1st sess. Washington, DC: Government Printing Office, 1902.

———. "Public Hearings Conducted Before a Subcommittee of the Public Lands Committee." Agana, Guam. November 21, 22, 23, 1949.

House of Representatives. Committee on Education and Labor. *Minimum Wages in Certain Territories, Possessions, and Oversea Areas of the United States*. 84th Congress, 2nd sess., 1956.

House of Representatives. Committee on Immigration, Citizenship, and International Law. *The Use of Temporary Alien Labor in Guam*. 95th Congress, 2nd sess., 1979.

House of Representatives. Committee on Insular Affairs. *Petition Relating to Permanent Government for the Island of Guam*. 57th Congress, 1st sess., February 27, 1902.

House of Representatives. Committee on Interior and Insular Affairs. *Economic Development of the Territory of Guam*. 89th Congress, 2nd sess., 1966. Committee Print No. 16.

———. *Guam Commonwealth: Hearings Before the Subcommittee on Insular and International Affairs*. Part 2. 101st Congress, 1st sess., 1989.

———. *Guam Mariana Islands*. 83rd Congress, 2nd sess., November 27 to December 4, 1954.

———. *United States–Guam Relationship: Oversight Hearing Before the Committee on Interior and Insular Affairs*. 99th Congress, 2nd sess., 1986.

House of Representatives. Committee on Public Lands. *Investigation of an Organic Act for Guam*. 81st Congress, 1st sess., November 21–23, 1949.

———. *Providing a Civil Government for Guam, and for Other Purposes*. 81st Congress, 2nd sess., February 22, 1950.

House of Representatives. Committee on Resources. *Hearing on H.R. 100, H.R. 2370, and 210: Guam Commonwealth Act, to Establish the Commonwealth of Guam, and for Other Purposes, Guam Judicial Empowerment Act of 1997, and to Amend the Organic Act of Guam*. 105th Congress, 1st sess., 1997.

Senate. Committee on Territories and Insular Affairs. *Citizenship for Residents of Guam*. 75th Congress, 1st sess., 1937.

Secondary Sources

Aaron, Jayne. "Regional Cold War History for Department of Defense Installations in Guam and the Northern Mariana Islands Project 09-454." Department of Defense Legacy Resource Management Program (July 2011). https://www.denix.osd.mil/cr/denix-files/sites/19/2016/03/24_Regional-Cold-War-History-for-Department-of-Defense-Installations-in-Gua.pdf.

Aboitiz, Nicole CuUnjieng. *Asian Place, Filipino Nation: A Global Intellectual History of the Philippine Revolution, 1887–1912*. New York: Columbia University Press, 2020.

———. "Philippine Asianist Thought and Pan-Asianist Action at the Turn of the Twentieth Century." In *The Anticolonial Transnational: Imaginaries, Mobilities, and Networks in the Struggle Against Empire of Global and International History*, edited by Erez Manela and Heather Streets Salter. Cambridge, UK: Cambridge University Press, 2023.

Ada, Joseph F. "The Quest for Commonwealth, the Quest for Change." In *Kinalamten Pulitikåt: Siñenten I Chamorro. Issues in Guam's Political Development: The Chamorro Perspective*, 125–203. Political Status and Education Coordinating Commission, 1996.

"Agueda Iglesias Johnston." In *Hale'ta: I Manfåyi*. Vol. 4. Hagåtña, Guam: Department of Chamorro Affairs, 2003.

Aguilar, Filipino V., Jr. "Tracing Origins: *Ilustrado* Nationalism and the Racial Science of Migration Waves." *Journal of Asian Studies* 64, no. 3 (August 2005): 605–37.
Aguon, Julian. "No Country for Eight Spot Butterflies." *Boston Review*, June 7, 2021, https://www.bostonreview.net/articles/no-country-for-eight-spot-butterflies/.
———. *The Properties of Perpetual Light*. Mangilao: University of Guam Press, 2021.
Aguon, Katherine. "The Guam Dilemma: The Need for a Pacific Island Education Perspective." In *Hale'ta Hinasso': Tinige' Put Chamorro Insights: The Chamorro Identity*. Agana, Guam: Political Status Education Coordinating Commission, 1993.
Akibayashi, Kozue. "Okinawa Women Act Against Military Violence: An Island Feminism Reclaiming Dignity." *Okinawan Journal of Island Studies* 1 (2020): 37–54.
Almaguer, Tomás. *Racial Fault Lines: The Historical Origins of White Supremacy in California*. Berkeley: University of California Press, 2009.
Alvarez, Hope Cristobal. "The Organization of People for Indigenous Rights: A Commitment Towards Self-Determination." In *Chamorro Self-Determination*, edited by Robert A. Underwood and Laura Torres Souder. Mangilao, Guam: Micronesia Area Research Center, 1987.
Anaya, S. James. *Indigenous Peoples in International Law*. 2nd ed. Oxford: Oxford University Press, 2004.
Arvin, Maile. *Possessing Polynesians: The Science of Settler Colonial Whiteness in Hawai'i and Oceania*. Durham, NC: Duke University Press, 2019.
Atienza, David. "Priests, Mayors and Indigenous Offices: Indigenous Agency and Adaptive Resistance in the Mariana Islands (1681–1758)." *Pacific Asia Inquiry* 5, no. 1 (2014): 31–48.
Baldoz, Rick. *The Third Asiatic Invasion: Empire and Migration in Filipino America, 1898–1946*. New York: NYU Press, 2011.
Bankoff, Greg. *Crime, Society, and the State in the Nineteenth-Century Philippines*. Quezon City, Philippines: Ateneo de Manila University Press, 1996.
Barker, Joanne. *Native Acts: Law, Recognition, and Cultural Authenticity*. Durham, NC: Duke University Press, 2011.
Barrett, W. Scott, and Walter S. Ferenz. "Peacetime Martial Law in Guam." *California Law Review* 48, no. 1 (March 1960).
Bettis, Leland. "Colonial Immigration on Guam." In *Kinalamten Pulitikåt: Siñenten I Chamorro: Issues in Guam's Political Development: The Chamorro Perspective*. Agaña, Guam: Political Status and Education Coordinating Commission, 1996.
Bevacqua, Michael. "Chamorros, Ghosts, Non-Voting Delegates: GUAM! Where the Production of America's Sovereignty Begins." PhD diss., University of California, San Diego, 2010.
Bevacqua, Michael Lujan, and Manuel Lujan Cruz. "The Banality of American Empire: The Curious Case of Guam, USA." *Journal of Transnational American Studies* 11, no. 1 (2020).
Black, Megan. *The Global Interior: Mineral Frontiers and American Power*. Cambridge, MA: Harvard University Press, 2018.
Blackhawk, Maggie. "Foreword: The Constitution of American Colonialism." *Harvard Law Review* 137, no. 1 (November 2023).

Bonus, Rick. *Locating Filipino Americans: Ethnicity and the Cultural Politics of Space.* Philadelphia: Temple University Press, 2000.
Brilliant, Mark. *The Color of America Has Changed: How Civil Rights Shaped Civil Rights Reform in California.* Oxford: Oxford University Press, 2010.
Byrd, Jodi. *The Transit of Empire: Indigenous Critiques of Colonialism.* Minneapolis: University of Minnesota Press, 2011.
Camacho, Keith L. *Cultures of Commemoration: The Politics of War, Memory, and History in the Mariana Islands.* Pacific Islands Monograph Series No. 25. Honolulu: Center for Pacific Islands Studies, School of Pacific and Asian Studies, University of Hawai'i. Mānoa: University of Hawai'i Press, 2011.
———."Enframing I Taotao Tano': Colonialism, Militarism, and Tourism in Twentieth Century Guam." Master's thesis, University of Hawai'i, 1998.
———. "Filipinos, Pacific Islanders, and the American Empire." In *The Oxford Handbook of Asian American History,* edited by David Yoo and Elichiro Azuma. Oxford: Oxford University Press, 2016.
———. *Sacred Men: Law, Torture, and Retribution in Guam.* Durham, NC: Duke University Press, 2019.
Campbell, Bruce. "The Filipino Community of Guam." Master's thesis, University of Guam, 1987.
Carano, Paul, and Pedro C. Sanchez. *A Complete History of Guam.* Rutland, VT: CE Tuttle, 1964.
Chang, David A. *The World and All the Things upon It: Native Hawaiian Geographies of Exploration.* Minneapolis: University of Minnesota Press, 2016.
Chin, Gabriel J., and Rose Cuison Villazor. *The Immigration and Nationality Act of 1965: Legislating a New America.* Cambridge, UK: Cambridge University Press, 2015.
Choy, Catherine Ceniza. *Empire of Care: Nursing and Migration in Filipino American History.* Durham, NC: Duke University Press, 2003.
Clement, Michael. "Bifurcating the Hagåtña Narrative: Garrison Folks, Indigenous Resettlement Villages, and the Long 18th Century in Marianas History." In *España y Las Islas Marianas: Una Historia Compartida,* edited by Carlos Madrid Álvarez-Piñer, David Atienza de Frutos, and Carlos Martínez Shaw. Madrid: Universidad Nacional de Educación a Distancia, 2022.
Clutario, Genevieve A. *Beauty Regimes: A History of Power and Modern Empire in the Philippines, 1898–1941.* Durham, NC: Duke University Press, 2023.
Cogan, Doloris Coulter. *We Fought the Navy and Won: Guam's Quest for Democracy—A Personal Memoir.* Honolulu: University of Hawai'i Press, 2008.
Cook, Mary Ellen. "A Survey of Exiles in the Mariana Islands." Master's thesis, Micronesian Area Research Center, University of Guam, 1980.
Cruz, Mary Therese F. "Identity and Self-determination in Guam: A Chamorro Homeland—An American Colony." *Micronesian Educator,* special edition, November 2015.
Cunningham, Lawrence J. *Ancient Chamorro Society.* Honolulu: Bess Press, 1992.
Dames, Vivian. "Rethinking the Circle of Belonging: American Citizenship and the Chamorros of Guam." PhD diss., University of Michigan, 2000.

Davis, Sasha. *The Empires' Edge: Militarization, Resistance, and Transcending Hegemony in the Pacific*. Athens: University of Georgia Press, 2015.
De Leon, Adrian. *Bundok: A Hinterland History of Filipino-America*. Chapel Hill: University of North Carolina Press, 2023.
———. "Sugarcane Sakadas: The Corporate Production of the Filipino on a Hawai'i Plantation." *Amerasia Journal* 45, no. 1 (2019): 50–67.
DeLisle, Christine Taitano. "Destination Chamorro Culture: Notes on Realignment, Rebranding, and Post-9/11 Militourism in Guam." *American Quarterly* 68, no. 3 (2016): 563–72.
———. "A History of Chamorro Nurse-Midwives in Guam and a 'Placental Politics' for Indigenous Feminism." *Intersections: Gender and Sexuality in Asia and the Pacific*, no. 37 (March 2015).
———. "Navy Wives/Native Lives: The Cultural and Historical Relations Between American Naval Wives and Chamorro Women in Guam, 1898–1945." PhD diss., University of Michigan, 2008.
———. *Placental Politics: CHamoru Women, White Womanhood, and Indigeneity Under U.S. Colonialism in Guam*. Chapel Hill: University of North Carolina Press, 2021.
Deloria, Philip Joseph. *Playing Indian*. New Haven, CT: Yale University Press, 1998.
De Viana, Agusto V. "The Development of the Philippine Foreign Service During the Revolutionary Period and the Filipino-American War (1896–1906): A Story of Struggle from the Formation of Diplomatic." *Antonious Journal* 2 (2015).
———. *In the Far Islands: The Role of Natives from the Philippines in the Conquest, Colonization and Repopulation of the Mariana Islands*. Manila: University of Santo Tomas, 2004.
Diaz, Vicente. "Bye Bye Ms. American Pie: The Historical Relations Between Chamorros and Filipinos and the American Dream." *ISLA: Journal of Micronesian Studies* 3, no. 1 (1995): 147–60.
———. "Deliberating Liberation Day: Identity, History, Memory, and War in Guam." In *Perilous Memories: The Asia-Pacific War(s)*, edited by T. Fujitani, Geoffrey M. White, and Lisa Yoneyama. Durham, NC: Duke University Press, 2001.
———. "Pious Sites: Chamorro Culture Between Spanish Catholicism and American Liberal Individualism." In *Cultures of United States Imperialism*, edited by Amy Kaplan. Durham, NC: Duke University Press, 1993.
———. *Repositioning the Missionary: Rewriting the Histories of Colonialism, Native Catholicism, and Indigeneity in Guam*. Honolulu: University of Hawai'i Press, 2017.
———. "Simply Chamorro: Telling Tales of Demise and Survival in Guam." *Contemporary Pacific* 6, no. 1 (April 1, 1994): 29–58.
———. "'TO "P" OR NOT TO "P"?': Marking the Territory Between Pacific Islander and Asian American Studies." *Journal of Asian American Studies* 7, no. 3 (October 2004): 183–208, 289.
———. "Voyaging for Anti-Colonial Recovery: Austronesian Seafaring, Archipelagic Rethinking, and Re-Mapping Indigeneity." *Pacific Asia Inquiry* 2, no. 1 (2011): 21–32.
Dizon, Joe. "Filipinos in Guam's 1970 Elections." *Guam Recorder* 2, no. 1 (January–March 1972): 56–59.
Droessler, Holger. *Coconut Colonialism: Workers and the Globalization of Samoa*. Cambridge, MA: Harvard University Press, 2022.

Dudziak, Mary L. *Cold War Civil Rights: Race and the Image of American Democracy.* Princeton, NJ: Princeton University Press, 2011.

Espina, Tabitha Caser. "Ali'e' and Asi'i: Unsettling the Rhetorics of Filipinos on Guåhan." *College English* 84, no. 1 (2021): 100–120.

———. "Unsettling the Rhetorics of the Politics of Filipinos on Guåhan." PhD diss., Washington State University, 2020.

Espina, Tabitha, and Josephine Faith Ong. "Bonds of Island Activism Among CHamoru and Filipino Women on Guåhan." *Okinawan Journal of Island Studies* 4, no. 2 (May 2023): 117–21.

Espina Velasco, Tabitha. "The Ube ('Roots') Generation." *Humanities Diliman* 13, no. 2 (2016): 75–101.

Espiritu, Yen Lê. *Asian American Panethnicity: Bridging Institutions and Identities.* Philadelphia: Temple University Press, 1992.

———. *Home Bound: Filipino American Lives Across Cultures, Communities, and Countries.* Berkeley: University of California Press, 2003.

Espiritu, Yên Lê, Lisa Lowe, and Lisa Yoneyama. "Transpacific Entanglements." In *Flashpoints for Asian American Studies,* edited by Cathy J. Schlund-Vials. New York: Fordham University Press, 2018.

Farrell, Don. "The Partition of the Marianas: A Diplomatic History." *ISLA: Journal of Micronesian Studies* 2, no. 2 (Dry Season 1994): 273–301.

Flores, Alfred. "'Little Island into Mighty Base': Indigeneity, Race, and U.S. Empire in Guam, 1944–1962." PhD diss., University of California, Los Angeles, 2015.

———. "'No Walk in the Park': US Empire and the Racialization of Civilian Military Labor in Guam, 1944–1962." *American Quarterly* 67, no. 3 (2015): 813–35.

———. *Tip of the Spear: Land, Labor, and US Settler Militarism in Guåhan, 1944–1962.* Ithaca, NY: Cornell University Press, 2023.

Frain, Sylvia C. "Resisting-Political-Colonization-and-American-Militarization-in-the-Marianas-Archipelago." *AlterNative: An International Journal of Indigenous Peoples* 12, no. 3 (September 1, 2016): 298–315.

———. "Women's Resistance in the Marianas Archipelago: A US Colonial Homefront and Militarized Frontline." *Feminist Formations* 29, no. 1 (Spring 2017): 97–135.

Friedman, Hal M. *Governing the American Lake: The US Defense and Administration of the Pacific, 1945–1947.* East Lansing: Michigan State University Press, 2007.

Fujikane, Candace. *Mapping Abundance for a Planetary Future: Kanaka Maoli and Critical Settler Cartographies in Hawai'i.* Durham, NC: Duke University Press, 2021.

Fujikane, Candace, and Jonathan Y. Okamura. *Asian Settler Colonialism: From Local Governance to the Habits of Everyday Life in Hawai'i.* Honolulu: University of Hawai'i Press, 2008.

Gabaccia, Donna R. *Foreign Relations: American Immigration in Global Perspective.* America in the World. Princeton, NJ: Princeton University Press, 2012.

Gaddis, John Lewis. *Strategies of Containment: A Critical Appraisal of American National Security Policy during the Cold War.* Oxford: Oxford University Press, 2005.

Gandhi, Evyn Lê Espiritu. *Archipelago of Resettlement: Vietnamese Refugee Settlers and Decolonization Across Guam and Israel-Palestine.* Berkeley: University of California Press, 2022.

Getachew, Adom. *Worldmaking After Empire: The Rise and Fall of Self-Determination.* Princeton, NJ: Princeton University Press, 2020.

Go, Julian. *American Empire and the Politics of Meaning: Elite Political Cultures in the Philippines and Puerto Rico During U.S. Colonialism.* Durham, NC: Duke University Press, 2008.

Goldstein, Alyosha. "Introduction: Toward a Genealogy of U.S. Colonial Present." In *Formations of United States Colonialism,* edited by Alyosha Goldstein. Durham, NC: Duke University Press, 2014.

Gonzalez, Vernadette Vicuña. *Securing Paradise: Tourism and Militarism in Hawai'i and the Philippines.* Durham, NC: Duke University Press, 2013.

Goodyear-Ka'ōpua, Noelani, Ikaika Hussey, and Erin Kahunawaika'ala Wright, eds. *A Nation Rising: Hawaiian Movements for Life, Land, and Sovereignty.* Durham, NC: Duke University Press, 2014.

Guam Humanities Council, *A Journey Home: Camp Roxas and Filipino American History on Guam.* Hagåtña: Guam Humanities Council, 2009.

Hale'ta I Manfåyi: Who's Who in Chamorro History. Vol. 2. Agaña, Guam: Political Status Education Coordinating Committee, 1997.

Hale'-ta I Manfåyi: Who's Who in Chamorro History. Vol. 3. Hagåtña, Guam: Department of Chamorro Affairs, 2002.

Hale'ta Kinalamten Pulitikåt: Siñenten I Chamorro; Issues in Guam's Political Development—The Chamorro Perspective. Agaña, Guam: Political Status and Education Coordinating Commission, 1996.

Hattori, Anne Perez. *Colonial Dis-Ease: US Navy Health Policies and the Chamorros of Guam, 1898–1941.* Pacific Islands Monograph Series No. 19. Honolulu: Center for Pacific Islands Studies, School of Hawaiian, Asian, and Pacific Studies, University of Hawai'i Press, 2004.

———. "Guardians of Our Soil: Indigenous Responses to Post–World War II Military Land Appropriation on Guam." In *Farms, Firms, and Runways: Perspectives on U.S. Military Bases in the Western Pacific,* edited by L. Eve Armetrout Ma. Chicago: Imprint, 2001.

———. "Navy Blues: Naval Rule on Guam and the Rough Road to Assimilation, 1898–1940." *Pacific Asia Inquiry* 5, no. 1 (Fall 2014): 13–30.

———. "Righting Civil Wrongs: The Guam Congress Walkout of 1949." *ISLA: Journal of Micronesian Studies* 3, no. 1 (Rainy Season, 1995): 1–27.

———. "A Take on Taking: Unwrapping Complexities of Oceanic Gifting in the Chamorro Context." President's Address. The Pacific Historical Association Conference, 2018.

Higuchi, Wakako. *The Japanese Administration of Guam, 1941–1944: A Study of Occupation and Integration Policies, with Japanese Oral Histories.* Jefferson, NC: McFarland, 2013.

———. "The Japanisation Policy for the Chamorros of Guam, 1941–1944." *Journal of Pacific History* 36, no. 1 (2001): 19–35.

Hofschneider, Penelope Bordallo. *A Campaign for Political Rights on the Island of Guam, 1899–1950.* Occasional Historic Papers Series No. 8. Saipan, CNMI: Division of Historical Preservation, 2001.

Hoganson, Kristin L. *Fighting for American Manhood: How Gender Politics Provoked the Spanish-American and Philippine-American Wars*. New Haven, CT: Yale University Press, 1998.

Jackson, Justin F. *The Work of Empire: War, Occupation, and the Making of American Colonialism in Cuba and the Philippines*. Chapel Hill: University of North Carolina Press, 2025.

Jung, Moon-Ho. *Coolies and Cane: Race, Labor, and Sugar in the Age of Emancipation*. Baltimore: Johns Hopkins University Press, 2008.

———. *Menace to Empire: Anticolonial Solidarities and the Transpacific Origins of the US Security State*. Berkeley: University of California Press, 2022.

Kalaw, Teodoro M. *The Philippine Revolution*. Manila: Manila Book Company, 1925.

Kaplan, Amy, and Donald E. Pease. *Cultures of United States Imperialism*. Durham, NC: Duke University Press, 1993.

Kasperbauer, Carmen Artero. "The Chamorro Culture." In *Hale'ta: Issues in Guam's Political Development: The Chamorro Perspective*. Agaña, Guam: Political Status Education Coordinating Committee, 1996.

Kim, Jodi. *Settler Garrison: Debt Imperialism, Militarism, and Transpacific Imaginaries*. Durham, NC: Duke University Press, 2022.

King, Katrina Quisumbing. "The Structural Sources of Ambiguity in the Modern State: Race, Empire, and Conflicts over Membership." *American Journal of Sociology* 128, no. 3 (November 2022): 768–819.

Kramer, Paul A. *The Blood of Government: Race, Empire, the United States, and the Philippines*. Chapel Hill: University of North Carolina Press, 2006.

Kruse, Line-Noue Memea. *The Pacific Insular Case of American Sāmoa: Land Rights and Law in Unincorporated US Territories*. London: Palgrave Macmillan, 2018.

Kauanui, J. Kehaulani. "False Dilemmas and Settler Colonial Studies: Response to Lorenzo Veracini: 'Is Settler Colonial Studies Even Useful.'" *Postcolonial Studies* 24, no. 2 (2021).

———. *Hawaiian Blood: Colonialism and the Politics of Sovereignty and Indigeneity*. Durham, NC: Duke University Press, 2008.

———. *The Paradoxes of Hawaiian Sovereignty: Land, Sex, and the Colonial Politics of State Nationalism*. Durham, NC: Duke University Press, 2018.

Kuper, Kenneth Gofigan. "Kontra I Peligru, Na'fansåfo' Ham: The Production of Military (In)Security in Guåhan." PhD diss., University of Hawai'i at Manoa, 2019.

Labrador, Roderick. *Building Filipino Hawai'i: Filipino Identity in Transition in Contemporary Hawai'i*. Champaign: University of Illinois Press, 2026.

Lee, Erika. *The Making of Asian America: A History*. New York: Simon & Schuster, 2016.

Leibowitz, Arnold H. *Defining Status: A Comprehensive Analysis of United States Territorial Relations*. Boston: Nijhoff, 1989.

Lew-Williams, Beth. *The Chinese Must Go: Violence, Exclusion, and the Making of the Alien in America*. Cambridge, MA: Harvard University Press, 2018.

Lowe, Lisa. *The Intimacies of Four Continents*. Durham, NC: Duke University Press, 2015.

Lutz, Catherine, ed. *The Bases of Empire: The Global Struggle Against U.S. Military Posts*. New York: NYU Press, 2009.

Mabalon, Dawn Bohulano. *Little Manila Is in the Heart: The Making of the Filipina/o American Community in Stockton, California.* Durham, NC: Duke University Press, 2013.

Mabini, Apolinario. *La revolución filipina (con otros documentos de la época).* Documentos de la Biblioteca nacional de Filipinas [. . .] ; no. 4–5. Manila: Bureau of Printing, 1931.

———. *Testament and Letters of Apolinario Mabini.* Translated from "Cartas Politicas de Mabini." Mabini Centennial ed. Quezon City: Asvel, 1964.

Madrid, Carlos. *Beyond Distances: Governance, Politics and Deportation in the Mariana Islands from 1870 to 1877.* Saipan: Northern Mariana Islands Council for Humanities, 2006.

Majul, Cesar Adib. "Mabini and the Philippine Revolution." *Diliman Review* 5, no. 1–4 (1957). Quezon City: University of the Philippines, 1960.

Man, Simeon. *Soldiering Through Empire: Race and the Making of the Decolonizing Pacific.* Oakland: University of California Press, 2018.

Manalansan, Martin F., and Augusto Espiritu. *Filipino Studies: Palimpsests of Nation and Diaspora.* New York: NYU Press, 2016.

Mar, Tracey Banivanua. *Decolonisation and the Pacific: Indigenous Globalization and the Ends of Empire.* Cambridge, UK: Cambridge University Press, 2016.

McCoy, Alfred W., and Francisco A. Scarano, eds. *Colonial Crucible: Empire in the Making of the Modern American State.* Madison: University of Wisconsin Press, 2009.

McCoy, Alfred W., Francisco A. Scarano, and Courtney Johnson. "On the Tropic of Cancer: Transitions and Transformations of U.S. Imperial State." In *Colonial Crucible: Empire in the Making of the Modern American State*, edited by Alfred W. McCoy and Francisco A. Scarano. Madison: University of Wisconsin Press, 2009.

Miles, Tiya. *Ties That Bind: The Story of an Afro-Cherokee Family in Slavery and Freedom.* Berkeley: University of California Press, 2015.

Miller-Davenport, Sarah. *Gateway State: Hawai'i and the Cultural Transformation of American Empire.* Princeton, NJ: Princeton University Press, 2019.

Molina, Natalia, Daniel Martinez HoSang, and Ramon A. Gutiérrez, eds. *Relational Formations of Race: Theory, Method, and Practice.* Berkeley: University of California Press, 2019.

Monnig, Laurel Anne. "'Proving Chamorro': Indigenous Narratives of Race, Identity, and Decolonization on Guam." PhD diss., University of Illinois, Urbana-Champaign, 2007.

Munoz, Alfred N. *The Filipinos in America.* Los Angeles: Mountainview, 1971.

Na'Puti, Tiara. "Archipelagic Rhetoric: Remapping the Marianas and Challenging Militarization from 'A Stirring Place.'" *Communication and Critical/Cultural Studies* 16, no. 1 (2019): 4–25.

———. "Contemporary Chamoru Activism: Anti-Militarization and Social Movements in Guåhan." PhD diss., University of Texas at Austin, 2013.

Na'Puti, Tiara, and Michael Bevacqua. "Militarization and Resistance from Guåhan: Protecting and Defending Pågat." *American Quarterly* 67, no. 3 (September 1, 2015): 837–58, 987, 990–91.

Navarro, Atoy M. "Philippines-Marianas Relations in History: Some Notes on Filipino Exiles in Guam." *Asian and Pacific Migration Journal* 8, no. 1–2 (1999): 117–30.

Nebolon, Juliet. "'Life Given Straight from the Heart': Settler Militarism, Biopolitics, and Public Health in Hawai'i during World War II." *American Quarterly* 69, no. 1 (2017): 23–45.

———. *Settler Militarism: World War II in Hawai'i and the Making of US Empire*. Durham, NC: Duke University Press, 2024.

Ngai, Mae M. *Impossible Subjects: Illegal Aliens and the Making of Modern America*. Princeton, NJ: Princeton University Press, 2004.

Oberiano, Kristin. "Guam's Quest for Indigenous Chamorro Self-Determination in the Age of Pacific Anticolonialism." In *The Anticolonial Transnational: Imaginaries, Mobilities, and Networks in the Struggle Against Empire*, edited by Erez Manela and Heather Streets-Salter. Cambridge, UK: Cambridge University Press, 2023.

———. "Race and Empire." In *Explaining the History of American Foreign Relations*, vol. 4, edited by Barbara Keys and Frank Costigliola. Cambridge, UK: Cambridge University Press, 2025.

Oberiano, Kristin, and Josephine Faith Ong. "Envisioning *Inafa'maolek* Solidarity: The Importance of CHamoru-Filipino Mutual Relations for a Decolonized Guåhan." *Critical Ethnic Studies*, special issue, *Interventions in Pacific Islands Studies and Trans-Pacific Studies* (September 2022).

Ong, Josephine Faith. "The Colonial Boundaries of Exilic Discourse: Contextualizing Mabini's Incarceration in Guåhan." Master's thesis, University of California, Los Angeles, 2019.

———. "Sculpted Memories: Apolinario Mabini's Memorialization and Chamorro–Filipino Relations in Guam." *Frontiers: A Journal of Women's Studies* 45, no. 1 (2024): 1–23.

Palomo, Tony. *An Island in Agony*. Self-published, 1984.

Perez, C. T. "Chamorro Re-Telling of 'Liberation.'" In *Hale'ta: Issues in Guam's Political Development: The Chamorro Perspective*. Agaña, Guam: Political Status Education Coordinating Committee, 1996.

Perez, Michael P. "Chamorro Resistance and Prospects for Sovereignty in Guam." In *Sovereignty Matters: Locations of Contestation and Possibility in Indigenous Struggles for Self-Determination*, edited by Joanne Barker. Lincoln: University of Nebraska Press, 2006.

———. "Contested Sites: Pacific Resistance in Guam to U.S. Empire." *Amerasia Journal* 27, no. 1 (January 1, 2001): 97–115.

———. "Interethnic Antagonism in the Wake of Colonialism: U.S. Territorial Racial and Ethnic Relations at the Margins." *Ethnic Studies Review* 23, no. 1–3 (April 30, 2000): 1.

Philips, Michael. "Land." In *Hale'ta: The Quest for Commonwealth, Issues in Guam's Political Development: The Chamorro Perspective*. Agaña, Guam: Political Status Education Coordinating Committee, 1996.

"Pio Del Pilar: 1865-1931." In *Filipinos in History*, vol. 2. Manila: National Historical Institute, 1990. https://dfa.gov.ph/images/AMabini/C__Managepoint_sessions_Diane_Rar1423.pdf.

Poblete, Joanna. *Islanders in the Empire: Filipino and Puerto Rican Laborers in Hawai'i*. Champaign: University of Illinois Press, 2014.

Pobutsky, Ann M., and Enrico I. Neri. "Patterns of Filipino Migration to Guam: United States Military Colonialism and Its Aftermath." *Philippine Studies: Historical and Ethnographic Viewpoints* 66, no. 1 (2018): 77–94.

Reyno, Adriano. *The Political, Social, and Moral Philosophy of Apolinario Mabini*. Manila: Catholic Trade School, 1964.

Rizal, Jose. *Noli Me Tangere*. Translated by Leon Ma. Guerrero. Mandaluyong City, Philippines: Anvil, 2020.

Roces, Mina. "Gender, Nation and the Politics of Dress in Twentieth-Century Philippines." *Gender & History* 17, no. 2 (2005): 354–77.

Rodriguez, Robyn Magalit. *Migrants for Export: How the Philippine State Brokers Labor to the World*. Minneapolis: University of Minnesota Press, 2010.

———. "Toward a Critical Filipino Studies Approach to Philippine Migration." In *Filipino Studies: Palimpsests of Nation and Diaspora*, edited by Martin F. Manalansan and Augusto Espiritu. New York: NYU Press, 2016.

Rogers, Robert F. *Destiny's Landfall: A History of Guam*. Revised ed. Honolulu: University of Hawai'i Press, 2011.

———."Guam's Quest for Political Identity." *Pacific Studies* 12, no. 1 (November 1, 1988): 49–70.

Rondilla, Joanne L. "The Filipino Question in Asia and the Pacific: Rethinking Regional Origins in Diaspora." In *Pacific Diaspora: Island Peoples in the United States and Across the Pacific*, edited by Paul Spickard, Joanne L. Rondilla, and Debbie Hippolite Wright. Honolulu: University of Hawai'i Press, 2002.

Sales, Joy N. "#NeverAgainToMartialLaw: Transnational Filipino American Activism in the Shadow of Marcos and the Age of Duterte." *Amerasia Journal* 45 (2019): 299–315.

Sanchez, Mark John. "Let the People Speak: Solidarity Culture and the Making of a Transnational Opposition to the Marcos Dictatorship, 1972–1986." PhD diss., University of Illinois at Urbana-Champaign, 2018.

Sanchez, Pedro. *Guåhan, Guam: The History of Our Island*. Agaña, Guam: Sanchez Publishing House, n.d.

Santos, Elyssa. "'Practicing Economy': Chamorro Agency and U.S. Colonial Agricultural Projects, 1898–1941." Master's thesis, University of Hawai'i at Manoa, 2018.

Saranillio, Dean Itsuji. "Colliding Histories: Hawai'i Statehood at the Intersection of Asians 'Ineligible to Citizenship' and Hawaiians 'Unfit for Self-Government.'" *Journal of Asian American Studies* 13, no. 3 (2010): 283–309.

———. "Settler Colonialism." In *Native Studies Keywords*, edited by Stephanie N. Teves, Andrea Smith, and Michelle H. Raheja. Tucson: University of Arizona Press, 2015.

———. *Unsustainable Empire: Alternative Histories of Hawai'i Statehood*. Durham, NC: Duke University Press, 2018.

———. "Why Asian Settler Colonialism Matters: A Thought Piece on Critiques, Debates, and Indigenous Difference." *Settler Colonial Studies* 3, no. 3–4 (2013): 280–94.

Schumacher, John N. "The Cavite Mutiny: Toward a Definitive History." *Philippine Studies* 59, no. 1 (March 2011).

Shah, Nayan. *Stranger Intimacy: Contesting Race, Sexuality, and the Law in the North American West*. Berkeley: University of California Press, 2011.

Shibusawa, Naoko. "U.S. Empire and Racial Capitalist Modernity." *Diplomatic History* 45, no. 5 (2021): 855–84.

Shigematsu, Setsu, and Keith L. Camacho. *Militarized Currents: Toward a Decolonized Future in Asia and the Pacific*. Minneapolis: University of Minnesota Press, 2010.

Simpson, Bradley. *The First Right: Self-Determination and the Transformation of International Order, 1941–2000*. Oxford: Oxford University Press, 2025.

Smith, Linda Tuhiwai. *Decolonizing Methodologies: Research and Indigenous Peoples*. 2nd ed. New York: Zed Books / Palgrave Macmillan, 2012.

Souder-Jaffery, Laura Marie Torres. *Daughters of the Island: Contemporary Chamorro Women Organizers on Gaum*. 2nd ed. MARC Monograph Series No. 1. Micronesian Area Research Center, University of Guam. Lanham, MD: University Press of America, 1992.

Stade, Ronald. *Pacific Passages: World Culture and Local Politics in Guam*. Stockholm Studies in Social Anthropology No. 42. Stockholm: Department of Social Anthropology, Stockholm University, 1998.

Stephens, Michelle Ann, and Brian Russell Roberts. *Archipelagic American Studies*. Durham, NC: Duke University Press, 2017.

Stoler, Anne. *Duress: Imperial Durabilities in Our Times*. Durham, NC: Duke University Press, 2016.

Tatour, Lana. "Citizenship as Domination: Settler Colonialism and the Making of Palestinian Citizenship in Israel." December 3, 2019. SSRN. https://ssrn.com/abstract=3533490 or http://dx.doi.org/10.2139/ssrn.3533490.

Teaiwa, Teresia. "Bikinis and Other s/Pacific n/Oceans." In *Voyaging Through the Contemporary Pacific*, edited by David L. Hanlon and Geoffrey M. White. Lanham, MD: Rowman & Littlefield, 2000.

———. "Postscript: Reflections on Militourism, US Imperialism, and American Studies." *American Quarterly* 68, no. 3 (2016): 847–53.

Teves, Stephanie Nohelani, and Maile Arvin. "Decolonizing API: Centering Indigenous Pacific Islander Feminism." In *Asian American Feminisms and Women of Color Politics*, edited by Lynn Fujiwara and Shireen Roshanravan. Seattle: University of Washington Press, 2018.

Thomas, Megan C. *Orientalists, Propagandists, and Ilustrados: Filipino Scholarship and the End of Spanish Colonialism*. Minneapolis: University of Minnesota Press, 2012.

Thompson, Lanny. "The Imperial Republic: A Comparison of the Insular Territories under U.S. Dominion After 1898." *Pacific Historical Review* 71, no. 4 (2002): 535–74.

Thompson, Laura. *Guam and Its People*. American Council Institute of Pacific Relations, 1941.

———."Guam's Bombed Out Capital." *Far Eastern Survey* 16, no. 6 (March 26, 1947).

Torres, Jose M. *The Massacre at Atåte*. Mangilao: University of Guam Press, 2014.

Trask, Haunani-Kay. *From a Native Daughter: Colonialism and Sovereignty in Hawai'i*. Revised ed. Honolulu: University of Hawai'i Press, 1999.

———. "Settlers of Color and 'Immigrant' Hegemony: 'Locals' in Hawai'i." In *Asian Settler Colonialism: From Local Governance to Habits of Everyday Life in Hawai'i*, edited by Candace Fujikane and Jonathan Y. Okamura. Honolulu: University of Hawai'i Press, 2008.

Underwood, Robert. "American Education and the Acculturation of Chamorros of Guam." PhD diss., University of Southern California, 1987.

———. "Dies Mit: The Origin and End of Chamorro Self-Determination." *Micronesian Educator* 22 (November 2015): 100–112.

———. "Excursions into Inauthenticity: The Chamorros of Guam." *Pacific Viewpoint* 26, no. 1 (1985).

———. "Immigration and Guam's Future." In *Chamorro Self-Determination*, edited by Robert A. Underwood and Laura Torres Souder. Mangilao: University of Guam, Micronesia Area Research Center, 1987.

———. "Uncle Sam, Sam My Dear Old Uncle Sam, Won't You Please Be Kind to Guam?," Guam Humanities Council Lecture Series (August, September, October, 2003).

Underwood, Robert A., and Laura Torres Souder, eds. *Chamorro Self-Determination.* Mangilao: University of Guam, Micronesia Area Research Center, 1987.

Veloso, Alfredo S., ed. *Testament and Political Letters of Apolinario Mabini.* Quezon City: Asvel, 1964.

Veracini, Lorenzo. *Settler Colonialism: A Theoretical Overview.* Houndmills, Basingstoke: Palgrave Macmillan, 2010.

Viernes, James. "Chamorro Men in the Making: Capitalism and Indigenous Masculinities Under US Naval Colonialism in Guam." *eJournal of the Australian Association for the Advancement of Pacific Studies*, no. 1.2 and 2.1 (April 2010).

———. "Fanhasso I Taotao Sumay: Displacement, Dispossession, and Survival in Guam." Master's thesis, University of Hawai'i at Manoa, 2008.

———. "Negotiating Manhood: Chamorro Masculinities and US Military Colonialism in Guam, 1898–1941." PhD diss., University of Hawai'i at Manoa, 2015.

Vine, David. *Base Nation: How U.S. Military Bases Abroad Harm America and the World.* New York: Metropolitan Books, 2015.

———."No Bases? Assessing the Impact of Social Movements Challenging US Foreign Military Bases." *Current Anthropology* 6, suppl. 19 (February 2019): S158–72.

Võ, Linda Trinh, and Rick Bonus. *Contemporary Asian American Communities: Intersections and Divergences.* Philadelphia: Temple University Press, 2002.

Weber, Benjamin D. "Fearing the Flood: Transportation as Counterinsurgency in the US-Occupied Philippines." In *Transportation, Deportation, and Exile: Perspectives from the Colonies in the Nineteenth and Twentieth Centuries*, special issue, *International Review of Social History* 63 (2018): 191–210.

Westad, Odd Arne. *The Global Cold War: Third World Interventions and the Making of Our Times.* Cambridge, UK: Cambridge University Press, 2005.

Willens, Howard P. *The Secret Guam Study: How President Ford's 1975 Approval of Commonwealth Was Blocked by Federal Officials.* The Occasional Historical Papers Series. Mangilao, Guam / Saipan: Micronesian Area Research Center; Commonwealth of the Northern Mariana Islands Division of Historic Preservation, 2004.

Willens, Howard P., and Dirk Anthony Ballendorf. *The Secret Guam Study: The Documents.* Washington, DC: Wilsie, 2005.

Williams, William Appleman. "Empire as a Way of Life." *Radical History Review* 50 (1991): 71–102.

Wolfe, Patrick. "Settler Colonialism and the Elimination of the Native." *Journal of Genocide Research* 8, no. 4 (December 1, 2006): 387–409.

———. *Traces of History: Elementary Structures of Race.* London: Verso, 2016.

Woods, Colleen. "Building Empire's Archipelago: The Imperial Politics of Filipino Labor in the Pacific." *Labor* 13, no. 3–4 (2016): 131–52.

Index

Italic page numbers refer to illustrations.

www.ingramcontent.com/pod-product-compliance
Lightning Source LLC
LaVergne TN
LVHW101545020926
846999LV00029B/236